MENTAL HEALTH: CULTURE, RACE, AND ETHNICITY

A SUPPLEMENT TO
MENTAL HEALTH: A REPORT OF THE SURGEON GENERAL

2001

U.S. DEPARTMENT OF HEALTH AND HUMAN SERVICES
Public Health Service
Office of the Surgeon General
Rockville, MD

National Library of Medicine Cataloging in Publication

Mental health : culture, race, and ethnicity : a supplement to
    Mental health : a report of the Surgeon General. — Rockville,
    MD. : U.S. Dept. of Health and Human Services, Public
    Health Service, Office of the Surgeon General ; Washington,
    D.C. : For sale by the Supt. of Docs., U.S. G.P.O., 2001.

    Includes bibliographical references.

    1. Mental Health. 2. Minority Groups. 3. Mental Health
Services. 4. Cross-Cultural Comparison. 5. Blacks. 6. Indians,
North American. 7. Asian Americans. 8. Hispanic Americans. 9.
United States. I. United States. Public Health Service. Office of
the Surgeon General. II. Center for Mental Health Services (U.S.)
III. United States. Substance Abuse and Mental Health Services
Administration.

02NLM: WA 305 M5485 2001

This publication is available on the World Wide Web at
http://www.surgeongeneral.gov/library.

For sale by the Superintendent of Documents, U.S. Government Printing Office,
Washington, D.C., 20402 ISBN# 0-16-050892-4

Center for Mental Health Services
*Substance Abuse and Mental Health
Services Administration*

Suggested Citation

U.S. Department of Health and Human Services. (2001). *Mental Health: Culture, Race, and Ethnicity—A Supplement to Mental Health: A Report of the Surgeon General*. Rockville, MD: U.S. Department of Health and Human Services, Public Health Service, Office of the Surgeon General.

Message from Tommy G. Thompson
Secretary of Health and Human Services

As a nation, we have only begun to come to terms with the reality and impact of mental illnesses on the health and well being of the American people. This groundbreaking publication makes clear that the tragic and devastating effects of mental illnesses touch people of all ages, colors, and cultures. And though *Mental Health: A Report of the Surgeon General* informed us that there are effective treatments available for most disorders, Americans do not share equally in the best that science has to offer. Through the process of conducting his comprehensive scientific review for this Supplement, and with recognition that mental illnesses are real, disabling conditions affecting all populations regardless of race or ethnicity, the Surgeon General has determined that disparities in mental health services exist for racial and ethnic minorities, and thus, mental illnesses exact a greater toll on their overall health and productivity.

Diversity is inherent to the American way of life, and so is equal opportunity. Ensuring that all Americans have equal access to high quality health care, including mental health care, is a primary goal of the Department of Health and Human Services. By identifying the many barriers to quality care faced by racial and ethnic minorities, this Supplement provides an important road map for Federal, State, and local leaders to follow in eliminating disparities in the availability, accessibility, and utilization of mental health services.

An exemplary feature of this Supplement is its consideration of the relevance of history and culture to our understanding of mental health, mental illness, and disparities in services. In particular, the national prevention agenda can be informed by understanding how the strengths of different groups' cultural and historical experiences might be drawn upon to help prevent the emergence of mental health problems or reduce the effects of mental illness when it strikes. This Supplement takes a promising first step in this direction.

One of the profound responsibilities of any government is to provide for its most vulnerable citizens. It is now incumbent upon the public health community to set in motion a plan for eliminating racial and ethnic disparities in mental health. To achieve this goal, we must first better understand the roles of culture, race, and ethnicity, and overcome obstacles that would keep anyone with mental health problems from seeking or receiving effective treatment. We must also endeavor to reduce variability in diagnostic and treatment procedures by encouraging the consistent use of evidence-based, state-of-the-art medications and psychotherapies throughout the mental health system. At the same time, research must continue to aid clinicians in understanding how to appropriately tailor interventions to the needs of the individual based on factors such as age, gender, race, culture, or ethnicity.

To ensure that the messages outlined by the Surgeon General in this document reach the American people, the Department of Health and Human Services encourages its State and local partners to engage communities and listen to their needs. We must understand how local leaders and communities, including schools, families, and faith organizations, can become vital allies in the battle against disparities. Together, we can develop a shared vision of equal access to effective mental health services, identify the opportunities and incentives for collaborative problem solving, and then seize them. From a commitment to health and mental health for all Americans, communities will benefit. States will benefit. The Nation will benefit.

Foreword

As was the case when *Mental Health: A Report of the Surgeon General* was released in 1999, *Mental Health: Culture, Race, and Ethnicity* provides cause for both celebration and concern for those of us at the Substance Abuse and Mental Health Services Administration (SAMHSA) and its Center for Mental Health Services (CMHS). We celebrate the Supplement's comprehensive coverage of issues relevant to the mental health of racial and ethnic minorities, its providing a historical and cultural context within which minority mental health may be better understood, and its appreciation of the hardships endured and the strength, energy, and optimism of racial and ethnic minorities in their quest for good mental health. The Supplement causes us concern because of its finding that very serious disparities do exist regarding the mental health services delivered to racial and ethnic minorities. We must eliminate these disparities.

SAMHSA and CMHS envision a Nation where all persons, regardless of their culture, race, or ethnicity, enjoy the benefits of effective mental health preventive and treatment services. To achieve this goal, cultural and historical context must be accounted for in designing, adapting, and implementing services and service delivery systems. Communities must ensure that prevention and treatment services are relevant, attractive, and effective for minority populations. As the field learns more about the meaning and effect of cultural competence, we will enrich our commitment to the delivery of evidence-based treatment, tailored to the cultural needs of consumers and families. This Supplement, and the activities it will inspire, represents both a Surgeon General and a Department striving to improve communication among stakeholders through a shared appreciation of science, culture, history, and social context.

Not only does this Supplement provide us with a framework for better understanding scientific evidence and its implications for eliminating disparities, it also reinforces a major finding of *Mental Health: A Report of the Surgeon General*. That is, it shows how stigma and shame deter many Americans, including racial and ethnic minorities, from seeking treatment. SAMHSA and CMHS have long been leaders in the fight to reduce the stigma of mental illness. We pledge to carry on our efforts in this fight.

SAMHSA and CMHS are proud to have developed this Supplement in consultation with the National Institute of Mental Health (NIMH) in the National Institutes of Health. NIMH has contributed to this Supplement in innumerable ways, and many of the future directions reflected herein, especially those related to the need for more research, can be addressed adequately only through NIMH's leadership. We are grateful that this leadership and the commitment to eliminating mental health disparities are well established at NIMH.

We again celebrate the publication of this Supplement, and we trust that you will see it as we do — as a platform upon which to build positive change in our mental health system for racial and ethnic minorities, and indeed, for our Nation as a whole.

Joseph H. Autry III, M.D
Acting Administrator
Substance Abuse and Mental Health Services
Administration

Bernard S. Arons, M.D.
Director
Center for Mental Health Services

Preface

from the Surgeon General
U.S. Public Health Service

Mental health is fundamental to health, according to *Mental Health: A Report of the Surgeon General*, the first Surgeon General's report ever to focus exclusively on mental health. That report of two years ago urged Americans to view mental health as paramount to personal well-being, family relationships, and successful contributions to society. It documented the disabling nature of mental illnesses, showcased the strong science base behind effective treatments, and recommended that people seek help for mental health problems or disorders.

The first mental health report also acknowledged that all Americans do not share equally in the hope for recovery from mental illnesses. This is especially true of members of racial and ethnic minority groups. That awareness galvanized me to ask for a supplemental report on the nature and extent of disparities in mental health care for racial and ethnic minorities and on promising directions for the elimination of these disparities. This Supplement documents that the science base on racial and ethnic minority mental health is inadequate; the best available research, however, indicates that these groups have less access to and availability of care, and tend to receive poorer quality mental health services. These disparities leave minority communities with a greater disability burden from unmet mental health needs.

A hallmark of this Supplement is its emphasis on the role that cultural factors play in mental health. The cultures from which people hail affect all aspects of mental health and illness, including the types of stresses they confront, whether they seek help, what types of help they seek, what symptoms and concerns they bring to clinical attention, and what types of coping styles and social supports they possess. Likewise, the cultures of clinicians and service systems influence the nature of mental health services.

Just as health disparities are a cause for public concern, so is our diversity a national asset. This Supplement carries with it a call to the people of the United States to understand and appreciate our many cultures and their impact on the mental health of all Americans. The main message of this Supplement — that culture counts — should echo through the corridors and communities of this Nation. In today's multicultural reality, distinct cultures and their relationship to the broader society are not just important for mental health and the mental health system, but for the broader health care system as well.

This Supplement encourages racial and ethnic minorities to seek help for mental health problems and mental illnesses. For this advice to be meaningful, it is essential that our Nation continues on the road toward eliminating racial and ethnic disparities in the accessibility, availability, and quality of mental health services. Researchers are working to fill gaps in the scientific literature regarding the exact roles of race, culture, and ethnicity in mental health, but much is already known. The mental health system must take advantage of the direction and insight offered by the research presented in this Supplement. Because State and local governments have primary oversight of public mental health spending, they have a clear and important role in assuring equal access to high quality mental health services for racial and ethnic minorities. Just as important, we need to redouble our efforts to support communities, especially consumers, families, and community leaders, in welcoming and demanding effective treatment for all. When it is easy for minorities to seek and use treatment, our vision of eliminating mental health disparities becomes a reality.

Finally, as noted in the previous report, it is inherently better to prevent an illness from occurring in the first place than to need to treat it once it develops. Just as other areas of medicine have promoted healthy lifestyles and thereby have reduced the incidence of conditions such as heart disease and some cancers, so now is the time for mental health providers, researchers, and policy makers to focus more on promoting mental health and preventing mental and behavioral disorders. Following this course will yield incalculable benefits, not only in terms of societal costs, but also in the significant decrease of human suffering.

David Satcher, M.D., Ph.D.
Surgeon General

Acknowledgments

This report was prepared by the Department of Health and Human Services under the direction of the Office of the Surgeon General, in partnership with the Substance Abuse and Mental Health Services Administration, Center for Mental Health Services, and in consultation with the National Institutes of Health, National Institute of Mental Health.

RADM Arthur Lawrence, Ph.D., R.Ph., Assistant Surgeon General, Acting Principal Deputy Assistant Secretary for Health, Office of Public Health and Science, Office of the Secretary, Washington, D.C.

RADM Kenneth Moritsugu, M.D., M.P.H., Deputy Surgeon General, Office of the Surgeon General, Office of the Secretary, Washington, D.C.

CAPT Allan Noonan, M.D., M.P.H., Senior Advisor, Office of the Surgeon General, Office of the Secretary, Washington, D.C.

Joseph H. Autry III, M.D., Acting Administrator, Substance Abuse and Mental Health Services Administration, Rockville, Maryland.

Bernard S. Arons, M.D., Director, Center for Mental Health Services, Substance Abuse and Mental Health Services Administration, Rockville, Maryland.

Camille Barry, Ph.D., Deputy Director, Center for Mental Health Services, Substance Abuse and Mental Health Services Administration, Rockville, Maryland.

Michael English, J.D., Director, Division of Knowledge Development and Systems Change, Center for Mental Health Services, Substance Abuse and Mental Health Services Administration, Rockville, Maryland.

RADM Brian Flynn, Ed.D., Director, Division of Program Development, Special Populations and Projects, Center for Mental Health Services, Substance Abuse and Mental Health Services Administration, Rockville, Maryland.

Anne Mathews-Younes, Ed.D., Chief, Special Programs Development Branch, Center for Mental Health Services, Substance Abuse and Mental Health Services Administration, Rockville, Maryland.

Ruth L. Kirschstein, M.D., Acting Director, National Institutes of Health, Bethesda, Maryland.

Steven E. Hyman, M.D., Director, National Institute of Mental Health, National Institutes of Health, Bethesda, Maryland.

Richard Nakamura, Ph.D., Deputy Director, National Institute of Mental Health, National Institutes of Health, Rockville, Maryland.

Science Editors

Jeanne Miranda, Ph.D., Senior Science Editor, Professor, Department of Psychiatry and Biobehavioral Sciences, University of California Los Angeles Neuropsychiatric Institute, Los Angeles, California.

Lonnie R. Snowden, Ph.D., Science Editor, Director, Center for Mental Health Services Research, Professor, School of Social Welfare, University of California, Berkeley, California.

Spero M. Manson, Ph.D., Science Editor, Professor and Head, American Indian and Alaska Native Programs, Department of Psychiatry, University of Colorado Health Sciences Center, Denver, Colorado.

Stanley Sue, Ph.D., Science Editor, Professor, Departments of Psychiatry and Psychology, Director, Asian American Studies Program, University of California, Davis, California.

Steven R. Lopez, Ph.D., Science Editor, Professor, Department of Psychology, University of California, Los Angeles, California.

Managing Editors

Nancy J. Davis, Ed.D., Managing Editor, Public Health Advisor, Center for Mental Health Services, Substance Abuse and Mental Health Services Administration, Rockville, Maryland.

Kana Enomoto, M.A., Associate Managing Editor, Public Health Advisor, Center for Mental Health Services, Substance Abuse and Mental Health Services Administration, Rockville, Maryland.

CAPT Norma J. Hatot, Associate Managing Editor, Senior Nurse Consultant, Center for Mental Health Services, Substance Abuse and Mental Health Services Administration, Rockville, Maryland.

Science Writers

Miriam Davis, Ph.D., Senior Science Writer, Medical Writer and Consultant, Silver Spring, Maryland.

Sharon Hogan, M.A., Science Writer, Hingham, Massachusetts.

Science Consultants

Donna Chen, M.D., Assistant Professor, University of Virginia, Charlottesville, Virginia.

Laura Kohn, Ph.D., Assistant Professor, Department of Psychology, University of Michigan.

David Takeuchi, Ph.D., Professor, Department of Sociology, Indiana University, Bloomington, Indiana.

Planning Board and Peer Reviewers

Margarita Alegria, Ph.D., Associate Professor, Department of Administration, School of Public Health, Center for Evaluation and Socioeconomic Research, University of Puerto Rico, San Juan, Puerto Rico.

James P. Allen, Ph.D., Professor, Department of Geography, California State University Northridge, Northridge, California.

Naleen Andrade, M.D., Department of Psychiatry, John A. Burns School of Medicine, University of Hawaii at Manoa, Honolulu, Hawaii.

Thomas E. Arthur, M.Ed., M.A., Liaison for Consumer/Family, Core Service Agencies and Community Affairs, Maryland Health Partners, Columbia, Maryland.

Carl C. Bell, M.D., President and CEO, Community Mental Health Council, Chicago, Illinois.

Kinike Bermudez, Consumer Advocate, National Asian American Pacific Islander Mental Health Association, Richardson, Texas.

Teresa Chapa, Ph.D., Senior Social Science Analyst, Center for Mental Health Services, Substance Abuse and Mental Health Services Administration, Rockville, Maryland.

Daniel P. Chapman, Ph.D., Psychiatric Epidemiologist, Center for Disease Control and Prevention, Atlanta, Georgia.

Peggy Clark, M.S.W., M.P.A., Technical Director, Disabled and Elderly Health Program Group, Center for Medicaid and State Operations, Centers for Medicare and Medicaid Services, Baltimore, Maryland.

H. Westley Clark, M.D., J.D., M.P.H., Director, Center for Substance Abuse Treatment, Substance Abuse and Mental Health Services Administration, Rockville, Maryland.

Kim Crocker, R.N., Special Assistant to the Deputy Commissioner for International and Constituent Relations, Office of the Commissioner, Food and Drug Administration, Rockville, Maryland.

Terry L. Cross, A.C.S.W., Executive Director, National Indian Child Welfare Association, Portland, Oregon.

Marsha Davenport, M.D., M.P.H., Chief Medical Officer, Office of Strategic Planning, Centers for Medicare and Medicaid Services, Baltimore, Maryland.

King Davis, Ph.D., Robert Lee Sutherland Chair in Mental Health and Social Policy, University of Texas, Austin, Texas.

Deborah Duran, Ph.D., Former Public Health Analyst, Office of Policy and Program Coordination, Substance Abuse and Mental Health Services Administration, Rockville, Maryland.

Tom Edwards, Chief, Clinical Interventions and Organizational Models Branch, Center for Substance Abuse Treatment, Substance Abuse and Mental Health Services Administration, Rockville, Maryland.

Lloyd C. Elam, M.D., Professor Emeritus, Department of Psychiatry, Meharry Medical College, Nashville, Tennessee

Kathryn Ellis, J.D., Principal Deputy Director, Office for Civil Rights, Office of the Secretary, Washington, D.C.

Jill Erickson, M.S.W., A.C.S.W., Public Health Advisor, Center for Mental Health Services, Substance Abuse and Mental Health Services Administration, Rockville, Maryland.

Javier Escobar, M.D. Professor and Chairman, Department of Psychiatry, Robert Wood Johnson Medical School, University of Medicine and Dentistry of New Jersey, Piscataway, New Jersey.

Loma K. Flowers, M.D., Clinical Professor of Psychiatry, University of California at San Francisco, San Francisco, California

Blanca Fuentes, M.P.A., Public Affairs Coordinator, Office of Rural Health Policy, Health Resources and Services Administration, Rockville, Maryland.

Rosa M. Gil, D.S.W., Special Advisor to the Mayor for Health Policy, New York City Mayor's Office of Health Services, New York, New York.

Sherry A. M. Glied, Ph.D., Associate Professor, Joseph L. Mailman School of Public Health, Columbia University, New York, New York.

Howard Goldman, M.D., Ph.D., Professor of Psychiatry, University of Maryland School of Medicine, Potomac, Maryland.

Junius Gonzales, M.D., Chief, Services Research and Clinical Epidemiology Branch, Division of Services Intervention Research, National Institute of Mental Health, National Institutes of Health, Bethesda, Maryland.

Eric Goplerud, Ph.D., Acting Associate Administrator, Office of Policy and Program Coordination, Substance Abuse and Mental Health Services Administration, Rockville, Maryland.

Maria Guajardo-Lucero, Ph.D., Executive Director, Assets for Colorado Youth, Denver, Colorado.

Peggy Halpern, Ph.D., Program Specialist, Administration on Aging, National Institutes of Health, Bethesda, Maryland.

Kevin Hennessy, M.P.P., Ph.D., Health Policy Analyst, Office of the Assistant Secretary for Planning and Evaluation, Washington, D.C.

Pablo Hernandez, M.D., Administrator, Wyoming State Commission for Mental Health, Division of Behavioral Health, Evanston, Wyoming.

Angelia Hill, Office of Minority Health, Substance Abuse and Mental Health Services Administration, Rockville, Maryland.

Tiffany Ho, M.D., Former Senior Medical Policy Advisor, Center for Mental Health Services, Substance Abuse and Mental Health Services Administration, Rockville, Maryland.

Michael F. Hogan, Ph.D., Director, Ohio Department of Mental Health, Columbus, Ohio.

Thomas Horvath, M.D., F.R.A.C.P., Chief of Staff, Houston VAMC, Houston, Texas.

Larke Nahme Huang, Ph.D., Director of Research, National Technical Assistance Center for Children's Mental Health, Georgetown University Medical Center, Washington, D.C.

DeLoris Hunter, Ph.D., Director, Office of Minority Health, Substance Abuse and Mental Health Services Administration, Rockville, Maryland.

D.J. Ida, Ph.D., Executive Director, National Asian American Pacific Islander Mental Health Association, Denver, Colorado.

Diane Justice, Principal Deputy Assistant Secretary, Office of the Assistant Secretary for Aging, Administration on Aging, Washington, D.C.

Mireille Kanda, M.D., M.P.H., Director, Health and Disabilities Services, Administration of Children, Youth and Families, Administration for Children and Families, Washington, D.C.

George Kanuck, Public Health Analyst, Office of Policy, Coordination and Planning, Center for Substance Abuse Treatment, Substance Abuse and Mental Health Services Administration, Rockville, Maryland.

Kelly J. Kelleher, M.D., Staunton Professor of Pediatrics, Psychiatry, and Health Services, Schools of Medicine and Public Health, University of Pittsburgh, Pittsburgh, Pennsylvania.

Teresa La Fromboise, Ph.D., Associate Professor, School of Education, Stanford University, Palo Alto, California.

Inez Larsen, Ph.D., Program Director, Youth Regional Treatment Center, Right Road Recovery Programs, Inc., Corning, California.

Keh-Ming Lin, M.D., M.P.H., Professor and Director of Research, Center on the Psycho-biology of Ethnicity, Harbor-UCLA Medical Center, Torrance, California.

Francis Lu, M.D., Professor of Clinical Psychiatry, Director, Cultural Competence and Diversity Program, Department of Psychiatry, University of California, San Francisco, California.

Gerrie Maccannon, M.P.H., Special Assistant to the Director, Office of Minority Health, Substance Abuse and Mental Health Services Administration, Rockville, Maryland.

Delores Macey, Ph.D., Director, Cultural Action Program, South Carolina Department of Mental Health, Columbia, South Carolina.

Maria Mar, Director, Rehabilitation Support Team, Community Support Network, Santa Rosa, California.

Anthony Marsella, Ph.D., D.H.C., Professor, Department of Psychology, University of Hawaii at Manoa, Honolulu, Hawaii.

Harriet G. McCombs, Ph.D., Senior Mental Health Advisor, Bureau of Primary Health Care, Health Resources and Services Administration, Bethesda, Maryland.

Jacki McKinney, M.S.W., Consultant, Philadelphia, Pennsylvania.

Denise Middlebrook, Ph.D., Public Health Advisor, Center for Mental Health Services, Substance Abuse and Mental Health Services Administration, Rockville, Maryland.

Charlotte Mullican, M.P.H., Health Scientist Administrator, Agency for Healthcare Research and Quality, Rockville, Maryland.

Hector Myers, Ph.D., Professor, Department of Psychology, University of California, Los Angeles, California.

Linda James Myers, Ph.D., Associate Professor, Department of African-American and African Studies, Ohio State University, Columbus, Ohio.

Harold W. Neighbors, Ph.D., Associate Professor, Department of Health Behavior and Health Education, School of Public Health, University of Michigan, Ann Arbor, Michigan.

James O'Brien, Program Specialist, Head Start Bureau, Administration for Children and Families, Washington, D.C.

Delores Parron, Ph.D., Deputy Assistant Secretary for Program Systems, Office of the Assistant Secretary for Planning and Evaluation, Washington, D.C.

Chester M. Pierce, M.D., Professor Emeritus, Psychiatry and Education, Harvard University School of Medicine, Harvard University Graduate School of Education, Boston, Massachusetts

Bernice Pescosolido, Ph.D., Professor, Department of Sociology, Indiana University, Bloomington, Indiana.

Aquila Powell, Special Assistant, Office of the Assistant Secretary for Legislation, Washington, D.C.

Andres J. Pumariega, M.D., Professor and Director, Child & Adolescent Psychiatry, James H. Quillen College of Medicine, East Tennessee State University, Johnson City, Tennessee.

Juan Ramos, Ph.D., Senior Advisor, Office of the Director, National Institute of Mental Health, National Institutes of Health, Bethesda, Maryland.

Rochelle Rollins, Ph.D., Special Assistant, Bureau of Primary Health Care, Health Resources and Services Administration, Rockville, Maryland.

Josie T. Romero, M.S.W., President, National Latino Behavioral Health Association, Gilroy, California.

Soledad Sambrano, Ph.D., Team Leader, Individual and Family Studies Unit, Center for Substance Abuse Prevention, Substance Abuse and Mental Health Services Administration, Rockville, Maryland.

Ruth Sanchez-Way, Ph.D., Acting Director, Center for Substance Abuse Prevention, Substance Abuse and Mental Health Services Administration, Rockville, Maryland.

Jean G. Spaulding, M.D., Vice Chancellor for Health Affairs, Duke University Medical Center, Durham, North Carolina

RADM Nathan Stinson, Jr., Ph.D., M.D., M.P.H., Deputy Assistant Secretary for Minority Health, Office of Public Health and Science, Office of the Secretary, Department of Health and Human Services, Rockville, Maryland.

Carolyn Strete, Ph.D., Associate Director for Health Disparities, Office of the Director, National Institute of Mental Health, National Institutes of Health, Bethesda, Maryland.

Gregg Taliaferro, Ph.D., Social Scientist, Agency for Healthcare Research and Quality, Rockville, Maryland.

Pamela Thurman, Ph.D., Research Associate, Tri-Ethnic Center for Prevention Research, Colorado State University, Fort Collins, Colorado.

RADM W. Craig Vanderwagen, M.D., Assistant Surgeon General, and Director, Office of Clinical and Preventive Services, Indian Health Service, Rockville, Maryland.

William Vega, Ph.D., Professor, Department of Psychiatry, Robert Wood Johnson Medical School, University of Medicine and Dentistry of New Jersey, New Brunswick, New Jersey.

Kenneth B. Wells, M.D., M.P.H., Professor, Department of Psychiatry and Biobehavioral Sciences, University of California Los Angeles Neuropsychiatric Institute, Los Angeles, California.

David R. Williams, Ph.D., Professor, Department of Sociology, University of Michigan, Ann Arbor, Michigan.

Roy C. Wilson, M.D., Director, Missouri Department of Mental Health, Jefferson City, Missouri.

Wilbur Woods, M.A., Management Analyst, Behavioral Health, Rockville, Maryland.

Participants in the Development of the Report

RADM Thomas Bornemann, Ed.D., Former Deputy Director, Center for Mental Health Services, Substance Abuse and Mental Health Services Administration, Rockville, Maryland.

Rhonda Baron-Hall, Ph.D., University of Pittsburgh at Bradford, Bradford, Pennsylvania.

Cheryl A. Boyce, Ph.D., Acting Chief, Sociocultural Processes and Health Disparities Program, National Institute of Mental Health, National Institutes of Health, Bethesda, Maryland.

Shelly Burgess, Office of External Liaison, Center for Mental Health Services, Substance Abuse and Mental Health Services Administration, Rockville, Maryland.

Nelba Chavez, Ph.D., Former Administrator, Substance Abuse and Mental Health Services Administration, Rockville, Maryland.

Jennifer Fiedelholtz, Ph.D., Office of Policy and Program Coordination, Substance Abuse and Mental Health Services Administration, Rockville, Maryland.

Theodora Fine, M.A., Senior Public Affairs Specialist and Director of Communications Policy and Strategy, Office of Communications, Substance Abuse and Mental Health Services Administration, Rockville, Maryland.

Charlotte Gordon, Writer/Editor, Office of the Director, Center for Mental Health Services, Substance Abuse and Mental Health Services Administration, Rockville, Maryland.

LTJG Christine L. Guthrie, M.P.H., Public Health Advisor, Center for Mental Health Services, Substance Abuse and Mental Health Services Administration, Rockville, Maryland.

Sabrina Harrison, Secretary, Office of the Director, Center for Mental Health Services, Substance Abuse and Mental Health Services Administration, Rockville, Maryland.

Timothy C. Hays, Ph.D., Special Assistant to the Deputy Director, Office of the Director, National Institute of Mental Health, National Institutes of Health, Bethesda, Maryland.

Denyse Hicks, Ph.D., African American Women's Mental Health Authority, Philadelphia, Pennsylvania.

Ann A. Hohmann, Ph.D., M.P.H., Chief, Methodological , Sociocultural Services, and Quality of Care Research Programs, National Institute of Mental Health, National Institutes of Health, Bethesda, Maryland.

Jeannette Johnson, Ph.D., Associate Professor, Department of Psychiatry, University of Maryland, Baltimore, Maryland.

Mary Knipmeyer, Ph.D., Program Director, HIV/AIDS Treatment Adherence, Health Outcomes, and Cost Study. Office of the Associate Director for Medical Affairs, Center for Mental Health Services, Rockville, Maryland.

Kathy L. Kopniski, Ph.D., Special Assistant to the Director, National Institute of Mental Health, National Institutes of Health, Bethesda, Maryland.

Nicole Lurie, M.D., M.S.P.H., Former Principal Deputy Assistant Secretary for Health, Office of Public Health and Science, Office of the Secretary, Washington, D.C.

Michael Malden, Public Affairs Specialist, Office of External Liaison, Center for Mental Health Services, Substance Abuse and Mental Health Services Administration, Rockville, Maryland.

Beverly L. Malone, Ph.D., R.N., F.A.A.N., Former Deputy Assistant Secretary for Health, Office of Public Health and Science, Office of the Secretary, Washington, D.C.

Lynn Mandujano, Editor, Program Support Center, Department of Health and Human Services, Rockville, Maryland.

Anna Marsh, Ph.D., Director, Office of Program Services, Division of Administrative Services, Substance Abuse and Mental Health Services Administration, Rockville, Maryland.

Leah McGee, Program Assistant, Office of the Director, Center for Mental Health Services, Substance Abuse and Mental Health Services Administration, Rockville, Maryland.

Carolyn O'Connor, Project Director, Program Support Center, Department of Health and Human Services, Rockville, Maryland.

Rajesh Rao, Office of the Director, National Institute of Mental Health, National Institutes of Health, Bethesda, Maryland.

CAPT Patricia Rye, J.D., M.S.W., Former Managing Editor, Office of the Director, Center for Mental Health Services, Substance Abuse and Mental Health Services Administration, Rockville, Maryland.

Juned Siddique, M.S., Statistician, Department of Psychiatry and Biobehavioral Sciences, University of California Los Angeles Neuropsychiatric Institute, Los Angeles, California.

Anne Thomas, Editor, Program Support Center, Department of Health and Human Services, Rockville, Maryland.

Damon Thompson, Director of Communications, Office of Public Health and Science, Office of the Assistant Secretary, Washington, D.C.

Mark Weber, Associate Administrator, Office of Communications, Substance Abuse and Mental Health Services Administration, Rockville, Maryland.

Special Thanks

Parklawn Health Library Staff, Rockville, Maryland.

Numerous interns from various programs including the Hispanic Association of Colleges and Universities and the National Association for Equal Opportunity in Higher Education.

MENTAL HEALTH:
A REPORT OF THE SURGEON GENERAL

Chapter 4

Chapter 5

Chapter 6

Chapter 7

Appendix A

Appendix B

CHAPTER 1
INTRODUCTION

Contents

CHAPTER 1

INTRODUCTION

America draws strength from its cultural diversity. The contributions of racial and ethnic minorities have suffused all areas of contemporary life. Diversity has made our Nation a more vibrant and open society, ablaze in ideas, perspectives, and innovations. But the full potential of our diverse, multicultural society cannot be realized until all Americans, including racial and ethnic minorities, gain access to quality health care that meets their needs.

This Supplement to *Mental Health: A Report of the Surgeon General* (U.S. Department of Health and Human Services [DHHS], 1999) documents the existence of striking disparities for minorities in mental health services and the underlying knowledge base. Racial and ethnic minorities have less access to mental health services than do whites.[1] They are less likely to receive needed care. When they receive care, it is more likely to be poor in quality.

These disparities have powerful significance for minority groups and for society as a whole. *A major finding of this Supplement is that racial and ethnic minorities bear a greater burden from unmet mental health needs and thus suffer a greater loss to their overall health and productivity.* This conclusion draws on prominent international and national findings. One is that mental disorders are highly disabling across all populations.[2] According to a landmark study by the World Health Organization, the World Bank, and Harvard University, mental disorders are so disabling that, in established market economies like the United States, they rank second only to cardiovascular disease in their impact on disability (Murray & Lopez, 1996). Another important finding comes from the largest disability study ever conducted in the United States It found that one-third of disabled[3] adults (ages 18–55)

living in the community[4] reported having a mental disorder contributing to their disability (Druss et al., 2000).

While neither of these studies addressed the disability burden for minorities relative to whites, key findings from this Supplement do: Most minority groups are less likely than whites to use services, and they receive poorer quality mental health care, despite having similar community rates of mental disorders. Similar prevalence, combined with lower utilization and poorer quality of care, means that minority communities have a higher proportion of individuals with unmet mental health needs. Further, minorities are overrepresented among the Nation's vulnerable, high-need[5] groups, such as homeless and incarcerated persons. These subpopulations have higher rates of mental disorders than do people living in the community (Koegel et al., 1988; Vernez et al., 1988; Breakey et al., 1989; Teplin, 1990). Taken together, the evidence suggests that the disability burden from unmet mental health needs is disproportionately high for racial and ethnic minorities relative to whites.

The greater disability burden to minorities is of grave concern to public health, and it has very real consequences. Ethnic and racial minorities do not yet completely share in the hope afforded by remarkable scientific advances in understanding and treating mental disorders. Because of preventable disparities in mental health services, a disproportionate number of minorities are not fully benefiting from, or contributing to, the opportunities and prosperity of our society.

More is known about the existence of disparities in mental health services — and their significance — than the reasons behind them. The most likely explanations, identified in *Mental Health: A Report of the Surgeon*

---

[1] This Supplement uses the term "whites" to denote non-Hispanic white Americans.

[2] Disability is measured in terms of lost years of healthy life from either disability or premature death.

[3] Disability is self-reported and defined as having a level of functional impairment sufficient to restrict major life activities.

[4] Most epidemiological studies using disorder-based definitions of mental illness are conducted in community household surveys. They fail to include nonhousehold members, such as persons without homes or persons residing in institutions such as residential treatment centers, jails, shelters, and hospitals.

[5] This Supplement defines vulnerable, high-need groups as any population subgroup (such as children or adults who are homeless, incarcerated, or in foster care) which has (1) a higher risk for mental illness, (2) a higher need for mental health services, or (3) a higher risk for not receiving mental health services.

General, are expanded upon throughout this Supplement. They trace to a mix of barriers deterring minorities from seeking treatment or operating to reduce its quality once they reach treatment.

The foremost barriers include the cost of care, societal stigma, and the fragmented organization of services. Additional barriers include clinicians' lack of awareness of cultural issues, bias, or inability to speak the client's language, and the client's fear and mistrust of treatment. More broadly, disparities also stem from minorities' historical and present day struggles with racism and discrimination, which affect their mental health and contribute to their lower economic, social, and political status.

The cumulative weight and interplay of all of these barriers, not any single one alone, is likely responsible for mental health disparities. Furthermore, these barriers operate to discernibly different degrees for different individuals and groups, depending on life circumstances, age, gender, sexual orientation, or spiritual beliefs. What becomes amply clear from this report is that there are no uniform racial or ethnic groups, white or nonwhite. Rather, each is highly heterogeneous, including a diverse mix of immigrants, refugees, and multigenerational Americans, with vastly different histories, languages, spiritual practices, demographic patterns, and cultures.

Origins and Purposes of the Supplement

This Supplement, *Mental Health: Culture, Race, and Ethnicity*, is an outgrowth of the 1999 report, *Mental Health: A Report of the Surgeon General*, the first Surgeon General's report ever issued on mental health and mental illness. That report (hereinafter called the SGR) called attention to several overarching points that resonate throughout this Supplement (Box 1–1). Through extensive documentation of the scientific literature, the report found that mental disorders are real and disabling conditions for which there are a range of effective treatments. It found that the efficacy of mental health treatment is well documented. On the basis of these findings, the Surgeon General made a single, explicit recommendation for everyone: *Seek help if you have a mental health problem or think you have symptoms of a mental disorder.* This Supplement affirms this vital recommendation and the major findings in which it is firmly anchored.

Overall, the SGR provided hope for people with, or at risk for, mental disorders by presenting the evidence for what can be done to prevent and treat mental illness. It also provided hope for recovery from mental illness. In his Preface, however, the Surgeon General pointed out that all Americans do not share this hope equally:

Even more than other areas of health and medicine, the mental health field is plagued by disparities in the availability of and access to its services. These disparities are viewed readily through the lenses of racial and cultural diversity, age, and gender. (DHHS, 1999, p. vi)

Box 1–1

Mental Health: A Report of the Surgeon General

Themes of the Report

- Mental health and mental illness require the broad focus of a public health approach.

- Mental disorders are disabling conditions.

- Mental health and mental illness are points on a continuum.

- Mind and body are inseparable.

- Stigma is a major obstacle preventing people from getting help.

Messages from the Surgeon General

- Mental health is fundamental to health.

- Mental illnesses are real health conditions.

- The efficacy of mental health treatments is well documented.

- A range of treatments exists for most mental disorders.

This Supplement was undertaken to probe more deeply into mental health disparities affecting racial and ethnic minorities. Drawing on scientific evidence from a wide-ranging body of empirical research, the Supplement has three purposes:

(1) To understand better the nature and extent of mental health disparities,

(2) To present the evidence on the need for mental health services and on the provision of services to meet those needs, and

(3) To document promising directions toward the elimination of mental health disparities and the promotion of mental health.

This Supplement covers the four most recognized racial and ethnic minority groups in the United States. According to Federal classifications, African Americans (blacks), American Indians and Alaska Natives, Asian Americans and Pacific Islanders, and white Americans (whites) are races. Hispanic American (Latino) is an ethnicity and may apply to a person of any race (U.S. Office of Management and Budget [OMB], 1978). For example, many people from the Dominican Republic identify their ethnicity as Hispanic or Latino and their race as black.

The U.S. Office of Management and Budget created these four categories for the collection of census and other types of information by Federal agencies. One limitation is that each category groups together an extremely heterogeneous array of ethnic groups. For example, the Bureau of Indian Affairs currently recognizes 561 American Indian and Alaska Native tribes. Further, the broad category labels are imprecise: People who are indigenous to the Americas, for example, may be called Hispanic if they are from Mexico but American Indian if they are from the United States. Despite these well recognized limitations, these categories are used for this Supplement because they serve as standard nomenclature for data collection and research.[6]

This Supplement employs the term "racial and ethnic minorities" to refer collectively to people who identify as African Americans, American Indians and Alaska Natives, Asian Americans and Pacific Islanders, and Hispanic Americans. The term "minority" is used to signify the groups' limited political power and social resources, as well as their unequal access to opportunities, social rewards, and social status. The term is not meant to connote inferiority or to indicate small demographic size.

The four major groups covered by this Supplement accounted for about 30 percent of the U.S. population in 2000. They are projected to account for almost 40 percent by 2025.[7] Figure 1–1 illustrates the growth in population size across racial and ethnic groups. The demographic surge in minority populations projected over the next two decades is expected to accompany continuing economic gaps between rich and poor. These gaps progressively narrowed from 1947 to 1968 but then reversed course: Income inequality rose over a 25-year period, from 1968 to 1993 (U.S. Census, 2000). These trends swelled the ranks of rich and poor, and reduced the size of the middle class. From 1993 to 1998, changes in income inequality leveled off, but significant disparities still exist.[8] Income status is relevant to mental health because of the strong association between lower income and higher rates of mental health problems and disorders (Chapter 2), and because of the association between health insurance and the ability to pay for mental health services (Brown et al., 2000) (Chapters 2–7).

Scope and Terminology

Mental Health and Mental Illness

The focus of this Supplement is on mental health and mental illness in racial and ethnic minorities. Mental health and mental illness are not polar opposites, but points on a continuum. Somewhere in the middle of that continuum are "mental health problems," which most people have experienced at some point in their lives. The experience of feeling low and dispirited in the face of a stressful job is a familiar example. The boundaries between mental health problems and milder forms of mental illness are often indistinct, just as they are in many other areas of health. Yet at the far end of the continuum lie disabling mental illnesses such as major depression, schizophrenia, and bipolar disorder. Left untreated, these disorders erase any doubt as to their devastating potential.

The SGR offered general definitions of mental health, mental illness, and mental health problems (Box 1–2). It described mental health as important for personal well-being, family and interpersonal relationships,

---

[6] In recognition of the limitations of the broad groupings, a major revision occurred with the 2000 census. The revision allows individuals to identify with more than one group (OMB, 2000). The U.S. Census Bureau anticipates that this change will result in approximately 63 different categories of racial and ethnic identifications.

[7] Wherever possible, this Supplement uses the most recent data from the 2000 census. However, because of the recency of results, more specialized analyses have yet to be performed. Therefore, this Supplement also draws on analyses of previous census data.

[8] Reasons behind growth in income inequality include the reduction in blue-collar jobs in manufacturing and less reliance on uneducated workers (Mishel & Bernstein, 1992). Also, there was a shift to technical service, information technology, and management (Drucker, 1993; U.S. Census Bureau, 2000).

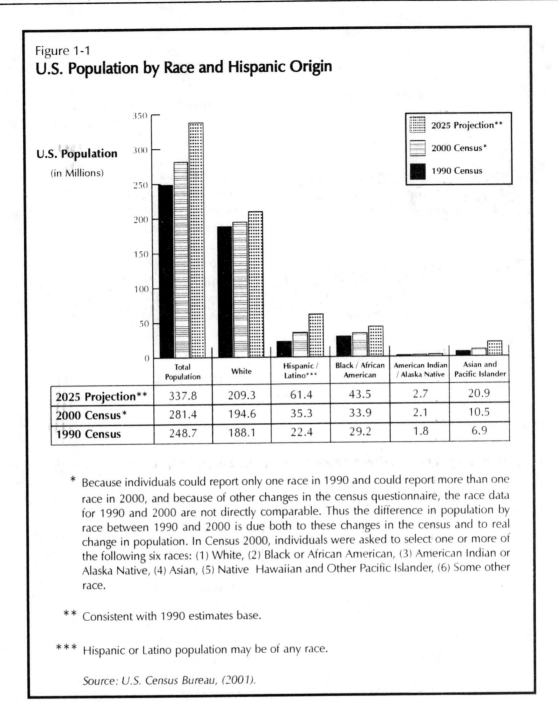

Figure 1-1
U.S. Population by Race and Hispanic Origin

	Total Population	White	Hispanic / Latino***	Black / African American	American Indian / Alaska Native	Asian and Pacific Islander
2025 Projection**	337.8	209.3	61.4	43.5	2.7	20.9
2000 Census*	281.4	194.6	35.3	33.9	2.1	10.5
1990 Census	248.7	188.1	22.4	29.2	1.8	6.9

* Because individuals could report only one race in 1990 and could report more than one race in 2000, and because of other changes in the census questionnaire, the race data for 1990 and 2000 are not directly comparable. Thus the difference in population by race between 1990 and 2000 is due both to these changes in the census and to real change in population. In Census 2000, individuals were asked to select one or more of the following six races: (1) White, (2) Black or African American, (3) American Indian or Alaska Native, (4) Asian, (5) Native Hawaiian and Other Pacific Islander, (6) Some other race.

** Consistent with 1990 estimates base.

*** Hispanic or Latino population may be of any race.

Source: U.S. Census Bureau, (2001).

and successful contributions to community or society. These are jeopardized by mental health problems and mental illnesses.

While these elements of mental health may be identifiable, mental health itself is not easy to define more precisely because any definition is rooted in value judgments that may vary across individuals and cultures. According to a distinguished leader in the field of mental health, "Because values differ across cultures as well as among some groups (and indeed individuals) within a culture, the ideal of the uniformly acceptable definition of [mental health] is illusory" (Cowen, 1994).

Mental illness refers collectively to all diagnosable mental disorders. Mental disorders feature abnormalities in cognition, emotion or mood, and the highest integrative aspects of human behavior, such as social interactions. Depression, anxiety, schizophrenia, and other mental disorders are commonly found in the U.S. population, affecting about 1 in 5 adults and children (DHHS, 1999). The prevalence rates for mental disorders in U.S. adults are presented in Table 1–1.

It would be helpful to be able to construct a similar table for racial and ethnic minorities. The patterns of specific mental disorders could then be compared

Box 1–2

Mental Health The successful performance of mental function, resulting in productive activities, fulfilling relationships with other people, and the ability to adapt to change and to cope with adversity.

Mental Illness The term that refers collectively to all mental disorders, which are health conditions characterized by alterations in thinking, mood, or behavior (or some combination thereof) associated with distress and/or impaired functioning.

Mental Health Problems Signs and symptoms of insufficient intensity or duration to meet the criteria for any mental disorder.

Source: DHHS (1999).

between each minority group and the U.S. population as a whole. Unfortunately, prevalence rates are not yet known for *each* mental disorder within a given minority population. The studies published thus far are not sufficiently nationally representative; however, such nationally representative studies are currently in progress. Nevertheless, this Supplement finds enough evidence from many smaller studies to conclude that the *overall* rate of mental illness among minorities is similar to the *overall* rate of about 21 percent across the U.S. population. In short, the patterns of prevalence for specific mental disorders within the overall rate may vary somewhat, but the *total* prevalence appears to be similar across populations living in community settings.[9]

Mental disorders reflect abnormal functioning of the brain. They alter mental life and behavior by affecting the function of neurocircuits, the elaborate pathways through which cells in the brain (neurons) communicate with one another and with other parts of the body. The precise causes of most mental disorders are not known; the broad forces that shape them are genetic, psychological, social, and cultural, which interact in ways not yet fully understood. The modern field of integrative neuroscience strives to explain how genes and environment (broadly defined to include culture) work together in a dynamic rather than a static manner to produce mental life and behavior. The field focuses on many levels of

investigation —molecular, cellular, systems, and behavior — to uncover the basis for mental health and mental illness. It does not separate nature from nurture, pitting them against one another. Rather, the field examines their interaction, the ways in which mental life and experience over time actually change the structure and function of neurocircuits. Through learning and memories that come with personal experience and socialization, neurocircuits are sculpted and shaped throughout life (Kandel, 1998; Hyman, 2000) .

Race, Ethnicity, and Culture

Any report of this magnitude needs to define the major terms it uses, all the more so when the terms are often controversial. The problem is that *precise* definitions of the terms "race," "ethnicity," and "culture" are elusive. As social concepts, they have so many different meanings, and those meanings evolve over time. With these caveats in mind, this section expands upon the general definitions of the terms adopted by the SGR.

Race

Most people think of "race" as a biological category — as a way to divide and label different groups according to a set of common inborn biological traits (e.g., skin color, or shape of eyes, nose, and face). Despite this popular view, there are no biological criteria for dividing races into distinct categories (Lewontin, 1972; Owens & King, 1999). No consistent racial groupings emerge when people are sorted by physical and biological characteristics. For example, the epicanthic eye fold that produces the so-called "Asian" eye shape is shared by the !Kung San Bushmen, members of an African nomadic tribe.

The visible physical traits associated with race, such as hair and skin color, are defined by a tiny fraction of our genes, and they do not reliably differentiate between the social categories of race. As more is learned about the 30,000 genes of the human genome, variations between groups are being identified, such as in genes that code for the enzymes active in drug metabolism (Chapter 2). While such information may prove to have clinical utility, it is important to note that these variations cannot be used to distinguish groups from one another as they are outweighed by overwhelming genetic similarities across so-called racial groups (Paabo, 2001).

The strongest, most compelling evidence to refute race as a biological category comes from genetic analysis of different racial groups. There is overwhelmingly

---

[9] Except as noted in Chapter 2 regarding the lack of data for some ethnic groups.

Table 1–1

Prevalence rates (1-year) of mental disorders: Best estimates for adults, ages 18–54

	ECA Prevalence (%)	NCS Prevalence (%)	Best Estimate **(%)
Any Anxiety Disorder	13.1	18.7	16.4
Simple Phobia	8.3	8.6	8.3
Social Phobia	2.0	7.4	2.0
Agoraphobia	4.9	3.7	4.9
GAD	(1.5)*	3.4	3.4
Panic Disorder	1.6	2.2	1.6
OCD	2.4	(0.9)*	2.4
PTSD	(1.9)*	3.6	3.6
Any Mood Disorder	7.1	11.1	7.1
MD Episode	6.5	10.1	6.5
Unipolar MD	5.3	8.9	5.3
Dysthymia	1.6	2.5	1.6
Bipolar I	1.1	1.3	1.1
Bipolar II	0.6	0.2	0.6
Schizophrenia	1.3	-	1.3
Nonaffective Psychosis	-	0.2	0.2
Somatization	0.2	-	0.2
ASP	2.1	-	2.1
Anorexia Nervosa	0.1	-	0.1
Severe Cognitive Impairment	1.2	-	1.2
Any Disorder	19.5	23.4	21.0

*Numbers in parentheses indicate the prevalence of the disorder without any comorbidity. These rates were calculated using the NCS data for GAD and PTSD, and the ECA data for OCD. The rates were not used in calculating the any anxiety disorder and any disorder totals for the ECA and NCS columns. The unduplicated GAD and PTSD rates were added to the best estimate total for any anxiety disorder (3.3%) and any disorder (1.5%).

**In developing best-estimate 1-year prevalence rates from the two studies, a conservative procedure was followed that had previously been used in an independent scientific analysis comparing these two data sets (Andrews, 1995). For any mood disorder and any anxiety disorder, the lower estimate of the two surveys was selected, which for these data was the ECA. The best estimate rates for the individual mood and anxiety disorders were then chosen from the ECA only, in order to maintain the relationships between the individual disorders. For other disorders that were not covered in both surveys, the available estimate was used.

Key to abbreviations: ECA, Epidemiologic Catchment Area; NCS, National Comorbidity Survey; GAD, generalized anxiety disorder; OCD, obsessive-compulsive disorder; PTSD, post-traumatic stress disorder; MD, major depression; ASP, antisocial personality disorder.

Table reprinted from *Mental Health: A Report of the Surgeon General*, DHHS, 1999.

greater genetic variation within a racial group than across racial groups. One study examined the variation in 109 DNA regions that were known to contain a high level of polymorphisms, or DNA sequence variations. Published in one of the most respected scientific journals and in agreement with earlier research, it found that 85 percent of human genetic diversity is found within a given racial group (Barbujani et al., 1997).

Race is not a biological category, but it does have meaning as a social category. Different cultures classify people into racial groups according to a set of characteristics that are *socially* significant. The concept of race is especially potent when certain social groups are separated, treated as inferior or superior, and given differential access to power and other valued resources. This is the definition adopted by this Supplement because of its significance in understanding the mental health of racial and ethnic minority groups in American society.

Ethnicity

Ethnicity refers to a common heritage shared by a particular group (Zenner, 1996). Heritage includes similar history, language, rituals, and preferences for music and foods. Historical experiences are so pivotal to understanding ethnic identity and current health status that they occupy the introductory portion of each chapter covering a racial or ethnic group (Chapters 3–6).

The term "race," when defined as a social category, may overlap with ethnicity, but each has a different social meaning. For example, in many national surveys and in the 1990 U.S. census, Native Hawaiians and Vietnamese Americans are classified together in the racial category of "Asian and Pacific Islander Americans." Native Hawaiians, however, have very little in common with Vietnamese Americans in terms of their heritage. Similarly, Caribbean blacks and Pacific Northwest Indians have different ethnicities than others within their same racial category. And, as noted earlier, because Hispanics are an ethnicity, not a race, the different Latino American ethnic subgroups such as Cubans, Dominicans, Mexicans, Puerto Ricans, and Peruvians include individuals of all races.

Culture

Culture is broadly defined as a common heritage or set of beliefs, norms, and values (DHHS, 1999). It refers to the shared, and largely learned, attributes of a group of people. Anthropologists often describe culture as a system of shared meanings. People who are placed, either by census categories or through self-identification, into

the same racial or ethnic group are often assumed to share the same culture. Yet this assumption is an over-generalization because not all members grouped together in a given category will share the same culture. Many may identify with other social groups to which they feel a stronger cultural tie such as being Catholic, Texan, teenaged, or gay.

Culture is as applicable to groups of whites, such as Irish Americans or German Americans, as it is to racial and ethnic minorities. As noted, the term "culture" is also applicable to the shared values, beliefs, and norms established in common social groupings, such as adults trained in the same profession or youth who belong to a gang. The culture of clinicians, for example, is discussed in Chapter 2 to help explain interactions between patients and clinicians.

The phrase "cultural identity" refers to the culture with which someone identifies and to which he or she looks for standards of behavior (Cooper & Denner, 1998). Given the variety of ways in which to define a cultural group, many people consider themselves to have multiple cultural identities.

A key aspect of any culture is that it is dynamic: Culture continually changes and is influenced both by people's beliefs and the demands of their environment (Lopez & Guarnaccia, 2000). Immigrants from different parts of the world arrive in the United States with their own culture but gradually begin to adapt. The term "acculturation" refers to the socialization process by which minority groups gradually learn and adopt selective elements of the dominant culture. Yet that dominant culture is itself transformed by its interaction with minority groups. And, to make matters more complex, the immigrant group may form its own culture, distinct from both its country of origin and the dominant culture. The Chinatowns of major cities in the United States often exemplify the blending of Chinese traditions and an American context.

The dominant culture for much of U.S. history has centered on the beliefs, norms, and values of white Americans of Judeo-Christian origin, but today's America is much more multicultural in character. Still, its societal institutions, including those that educate and train mental health professionals, have been shaped by white American culture and, in a broader characterization, Western culture. That cultural legacy has left its imprint on how mental health professionals respond to patients in all facets of care, beginning with their very first encounter, the diagnostic interview.

Diagnosis and Culture

Western medicine has become a cornerstone of health worldwide because it is based on evidence from scientific research. A hallmark of Western medicine is its reliance on accurate diagnosis, the identification and classification of disease. An accurate diagnosis dictates the type of treatment and supportive care, and it sheds light on prognosis and course of illness. The diagnosis of a mental disorder is arguably more difficult than diagnoses in other areas of medicine and health because there are usually no definitive lesions (pathological abnormalities) or laboratory tests. Rather, a diagnosis depends on a pattern, or clustering, of symptoms (i.e., subjective complaints), observable signs, and behavior associated with distress or disability. Disability is impairment in one or more areas of functioning at home, work, school, or in the community (American Psychiatric Association [APA], 1994).

The formal diagnosis of a mental disorder is made by a clinician and hinges upon three components: a patient's description of the nature, intensity, and duration of symptoms; signs from a mental status examination; and a clinician's observation and interpretation of the patient's behavior, including functional impairment. The final diagnosis rests on the clinician's judgment about whether the patient's signs, symptom patterns, and impairments of functioning meet the criteria for a given diagnosis. The American Psychiatric Association sets forth those diagnostic criteria in a standard manual known as the *Diagnostic and Statistical Manual of Mental Disorders*. This is the most widely used classification system, both nationally and internationally, for teaching, research, and clinical practice (Maser et al., 1991).

Mental disorders are found worldwide. Schizophrenia, bipolar disorder, panic disorder, and depression have similar symptom profiles across several continents (Weissman et al., 1994, 1996, 1997, 1998). Yet diagnosis can be extremely challenging, even to the most gifted clinicians, because the manifestations of mental disorders and other physical disorders vary with age, gender, race, ethnicity, and culture. Take some of the symptoms of depression — persistent sadness or despair, hopelessness, social withdrawal — and imagine the difficulty of communication and interpretation within a culture, much less from one culture to another. The challenge rests not only with the patient, but also with the clinician, as well as with their dynamic interactions. Patients from one culture may manifest and communicate symptoms in a way poorly understood in the culture of the clinician. Consider that words such as "depressed" and "anxious" are absent from the languages of some American Indians and Alaska Natives (Manson et al., 1985). However, this does not preclude them from having depression or anxiety.

To arrive at a diagnosis, clinicians must determine whether patients' signs and symptoms significantly impair their functioning at home, school, work, and in their communities. This judgment is based on deviation from social norms (cultural standards of acceptable behavior) (Scadding, 1996). For example, among some cultural groups, perceiving visions or voices of religious figures might be part of normal religious experience on some occasions and aberrant social functioning on other occasions. It becomes obvious that the interaction between clinician and patient is rife with possibilities for miscommunication and misunderstanding when they are from different cultures. According to the American Psychiatric Association,

> *Diagnostic assessment can be especially challenging when a clinician from one ethnic or cultural group uses the DSM–IV Classification to evaluate an individual from a different ethnic or cultural group. A clinician who is unfamiliar with the nuances of an individual's cultural frame of reference may incorrectly judge as psychopathology those normal variations in behavior, beliefs, or experience that are particular to the individual's culture. (APA, 1994)*

The multifaceted ways that culture influences mental illness and mental health services are discussed at length in Chapter 2.

The issuance in 1994 of the fourth edition of the *Diagnostic and Statistical Manual of Mental Disorders* (DSM–IV) marked a new level of acknowledgment of the role of culture in shaping the symptom presentation, expression, and course of mental disorders. Whereas prior editions referred to such matters only in passing, this edition specifically included some discussion of cultural variations in the clinical presentation of each DSM–IV disorder, a glossary of some idioms of distress and "culture-bound syndromes" (Box 1–3), and a brief outline to assist the clinician in formulating the cultural dimensions for an individual patient (APA, 1994).

The "Outline for Cultural Formulation" in DSM–IV systematically calls attention to five distinct aspects of the cultural context of illness and their relevance to diagnosis and care. The clinician is encouraged to:

Box 1–3

Idioms of Distress and Culture-Bound Syndromes

Idioms of distress are ways in which different cultures express, experience, and cope with feelings of distress. One example is *somatization*, or the expression of distress through physical symptoms (Kirmayer & Young, 1998). Stomach disturbances, excessive gas, palpitations, and chest pain are common forms of *somatization* in Puerto Ricans, Mexican Americans, and whites (Escobar et al., 1987). Some Asian groups express more cardiopulmonary and vestibular symptoms, such as dizziness, vertigo, and blurred vision (Hsu & Folstein, 1997). In Africa and South Asia, *somatization* sometimes takes the form of burning hands and feet, or the experience of worms in the head or ants crawling under the skin (APA, 1994).

Culture-bound syndromes are clusters of symptoms much more common in some cultures than in others. For example, some Latino patients, especially women from the Caribbean, display *ataque de nervios*, a condition that includes screaming uncontrollably, attacks of crying, trembling, and verbal or physical aggression. Fainting or seizure-like episodes and suicidal gestures may sometimes accompany these symptoms (Guarnaccia et al., 1993). A culture-bound syndrome from Japan is *taijin kyofusho*, an intense fear that one's body or bodily functions give offense to others. This syndrome is listed as a diagnosis in the Japanese clinical modification of the World Health Organization (WHO) International Classification of Diseases, 10th edition (1993).

Numerous other culture-bound syndromes are given in the DSM–IV "Glossary of Culture-Bound Syndromes." Researchers have taken initial steps to examine the interrelationships between culture-bound syndromes and the diagnostic classifications of DSM–IV. For example, in a sample of Latinos seeking care for anxiety disorders, 70 percent reported having at least one *ataque*. Of those, over 40 percent met DSM–IV criteria for panic disorder, and nearly 25 percent met criteria for major depression (Liebowitz et al., 1994). In past research, there has been an effort to fit culture-bound syndromes into variants of DSM diagnoses. Rather than assume that DSM diagnostic entities or culture-bound syndromes are the basic patterns of illness, current investigators are interested in examining how the social, cultural, and biological contexts interact to shape illnesses and reactions to them. This is an important area of research in a field known as cultural psychiatry or ethnopsychiatry.

(1) Inquire about patients' **cultural identity** to determine their ethnic or cultural reference group, language abilities, language use, and language preference,

(2) Explore possible **cultural explanations of the illness**, including patients' idioms of distress, the meaning and perceived severity of their symptoms in relation to the norms of the patients' cultural reference group, and their current preferences for, as well as past experiences with, professional and popular sources of care,

(3) Consider **cultural factors related to the psychosocial environment and levels of functioning.** This assessment includes culturally relevant interpretations of social stressors, available support, and levels of functioning, as well as patients' disability,

(4) Critically examine **cultural elements in the patient-clinician relationship** to determine differences in culture and social status between them and how those differences affect the clinical encounter, ranging from communication to rapport and disclosure,

(5) Render an **overall cultural assessment for diagnosis and care**, meaning that the clinician synthesizes all of the information to determine a course of care.

The "Outline for Cultural Formulation" has been heralded as a major step forward, but with limitations related to its scope, depth, and placement in an appendix (see review in Lopez & Guarnaccia, 2000). Because major areas were omitted in the final version of the Outline, some assert that the scope is too narrow to reflect the dynamic role of culture in mental health problems and disorders (Lewis-Fernandez & Kleinman, 1995; Mezzich et al., 1999).

Other mental health experts point out that the discussion of idioms of distress is too limited and fails to capture their nuances, from their everyday meanings within a culture to their significance as symptoms of distress and their possible application to many different disorders across cultures (Kirmayer & Young, 1998; see also Chapter 6). Finally, placement of the Outline in an appendix is seen as marginalizing the role of culture, instead of appreciating its multifaceted roles across all mental disorders and cultures, including white American culture.

In recognition of the evolving nature of diagnosis, the American Psychiatric Association has an explicit revision process for DSM, which is updated roughly every 10 years to achieve greater objectivity, diagnostic precision, and diagnostic reliability in light of new empirical findings and field testing. Limitations of the current cultural formulation are expected to be addressed in future revisions of DSM. Interest in the role of culture in mental health and mental illness is consistent with the broader trend in neuroscience and genetics, *integrative neuroscience*. This field strives to explain the powerful effect of experience, in the broadest possible sense, on the structure and function of the brain. Leaders in the field envision that the study of genes and their interaction with the environment will yield new boundaries between mental disorders, which now are divided mostly on the basis of symptom clusters, course of illness, response to treatment, and family history (Hyman, 2000).

The Public Health Approach

The public health field in the United States traces its origins to attempts to control infectious diseases in the late 18th century (Mullan, 1989). Its expansion during the 19th and 20th centuries was tied to the growing awareness of the importance of income, employment, lifestyle, and diet in health and disease (Porter, 1997). The first reports on public health documented higher rates of disease in impoverished, overcrowded communities. The documented effects of population growth, migration to cities, and industrialization brought to light the roles of social forces and the environment in disease causation. By the mid-19th century, public health became a new field grounded in scientific observation and stunning developments in bacteriology (Institute of Medicine [IOM], 1988).

Today the public health approach underpins the Nation's commitment to health and medicine. This population-based approach is concerned with the health of an entire population, including its link to the physical, psychological, cultural, and social environments in which people live, work, and go to school (Chapter 2).

Public health focuses not only on traditional areas of medicine — diagnosis, treatment, and etiology or cause of an illness — but also on disease surveillance, health promotion, disease prevention, and access to and evaluation of services (Last & Wallace, 1992). The public health approach is premised on the conviction that it is inherently better to promote health and to prevent illness before it begins. Prevention also holds the promise of being more cost-effective.

Promoting Mental Health and Preventing Mental Disorders

The mental health field traditionally focused on mental illness in an attempt to serve individuals with the most severe disorders. As the field matures, however, it has begun to embrace activities that may promote mental health or prevent some mental illnesses and behavioral disorders. More specifically, it is employing the public health approach to identify problems and develop solutions for entire population groups. This approach:

- Defines the problem using surveillance processes designed to gather data that establish the nature of the problem and the trends in its incidence and prevalence;

- Identifies potential causes through epidemiological analyses that identify risk and protective factors associated with the problem;

- Designs, develops, and evaluates the effectiveness and generalizability of interventions; and

- Disseminates successful models as part of a coordinated effort to educate and reach out to the public (Hamburg, 1998; Mercy et al., 1993).

Just as mental health and mental illness are points on a continuum, so too are the public health goals of mental health promotion and mental illness prevention. Promotion refers to active steps to enhance mental health, while prevention refers to active steps to protect against the onset of mental health problems or illnesses.[10]

Promotion and prevention hinge on the identification of modifiable *risk* and *protective* factors, i.e., characteristics or conditions that, if present, increase or diminish, respectively, the likelihood that people will develop mental health problems or disorders (see full discussion in DHHS, 1999, p. 63–64). The *modifiabili-*

---

[10] This definition technically refers to *primary* prevention, i.e., prevention of a disorder before its initial onset. *Secondary* prevention refers to the prevention of recurrences or exacerbations of already diagnosed disorders. *Tertiary* prevention refers to the prevention or reduction of disability caused by a disorder. There also are other ways to define comprehensive efforts at prevention (IOM, 1994).

ty of a risk or protective factor is a prerequisite for developing interventions targeted at these factors.

Risk and protective factors may be biological, psychological, or social in nature. They can operate within an individual, family, community, culture, or the larger society (Boxes 1–4, 1–5). A single risk or protective factor, in most cases, increases the *probability*, but is not necessarily the *cause* of a harmful or healthful effect. That is, one factor rarely is either necessary or sufficient to produce a given outcome. Each person is exposed to a unique constellation of risk and protective factors that act not in isolation, but rather through complex and often perplexing interactions. It is the accumulation and interaction of risk and protective factors that contribute to mental health, mental health problems, or mental illness, not a single risk or protective factor (IOM, 1994).

Risk and protective factors not only vary across individuals, but also across age, gender, and culture. A prime goal of the SGR was to sift through risk and protective factors affecting different age groups. This Supplement focuses on risk and protective factors that disproportionately affect racial and ethnic minorities. Such risk factors include poverty, immigration, violence, racism, and discrimination, whereas protective factors include spirituality and community and family support (Chapter 2).

Several well-designed studies have demonstrated that interventions can successfully reduce the severity of certain mental disorders and enhance mental health. Some of these studies have been conducted with ethnic and racial minority samples. For example, low-income minority adults at risk for depression participated in a course on cognitive-behavioral methods adapted to their culture to control their moods. At the end of the course and at 1-year followup, these adults showed fewer symptoms of depression than did a control group (Munoz et al., 1995). For low-income, Spanish-speaking immigrant families at risk for attachment disorders, a home visitor program for mothers and infants led to more secure attachments (Lieberman et al., 1991). These findings, while quite promising, must be understood in context: At this point, the mental health field does not have sufficient knowledge of causation to prevent the onset of major mental disorders like schizophrenia and bipolar disorder (DHHS, 1999).

The recently issued report, *Youth Violence: A Report of the Surgeon General*, spotlighted 27 effective interventions designed to prevent youth violence (DHHS, 2001). Many of these programs target high-risk racial and ethnic minority youth. Violence in youth not only produces injuries, disability, and death, but it also often

---

Box 1–4

Examples of Risk Factors Common to Mental Health Problems and Mental Disorders

Individual

Genetic vulnerability*
Gender
Low birth weight
Neuropsychological deficits
Language disabilities
Chronic physical illness
Below-average intelligence
Child abuse or neglect

Family

Severe marital discord
Social disadvantage
Overcrowding or large family size
Paternal criminality
Maternal mental disorder
Admission to foster care

Community or social

Violence
Poverty
Community disorganization
Inadequate schools
Racism and discrimination

* Genetic vulnerability varies by mental disorder

Sources: DHHS, 2001; DHHS, 1999; IOM, 1994

---

has enduring negative consequences for the mental health of victims, perpetrators, their families, and their communities. There is little doubt that our poorest neighborhoods, where a disproportionate percentage of minorities live, are fraught with violence. Preventing violence is a vital public health goal with the potential to improve the mental health and overall health of our Nation.

Resilience

One area of mental health promotion that has received considerable attention in recent years is resilience, or the capacity to bounce back from adversity. Increasingly

Box 1–5

Examples of Protective Factors Against Mental Health Problems and Mental Disorders

Individual

> Positive temperament
> Above-average intelligence
> Social competence
> Spirituality or religion

Family

> Smaller family structure
> Supportive relationships with parents
> Good sibling relationships
> Adequate rule setting and monitoring by parents

Community or social

> Commitment to schools
> Availability of health and social services
> Social cohesion

Sources: DHHS, 2001; DHHS, 1999; IOM, 1994

researchers emphasize that *resilience is by no means a fixed trait of an individual.* Rather, resilient adaptation comes about as a result of an individual's situation in interaction with protective factors in the social environment. Resilience research and programs take a "strengths-based approach" to human development and functioning: Rather than focusing on deficits and illnesses, they seek to understand and promote "self-righting tendencies" in individuals, families, and communities (Werner, 1989).

The formal study of resilience stems from research begun in the 1970s on children of parents with schizophrenia (Garmezy, 1971). The investigator found that having a parent with schizophrenia does indeed increase someone's risk for the illness, yet about 90 percent of the children in the study did *not* develop the illness. Further, most fared well in terms of peer relations, academic achievement, and other measures of mental health (Garmezy, 1971, 1991). This seminal research spawned a new line of investigations on children and other groups living in high-risk conditions such as poverty, war, and natural disasters.

Consistent with the public health approach, resilience research focuses on the promotion of protective factors. Key protective factors in racial and ethnic minority communities are supportive families, strong communities, spirituality, and religion.

Supportive Families and Communities

Researchers find that the support of other people is key to helping people cope with adversity. According to a nationally representative survey, families and friends are the first sources to which people say they will turn if they develop a mental illness (Pescosolido et al., 2000).

As early as 1983, researchers identified the following 10 characteristics of resilient African American families:

(1) Strong economic base

(2) Achievement orientation

(3) Role adaptability

(4) Spirituality

(5) Extended family bonds

(6) Racial pride

(7) Respect and love

(8) Resourcefulness

(9) Community involvement

(10) Family unity (Gary et al., 1983)

Other researchers have looked at the role of extended family members and other people in the community in helping children function well. A literature review on resilient African American children raised in inner-city neighborhoods concluded that "there was at least one adequate significant adult who was able to serve as an identification figure. In turn, the achieving youngsters seemed to hold a more positive attitude toward adults and authority figures in general" (Garmezy & Neuchterlein, 1972). In another study, African American children of low-income, divorced or separated parents were less likely to drop out of school if influenced by grandparents who provided continuity and support (Robins, et al., 1975). Similarly, for urban elementary students chronically exposed to violence, support of teachers enhanced their social competence in the classroom, as did support from peers and family. Family support was also critical in relieving the children's anxiety (Hill & Madhere, 1996; Hill et al.,1996).

One ground-breaking ethnographic study focused on the children of Vietnamese refugees who were forced to leave Vietnam when Saigon fell in 1975. Many parents were subjected to severe trauma prior to immigration and then to the stress of resettlement in the United States. The children of these refugees showed remarkable resilience, at least in terms of school performance and academic ambitions. In an examination of Vietnamese students attending public high schools in a low-income resettlement area in New Orleans, approximately one-fourth of the students had an A average, and over half had a B average. Only 5 percent did not want to go to college. This study concluded that several factors contributed to the resilience of these children, including strong family and community ties, and "selective Americanization," i.e., integrating the best of American values while maintaining the best Vietnamese values (Zhou & Bankston, 1998).

For racial and ethnic minority groups, supportive families and communities help arriving immigrants with practical assistance in housing, transportation, and employment. In addition, they offer enduring emotional support and a haven against racism and discrimination. They also affirm cultural identity. The contributions of family and community are so ubiquitous and expected, that they only become obvious by their absence. A recurring theme of this Supplement is the essential nature of community and family support.

Spirituality and Religion

Spirituality and religion are gaining increased research attention because of their possible link to mental health promotion and mental illness prevention. Research findings, while somewhat equivocal, suggest that various aspects of religious practice, affiliation, and belief are beneficial for mental health. The findings are strongest for a link between spirituality and certain *aspects* of mental health, such as subjective well-being and life satisfaction (e.g., Witter et al., 1985; Koenig et al., 1988; Ellison, 1991; Schumaker, 1992; Levin, 1994).

Research findings are somewhat contradictory about whether spirituality is associated with less psychological distress and fewer symptoms of depression in adults (e.g., Idler, 1987; Williams et al., 1991). For prevention purposes, the role of spirituality may be tied to family relationships, as demonstrated by one recent, long-term study. It examined whether the mother's religious devotion was correlated with whether her children developed depression. The study found, over a 10-year period, that two factors were correlated with the children's not developing depression — the mother's religiosity and

her having the same religious denomination as her children (Miller et al., 1997).

The association between religious involvement and mental health also has been studied directly in African Americans. Using data from five large national samples, researchers found that African Americans report significantly higher levels of subjective religiosity than do whites (Taylor et al., 1999). Other studies show that religious factors are strong predictors of life satisfaction for African Americans (St. George & McNamara, 1984; Thomas & Holmes, 1992). Studies also find that public and private aspects of religious involvement are associated with improved self-perceptions and self-esteem (Krause & Tran, 1989; Ellison, 1993).

Spirituality plays a prominent role in the lives of the majority of Americans, including many racial and ethnic minorities. For example, many American Indian and Alaska Native communities participate in spiritual and religious traditions, including the Native American Church, where Christian and Native beliefs coexist. Less is known about how these traditions relate to mental health. To study the relationship, researchers may need to develop new approaches and different types of outcome measures (The Fetzer Institute & National Institute on Aging, 1999).

How might spirituality and religion exert an influence on health? This provocative question has led to the development of theories to guide empirical research. Some hypotheses are that spirituality and religion influence health by adherence to health-related behaviors and lifestyles, by having an impact on marriage patterns and hence heritability, by providing social support, by psychophysiology via ritual, or by promoting healthy cognitions via belief or faith (Levin, 1996).

Organization of Supplement and Major Topics Covered

Chapter 2 lays the foundations for understanding the relationships between culture, mental health, mental illness, and mental health services. Chapters 3 through 6 provide information about each racial and ethnic minority group. Chapter 7 concludes with promising directions and courses of action to reduce disparities and improve the mental health of racial and ethnic minorities.

Each chapter concerning a racial or ethnic minority group follows a common format. The chapter begins with facets of the group's history in the United States and its demographic patterns, which include family structure, income, education, and health status. These factors are important for understanding contemporary ethnic identity issues and mental health, and the need for mental health services. The chapter then reviews the available scientific evidence regarding the need for mental health services (as measured by prevalence), the availability, accessibility, and utilization of services, and the appropriateness and outcomes of mental health services.

Need

In this Supplement, the need for mental health services is equated with prevalence, i.e., new and existing cases of mental disorders. Prevalence rates, however, are imperfect measures of need. A mental health problem may impair someone sufficiently to warrant treatment or other types of services (e.g., preventive care), while some milder forms of mental illness may not impair someone enough to warrant professional treatment. The problem is that the mental health field has not yet developed standard measures of "need for treatment" in the general population, much less for a given racial or ethnic group (DHHS, 1999). Where relevant, this Supplement also uses the diagnosis of a culture-bound syndrome as indicating a need for treatment.

This Supplement pays special attention to vulnerable, high-need populations, such as people who are homeless or incarcerated, or children in foster care. These are among the populations of most concern because they have the greatest need for services, defined by a higher risk for or prevalence of mental disorder than a relevant comparison population (Aday, 1994). Other populations, such as persons with co-occurring disorders or those living in migrant or rural communities, are also likely to be underserved or to have difficulty accessing needed treatment.

The chapters for each minority group vary somewhat in terms of which high-need populations they cover. High-need populations were included in specific chapters on the basis of having overrepresentation by that particular minority group. For example, the chapter on Hispanic Americans covers refugees, whereas the chapter on American Indians and Alaska Natives covers children in foster care and people who abuse alcohol and drugs. The placements of these emphases should not be used to stereotype the group. High-need populations of all types exist in every group.

Availability

Availability of services refers to the number of providers in a given area and to whether these providers are able to offer mental health services that meet the needs of the population(s) they serve. The development of such services requires recognizing and responding to cultural concerns of racial and ethnic groups, including histories, traditions, beliefs, and value systems (U.S. Center for Mental Health Services [CMHS], 2000).

Accessibility

Access is defined as probability of use, given need for services. Because of the difficulty of operationalizing this definition, this Supplement relies on a commonly accepted measure of access, insurance status, i.e., whether or not people have private or public insurance to cover some or all of the cost of services (Brown et al., 2000). People with health insurance have greater access to services than those who do not (Newhouse, 1993). The nature of the coverage is also important — details such as coverage limits, deductibles, and the like — but few studies of minorities provide this level of specificity. Other cultural and organizational factors impede access, such as attitudes against treatment, mistrust, stigma, and fragmentation of services.

Utilization

Utilization of services is generally reported in this Supplement by rates of use of mental health services in any of the settings and sectors where they are provided. The chapters also provide some insight into more specific aspects of use such as intensity and duration of treatment, timing of care from first onset of symptoms, dropout rates, type of provider (e.g., specialist or primary care), sector, setting, and treatment modality. Many of these characteristics are described in the section on Service Settings (Chapter 2). Utilization is conceptualized as a combined function of all the previous topics — need, availability, and access.

Utilization is also reported for alternative or complementary sources of care including acupuncture, meditation, spiritual healing, herbal remedies, and/or traditional Chinese or American Indian medicine. The need to report these sources of care was prompted by the first national study of more than 16,000 people that found that about 10 percent of people reporting a mental condition used practitioner-based alternative or complementary treatments. This rate of use was greater than that for people reporting a chronic medical condition (Druss & Rosenheck, 1999, 2000). The study also suggested that consumers[11] tend to use these therapies for

---

[11] Although a number of terms identify people who use or have used mental health services (e.g., mental health consumer, survivor, ex-patient, client), the terms "consumer" and "patient" will be used interchangably throughout this Supplement.

milder mental health problems and continue to use mainstream medical services for more severe mental illnesses. Studies of the overall population in primary care clinics and in clinics specializing in complementary health care note that anxiety and depression are two of the disorders for which individuals use complementary care (Elder et al., 1997; Davidson, et al., 1998; Eisenberg et al., 1998).

Appropriateness and Outcomes

Appropriateness is defined herein as receiving an accurate diagnosis or guideline-based treatment. An accurate diagnosis is one in which a careful evaluation of a patient's symptoms show that they correspond to diagnostic criteria in the *Diagnostic and Statistical Manual of Mental Disorders* published by the American Psychiatric Association. An appropriate treatment conforms to the treatment guidelines for that disorder published by professional mental health associations or evidence-based reports on healthcare outcomes (drawn from comprehensive syntheses and analyses of relevant scientific literature) supported by government agencies.

Outcomes of treatment ordinarily refer either to the efficacy or effectiveness of treatment. Efficacy is whether treatment works in highly controlled research settings, whereas effectiveness is whether treatment works in clinical practice settings. Common outcomes that are measured are improved mortality and morbidity — such as less suicide or a reduction in symptoms or levels of distress — and improvement in mental health. Outcomes also cover improvements in disability, work performance, and other functional measures. Outcomes are studied in relation to any type of treatment, including those that are culturally responsive.

Science Base

Standards of Scientific Evidence

This Supplement draws on the best available science coming from many disciplines — mental health, health services, history, sociology, and anthropology. The statements made in this Supplement are documented by reference to studies published in the professional literature. Publications are first required to be peer-reviewed by fellow experts to ensure their quality. Quality depends on scientifically rigorous methods of data collection, analysis, and interpretation.

No single study, regardless of the quality of its design, is sufficient by itself to serve as the basis for a conclusion in this Supplement. Findings must be replicated in several studies, and findings must be consistent. The strength or degree of evidence amassed for any conclusion is referred to as the level of evidence.

Assessing the level of evidence is often difficult when findings transcend disciplinary boundaries. Distinct disciplines formulate questions differently. This, in turn, dictates different approaches to designing and conducting research, and the approach often determines how researchers report their findings and conclusions. Even when approaches are similar, investigators in different disciplines frequently employ different terms to describe similar concepts. In seeking to apply scientific standards consistently across the many fields of research reviewed, this Supplement emphasizes two criteria: rigorous methods of inquiry and sufficient data to support major conclusions.

Methodological Issues in Studying Minorities

Because race and ethnicity are hard to define, many scientists discourage the use of these terms in the analysis of disease, unless there is reason to suspect, based on other sources of evidence, that a relationship exists. In general, cause and effect relationships between health status and race and ethnicity have been rare, and when they have been found, they are usually related to lifestyle or other behavioral factors that tend to correlate with racial and ethnic categories. Observed differences between racial and ethnic groups are less likely to be caused by underlying biological differences but rather by factors that co-vary with race, such as income, education, or environment. Even central tendency differences in metabolic rates are overshadowed by the complete overlap in the distribution of metabolic rates across American racial and ethnic groups. Some editors of scientific journals actively discourage presentation of racial and ethnic data unless there is a specific rationale for such analyses.

NIH insists that clinical trials to test treatments include a strongly diverse population of volunteers. This diversity is necessary to ensure that the results of the trials will apply broadly to all populations, including minority groups. According to the theory of clinical trials, it is not necessary to separately analyze subpopulations unless there are empirically based hypotheses about group differences.

Still, the study of mental health in minorities is flourishing, even though researchers face methodological hurdles that make these studies more complex, costly, and difficult to conduct than similar types of investigations in predominantly white communities.

One major consideration is related to the measurement of mental disorders. For example, even when using the DSM system to establish the criteria for different mental disorders and a standardized instrument such as the Composite International Diagnostic Interview Schedule (CIDI) to measure disorders, cultural factors affect how individuals define, evaluate, seek help for, and present their health problems to family members, friends, and service providers. Considering culture in a standardized measure of mental disorders is reliant on at least three types of equivalence: conceptual, scale, and norm. Conceptual equivalence refers to similarities in the meaning of concepts used in assessment: e.g., Do minorities and whites think of well-being, depression, or self-esteem in the same way? Scale equivalence refers to the use of standard formats in questionnaire items that are familiar to all groups. Western-educated people of all groups are familiar with responding to questions that have choices such as "strongly agree," "agree," and so on, or a true-false dichotomy. Recent immigrants, particularly individuals who have not been educated in the Western system, may not understand this format. Accordingly, their answers to questions using these response options may not be valid or reliable. Norm equivalence refers to the application of standard norms developed in one sample and used with another group. Because population or sub-population statistics form one standard by which we judge normal and abnormal or high and low functioning, it is important to understand whether the population on which the norms are based is similar to the study group.

Over the past decade, social scientists have used focus groups, ethnographies, and detailed interviews to help modify standardized measures to make them more equivalent for use with racial and ethnic minority groups. Although refining instruments for different racial and ethnic minorities has been made more systematic and efficient, making measures equivalent remains a time-consuming process.

For researchers who use surveys to collect data, a major methodological hurdle is the issue of sampling. Compared with interviewing all members living in a geographic area, sampling is a scientific and cost-effective means to estimate the rates of mental disorder and use of services for a particular group or community. Because ethnic and racial minority groups are relatively rare in most communities, it is difficult to recruit adequate samples for any one particular study. When a study requires large samples of a specific ethnic group, the screening time to locate respondents is quite high. For example, in a study in Los Angeles, nearly 17,000 households were approached to secure a final sample size of 1,747 Chinese American respondents (Takeuchi et al., 1998). If the study design looks for certain subgroups (e.g., adults, children, and older adults), the cost and time for screening individuals can become even higher.

Another potential obstacle is that racial and ethnic minorities may be reluctant to participate in research studies. For some, like American Indians and African Americans, research raises past breaches of ethics and harm to individuals (Krieger, 1987). For others, like recent Asian or Latino immigrants, participation in research may be a strange concept, and recruitment may be difficult.

In addition to the difficulties of recruiting individual respondents, some racial and ethnic minority communities may resist being part of a research study. Researchers often conduct studies in minority communities because they want their work to have an impact in resolving social problems, guiding policy, or serving as a basis for programs that will improve the quality of life in the community. These investigations can provide communities with needed data to secure resources for new programs, assess interventions that may be useful in the community, or identify high-risk groups. To conduct studies, however, investigators must rely on community cooperation to help identify people and encourage participation. Frequently, an uneasy tension exists between researchers and the communities they study. Community leaders may see researchers as exploitative and divorced from real issues and real-life problems, while researchers view community leaders as compromising research methods and thereby diminishing outcomes, which would have eventually benefited the community. Such tensions can hinder the initiation of research projects in both white and nonwhite communities.

Preparation of the Supplement

In February 2000, the Surgeon General commissioned this Supplement to examine racial and ethnic minority mental health. Accordingly, it selectively expands on parts of the main report, *Mental Health: A Report of the Surgeon General* (DHHS, 1999).

As was the case with that report, the Office of the Surgeon General, with the approval of the Secretary of the Department of Health and Human Services, authorized the Substance Abuse and Mental Health Services Administration (SAMHSA) to serve as the lead operating division for preparing the Supplement. SAMHSA's Center for Mental Health Services worked in consultation with the National Institute of Mental Health (NIMH) of the National Institutes of Health to develop this Supplement under the guidance of the Surgeon General, Dr. David Satcher.

References

Aday, L. A. (1994). Health status of vulnerable populations. *Annual Review of Public Health, 15*, 487–509.

American Psychiatric Association. (1994). *The diagnostic and statistical manual of mental disorders* (4th ed.). Washington, DC: Author.

Barbujani, G., Magagni, A., Minch, E., & Cavalli-Sforza, L. L. (1997). An apportionment of human DNA diversity. *Proceedings of the National Academy of Sciences USA, 94*, 4516–4519.

Borowsky, S. J., Rubenstein, L. V., Meredith, L. S., Camp, P., Jackson-Triche, M., & Wells, K.B. (2000). Who is at risk of nondetection of mental health problems in primary care? *Journal of General Internal Medicine, 15*, 381–388.

Breakey, W. R., Fischer, P. J., Kramer, M., Nestadt, G., Romanoski, A. J., Ross, A., Royall, R. M., & Stine, O. (1989). Health and mental health problems of homeless men and women in Baltimore. *Journal of the American Medical Association, 262*, 1352–1357.

Brown, E. R., Ojeda, V. D., Wyn, R., & Levan, R. (2000). *Racial and ethnic disparities in access to health insurance and health care.* Los Angeles: UCLA Center for Health Policy Research and The Henry J. Kaiser Family Foundation.

Cooper, C. R., & Denner, J. (1998). Theories linking culture and psychopathology: Universal and community-specific processes. *Annual Review of Psychology, 49*, 559–584.

Cowen, E. L. (1994). The enhancement of psychological wellness: Challenges and opportunities. *American Journal of Community Psychology, 22*, 149–179.

Davidson, J. R. T., Rampes, H., Eisen, M., Fisher, P., Smith, R. D., & Malik, M. (1998). Psychiatric disorders in primary care patients receiving complementary medical treatments. *Comparative Psychiatry, 39*, 16–20.

Drucker, P. F. (1993). *The Post-Capitalist Society.* New York: HarperCollins.

Druss, B. G., Marcus, S. C., Rosenheck, R. A., Olfson, M., Tanielian, T., & Pincus, H. A. (2000). Understanding disability in mental and general medical conditions. *American Journal of Psychiatry, 157*, 1485–1491.

Druss, B. G., & Rosenheck, R. A. (1999). Association between use of unconventional therapies and conventional medical services. *Journal of the American Medical Association, 282*, 651–656.

Druss, B.G., & Rosenheck, R. A. (2000). Use of practitioner-based complementary therapies by persons reporting mental conditions in the United States. *Archives of General Psychiatry, 57*, 708–714.

Eisenberg, D., Davis, R., Ettner, S., Appel, S., Wilkey, S., Van Rompay, M., & Kessler, R. C. (1998). Trends in alternative medicine use in the United States, 1990–1997: Results of a follow-up national survey. *Journal of the American Medical Association, 280*, 1569–1575.

Ellison, C. G. (1991). Religious involvement and subjective well-being. *Journal of Health and Social Behavior, 32*, 80–99.

Ellison, C. G. (1993). Religion, the life stress paradigm, and the study of depression. In J. S. Levin (Ed.), *Religion in aging and mental health.* Thousand Oaks, CA: Sage.

Escobar, J. I., Burnam, M. A., Karno, M., Forsythe, A., & Golding, J. M. (1987). Somatization in the community. *Archives of General Psychiatry, 44*, 713–718.

Fetzer Institute and the National Institute on Aging. (1999). *Measurement of religiousness and spirituality.* Kalamazoo, MI: Author.

Garmezy, N. (1971). Vulnerability research and the issue of primary prevention. *American Journal of Orthopsychiatry, 41*, 101–116.

Garmezy, N. (1991). Resilience in children's adaptation to negative life events and stressed environments. *Pediatrics Annals, 20*, 459–460, 463–466.

Garmezy, N., & Neuchterlein, K. (1972). Invulnerable children: The fact and fiction of competence and disadvantage. *American Journal of Orthopsychiatry, 42*, 328–329.

Gary, L. E., Beatty, L. A., Berry, G. I., & Price, M. D. (1983). *Stable black families: Final report.* Washington, DC: Institute for Urban Affairs and Research, Howard University.

Guarnaccia, P. J., Canino, G., Rubio-Stipec, M., & Bravo, M. (1993). The prevalence of ataques de nervios in the Puerto Rico disaster study. The role of culture in psychiatric epidemiology. *Journal of Nervous and Mental Disease, 181*, 157–165.

Hamburg, M. A. (1998). Youth violence is a public health concern. In D. S. Elliott, B. A. Hamburg, & K. R. Williams (Eds.), *Violence in American schools: A new perspective* (pp. 31–54). New York: Cambridge University Press.

Hill, H. M., & Madhere, S. (1996). Exposure to community violence and African American children: A multidimensional model of risks and resources. *Journal of Community Psychology, 24*, 26–43.

Hill, H. M., Levermore, M., Twaite, J., & Jones, L .P. (1996). Exposure to community violence and social support as predictors of anxiety and social and emotional behavior among African American children. *Journal of Child and Family Studies, 5*, 399–414.

Hsu, L. K., & Folstein, M. F. (1997). Somatoform disorders in Caucasian and Chinese Americans. *Journal of Nervous and Mental Disease, 185*, 382–387.

Hyman, S. E. (2000). The genetics of mental illness: Implications for practice. *Bulletin of the World Health Organization, 78*, 455–463.

Idler, E. (1987). Religious involvement and the health of the elderly: Some hypotheses and an initial test. *Social Forces, 66*, 226–238.

Institute of Medicine. (1988). *The future of public health.* Washington, DC: National Academy Press.

Institute of Medicine. (1994). *Reducing risks for mental disorders: Frontiers for preventive intervention research.* Washington, DC: National Academy Press.

Kandel, E. R. (1998). A new intellectual framework for psychiatry. *American Journal of Psychiatry, 155*, 457–69.

Kirmayer, L. J. (1998). Editorial: The fate of culture in DSM–IV. *Transcultural Psychiatry, 35*, 339–342.

Kirmayer, L. J., & Young, A. (1998). Culture and somatization: Clinical, epidemiological, and ethnographic perspectives. *Psychosomatic Medicine, 60*, 420–430.

Koegel, P. M., Burnam, A., & Farr, R. K. (1988). The prevalence of specific psychiatric disorders among homeless individuals in the inner city of Los Angeles. *Archives of General Psychiatry, 45*, 1085–1093.

Koenig, H. G., Smiley, M., & Gonzales, J. A. P. (1988). *Religion, health, and aging.* New York: Greenwood Press.

Krause, N., & Tran, T. V. (1989). Stress and religious involvement among older blacks. *Journal of Gerontology: Social Sciences, 44*, 4–13.

Krieger, N. (1987). Shades of difference: Theoretical underpinnings of the medical controversy on black/white differences in the United States, 1830–1870. *International Journal of Health Services, 17*, 259–278.

Last, J. M., & Wallace, R. B. (Eds.). (1992). *Maxcy-Rosenau-Last public health and preventive medicine* (13th ed.). Norwalk, CT: Appleton and Lange.

Levin, J. S. (1994). Religion and health: Is there an association, is it valid, and is it causal? *Social Science and Medicine, 38*, 1475–1484.

Levin, J. S. (1996). How religion influences morbidity and health: Reflections on natural history, salutogenesis and host resistance. *Social Science and Medicine, 43*, 849–64.

Lewis-Fernandez, R., & Kleinman, A. (1995). Cultural psychiatry: Theoretical, clinical and research issues. *Cultural Psychiatry, 18*, 433–445

Lewontin, R. C. (1972). The apportionment of human diversity. *Evolutionary Biology, 6*, 381–398.

Lieberman, A. F., Weston, D. R., & Pawl, J. H. (1991). Preventive intervention and outcome with anxiously attached dyads. *Child Development, 62*, 199–209.

Liebowitz, M. R., Salman, E., Jusino, C. M., Garfinkel, R., Street, L., Cardenas, D. L., Silvestre, J., Fyer, A. J., Carrasco, J. L., Davies, S., Guarnaccia, P., & Klein, D. L. (1994). Ataque de nervios and panic disorder. *American Journal of Psychiatry, 151*, 871–875.

Lopez, S. R., & Guarnaccia, P. J. (2000). Cultural psychopathology: Uncovering the social world of mental illness. *Annual Review of Psychology, 51*, 571–598.

Manson, S. M., Shore, J. H., & Bloom, J. D. (1985). The depressive experience in American Indian communities: A challenge for psychiatric theory and diagnosis. In A. Kleinman & B. Good (Eds.), *Culture and depression* (pp. 331–338). Berkeley, CA: University of California Press.

Maser, J. D., Kaelber, C., & Weise, R. E. (1991). International use and attitudes toward DSM–III and DSM–III–R: Growing consensus in psychiatric classification. *Journal of Abnormal Psychology, 100*, 271–279.

Mercy, J. A., Rosenberg, M. L., Powell, K. E., Broome, C. V., & Roper, W. L. (1993). Public policy for violence prevention. *Health Affairs, 12*, 7–29.

Mezzich, J. E., Kirmayer, L. J., Kleinman, A., Fabrega, H., Parron, D. L., Good, B. J., Lin, K. M., & Manson, S. M. (1999). The place of culture in DSM–IV. *Journal of Nervous and Mental Disease, 187*, 457–464.

Miller, D. B., & MacIntosh, R. (1999). Promoting resilience in urban African-American adolescents: Racial socialization and identity as protective factors. *Social Work Research, 23*, 159–161.

Mishel, L., & Bernstein, J. (1992). *Declining wages for high school and college graduates: Pay and benefits trends by education, gender, occupation and state, 1979–1991* (Briefing Paper No. 31). Washington, DC: Economic Policy Institute.

Mullan, F. (1989). *Plagues and politics: The story of the United States Public Health Service*. New York: Basic Books.

Munoz, R. F., Ying, Y. W., Bernal, G., Perez-Stable, E. J., Sorensen, J. L., Hargreaves, W. A., Miranda, J., & Miller, L. S. (1995). Prevention of depression with primary care patients: A randomized controlled trial. *American Journal of Community Psychology, 23*, 199–222.

Murray, C. J. L., & Lopez, A. D. (Eds.). (1996). *The global burden of disease. A comprehensive assessment of mortality and disability from diseases, injuries, and risk factors in 1990 and projected to 2020*. Cambridge, MA: Harvard School of Public Health.

Newhouse, J. P. (1993). *Free for all: Lessons from the RAND health insurance experiment*. Cambridge, MA: Harvard University Press.

Owens, K., & King, M. C. (1999). Genomic views of human history. *Science, 286*, 451–453.

Paabo, S. (2001). Genomics and society. The human genome and our view of ourselves. *Science, 291* (5,507), 1219–1220.

Pescosolido, B., Martin, J. K., Link, B. G., Kikuzawa, S., Burgos, G., Swindle, R., & Phelan, J. (2000). *Americans' views of mental health and illness at century's end: Continuity and change*. Public report on the MacArthur Mental Health Module, 1996 General Social Survey. Bloomington, IN: Indiana Consortium of Mental Health Services Research, Indiana University and the Joseph P. Mailman School of Public Health, Columbia University.

Porter, R. (1997). *The greatest benefit to mankind: A medical history of humanity*. New York: Norton.

Robins, L. N., West, P. A., & Herjanic, B. L. (1975). Arrests and delinquency: A study of black urban families and their children. *Journal of Child Psychology and Psychiatry, 16*, 25–140.

St. George, A., & McNamara, P. H. (1984). Religion, race and psychological well-being. *Journal for the Scientific Study of Religion, 23*, 351–363.

Scadding, J. G. (1996). Essentialism and nominalism in medicine: Logic of diagnosis in disease terminology. *Lancet, 348* (9,027), 594–596.

Schumaker, J. F. (1992). Mental health consequences of irreligion. In J. F. Schumaker (Ed.), *Religion and mental health*. New York: Oxford University Press.

Takeuchi, D. T., Chung, R. C., Lin, K. M., Shen, H., Kurasaki, K., Chung, C. A., & Sue, S. (1998). Lifetime and twelve-month prevalence rates of major depressive episodes and dysthymia among Chinese Americans in Los Angeles. *American Journal of Psychiatry, 155*, 1407–1414.

Taylor, R. J., Mattis, J. S., & Chatters, L. M. (1999). Subjective religiosity among African-Americans: A synthesis of findings from five national samples. *Journal of Black Psychology, 25*, 524–543.

Teplin, L. A. (1990). The prevalence of severe mental disorder among male urban jail detainees: Comparison with the Epidemiologic Catchment Area program. *American Journal of Public Health, 80*, 663–669.

Thomas, M., & Holmes, B. (1992). Determinants of satisfaction for Blacks and whites. *Sociological Quarterly, 33*, 459–472.

U.S. Census Bureau. (2000). *Changing shape of the nation's income distribution*, 1947–1998. Retrieved April 4, 2001, from http://www.census.gov/prod/2000pubs/p60-204.pdf.

U.S. Census Bureau. (2001). *Profiles of general demographic characteristics: 2000 Census of Population and Housing, United States*. Retrieved June 22, 2001, from http://www2.census.gov/census_2000/datasets/demographic_profile/0_National_Summary/.

U.S. Center for Mental Health Services. (2000). *Cultural competence standards in managed care mental health services: Four underserved/underrepresented racial/ethnic groups*. Rockville, MD: Author.

U.S. Department of Health and Human Services. (1999). *Mental health: A report of the Surgeon General*. Rockville, MD: Author.

U.S. Department of Health and Human Services. (2001). *Youth violence: A report of the Surgeon General*. Rockville, MD: Author.

U.S. Office of Management and Budget. (1978). *Directive No. 15: Race and ethnic standards for Federal statistics and administrative reporting*. Washington, DC: Author.

U.S. Office of Management and Budget. (2000). *Guidance on aggregation and allocation of data on race for use in civil rights monitoring and enforcement* (OMB Bulletin No. 00–02). Retrieved July 20, 2001, from http://www.whitehouse.gov/omb/bulletins/b00-02.html.

Vernez, G. M., Burnam, M. A., McGlynn, E. A., Trude, S., & Mittman, B. (1988). *Review of California's program for the homeless mentally ill disabled* (Report No. R3631–CDMH). Santa Monica, CA: RAND.

Weissman, M. M., Bland, R. C., Canino, G. J., Faravelli, C., Greenwald, S., Hwu, H. G., Joyce, P. R., Karam, E. G., Lee, C. K., Lellouch, J., Lepine, J. P., Newman, S. C., Rubio-Stipec, M., Wells, J. E., Wickramaratne, P. J., Wittchen, H., & Yeh, E. K. (1996). Cross-national epidemiology of major depression and bipolar disorder. *Journal of the American Medical Association, 276,* 293–299.

Weissman, M. M., Bland, R. C., Canino, G. J., Faravelli, C., Greenwald, S., Hwu, H. G., Joyce, P. R., Karam, E. G., Lee, C. K., Lellouch, J., Lepine, J. P., Newman, S. C., Rubio-Stipec, M., Wells, J. E., Wickramaratne, P. J., Wittchen, H., & Yeh, E. K. (1997). The cross-national epidemiology of panic disorder. *Archives of General Psychiatry, 54,* 305–309.

Weissman, M. M., Bland, R. C., Canino, G. J., Greenwald, S., Hwu, H. G., Lee, C. K., Newman, S. C., Oakley-Browne, M. A., Rubio-Stipec, M., Wickramaratne, P. J., Wittchen, H.U., & Yeh, E.K. (1994). The cross national epidemiology of obsessive compulsive disorder. The Cross National Collaborative Group. *Journal of Clinical Psychiatry, 55* (Suppl.), 5–10.

Weissman, M. M., Broadhead, W. E., Olfson, M., Sheehan, D. V., Hoven, C., Conolly, P., Fireman, B. H., Farber, L., Blacklow, R. S., Higgins, E. S., & Leon, A. C. (1998). A diagnostic aid for detecting (DSM–IV) mental disorders in primary care. *General Hospital Psychiatry, 20,* 1–11.

Werner, E. E. (1989). High-risk children in young adulthood: A longitudinal study from birth to 32 years. *American Journal of Orthopsychiatry, 59,* 72–81.

Williams, D. R., Larson, D. B., Buckler, R. E., Heckman, R. C., & Pyle, C. M. (1991). Religion and psychological distress in a community sample. *Social Science and Medicine, 32,* 1257–1262.

Witter, R. A., Stock, W. A., Okun, M. A., & Haring, M. J. (1985). Religion and subjective well-being in adulthood: A quantitative synthesis. *Review of Religious Research, 26,* 332–342.

World Health Organization. (1992). *International statistical classification of diseases and related health problems* (10th revision, ICD–10). Geneva: Author.

Zenner, W. (1996). Ethnicity. In D. Levinson & M. Ember (Eds.), *Encyclopedia of Cultural Anthropology* (pp. 393–395). New York: Holt.

Zhou, M., & Bankston, C. L. (1998). *Growing up American: How Vietnamese children adapt to life in the United States.* New York: Russell Sage Foundation.

CHAPTER 2

CULTURE COUNTS: THE INFLUENCE OF CULTURE AND SOCIETY ON MENTAL HEALTH

Contents

Contents, *continued*

CULTURE COUNTS: THE INFLUENCE OF CULTURE AND SOCIETY ON MENTAL HEALTH, MENTAL ILLNESS

Introduction

To better understand what happens inside the clinical setting, this chapter looks outside. It reveals the diverse effects of culture and society on mental health, mental illness, and mental health services. This understanding is key to developing mental health services that are more responsive to the cultural and social contexts of racial and ethnic minorities.

With a seemingly endless range of subgroups and individual variations, culture is important because it bears upon what *all* people bring to the clinical setting. It can account for minor variations in how people communicate their symptoms and which ones they report. Some aspects of culture may also underlie *culture-bound syndromes* — sets of symptoms much more common in some societies than in others. More often, culture bears on whether people even seek help in the first place, what types of help they seek, what types of coping styles and social supports they have, and how much stigma they attach to mental illness. Culture also influences the *meanings* that people impart to their illness. Consumers of mental health services, whose cultures vary both between and within groups, naturally carry this diversity directly to the service setting.

The cultures of the clinician and the service system also factor into the clinical equation. Those cultures most visibly shape the interaction with the mental health consumer through diagnosis, treatment, and organization and financing of services. It is all too easy to lose sight of the importance of culture — until one leaves the country. Travelers from the United States, while visiting some distant frontier, may find themselves stranded in miscommunications and seemingly unorthodox treatments if they seek care for a sudden deterioration in their mental health.

Health and mental health care in the United States are embedded in Western science and medicine, which emphasize scientific inquiry and objective evidence. The self-correcting features of modern science — new methods, peer review, and openness to scrutiny through publication in professional journals — ensure that as knowledge is developed, it builds on, refines, and often replaces older theories and discoveries. The achievements of Western medicine have become the cornerstone of health care worldwide.

What follows are numerous examples of the ways in which culture influences mental health, mental illness, and mental health services. This chapter is meant to be illustrative, not exhaustive. It looks at the culture of the patient, the culture of the clinician, and the specialty in which the clinician works. With respect to the context of mental health services, the chapter deals with the organization, delivery, and financing of services, as well as with broader social issues — racism, discrimination, and poverty — which affect mental health.

Culture refers to a group's shared set of beliefs, norms, and values (Chapter 1). Because common social groupings (e.g., people who share a religion, youth who participate in the same sport, or adults trained in the same profession) have their own cultures, this chapter has separate sections on the culture of the patient as well as the culture of the clinician. Where cultural influences end and larger societal influences begin, there are contours not easily demarcated by social scientists. This chapter takes a broad view about the importance of both culture and society, yet recognizes that they overlap in ways that are difficult to disentangle through research.

What becomes clear is that culture and social contexts, while not the only determinants, shape the mental health of minorities and alter the types of mental health services they use. Cultural misunderstandings between patient and clinician, clinician bias, and the fragmentation of mental health services deter minorities from accessing and utilizing care and prevent them from receiving appropriate care. These possibilities intensify with the demographic trends highlighted at the end of the chapter.

Culture of the Patient

The culture of the patient, also known as the consumer of mental health services, influences many aspects of mental health, mental illness, and patterns of health care utilization. One important cautionary note, however, is that general statements about cultural characteristics of a given group may invite stereotyping of individuals based on their appearance or affiliation. Because there is usually more diversity within a population than there is between populations (e.g., in terms of level of acculturation, age, income, health status, and social class), information in the following sections should not be treated as stereotypes to be broadly applied to any individual member of a racial, ethnic, or cultural group.

Symptoms, Presentation, and Meaning

The symptoms of mental disorders are found worldwide. They cluster into discrete disorders that are real and disabling (U.S. Department of Health and Human Services [DHHS], 1999). As noted in Chapter 1, mental disorders are defined in the *Diagnostic and Statistical Manual of Mental Disorders* (American Psychiatric Association [APA], 1994). Schizophrenia, bipolar disorder, panic disorder, obsessive compulsive disorder, depression, and other disorders have similar and recognizable symptoms throughout the world (Weissman et al., 1994, 1996, 1997, 1998). Culture-bound syndromes, which appear to be distinctive to certain ethnic groups, are the exception to this general statement. Research has not yet determined whether culture-bound syndromes are distinct[1] from established mental disorders, are variants of them, or whether *both* mental disorders and culture-bound syndromes reflect different ways in which the cultural and social environment interacts with genes to shape illness (Chapter 1).

One way in which culture affects mental illness is through how patients describe (or present) their symptoms to their clinicians. There are some well recognized differences in symptom presentation across cultures. The previous chapter described ethnic variation in symptoms of somatization, the expression of distress through one or more physical (somatic) symptoms (Box 1-3). Asian patients, for example, are more likely to report their somatic symptoms, such as dizziness, while not reporting their emotional symptoms. Yet, when questioned further, they do acknowledge having emotional symptoms (Lin & Cheung, 1999). This finding supports the view that patients in different cultures tend to selectively express or present symptoms in culturally acceptable ways (Kleinman, 1977, 1988).

Cultures also vary with respect to the *meaning* they impart to illness, their way of making sense of the subjective experience of illness and distress (Kleinman, 1988). The meaning of an illness refers to deep-seated

attitudes and beliefs a culture holds about whether an illness is "real" or "imagined," whether it is of the body or the mind (or both), whether it warrants sympathy, how much stigma surrounds it, what might cause it, and what type of person might succumb to it. Cultural meanings of illness have real consequences in terms of whether people are motivated to seek treatment, how they cope with their symptoms, how supportive their families and communities are, where they seek help (mental health specialist, primary care provider, clergy, and/or traditional healer), the pathways they take to get services, and how well they fare in treatment. The consequences can be grave — extreme distress, disability, and possibly, suicide — when people with severe mental illness do not receive appropriate treatment.

Causation and Prevalence

Cultural and social factors contribute to the causation of mental illness, yet that contribution varies by disorder. Mental illness is considered the product of a complex interaction among biological, psychological, social, and cultural factors. The role of any one of these major factors can be stronger or weaker depending on the disorder (DHHS, 1999).

The prevalence of schizophrenia, for example, is similar throughout the world (about 1 percent of the population), according to the *International Pilot Study on Schizophrenia*, which examined over 1,300 people in 10 countries (World Health Organization [WHO], 1973). International studies using similarly rigorous research methodology have extended the WHO's findings to two other disorders: The lifetime prevalence of bipolar disorder (0.3–1.5%) and panic disorder (0.4–2.9%) were shown to be relatively consistent across parts of Asia, Europe, and North America (Weissman et al., 1994, 1996, 1997, 1998). The global consistency in symptoms and prevalence of these disorders, combined with results of family and molecular genetic studies, indicates that they have high heritability (genetic contribution to the variation of a disease in a population) (National Institute of Mental Health [NIMH], 1998). In other words, it seems that culture and societal factors play a more subordinate role in causation of these disorders.

Cultural and social context weigh more heavily in causation of depression. In the same international studies cited above, prevalence rates for major depression varied from 2 to 19 percent across countries (Weissman et al., 1996). Family and molecular biology studies also indicate less heritability for major depression than for bipolar disorder and schizophrenia (NIMH, 1998). Taken together, the evidence points to social and cultural fac-

---

[1] In medicine, each disease or disorder is considered mutually exclusive from another (WHO, 1992). Each disorder is presumed, but rarely proven, to have unique pathophysiology (Scadding, 1996).

tors, including exposure to poverty and violence, playing a greater role in the onset of major depression. *In this context, it is important to note that poverty, violence, and other stressful social environments are not unique to any part of the globe, nor are the symptoms and manifestations they produce. However, factors often linked to race or ethnicity, such as socioeconomic status or country of origin can increase the likelihood of exposure to these types of stressors.*

Cultural and social factors have the most direct role in the causation of post-traumatic stress disorder (PTSD). PTSD is a mental disorder caused by exposure to severe trauma, such as genocide, war combat, torture, or the extreme threat of death or serious injury (APA, 1994). These traumatic experiences are associated with the later development of a longstanding pattern of symptoms accompanied by biological changes (Yehuda, 2000). Traumatic experiences are particularly common for certain populations, such as U.S. combat veterans, inner-city residents, and immigrants from countries in turmoil. Studies described in the chapters on Asian Americans and Hispanic Americans reveal alarming rates of PTSD in communities with a high degree of pre-immigration exposure to trauma (Chapters 5 and 6). For example, in some samples, up to 70 percent of refugees from Vietnam, Cambodia, and Laos met diagnostic criteria for PTSD. By contrast, studies of the U.S. population as a whole find PTSD to have a prevalence of about 4 percent (DHHS, 1999).

Suicide rates vary greatly across countries, as well as across U.S. ethnic sub-groups (Moscicki, 1995). Suicide rates among males in the United States are highest for American Indians and Alaska Natives (Kachur et al., 1995). Rates are lowest for African American women (Kachur et al., 1995). The reasons for the wide divergence in rates are not well understood, but they are likely influenced by variations in the social and cultural contexts for each subgroup (van Heeringen et al., 2000; Ji et al., 2001).

Even though there are similarities and differences in the distribution of certain mental disorders across populations, the United States has an aggregate rate of about 20 percent of adults and children with diagnosable mental disorders (DHHS, 1999; Table 1-1). As noted in Chapter 1, this aggregate rate for the population as a whole does not have sufficient representation from most minority groups to permit comparisons between whites and other ethnic groups. The rates of mental disorder are not sufficiently studied in many smaller ethnic groups to permit firm conclusions about overall prevalence; however, several epidemiological studies of ethnic popula-

tions, supported by the NIMH, are currently in progress (Chapter 7). Until more definitive findings are available, *this Supplement concludes, on the basis of smaller studies, that overall prevalence rates for mental disorders in the United States are similar across minority and majority populations.* As noted in Chapter 1, this general conclusion applies to racial and ethnic minority populations living in the community, because high-need subgroups are not well captured in community household surveys.

Family Factors

Many features of family life have a bearing on mental health and mental illness. Starting with etiology, Chapter 1 highlighted that family factors can protect against, or contribute to, the risk of developing a mental illness. For example, supportive families and good sibling relationships can protect against the onset of mental illness. On the other hand, a family environment marked by severe marital discord, overcrowding, and social disadvantage can contribute to the onset of mental illness. Conditions such as child abuse, neglect, and sexual abuse also place children at risk for mental disorders and suicide (Brown et al., 1999; Dinwiddie et al., 2000).

Family risk and protective factors for mental illness vary across ethnic groups. But research has not yet reached the point of identifying whether the variation across ethnic groups is a result of that group's culture, its social class and relationship to the broader society, or individual features of family members.

One of the most developed lines of research on family factors and mental illness deals with relapse in schizophrenia. The first studies, conducted in Great Britain, found that people with schizophrenia who returned from hospitalizations to live with family members who expressed criticism, hostility, or emotional involvement (called *high expressed emotion*) were more likely to relapse than were those who returned to family members who expressed lower levels of negative emotion (Leff & Vaughn, 1985; Kavanaugh, 1992; Bebbington & Kuipers, 1994; Lopez & Guarnaccia, 2000). Later studies extended this line of research to Mexican American samples. These studies reconceptualized the role of family as a dynamic interaction between patients and their families, rather than as static family characteristics (Jenkins, Kleinman, & Good, 1991; Jenkins, 1993). Using this approach, a study comparing Mexican American and white families found that different types of interactions predicted relapse. For the Mexican American families, interactions featuring distance or lack of warmth predicted relapse for the individual with schizophrenia better than interactions featuring criticism. For whites, the converse was true (Lopez et al., 1998). This example, while not necessarily generalizable to other Hispanic groups, suggests avenues by which other culturally based family differences may be related to the course of mental illness.

Coping Styles

Culture relates to how people cope with everyday problems and more extreme types of adversity. Some Asian American groups, for example, tend not to dwell on upsetting thoughts, thinking that reticence or avoidance is better than outward expression. They place a higher emphasis on suppression of affect (Hsu, 1971; Kleinman, 1977), with some tending first to rely on themselves to cope with distress (Narikiyo & Kameoka, 1992). African Americans tend to take an active approach in facing personal problems, rather than avoiding them (Broman, 1996). They are more inclined than whites to depend on handling distress on their own (Sussman et al., 1987). They also appear to rely more on spirituality to help them cope with adversity and symptoms of mental illness (Broman, 1996; Cooper-Patrick et al., 1997; Neighbors et al., 1998).

Few doubt the importance of culture in fostering different ways of coping, but research is sparse. One of the few, yet well developed lines of research on coping styles comes from comparisons of children living in Thailand versus America. Thailand's largely Buddhist religion and culture encourage self-control, emotional restraint, and social inhibition. In a recent study, Thai children were two times more likely than American children to report reliance on covert coping methods such as "not talking back," than on overt coping methods such as "screaming" and "running away" (McCarty et al., 1999). Other studies by these investigators established that different coping styles are associated with different types and degrees of problem behaviors in children (Weisz et al., 1997).

The studies noted here suggest that better understanding of coping styles among racial and ethnic minorities has implications for the promotion of mental health, the prevention of mental illness, and the nature and severity of mental health problems.

Treatment Seeking

It is well documented that racial and ethnic minorities in the United States are less likely than whites to seek mental health treatment, which largely accounts for their underrepresentation in most mental health services (Sussman et al., 1987; Kessler et al., 1996; Vega et al. 1998; Zhang et al., 1998). Treatment seeking denotes the pathways taken to reach treatment and the types of treatments sought (Rogler & Cortes, 1993). The pathways are the sequence of contacts and their duration once someone (or their family) recognizes their distress as a health problem.

Research indicates that some minority groups are more likely than whites to delay seeking treatment until symptoms are more severe (See Chapters 3 & 5). Further, racial and ethnic minorities are less inclined than whites to seek treatment from mental health specialists (Gallo et al., 1995; Chun et al., 1996; Zhang et al., 1998). Instead, studies indicate that minorities turn more often to primary care (Cooper-Patrick et al., 1999a; see later section on *Primary Care*). They also turn to informal sources of care such as clergy, traditional healers, and family and friends (Neighbors & Jackson, 1984; Peifer et al., 2000). In particular, American Indians and Alaska Natives often rely on traditional healers, who frequently work side-by-side with formal providers in tribal mental health programs (Chapter 4). African Americans often rely on ministers, who may play various mental health roles as counselor, diagnostician, or referral agent (Levin, 1986). The extent to which minority groups rely on informal sources in lieu of, or in addition to, formal mental health services in primary or specialty care is not well studied.

When they use mental health services, Some African Americans prefer therapists of the same race or ethnicity. This preference has encouraged the development of ethnic-specific programs that match patients to therapists of the same culture or ethnicity (Sue, 1998). Many African Americans also prefer counseling to drug therapy (Dwight-Johnson et al., 2000). Their concerns revolve around side effects, effectiveness, and addiction potential of medications (Cooper-Patrick et al., 1997).

The fundamental question raised by this line of research is: Why are many racial and ethnic minorities less inclined than whites to seek mental health treatment? Certainly, the constellation of barriers deterring whites also operates to various degrees for minorities — cost, fragmentation of services, and the societal stigma on mental illness (DHHS, 1999). But there are extra barriers deterring racial and ethnic minorities such as mistrust and limited English proficiency.

Mistrust

Mistrust was identified by the SGR as a major barrier to the receipt of mental health treatment by racial and ethnic minorities (DHHS, 1999). Mistrust is widely accepted as pervasive among minorities, yet there is surprisingly little empirical research to document it (Cooper-Patrick et al., 1999). One of the few studies on this topic looked at African Americans and whites surveyed in the early 1980s in a national study known as the Epidemiologic Catchment Area (ECA) study. This study found that African Americans with major depression were more likely to cite their fears of hospitalization and of treatment as reasons for not seeking mental health treatment. For instance, almost half of African Americans, as opposed to 20 percent of whites, reported being afraid of mental health treatment (Sussman et al., 1987).

What are the reasons behind the lack of trust? Mistrust of clinicians by minorities arises, in the broadest sense, from historical persecution and from present-day struggles with racism and discrimination. It also arises from documented abuses and perceived mistreatment, both in the past and more recently, by medical and mental health professionals (Neal-Barnett & Smith, 1997; see later section on "Clinician Bias and Stereotyping"). A recent survey conducted for the Kaiser Family Foundation (Brown et al., 1999) found that 12 percent of African Americans and 15 percent of Latinos, in comparison with 1 percent of whites, felt that a doctor or health provider judged them unfairly or treated them with disrespect because of their race or ethnic background. Even stronger ethnic differences were reported in the Commonwealth Fund Minority Health Survey: It found that 43 percent of African Americans and 28 percent of Latinos, in comparison with 5 percent of whites, felt that a health care provider treated them badly because of their race or ethnic background (LaVeist et al., 2000). Mistrust of mental health professionals is exploited by present day antipsychiatry groups that target the African American community with incendiary material about purported abuses and mistreatment (Bell, 1996).

Mistrustful attitudes also may be commonplace among other groups. While insufficiently studied, mistrust toward health care providers can be inferred from a group's attitudes toward government-operated institutions. Immigrants and refugees from many regions of the world, including Central and South America and Southeast Asia, feel extreme mistrust of government, based on atrocities committed in their country of origin and on fear of deportation by U.S. authorities. Similarly, many American Indians and Alaska Natives are mistrustful of health care institutions; this dates back through centuries of legalized discrimination and segregation, as discussed in Chapter 4.

Stigma

Stigma was portrayed by the SGR as the "most formidable obstacle to future progress in the arena of mental illness and health" (DHHS, 1999). It refers to a cluster of negative attitudes and beliefs that motivate the general public to fear, reject, avoid, and discriminate against people with mental illness (Corrigan & Penn, 1999).

Stigma is widespread in the United States and other Western nations (Bhugra, 1989; Brockington et al., 1993) and in Asian nations (Ng, 1997). In response to societal stigma, people with mental problems internalize public attitudes and become so embarrassed or ashamed that they often conceal symptoms and fail to seek treatment (Sussman et al., 1987; Wahl, 1999). Stigma also lowers their access to resources and opportunities, such as housing and employment, and leads to diminished self-esteem and greater isolation and hopelessness (Penn & Martin, 1998; Corrigan & Penn, 1999). Stigma can also be against family members; this damages the consumer's self-esteem and family relationships (Wahl & Harman, 1989). In some Asian cultures, stigma is so extreme that mental illness is thought to reflect poorly on family lineage and thereby diminishes marriage and economic prospects for other family members as well (Sue & Morishima, 1982; Ng, 1997).

Stigma is such a major problem that the very topic itself poses a challenge to research. Researchers have to contend with people's reluctance to disclose attitudes often deemed socially unacceptable. How stigma varies by culture can be studied from two perspectives. One perspective is that of the targets of stigma, i.e., the people with symptoms: If they are members of a racial or ethnic minority, are they more likely than whites to experience stigma? The other perspective is that of the public in their attitudes toward people with mental illness: Are members of each racial or ethnic minority group more likely than whites to hold stigmatizing attitudes toward mental illness? The answers to these cross-cultural questions are far from definitive, but there are some interesting clues from research.

Turning first to those who experience symptoms, one of the few cross-cultural studies questioned Asian Americans living in Los Angeles. The findings were eye-opening: Only 12 percent of Asians would mention their mental health problems to a friend or relative (versus 25 percent of whites). A meager 4 percent of Asians would seek help from a psychiatrist or specialist (versus 26 percent of whites). And only 3 percent of Asians would seek help from a physician (versus 13 percent of whites). The study concluded that stigma was pervasive and pronounced for Asian Americans in Los Angeles (Zhang et al., 1998).

Turning to the question of public attitudes toward mental illness, the largest and most detailed study of stigma in the United States was performed in 1996 as part of the General Social Survey, a respected, nationally representative survey being conducted by the National Opinion Research Center since the 1970s. In this study, a representative sample was asked in personal interviews to respond to different vignettes depicting people with mental illness. The respondents generally viewed people with mental illness as dangerous and less competent to handle their own affairs, with their harshest judgments reserved for people with schizophrenia and substance use disorders. Interestingly, neither the ethnicity of the respondent, nor the ethnicity of the person portrayed in the vignette, seemed to influence the degree of stigma (Pescosolido et al., 1999).

By contrast, another large, nationally representative study found a different relationship between race, ethnicity, and attitudes towards patients with mental illness. Asian and Hispanic Americans saw them as more dangerous than did whites. Although having contact with individuals with mental illness helped to reduce stigma for whites, it did not for African Americans. American Indians, on the other hand, held attitudes similar to whites (Whaley, 1997).

Taken together, these results suggest that minorities hold similar, and in some cases stronger, stigmatizing attitudes toward mental illness than do whites. Societal stigma keeps minorities from seeking needed mental health care, much as it does for whites. Stigma is so potent that it not only affects the self-esteem of people with mental illness, but also that of family members. The bottom line is that stigma does deter major segments of the population, majority and minority alike, from seeking help. It bears repeating that a majority of *all* people with diagnosable mental disorders do not get treatment (DHHS, 1999).

Immigration

Migration, a stressful life event, can influence mental health. Often called acculturative stress, it occurs during the process of adapting to a new culture (Berry et al., 1987). Refugees who leave their homelands because of extreme threat from political forces tend to experience more trauma, more undesirable change, and less control over the events that define their exits than do voluntary immigrants (Rumbaut, 1985; Meinhardt et al., 1986).

The psychological stress associated with immigration tends to be concentrated in the first three years after arrival in the United States (Vega & Rumbaut, 1991). According to studies of Southeast Asian refugees, an initial euphoria often characterizes the first year following migration, followed by a strong disenchantment and demoralization reaction during the second year. The

third year includes a gradual return to well-being and satisfaction (Rumbaut, 1985, 1989). This U-shaped curve has been observed in Cubans and Eastern Europeans (Portes & Rumbaut, 1990). Similarly, Ying (1988) finds that Chinese immigrants who have been in the United States less than one year have fewer symptoms of distress than those residing here for several years. Korean American immigrants have been found to have the highest levels of depressive symptoms in the one to two years following immigration; after three years, these symptoms remit (Hurh & Kim, 1988).

Although immigration can bring stress and subsequent psychological distress, research results do not suggest that immigration *per se* results in higher rates of mental disorders (e.g., Vega et al., 1998). However, as described in the chapters on Asian Americans and Latinos, the traumas experienced by adults and children from war-torn countries before and after immigrating to the United States seem to result in high rates of posttraumatic stress disorder (PTSD) among these populations.

Overall Health Status

The burden of illness in the United States is higher in racial and ethnic minorities than whites. The National Institutes of Health (NIH) recently reported that compared with the majority populations, U.S. minority populations have shorter overall life expectancies and higher rates of cardiovascular disease, cancer, infant mortality, birth defects, asthma, diabetes, stroke, adverse consequences of substance abuse, and sexually transmitted diseases (DHHS, 2000; NIH, 2000). The list of illnesses is overpoweringly long.

Disparities in health status have led to high-profile research and policy initiatives. One long-standing policy initiative is *Healthy People*, a comprehensive set of national health objectives issued every decade by the Department of Health and Human Services. The most recent is *Healthy People 2010*, which contains both well defined objectives for reducing health disparities and the means for monitoring progress (DHHS, 2000).

Higher rates of physical (somatic) disorders among racial and ethnic minorities hold significant implications for mental health. For example, minority individuals who do not have mental disorders are at higher risk for developing problems such as depression and anxiety because chronic physical illness is a risk factor for mental disorders (DHHS, 1999; see also earlier section). Moreover, individuals from racial and ethnic minority groups who *already* have both a mental and a physical disorder (known as comorbidity) are more likely to have their mental disorder missed or misdiagnosed, owing to competing demands on primary care providers who are preoccupied with the treatment of the somatic disorder (Borowsky, et al., 2000; Rost et al., 2000). Even if their mental disorder is recognized and treated, people with comorbid disorders are saddled by more drug interactions and side effects, given their higher usage of medications. Finally, people with comorbid disorders are much more likely to be unemployed and disabled, compared with people who have a single disability (Druss et al., 2000).

Thus, poor somatic health takes a toll on mental health. And it is probable that some of the mental health disparities described in this Supplement are linked to the poorer somatic health status of racial and ethnic minorities. The interrelationships between mind and body are inescapably evident.

Culture of the Clinician

As noted earlier, a group of professionals can be said to have a "culture" in the sense that they have a shared set of beliefs, norms, and values. This culture is reflected in the jargon members of a group use, in the orientation and emphasis in their textbooks, and in their mindset, or way of looking at the world.

Health professionals in the United States, and the institutions in which they train and practice, are rooted in Western medicine. The culture of Western medicine, launched in ancient Greece, emphasizes the primacy of the human body in disease.[2] Further, Western medicine emphasizes the acquisition of knowledge through scientific and empirical methods, which hold objectivity paramount. Through these methods, Western medicine strives to uncover universal truths about disease, its causation, diagnosis, and treatment.

Around 1900, Western medicine started to conceptualize disease as affected by social, as well as by biological phenomena. Its scope began to incorporate wider questions of income, lifestyle, diet, employment, and family structure, thereby ushering in the broader field of public health (Porter, 1997; see also Chapter 1).

Mental health professionals trace their roots to Western medicine and, more particularly, to two major European milestones — the first forms of biological psychiatry in the mid-19th century and the advent of psychotherapy (or "talk therapy") near the end of that century (Shorter, 1997). The earliest forms of biological psy-

chiatry primed the path for more than a century of advances in pharmacological therapy, or drug treatment, for mental illness. The original psychotherapy, known as psychoanalysis, was founded in Vienna by Sigmund Freud. While many forms of psychotherapy are available today, with vastly different orientations, all emphasize verbal communication between patient and therapist as the basis of treatment. Today's treatments for specific mental disorders also may combine pharmacological therapy and psychotherapy; this approach is known as multimodal therapy. These two types of treatment and the intellectual and scientific traditions that galvanized their development are an outgrowth of Western medicine.

To say that physicians or mental health professionals have their own culture does not detract from the universal truths discovered by their fields. Rather, it means that most clinicians share a worldview about the interrelationship among body, mind, and environment, informed by knowledge acquired through the scientific method. It also means that clinicians view symptoms, diagnoses, and treatments in a manner that sometimes diverges from their patients. "[Clinicians'] conceptions of disease and [their] responses to it unquestionably show the imprint of [a] particular culture, especially its individualist and activist therapeutic mentality," writes sociologist of medicine Paul Starr (1982).

Because of the professional culture of the clinician, some degree of distance between clinician and patient always exists, regardless of the ethnicity of each (Burkett, 1991). Clinicians also bring to the therapeutic setting their own personal cultures (Hunt, 1995; Porter, 1997). Thus, when clinician and patient do not come from the same ethnic or cultural background, there is greater potential for cultural differences to emerge. Clinicians may be more likely to ignore symptoms that the patient deems important, or less likely to understand the patient's fears, concerns, and needs. The clinician and the patient also may harbor different assumptions about what a clinician is supposed to do, how a patient should act, what causes the illness, and what treatments are available. For these reasons, *DSM-IV* exhorts clinicians to understand how their relationship with the patient is affected by cultural differences (Chapter 1).

Communication

The emphasis on verbal communication is a distinguishing feature of the mental health field. The diagnosis and treatment of mental disorders depend to a large extent on verbal communication between patient and clinician about symptoms, their nature, intensity, and impact on functioning (Chapter 1). While many mental health pro-

---

[2] In very general terms, most other healing systems throughout history conceived of sickness and health in the context of understanding relations of human beings to the cosmos, including planets, stars, mountains, rivers, deities, spirits, and ancestors (Porter 1997).

fessionals strive to deliver treatment that is sensitive to the culture of the patient, problems can occur.

The emphasis on verbal communication yields greater potential for miscommunication when clinician and patient come from different cultural backgrounds, even if they speak the same language. Overt and subtle forms of miscommunication and misunderstanding can lead to misdiagnosis, conflicts over treatment, and poor adherence to a treatment plan. But when patient and clinician do not speak the same language, these problems intensify. The importance of cross-cultural communication in establishing trusting relationships between clinician and patient is just beginning to be explored through research in family practice (Cooper-Patrick et al., 1999) and mental health (see later section on "Culturally Competent Services").

Primary Care

Primary care is a critical portal to mental health treatment for ethnic and racial minorities. Minorities are more likely to seek help in primary care as opposed to specialty care, and cross-cultural problems may surface in either setting (Cooper-Patrick et al., 1999). Primary care providers, particularly under the constraints of managed care, may not have the time or capacity to recognize and diagnose mental disorders or to treat them adequately, especially if patients have co-existing physical disorders (Rost et al., 2000). Some estimates suggest that about one–third to one–half of patients with mental disorders go undiagnosed in primary care settings (Higgins, 1994; Williams et al., 1999). Minority patients are among those at greatest risk of nondetection of mental disorders in primary care (Borowsky et al., 2000). Missed or incorrect diagnoses carry severe consequences if patients are given inappropriate or possibly harmful treatments, while their underlying mental disorder is left untreated.

Clinician Bias and Stereotyping

Misdiagnosis also can arise from clinician bias and stereotyping of ethnic and racial minorities. Clinicians often reflect the attitudes and discriminatory practices of their society (Whaley, 1998). This institutional racism was evident over a century ago with the establishment of a separate, completely segregated mental hospital in Virginia for African American patients (Prudhomme & Musto, 1973). While racism and discrimination have certainly diminished over time, there are traces today which are manifest in less overt medical practices concerning diagnosis, treatment, prescribing medications, and referrals (Giles et al., 1995; Shiefer, Escarce, &

Schulman, 2000). One study from the mental health field found that African American youth were four times more likely than whites to be physically restrained after acting in similarly aggressive ways, suggesting that racial stereotypes of blacks as violent motivated the professional judgment to have them restrained (Bond et al., 1988). Another study found that white therapists rated a videotape of an African American client with depression more negatively than they did a white patient with identical symptoms (Jenkins-Hall & Sacco, 1991).

There is ample documentation provided in Chapter 3 that African American patients are subject to overdiagnosis of schizophrenia. African Americans are also underdiagnosed for bipolar disorder (Bell et al., 1980, 1981; Mukherjee, et al., 1983), depression, and, possibly, anxiety (Neal-Barnett & Smith, 1997; Baker & Bell, 1999; Borowsky et al., 2000). The problems extend beyond African Americans. Widely held stereotypes of Asian Americans as "problem free" may prompt clinicians to overlook their mental health problems (Takeuchi & Uehara, 1996).

The following chapters of this Supplement each cover diagnostic errors and inappropriate treatment in greater detail. They also address the extent to which each racial or ethnic minority group utilizes services or receives treatment in conformance with treatment guidelines developed from controlled clinical trials. For example, minority patients are less likely than whites to receive the best available treatments for depression and anxiety (Wang et al., 2000; Young et al., 2001).

To infer a role for bias and stereotyping by clinicians does not prove that it is actually occurring, nor does it indicate the extent to which it explains disparities in mental health services. Some of the racial and ethnic disparities described in this Supplement are likely the result of racism[3] and discrimination by white clinicians; however, the limited research on this topic suggests that the issue is more complex. A large study of cardiac patients could not attribute African Americans' lower utilization of a cardiac procedure to the race of the physician. Lower utilization by African American versus white patients was independent of whether patients were treated by white or black physicians (Chen et al., 2001). The study authors suggested the possibility that institutional factors and attitudes that were common to black and white physicians contributed to lower rates of utilization by black patients. Some have suggested that what

---

[3] Defined in the next section of this chapter as "beliefs, attitudes, and practices that denigrate individuals or groups because of phenotypic characteristics or ethnic group affiliation...[which] can be perpetrated by institutions or individuals, acting intentionally or unintentionally."

appears to be racial bias by clinicians might instead reflect biases of their socioeconomic status or their professional culture (Epstein & Ayanian, 2001). These biases, whether intentional or unintentional, may be more powerful influences on care than the influence of the clinician's own race or ethnicity.

Culture, Society, and Mental Health Services

Every society influences mental health treatment by how it organizes, delivers, and pays for mental health services. In the United States, services are financed and delivered in vastly different ways than in other nations. That organization was shaped by and reflects a unique set of historical, economic, political, and social forces, which were summarized in the SGR (DHHS, 1999). The mental health service system is a fragmented patchwork, often referred to as the "*de facto* mental health system" because of its lack of a single set of organizing principles (Regier et al., 1993). While this hybrid system serves a range of functions for many people, it has not successfully addressed the problem that people with the most complex needs and the fewest financial resources often find it difficult to use. This problem is magnified for minority groups. To understand the obstacles that minorities face, this section provides background on mental health service settings, financing, and the concept of culturally competent services.

Service Settings and Sectors

Mental health services are provided by numerous types of practitioners in a diverse array of environments, variously called settings and sectors. Settings range from home and community to institutions, and sectors include public or private primary care and specialty care. This section provides a broad overview of mental health services, patterns of use, and trends in financing. Interested readers are referred to the SGR, which covers these topics in greater detail.

The burgeoning types of community services available today stand in sharp contrast to the institutional orientation of the past. Propelled by reform movements, advocacy, and the advent of managed care, today's best mental health services extend beyond diagnosis and treatment to cover prevention and the fulfillment of broader needs, including housing and employment. Services are formal (provided by professionals) or informal (provided by lay volunteers). The most fundamental shift has been

in the setting for service delivery, from the institution to the community.

There are four major sectors for receiving mental health care:

(1) The specialty mental health sector is designed solely for the provision of mental health services. It refers to mental hospitals, residential treatment facilities, and psychiatric units of general hospitals. It also refers to specialized agencies and programs in the community, such as community mental health centers, day treatment programs, and rehabilitation programs. Within these settings, services are furnished by specialized mental health professionals, such as psychologists, psychiatric nurses, psychiatrists, and psychiatric social workers;

(2) The general medical and primary care sector offers a comprehensive range of health care services including, but not limited to, mental health services. Primary care physicians, nurse practitioners, internists, and pediatricians are the general types of professionals who practice in a range of settings that include clinics, offices, community health centers, and hospitals;

(3) The human services sector is made up of social welfare (housing, transportation, and employment), criminal justice, educational, religious, and charitable services. These services are delivered in a full range of settings — home, community, and institutions;

(4) The voluntary support network refers to self-help groups and organizations devoted to education, communication, and support. Services provided by the voluntary support network are largely found in the community. Typically informal in nature, they often help patients and families increase knowledge, reduce feelings of isolation, obtain referrals to formal treatment, and cope with mental health problems and illnesses.

Consumers can exercise choice in treatment largely because of the range of effective treatments for mental illness and the diversity of settings and sectors in which these treatments are offered. Consumers can choose, too, between distinct treatment modalities, such as psychotherapy, counseling, pharmacotherapy (medications), or rehabilitation. For severe mental illnesses, however, all types are usually essential, as are delivery systems to integrate their services (DHHS, 1999).

Consumer preferences cannot necessarily be inferred from the types of treatment they actually use because costs, reimbursement, or availability of services — rather than preferences — may drive their utilization. For example, minority patients who wish to see mental health professionals of similar racial or ethnic backgrounds may often find it difficult or impossible, because most mental health practitioners are white. Because there are only 1.5 American Indian/Alaska Native psychiatrists per 100,000 American Indians/Alaska Natives in this country, and only 2.0 Hispanic psychiatrists per 100,000 Hispanics, the chance of an ethnic match between Native or Hispanic American patient and provider is highly unlikely (Manderscheid & Henderson, 1999).

Financing of Mental Health Services and Managed Care

Mental health services are financed from many funding streams that originate in the public and private sectors. In 1996, slightly more than half of the $69 billion in mental health spending was by public payers, including Medicaid and Medicare. The remainder came mostly from either private insurance (27%) or out-of-pocket payments (17%) by patients and their families (DHHS, 1999).

One of the most significant changes affecting both privately and publicly funded services has been the striking shift to managed care. Relatively uncommon two decades ago, managed care in some form now covers the majority of Americans, regardless of whether their care is paid for through the public or the private sector (Levit & Lundy, 1998). The term "managed care" technically refers to a variety of mechanisms for organizing, delivering, and paying for health services. It is attractive to purchasers because it holds the promise of containing costs, increasing access to care, improving coordination of care, promoting evidence-based quality care, and emphasizing prevention. Attainment of these goals for all racial and ethnic groups is difficult to verify through research because of the breathtaking pace of change in the health care marketplace. Study in this area is also challenging because claims data are closely held by private companies and thus are often unavailable to researchers, and because insurers and providers often do not collect information about ethnicity or race (Fraser, 1997).

Almost 72 percent of Americans with health insurance in 1999 were enrolled in managed *behavioral* health organizations for mental or addictive disorders (OPEN MINDS, 1999). Managed care has far-reaching implications for mental health services in terms of access, utilization, and quality, yet there has been only a limited body of research on its effectiveness in these areas (DHHS, 1999).

Through lower costs, managed care was expected to boost access to care, which is especially critical for racial and ethnic minorities. However, there is preliminary evidence that managed care is perceived by some racial and ethnic minorities as imposing more barriers to treatment than does fee-for-service care (Scholle & Kelleher, 1997; Provan & Carle, 2000). Yet, improved access alone will not eliminate disparities (Chapter 3). Other compelling factors curtail utilization of services by racial and ethnic minorities, and they need to be addressed to reduce the gap between minorities and whites (Chapter 7).

In terms of quality of care, the SGR noted ongoing efforts within behavioral health care to develop quality reporting systems. It also pointed out that existing incentives within and outside managed care do not encourage an emphasis on quality of care (DHHS, 1999). While the SGR concluded that there is little direct evidence of problems with quality in well implemented managed care programs, it cautioned that "the risk for more impaired populations and children remains a serious concern."

Finally, managed care has been coupled with legislative proposals to impose parity in financing of mental health services. Intended to reverse decades of inequity, parity seeks coverage for mental health services on a par with that for somatic (physical) illness. Managed care's potential to control costs through various management strategies that prevent overuse of services makes parity more economically feasible (DHHS, 1999). Studies described in the SGR found negligible cost increases under existing parity programs within several States. Further, several studies have shown that racial and ethnic disparities in access to health care and in treatment outcomes are reduced or eliminated under equal access systems such as the Department of Defense health care system (Optenberg et al., 1995; Taylor et al., 1997), the VA medical system for some disease conditions, and in some health maintenance organizations (Tambor et al., 1994; Martin, Shelby, & Zhang, 1995; Clancy & Franks, 1997).

Evidence-Based Treatment and Minorities

The SGR documented a comprehensive range of effective treatments for many mental disorders (DHHS, 1999). These evidence-based treatments rely on consistent scientific evidence, from controlled clinical trials, that they significantly improve patients' outcomes (Drake et al., 2001). Despite strong and consistent evidence of efficacy, the SGR spotlighted the problem that evidence-based treatments are not being translated into community settings and are not being provided to everyone who comes in for care.

Many reasons have been cited as underlying the gap between research and practice. The most significant are practitioners' lack of knowledge of research results, the lag time between reporting of results and their translation into the practice setting, and the cost of introducing innovative services into health systems, most of which are operating within a highly competitive marketplace. There are also fundamental differences in the health characteristics of patients studied in academic settings where the research is conducted versus practice settings where patients are much more heterogeneous and often disabled by more than one disorder (DHHS, 1999).

The gap between research and practice is even worse for racial and ethnic minorities. Problems span both research and practice settings. A special analysis performed for this Supplement reveals that controlled clinical trials used to generate professional treatment guidelines did not conduct specific analyses for any minority group (See Appendix A for complete analysis). Controlled clinical trials offer the highest level of scientific rigor for establishing that a given treatment works.

Several professional associations and government agencies have formulated treatment guidelines or evidence-based reports on treatment outcomes for certain disorders on the basis of consistent scientific evidence, across multiple controlled clinical trials. Since 1986, nearly 10,000 participants have been included in randomized clinical trials evaluating the efficacy of treatments for bipolar disorder, major depression, schizophrenia, and attention-deficit/hyperactivity disorder. However, for nearly half of these participants (4,991), no information on race or ethnicity is available.[4] For another 7 percent of participants (N = 656), studies only reported the designation "non-white," without indicating a specific minority group. For the remaining 47 percent of participants (N = 4,335), Table 2-1 shows the breakdown by ethnicity. *In all clinical trials reporting data on ethnicity, very few*

minorities were included and not a single study analyzed the efficacy of the treatment by ethnicity or race.[5] A similar conclusion was reached by the American Psychological Association in a careful analysis of all empirically validated psychotherapies: "We know of no psychotherapy treatment research that meets basic criteria important for demonstrating treatment efficacy for ethnic minority populations..." (Chambless et al., 1996).

The failure to conduct ethnic-specific analyses in clinical research is a problem that must be addressed

Table 2-1

Ethnic Specific Analyses in Clinical Trials for Developing Evidence Based Treatment Guidelines

STUDIES	Total Number of Participants	N (% of total sample)	NUMBER OF PARTICIPANTS FOR WHOM ETHNICITY IS REPORTED						Total Number of Ethnic Specific Analyses Conducted
			White	Unspecified Non-White	Black	Hispanic	AA/PI	AI/AN	
Bipolar Disorder	921	305 (33%)	234	39	32	0	0	0	0
Schizophrenia	2813	2044 (73%)	1314	305	376	44	5	0	0
Depression	3860	1841 (48%)	1571	241	27	0	2	0	0
ADHD	1672	801 (48%)	545	71	126	55	4	0	0
Total	9266	4991 (54%)	3664	656	561	99	11	0	0

See Appendix A

(Chapter 7). This problem is not unique to the mental health field; it affects all areas of health research. In 1993, Congress passed legislation creating the National Institute of Health's Office of Research on Minority Health to increase the representation of minorities in all aspects of biomedical and behavioral research (National Institutes of Health, 2001). In November 2000, the Minority Health Disparities Research and Education Act elevated the Office of Research on Minority Health to the National Center on Minority Health and Health Disparities. This gave NIH increased programmatic and budget authority for research on minority health issues and health disparities. The law also promotes more training and education of health professionals, the evaluation

---

[4] Researchers may have collected this information but did not report it in their published studies.

[5] One study of attention-deficit/hyperactivity disorder (AD/HD), the NIMH Multimodal Treatment Study of AD/HD, plans to conduct ethnic-specific analyses.

of data collection systems, and a national public awareness campaign.

Even though the treatment guidelines are extrapolated from largely white populations, they are, as a matter of public health prudence, the best available treatments for everyone, regardless of race or ethnicity. Yet evidence suggests that in clinical practice settings, minorities are less likely than whites to receive treatment that adheres to treatment guidelines (Chapters 3–6; see also Lehman & Steinwachs, 1998; Sclar et al., 1999; Blazer et al., 2000; Young et al., 2001). *Existing treatment guidelines should be used for all people with mental disorders, regardless of ethnicity or race.* But to be most effective, treatments need to be tailored and delivered appropriately for individuals according to age, gender, race, ethnicity, and culture (DHHS, 1999).

Culturally Competent Services

The last four decades have witnessed tremendous changes in mental health service delivery. The civil rights movement, the expansion of mental health services into the community, and the demographic shift toward greater population diversity led to a growing awareness of inadequacies of the mental health system in meeting the needs of ethnic and racial minorities (Rogler et al., 1987; Takeuchi & Uehara, 1996). Research documented huge variations in utilization between minorities and whites, and it began to uncover the influence of culture on mental health and mental illness (Snowden & Cheung, 1990; Sue et al., 1991). Major differences were found in some manifestations of mental disorders, idioms for communicating distress, and patterns of help-seeking. The natural outgrowth of research and public awareness was self-examination by the mental health field and the advent of consumer and family advocacy. As noted in Chapter 1, major recognition was given to the importance of culture in the assessment of mental illness with the publication of the *"Outline for Culture Formulation"* in DSM–IV (APA, 1994).

Another innovation was to take stock of the mental health treatment setting. This setting is arguably unique in terms of its strong reliance on language, communication, and trust between patients and providers. Key elements of therapeutic success depend on rapport and on the clinicians' understanding of patients' cultural identity, social supports, self-esteem, and reticence about treatment due to societal stigma. Advocates, practitioners, and policymakers, driven by widespread awareness of treatment inadequacies for minorities, began to press for a new treatment approach: the delivery of services responsive to the cultural concerns of racial and ethnic minority groups, including their languages, histories, traditions, beliefs, and values. This approach to service delivery, often referred to as cultural competence, has been promoted largely on the basis of humanistic values and intuitive sensibility rather than empirical evidence. Nevertheless, substantive data from consumer and family self-reports, ethnic match, and ethnic-specific services outcome studies suggest that tailoring services to the specific needs of these groups will improve utilization and outcomes.

Cultural competence underscores the recognition of patients' cultures and then develops a set of skills, knowledge, and policies to deliver effective treatments (Sue & Sue, 1999). Underlying cultural competence is the conviction that services tailored to culture would be more inviting, would encourage minorities to get treatment, and would improve their outcome once in treatment. Cultural competence represents a fundamental shift in ethnic and race relations (Sue et al., 1998). The term *competence* places the responsibility on mental health services organizations and practitioners — most of whom are white (Peterson et al., 1996) — and challenges them to deliver culturally appropriate services. Yet the participation of consumers, families, and communities helping service systems design and carry out culturally appropriate services is also essential (Chapter 7).

Many models of cultural competence have been proposed. One of the most frequently cited models was developed in the context of care for children and adolescents with serious emotional disturbance (Cross et al., 1989). At the Federal level, efforts have begun to operationalize cultural competence for applied behavioral healthcare settings (CMHS, 2000). Though these and many other models have been proposed, few if any have been subject to empirical test. No empirical data are yet available as to what the key ingredients of cultural competence are and what influence, if any, they have on clinical outcomes for racial and ethnic minorities (e.g., Sue & Zane, 1987; Ramirez, 1991; Pedersen & Ivey, 1993; Ridley et al., 1994; Lopez, 1997; Szapocznik et al. 1997; Falicov, 1998; Koss-Chioino & Vargas, 1999; Sue & Sue, 1999). A common theme across models of cultural competence, however, is that they make treatment effectiveness for a culturally diverse clientele the responsibility of the system, not of the people seeking treatment.

Later chapters of this Supplement describe the findings to date in relation to each ethnic or racial group. The main point is that cultural competence is more than the sum of its parts: It is a broad-based approach to transform the organization and delivery of all mental health services to meet the diverse needs of all patients.

Medications and Minorities

The introductory chapter of this Supplement emphasized the overall genetic similarities across ethnic groups and noted that while there may be some genetic polymorphisms that show mean differences between groups, these variations cannot be used to distinguish one population from another. Observed group differences are outweighed by shared genetic variation and may be correlates of lifestyle rather than genetic factors (Paabo, 2001). For example, researchers are finding some racial and ethnic differences in response to a heart medication (Exner et al., 2001) that appear to reflect both genetic and environmental factors. It is nevertheless reasonable to assume that medications for mental disorders, in the absence of data to the contrary, are as effective for racial and ethnic minority groups as they are for whites. *Therefore, this Supplement encourages people with mental illness, regardless of race or ethnicity, to take advantage of scientific advances and seek effective pharmacological treatments for mental illness.* As part of the standard practice of delivering medicine, clinicians always need to individualize therapies according to the age, gender, culture, ethnicity, and other life circumstances of the patient.

There is a growing body of research on subtle genetic differences in how medications are metabolized across certain ethnic populations. Similarly, this body of research also focuses on how lifestyles that are more common to a given ethnic group affect drug metabolism. Lifestyle factors include diet, rates of smoking, alcohol consumption, and use of alternative or complementary treatments. These factors can interact with drugs to alter their safety or effectiveness.

The relatively new field known as ethnopsychopharmacology investigates ethnic variations that affect medication dosing and other aspects of pharmacology. Most research in this field has focused on gene polymorphisms (DNA variations) affecting drug metabolizing enzymes. After drugs are taken by mouth, they enter the blood and are circulated to the liver, where they are metabolized by enzymes (proteins encoded by genes). Certain genetic variations affecting the functions of these enzymes are more common to particular racial or ethnic groups. The variations can affect the pace of drug metabolism: A faster rate of metabolism leaves less drug in the circulation, whereas a slower rate allows more drug to be recirculated to other parts of the body. For example, African Americans and Asians are, on average, more likely than whites to be slow metabolizers of several medications for psychosis and depression (Lin et al., 1997). Clinicians who are unaware of these differences may inadvertently prescribe doses that are too high for minority patients by giving them the dose normally prescribed for whites. This would lead to more medication side effects, patient nonadherence, and possibly greater risk of long-term, severe side effects such as tardive dyskinesia (Lin et al., 1997; Lin & Cheung, 1999).

A key point is that this area of research looks for frequency differences across populations, rather than between individuals. For example, one research study reported on population frequencies for a polymorphism linked to the breakdown of neurotransmitters. It found the particular polymorphism in 15 to 31 percent of East Asians, compared with 7 to 40 percent of Africans, and 33 to 62 percent of Europeans and Southwest Asians (Palmatier et al., 1999). It is important to note that these differences become apparent across populations, but do not apply to an individual seeking treatment (unless the clinician has specific knowledge about that person's genetic makeup, or genotype, or their medication blood levels). The concern about applying research regarding ethnically based differences in population frequencies of gene polymorphisms is that it will lead to stereotyping and racial profiling of individuals based on their physical appearance (Schwartz, 2001). For any individual, genetic variation in response to medications cannot be inferred from racial or ethnic group membership alone.

Racism, Discrimination, and Mental Health

Since its inception, America has struggled with its handling of matters related to race, ethnicity, and immigration. The histories of each racial and ethnic minority group attest to long periods of legalized discrimination — and more subtle forms of discrimination — within U.S. borders (Takaki, 1993). Ancestors of many of today's African Americans were forcibly brought to the United States as slaves. The Indian Removal Act of 1830 forced American Indians off their land and onto reservations in remote areas of the country that lacked natural resources and economic opportunities. The Chinese Exclusion Act of 1882 barred immigration from China to the U.S. and denied citizenship to Chinese Americans until it was repealed in 1952. Over 100,000 Japanese Americans were unconstitutionally incarcerated during World War II, yet none was ever shown to be disloyal. Many Mexican Americans, Puerto Ricans, and Pacific Islanders became U.S. citizens through conquest, not choice. Although racial and ethnic minorities cannot lay claim to being the sole recipients of maltreatment in the United States, legally sanctioned discrimination and exclusion of racial and ethnic minorities have been the rule, rather than the exception, for much of the history of this country. Each of the later chapters of this Supplement describes some of the key historical events that helped shape the contemporary mental health status of each group.

Racism and discrimination are umbrella terms referring to beliefs, attitudes, and practices that denigrate individuals or groups because of phenotypic characteristics (e.g., skin color and facial features) or ethnic group affiliation. Despite improvements over the last three decades, research continues to document racial discrimination in housing rentals and sales (Yinger, 1995) and in hiring practices (Kirschenman & Neckerman, 1991). Racism and discrimination also have been documented in the administration of medical care. They are manifest, for example, in fewer diagnostic and treatment procedures for African Americans versus whites (Giles et al., 1995; Shiefer et al., 2000). More generally, racism and discrimination take forms from demeaning daily insults to more severe events, such as hate crimes and other violence (Krieger et al., 1999). Racism and discrimination can be perpetrated by institutions or individuals, acting intentionally or unintentionally.

Public attitudes underlying discriminatory practices have been studied in several national surveys conducted over many decades. One of the most respected and nationally representative surveys is the General Social Survey, which in 1990 found that a significant percentage of whites held disparaging stereotypes of African Americans, Hispanics, and Asians. The most extreme findings were that 40 to 56 percent of whites endorsed the view that African Americans and Hispanics "prefer to live off welfare" and "are prone to violence" (Davis & Smith, 1990).

Minority groups commonly report experiences with racism and discrimination, and they consider these experiences to be stressful (Clark et al., 1999). In a national probability sample of minority groups and whites, African Americans and Hispanic Americans reported experiencing higher overall levels of global stress than did whites (Williams, 2000). The differences were greatest for two specific types: financial stress and stress from racial bias. Asian Americans also reported higher overall levels of stress and higher levels of stress from racial bias, but sampling methods did not permit statistical comparisons with other groups. American Indians and Alaska Natives were not studied (Williams, 2000).

Recent studies link the experience of racism to poorer mental and physical health. For example, racial inequalities may be the primary cause of differences in reported quality of life between African Americans and whites (Hughes & Thomas, 1998). Experiences of racism have been linked with hypertension among African Americans (Krieger & Sidney, 1996; Krieger et al., 1999). A study of African Americans found perceived[6] discrimination to be associated with psychological distress, lower well-being, self-reported ill health, and number of days confined to bed (Williams et al., 1997; Ren et al., 1999).

A recent, nationally representative telephone survey looked more closely at two overall types of racism, their prevalence, and how they may differentially affect mental health (Kessler et al., 1999). One type of racism was termed "major discrimination" in reference to dramatic events like being "hassled by police" or "fired from a job." This form of discrimination was reported with a lifetime prevalence of 50 percent of African Americans, in contrast to 31 percent of whites. Major discrimination was associated with psychological distress and major depression in both groups. The other form of discrimination, termed "day-to-day perceived discrimination," was reported to be experienced "often" by almost 25 percent of African Americans and only 3 percent of whites. This form of discrimination was related to the development of distress and diagnoses of generalized anxiety and depression in African Americans and whites. The magnitude of the association between these two forms of discrimination and poorer mental health was similar to other commonly studied stressful life events, such as death of a loved one, divorce, or job loss.

While this line of research is largely focused on African Americans, there are a few studies of racism's impact on other racial and ethnic minorities. Perceived discrimination was linked to symptoms of depression in a large sample of 5,000 children of Asian, Latin American, and Caribbean immigrants (Rumbaut, 1994). Two recent studies found that perceived discrimination was highly related to depressive symptoms among adults of Mexican origin (Finch et al., 2000) and among Asians (Noh et al., 1999).

In summary, the findings indicate that racism and discrimination are clearly stressful events (see also Clark et al., 1999). Racism and discrimination adversely affect health and mental health, and they place minorities *at risk for* mental disorders such as depression and anxiety. Whether racism and discrimination can by themselves cause these disorders is less clear, yet deserves research attention.

---

[6] "Perceived discrimination" is the term used by researchers in reference to the self-reports of individuals about being the target of discrimination or racism. The term is not meant to imply that racism did not take place.

These and related findings have prompted researchers to ask how racism may jeopardize the mental health of minorities. Three general ways are proposed:

(1) Racial stereotypes and negative images can be internalized, denigrating individuals' self-worth and adversely affecting their social and psychological functioning;

(2) Racism and discrimination by societal institutions have resulted in minorities' lower socioeconomic status and poorer living conditions in which poverty, crime, and violence are persistent stressors that can affect mental health (see next section); and

(3) Racism and discrimination are stressful events that can directly lead to psychological distress and physiological changes affecting mental health (Williams & Williams-Morris, 2000).

Poverty, Marginal Neighborhoods, and Community Violence

Poverty disproportionately affects racial and ethnic minorities. The overall rate of poverty in the United States, 12 percent in 1999, masks great variation. While 8 percent of whites are poor, rates are much higher among racial and ethnic minorities: 11 percent of Asian Americans and Pacific Islanders, 23 percent of Hispanic Americans, 24 percent of African Americans, and 26 percent of American Indians and Alaska Natives (U. S. Census Bureau, 1999). Measured another way, the per capita income for racial and ethnic minority groups is much lower than that for whites (Table 2-2).

For centuries, it has been known that people living in poverty, whatever their race or ethnicity, have the poorest overall health (see reviews by Krieger, 1993; Adler et al., 1994; Yen & Syme, 1999). It comes as no surprise then that poverty is also linked to poorer mental health (Adler et al., 1994). Studies have consistently shown that people in the lowest strata of income, education, and occupation (known as socioeconomic status, or SES) are about two to three times more likely than those in the highest strata to have a mental disorder (Holzer et al., 1986; Regier et al., 1993; Muntaner et al., 1998). They also are more likely to have higher levels of psychological distress (Eaton & Muntaner, 1999).

Poverty in the United States has become concentrated in urban areas

(Herbers, 1986). Poor neighborhoods have few resources and suffer from considerable distress and disadvantage in terms of high unemployment rates, homelessness, substance abuse, and crime. A disadvantaged community marked by economic and social flux, high turnover of residents, and low levels of supervision of teenagers and young adults creates an environment conducive to violence. Young racial and ethnic minority men from such environments are often perceived as being especially prone to violent behavior, and indeed they are disproportionately arrested for violent crimes. However, the recent Surgeon General's Report on Youth Violence cites self-reports of youth from both majority and minority populations *that indicate that differences in violent acts committed* may not be as large as arrest records suggest. The Report on Youth Violence concludes that race and ethnicity, considered in isolation from other life circumstances, shed little light on a given child's or adolescent's propensity for engaging in violence (DHHS, 2001).

Regardless of who is perpetrating violence, it disproportionately affects the lives of racial and ethnic minorities. The rate of victimization for crimes of violence is higher for African Americans than for any other ethnic or racial group (Maguire & Pastore, 1999). More than 40 percent of inner city young people have seen someone shot or stabbed (Schwab-Stone et al., 1995). Exposure to community violence, as victim or witness, leaves immediate and sometimes long-term effects on mental health, especially for youth (Bell & Jenkins, 1993; Gorman-Smith & Tolan, 1998; Miller et al., 1999).

How is poverty so clearly related to poorer mental health? This question can be answered in two ways. People who are poor are more likely to be exposed to stressful social environments (e.g., violence and unem-

Table 2-2: Per Capita Income By Ethnicity in 1999

	Per Capita Incomes
African Americans	$14,397
Hispanic Americans	$11,621
Asian Americans & Pacific Islanders	$21,134
American Indians/Alaska Natives	Not Available
White Americans	$24,109

Source: U.S. Census Bureau, Current Population Reports, Money Income in the U.S., 1999.

ployment) and to be cushioned less by social or material resources (Dohrenwend, 1973; McLeod & Kessler, 1990). In this way, poverty among whites and nonwhites is a risk factor for poor mental health. Also, having a mental disorder, such as schizophrenia, takes such a toll on individual functioning and productivity that it can lead to poverty. In this way, poverty is a consequence of mental illness (Dohrenwend et al., 1992). Both are plausible explanations for the robust relationship between poverty and mental illness (DHHS, 1999).

Scholars have debated whether low SES alone can explain cultural differences in health or health care utilization (e.g. Lillie-Blanton et al., 1996; Williams, 1996; Stolley, 1999, 2000; LaVeist, 2000; Krieger, 2000). Most scholars agree that poverty and socioeconomic status do play a strong role, but the question is whether they play an exclusive role. The answer to this question is "no." Evidence contained within this Supplement is clearly contrary to the simple assertion that lower SES by itself explains ethnic and racial disparities. An excellent example is presented in Chapter 6. Mexican American immigrants to the United States, although quite impoverished, enjoy excellent mental health (Vega et al., 1998). In this study, immigrants' culture was interpreted as protecting them against the impact of poverty. In other studies of African Americans and Hispanics (cited in Chapters 3 and 6), more generous mental health coverage for minorities did not eliminate disparities in their utilization of mental health services. Minorities of the same SES as whites still used fewer mental health services, despite good access.

The debate separates poverty from other factors that might influence the outcome — such as experiences with racism, help-seeking behavior, or attitudes — as if they were isolated or independent from one another. In fact, poverty is caused in part by a historical legacy of racism and discrimination against minorities. And minority groups have developed coping skills to help them endure generations of poverty. In other words, poverty and other factors are overlapping and interdependent for different ethnic groups and different individuals. As but one example, the experience of poverty for immigrants who previously had been wealthy in their homeland cannot be equated with the experience of poverty for immigrants coming from economically disadvantaged backgrounds.

An important caveat in reviewing this evidence is that while most researchers measure and control for SES they do not carefully define and measure aspects of culture. Many studies report the ethnic or racial backgrounds of study participants as a shorthand for their culture, without systematically examining more specific information about their living circumstances, social class, attitudes, beliefs, and behavior. In the future, defining and measuring different aspects of culture will strengthen our understanding ethnic differences that occur, beyond those explained by poverty and socioeconomic status.

Demographic Trends

The United States is undergoing a major demographic transformation in racial and ethnic composition of its population. In 1990, 23 percent of U.S. adults and 31 percent of children were from racial and ethnic minority groups (Hollmann, 1993). In 25 years, it is projected that about 40 percent of adults and 48 percent of children will be from racial and ethnic minority groups (U.S. Census Bureau, 2000; Lewit & Baker, 1994). While these changes bring with them the enormous richness of diverse cultures, significant changes are needed in the mental health system to meet the associated challenges, a topic addressed in Chapter 7.

Diversity within Racial and Ethnic Groups

The four most recognized racial and ethnic minority groups are themselves quite diverse. For instance, Asian Americans and Pacific Islanders include at least 43 separate subgroups who speak over 100 languages. Hispanics are of Mexican, Puerto Rican, Cuban, Central and South American, or other Hispanic heritage (U.S. Census Bureau, 2000). American Indian/Alaskan Natives consist of more than 500 tribes with different cultural traditions, languages, and ancestry. Even among African Americans, diversity has recently increased as black immigrants arrive from the Caribbean, South America, and Africa. Some members of these subgroups have largely acculturated or assimilated into mainstream U.S. culture, whereas others speak English with difficulty and interact almost exclusively with members of their own ethnic group.

Growth Rates

African Americans had long been the country's largest ethnic minority group. However, over the past decade, they have grown by just 13 percent to 34.7 million people. In contrast, higher birth and immigration rates led Hispanics to grow by 56 percent, to 35.3 million people, while the whites grew just 1 percent from 209 million to 212 million. According to 2000 census figures, Hispanics have replaced African Americans as the second largest ethnic group after whites (U.S. Census Bureau, 2001).

Hispanics grew faster than any other ethnic minority group in terms of the actual number of individuals and the rate of population growth. The group with the second highest rate of population growth was Asian Americans, who in the 2000 census were counted separately from Native Hawaiians and Other Pacific Islanders. Because of immigration, the Asian American population grew 40.7 percent to 10.6 million people, and this growth is projected to continue throughout the century (U.S. Census Bureau, 2001).

American Indians and Alaska Natives surged between 38 and 50 percent over each of the decades from the 1960s through the 1980s. However, during the 1990s, the rate of growth was slightly slower (19%). Even so, the rate is still greater than that for the general population. One factor accounting for this higher-than-average growth rate is an increase in the number of people who now identify themselves as American Indian or Alaska Native. The current size of the American Indian and Alaska Native population is just under 1 percent of the total U.S. population, or about 2.5 million people. This number nearly doubles, however, when including individuals who identify as being American Indian and Alaska Native as well as one or more other races (U.S. Census Bureau, 2001).

The numbers of ethnic minority children and youth are increasing most rapidly. Between 1995 and 2015, the numbers of black youth are expected to increase by 19 percent, American Indian and Alaska Native youth by 17 percent, Hispanic youth by 59 percent, and Asian and Pacific Islander youth by 74 percent. During the same period, the white youth population is expected to increase by 3 percent (Snyder & Sickmund, 1999).

Geographic Distribution

Until the 1960s, American Indians, Asian Americans, and Hispanic Americans were geographically isolated. Before then, American Indians lived primarily on reservations to which the government assigned them. Few Asian Americans lived outside California, Hawaii, Washington, and New York City. Latinos resided primarily in the southwestern border States, New York City, and a few midwestern industrial cities (Harrison & Bennett, 1995).

Today, although they are not evenly distributed, members of each of the four major racial and ethnic minority groups reside throughout the United States. The western States are the most ethnically diverse in the United States, and they are home to many Latinos, Asian

Americans, and American Indians. In the Midwest, which is less ethnically diverse, over 85 percent of the population is white, and most of the remainder is black. This proportion has remained relatively unchanged since the 1970s.

Although the Nation as a whole is becoming more ethnically diverse, this diversity remains relatively concentrated in a few States and large metropolitan areas. In general, minorities are more likely than whites to live in urban areas. In 1997, 88 percent of minorities lived in cities and their surrounding areas, compared to 77 percent of whites. American Indians/Alaska Natives and African Americans are the only minority groups with any considerable rural population. (U.S. Census Bureau, 1999).

Impact of Immigration Laws

During the last century, U.S. immigration laws alternately closed and opened the doors of immigration to different foreign populations. For example, the 1924 Immigration Act established the National Origins System, which restricted annual immigration from any foreign country to 2 percent of that country's population living in the United States, as counted in the census of 1890. Since most of the foreign-born counted in the 1890 census were from northern and western European countries, the 1924 Immigration Act reinforced patterns of white immigration and staved off immigration from other areas, including Asia, Latin America, and Africa.

Until the 1960s, approximately two-thirds of all legal immigrants to the United States were from Europe and Canada. The Immigration Act of 1965 replaced the National Origins System and allowed an annual immigration quota of 20,000 individuals from each country in the Eastern Hemisphere. The Act also gave preference to individuals in certain occupations. The effect was striking: Immigration from Asia skyrocketed from 6 percent of all immigrants in the 1950s to 37 percent by the 1980s. Yet another provision of the Act supported family reunification and gave preference to people with relatives in the United States, one factor behind the growth in immigration from Mexico and other Latin American countries (U.S. Census Bureau, 1999). Over this same period of time, the percentage of immigrants from Europe and Canada fell from 68 percent to 12 percent (U.S. Immigration and Naturalization Service, 1999).

In the past 20 years, immigration has led to a shift in the racial and ethnic composition of the United States not witnessed since the late 17th century, when black slaves became part of the labor force in the South (Muller, 1993). Though this wave of immigration is similar to the surge of immigration that occurred in the early part of this century, a critical difference is in the countries of origin. In the early 1900s, immigrants primarily came from Europe and Canada, while recent immigration is primarily from Asian and Latin American countries.

Overall, the racial and ethnic makeup of the United States has changed more rapidly since 1965 than during any other period in history. The reform in immigration policy in 1965, the increase in self-identification by ethnic minorities, and the slowing of the country's birth rates, especially among non-Hispanic white Americans, have all led to an increasing, and increasingly diverse, racial and ethnic minority population in the United States.

Conclusions

(1) Culture influences many aspects of mental illness, including how patients from a given culture express and manifest their symptoms, their style of coping, their family and community supports, and their willingness to seek treatment. Likewise, the cultures of the clinician and the service system influence diagnosis, treatment, and service delivery. Cultural and social influences are not the only determinants of mental illness and patterns of service utilization for racial and ethnic minorities, but they do play important roles.

(2) Mental disorders are highly prevalent across all populations, regardless of race or ethnicity. Cultural and social factors contribute to the causation of mental illness, yet that contribution varies by disorder. Mental illness is considered the product of a complex interaction among biological, psychological, social, and cultural factors. The role of any one of these major factors can be stronger or weaker depending on the specific disorder

(3) Within the United States, overall rates of mental disorders for most minority groups are largely similar to those for whites. This general conclusion does not apply to vulnerable, high-need subgroups, who have higher rates and are often not captured in community surveys. The overall rates of mental disorder for many smaller racial and ethnic groups, most notably American Indians, Alaska Natives, Asian Americans and Pacific Islanders are not sufficiently studied to permit definitive conclusions.

(4) Ethnic and racial minorities in the United States face a social and economic environment of inequality that includes greater exposure to racism and discrimination, violence, and poverty, all of which take a toll on mental health. Living in poverty has the most measurable impact on rates of mental illness. People in the lowest stratum of income, education, and occupation are about two to three times more likely than those in the highest stratum to have a mental disorder.

(5) Racism and discrimination are stressful events that adversely affect health and mental health. They place minorities at risk for mental disorders such as depression and anxiety. Whether racism and discrimination can by themselves cause these disorders is less clear, yet deserves research attention.

(6) Stigma discourages major segments of the population, majority and minority alike, from seeking help. Attitudes toward mental illness held by minorities are as unfavorable, or even more unfavorable, than attitudes held by whites.

(7) Mistrust of mental health services is an important reason deterring minorities from seeking treatment. Their concerns are reinforced by evidence, both direct and indirect, of clinician bias and stereotyping. The extent to which clinician bias and stereotyping explain disparities in mental health services is not known.

(8) The cultures of ethnic and racial minorities alter the types of mental health services they use. Cultural misunderstandings or communication problems between patients and clinicians may prevent minorities from using services and receiving appropriate care.

References

Adler, N. E., Boyce, T., Chesney, M. A., Cohen, S., Folkman, S., Kahn, R. L., & Syme, S. L. (1994). Socioeconomic status and health: The challenge of the gradient. *American Psychologist, 49,* 15–24.

American Psychiatric Association. (1994). *Diagnostic and statistical manual of mental disorders* (4th ed.). Washington, DC: Author.

Baker, F. M., & Bell, C. C. (1999). Issues in the psychiatric treatment of African Americans. *Psychiatric Services, 50,* 362–368.

Bebbington, P., & Kuipers, L. (1994). The predictive utility of expressed emotion in schizophrenia: An aggregate analysis. *Psychological Medicine, 24*, 707–718.

Bell, C. C. (1996). Pimping the African-American community. *Psychiatric Services, 47*, 1025.

Bell, C. C., & Jenkins, E. J. (1993). Community violence and children on Chicago's southside. *Psychiatry, 56*, 46–54.

Bell, C. C. & Mehta, H. (1980). The misdiagnosis of black patients with manic depressive illness. *Journal of the National Medical Association, 72*, 141–145.

Bell, C. C. & Mehta, H. (1981). The misdiagnosis of black patients with manic depressive illness: Second in a series. *Journal of the National Medical Association, 73*, 101–107.

Berry, J. W., Kim, U., Minde, T., & Mok, D. (1987). Comparative studies of acculturative stress. *International Migration Review, 21*, 491–511.

Bhugra, D. (1989). Attitudes towards mental illness: A review of the literature. *Acta Psychiatrica Scandinavia, 80*, 1–12.

Blazer, D. G., Hybels, C. F., Simonsick, E. G., et al. (2000). Marked differences in antidepressant use by race in an elderly community sample: 1986–1996. *American Journal of Psychiatry. 157*, 1089–1094.

Bond, C. F., DiCandia, C. G., MacKinnon, J. R. (1988). Responses to violence in a psychiatric setting: The role of patient's race. *Personality and Social Psychology Bulletin, 14*, 448–458.

Borowsky, S. J., Rubenstein, L. V., Meredith, L. S., Camp, P., Jackson-Triche, M., & Wells, K B. (2000). Who is at risk of nondetection of mental health problems in primary care? *Journal of General Internal Medicine, 15*, 381–388.

Brockington, I., Hall, P. Levings, J., & Murphy, C. (1993). The community`s tolerance of the mentally ill. *British Journal of Psychiatry, 162*, 93–99.

Broman, C. L. (1996). Coping with personal problems. In H. W. Neighbors & J. S. Jackson (Eds.), *Mental health in black America* (pp. 117–129). Thousand Oaks, CA: Sage.

Brown, E. R., Ojeda, V. D., Wyn, R., & Levan, R. (2000). *Racial and ethnic disparities in access to health insurance and health care.* Los Angeles: UCLA Center for Health Policy Research and The Henry J. Kaiser Family Foundation.

Brown, J., Cohen, P., Johnson, J. G., & Smailes, E. M. (1999). Childhood abuse and neglect: Specificity of effects on adolescent and young adult depression and suicidality. *Journal of the American Academy of Child and Adolescent Psychiatry, 38*, 1490–1496.

Burkett, G. L. (1991). Culture, illness, and the biopsychosocial model. *Family Medicine, 23*, 287–291.

Chambless, D. L., Sanderson, W. C., Shoham, V., Bennett Johnson, S., Pope, K. S., Crits-Christoph, P., Baker, M., Johnson, B., Woody, S. R., Sue, S., Beutler, L., Williams, D. A., & McCurry, S. (1996). An update on empirically validated therapies. *The Clinical Psychologist, 49*, 5–18.

Chen, J., Rathore, S. S., Radford, M. J., Wang, Y., & Krumholz, H. M. (2001). Racial differences in the use of cardiac catheterization after acute myocardial infarction. *New England Journal of Medicine, 344*, 1443–1449.

Chun, C., Enomoto, K., & Sue, S. (1996). Health-care issues among Asian Americans: Implications of somatization. In P. M. Kata & T. Mann (Eds.), *Handbook of diversity issues in health psychology* (pp. 347–366). New York: Plenum.

Clancy, C. M., & Franks, P. (1997). Utilization of specialty and primary care: The impact of HMO insurance and patient-related factors. *Journal of Family Practice, 45*, 500–508.

Clark, R., Anderson, N. B., Clark, V. R., & Williams, D. R. (1999). Racism as a stressor for African Americans. A biopsychosocial model. *American Psychologist, 54*, 805–816.

Cooper-Patrick, L., Gallo, J. J., Gonzales, J. J., Vu, H. T., Powe, N. R., Nelson, C., & Ford, D. E. (1999). Race, gender, and partnership in the patient–physician relationship. *Journal of the American Medical Association, 282*, 583–589.

Cooper-Patrick, L., Gallo, J. J., Powe, N. R., Steinwachs, D. M., Eaton, W. W., & Ford, D. E. (1999). Mental health service utilization by African Americans and whites: The Baltimore Epidemiologic Catchment Area follow-up. *Medical Care, 37*, 1034–1045.

Cooper-Patrick, L., Powe, N. R., Jenckes, M. W., Gonzales, J. J., Levine, D. M., & Ford, D. E. (1997). Identification of patient attitudes and preferences regarding treatment of depression. *Journal of General Internal Medicine, 12*, 431–438.

Corrigan, P. W., & Penn, D. L. (1998). Lessons from social psychology on discrediting psychiatric stigma. *American Psychologist, 54*, 765–776.

Cross, T. L., Bazron, B. J., Dennis, K. W., & Isaacs, M. R. (1989). *Towards a culturally competent system of care.* Washington, DC: CAASP Technical Assistance Center.

Davis, J. A., & Smith, T. W. (1990). *General social surveys, 1972–1990.* Chicago: National Opinion Research Center.

Dinwiddie, S., Heath, A. C., Dunne, M. P., Bucholz, K. K., Madden, P. A., Slutske, W. S., Bierut, L. J., Statham, D. B., & Martin, N. G. (2000). Early sexual abuse and lifetime psychopathology: A co-twin-control study. *Psychology and Medicine, 30*, 41–52.

Dohrenwend, B. P. (1973). Social status and stressful life events. *Journal of Personality and Social Psychology, 28,* 225–235.

Dohrenwend, B. P., Levav, I., Shrout, P. E., Schwartz, S., Naveh, G., Link, B. G., Skodol, A. E., & Stueve, A. (1992). Socioeconomic status and psychiatric disorders: The causation–selection issue. *Science, 255,* 946–952.

Drake, R. E., Goldman, H. H., Leff, H. S., Lehman, A. F., Dixon, L., Mueser, K. T., & Torrey, W. C. (2001). Implementing evidence-based practices in routine mental health service settings. *Psychiatric Services 52,* 179–182.

Druss, B. G., Marcus, S. C., Rosenheck, R. A., Olfson, M., Tanielian, T., & Pincus, H. A. (2000). Understanding disability in mental and general medical conditions. *American Journal of Psychiatry, 157,* 1485–1491

Dwight-Johnson, M., Sherbourne, C. D., Liao, D., & Wells, K. B. (2000). Treatment preferences among primary care patients. *Journal of General Internal Medicine, 15,* 527–534.

Eaton, W. W., & Muntaner, C. (1999). Socioeconomic stratification and mental disorder. In A. V. Horwitz & T. K. Scheid (Eds.), *A handbook for the study of mental health: Social contexts, theories, and systems* (pp. 259–283). New York: Cambridge University Press.

Epstein, A. M., & Ayanian, J. Z. (2001). Racial disparities in medical care. *New England Journal of Medicine, 344,* 1471–1473.

Exner, D. V., Dries, D. L., Domanski, M. J., & Cohn, J. N. (2001). Lesser response to angiotensin-converting-enzyme inhibitor therapy in black as compared with white patients with left ventricular dysfunction. *New England Journal of Medicine, 344,* 1351–1357.

Falicov, C. J. (1998). *Latino families in therapy: A guide to multicultural practice.* New York: Guilford Press.

Finch, B. K., Kolody, B., & Vega, W. A. (2000). Perceived discrimination and depression among Mexican origin adults in California. *Journal of Health and Social Behavior, 41,* 295–313.

Fraser, I. (1997). Introduction: Research on health care organizations and markets—the best and worst of times. *Health Services Research, 32,* 669–678.

Gallo, J. J., Marino, S., Ford, D., & Anthony, J. C. (1995). Filters on the pathway to mental health care, II. Sociodemographic factors. *Psychological Medicine, 25,* 1149–1160.

Giles, W. H., Anda, R. F., Casper, M. L., Escobedo, L. G., & Taylor, H. A. (1995). Race and sex differences in rates of invasive cardiac procedures in U.S. hospitals. Data from the National Hospital Discharge Survey. *Archives of Internal Medicine, 155,* 318–324.

Gorman-Smith, D., & Tolan, P. (1998). The role of exposure to community violence and developmental problems among inner-city youth. *Development and Psychopathology, 10,* 101–116.

Harrison, R. J., & Bennett, C. (1995). Racial and ethnic diversity. In R. Farley (Ed.), *State of the Union: America in the 1990s. Vol. 2, Social Trends.* New York: Russell Sage.

Herbers, J. (1986). *The new heartland: America's flight beyond the suburbs and how it is changing our future.* New York: Times Books.

Higgins, E. S. (1994). A review of unrecognized mental illness in primary care: Prevalence, natural history, and efforts to change the course. *Archives of Family Medicine, 3,* 908–917.

Hollmann, F. W. (1993). *U.S. population estimates, by age, sex, race, and Hispanic origin: 1980 to 1991* (U.S. Bureau of the Census, Current Population Reports Series P25, No. 1095). Washington, DC: U.S. Government Printing Office.

Holzer, C., Shea, B., Swanson, J., Leaf, P., Myers, J., George, L., Weissman, M., & Bednarski, P. (1986). The increased risk for specific psychiatric disorders among persons of low socioeconomic status. *American Journal of Social Psychiatry, 6,* 259–271.

Hsu, F. L. K. (1971). Psychosocial homeostasis and jen: Conceptual tools for advancing psychological anthropology. *American Anthropologist, 73,* 23–44.

Hughes, M., Thomas, M. E. (1998). The continuing significance of race revisited: A study of race, class and quality of life in America, 1972 –1996. *American Sociological Review, 63,* 785–795.

Hunt, G. J. (1995). Social and cultural aspects of health, illness, and treatment. In H. H. Goldman (Ed.), *Review of general psychiatry.* Norwalk, CT: Appleton and Lange.

Hurh, W. M., & Kim, K. C. (1988). *Uprooting and adjustment: A sociological study of Korean immigrants' mental health* (Final report to the National Institute of Mental Health). Macomb, IL: Western Illinois University, Department of Sociology and Anthropology.

Jenkins, J. H. (1993). Too close for comfort: Schizophrenia and emotional overinvolvement among Mexicano families. In A. D. Gaines (Ed.), *Ethnopsychiatry* (pp. 203–221). Albany, NY: State University of New York Press.

Jenkins, J. H., Kleinman, A., & Good, B. J. (1991). Cross-cultural studies of depression. In J. Becker & A. Kleinman (Eds.), *Psychosocial aspects of depression* (pp. 67–99). Hillsdale, NJ: Erlbaum.

Jenkins-Hall, K. D., & Sacco, W. P. (1991). Effect of client race and depression on evaluations by white therapists. *Journal of Social and Clinical Psychology, 10,* 322–333.

Ji, J., Kleinman, A., & Becker, A. E. (2001). Suicide in contemporary China: A review of China's distinctive suicide demographics in their sociocultural context. *Harvard Review of Psychiatry, 9,* 1–12

Kachur, S. P., Potter, L. B., James, S. P., & Powell, K. E. (1995). *Suicide in the United States, 1980–1992* (Violence Surveillance Summary Series, No. 1). Atlanta, GA: Centers for Disease Control and Prevention.

Kavanaugh, D. (1992). Recent developments in expressed emotion and schizophrenia. *British Journal of Psychiatry, 160,* 601–620.

Kessler, R. C., Berglund, P. A., Zhao, S., Leaf, P. J., Kouzis, A. C., Bruce, M. L., Freidman, R. L., Grosser, R. C., Kennedy, C., Narrow, W. E., Kuehnel, T. G., Laska, E. M., Manderscheid, R. W., Rosenheck, R. A., Santoni, T. W., & Schneier, M. (1996). The 12-month prevalence and correlates of serious mental illness (SMI). In R. W. Manderscheid & M. A. Sonnenschein (Eds.), *Mental health, United States* (Pub. No. [SMA] 96–3098). Rockville, MD: Center for Mental Health Services.

Kessler, R. C., Mickelson, K. D., Williams, D. R. (1999). The prevalence, distribution, and mental health correlates of perceived discrimination in the United States. *Journal of Health and Social Behavior, 40,* 208–230.

Kirschenman, J., & Neckerman, K. M. (1991). "We'd love to hire them, but...": The meaning of race for employers. In C. Jencks and P.E. Peterson (Eds.), *The urban underclass* (pp. 203–234). Washington, DC: Brookings Institution.

Kleinman, A. (1977). Depression, somatization and the "new cross-cultural psychiatry." *Social Science and Medicine, 11,* 3–10.

Kleinman, A. (1988). *Rethinking psychiatry: From cultural category to personal experience.* New York: Free Press.

Koss-Chioino, J. D., & Vargas, L. A. (1999). *Working with Latino youth: Culture, development and context.* San Francisco: Jossey-Bass.

Krieger N. (1993). Epidemiologic theory and societal patterns of disease. *Epidemiology, 4,* 276–278.

Krieger, N., (2000). Refiguring "race": Epidemiology, racialized biology, and biological expressions of race relations. *International Journal of Health Services, 30,* 211–216.

Krieger, N., & Sidney, S. (1996). Racial discrimination and blood pressure: The CARDIA study of young black and white adults. *American Journal of Public Health, 86,* 1370–1378.

Krieger, N., Sidney, S., & Coakley, E. (1999). Racial discrimination and skin color in the CARDIA study: Implications for public health research. *American Journal of Public Health, 88,* 1308–1313.

LaVeist, T. A. (2000). On the study of race, racism, and health: A shift from description to explanation. *International Journal of Health Services, 30,* 217–219.

LaVeist, T. A., Diala, C., & Jarrett, N. C. (2000). Social status and perceived discrimination: Who experiences discrimination in the health care system, how, and why? In C. Hogue, M. Hargraves, & K. Scott-Collins (Eds.), *Minority health in America* (pp. 194–208). Baltimore, MD: Johns Hopkins University Press.

Leff, J., & Vaughn, C. (1985). *Expressed emotion in families: Its significance for mental illness.* New York: Guilford.

Lehman, A. F., & Steinwachs, D. M. (1998). Patterns of usual care for schizophrenia: Initial results from the Schizophrenia Patient Outcomes Research Team (PORT) Client Survey (Discussion 20–32). *Schizophrenia Bulletin, 24,* 11–20.

Levin, J. (1986). Roles for the black pastor in preventive medicine. *Pastoral Psychology, 35,* 94–103.

Levit, L., & Lundy, J. (1998). Trends and indicators in the changing health care market place: Chartbook. Menlo Park, CA: Henry J. Kaiser Family Foundation.

Lewit, E. M., & Baker, L. S. (1994). Children's health and the environment. *Future of Children, 5,* 8–10.

Lillie-Blanton, M., Parsons, P. E., Gayle, H., & Dievler, A. (1996). Racial differences in health: Not just black and white, but shades of gray. *Annual Review of Public Health, 17,* 411–448.

Lin, K. M., & Cheung, F. (1999). Mental health issues for Asian Americans. *Psychiatric Services 50,* 774–780.

Lin, K. M., Cheung, F., Smith, M., & Poland, R. E. (1997). The use of psychotropic medications in working with Asian patients. In E. Lee (Ed.), *Working with Asian Americans: A guide for clinicians* (pp.388–399). New York: Guilford.

Lopez, S. R. (1997). Cultural competence in psychotherapy: A guide for clinicians and their supervisors. In C. E. Watkins, Jr. (Ed.), *Handbook of psychotherapy supervision.* New York: Wiley.

Lopez, S. R., Nelson, K. A., Polo, J. A., Jenkins, J., Karno, M., & Snyder, K. (1998, August). *Family warmth and the course of schizophrenia of Mexican Americans and Anglo Americans.* Paper presented at the International Congress of Applied Psychology, San Francisco, CA.

Lopez, S. R., & Guarnaccia, P. J. (2000). Cultural psychopathology: Uncovering the social world of mental illness. *Annual Review of Psychology, 51,* 571–598.

Maguire, K., & Pastore, E. (Eds.). (1999). *Sourcebook of criminal justice statistics 1998.* Washington, DC: U.S. Government Printing Office.

Manderscheid, R. W., & Henderson, M. J., Eds. (1999). *Mental Health, United States: 1998.* Rockville, MD: Center for Mental Health Services.

Martin, T. L., Shelby, J. V., & Zhang, D. (1995). Physician and patient prevention practices in NIDDM in a large urban managed-care organization. *Diabetes Care, 18,* 1124–1132.

McCarty, C. A., Weisz, J. R., Wanitromanee, K., Eastman, K. L., Suwanlert, S., Chaiyasit, W., & Band, E. B. (1999). Culture, coping, and context: Primary and secondary control among Thai and American youth. *Journal of Child Psychology and Psychiatry, 40,* 809–818.

McLeod, J. D., & Kessler, R. C. (1990). Socioeconomic status differences in vulnerability to undesirable life events. *Journal of Health and Social Behavior, 31,* 162–172.

Meinhardt, K., Tom, S., Tse, P., & Yu, C. Y. (1986). Southeast Asian refugees in the "Silicon Valley": The Asian Health Assessment Project. *Amerasia Journal, 12,* 43–65.

Miller, L. S., Wasserman, G. A., Neugebauer, R., Gorman-Smith, D., & Kamboukos, D. (1999). Witnessed community violence and antisocial behavior in high-risk, urban boys. *Journal of Clinical Child Psychology, 28,* 2–11.

Moscicki, E. K. (1995). Epidemiology of suicide. *International Psychogeriatrics, 7,* 137–148.

Mukherjee, S., Shukla, S., Woodle, J., Rosen, A. M., & Olarte, S. (1983). Misdiagnosis of schizophrenia in bipolar patients: A multiethnic comparison. *American Journal of Psychiatry, 140,* 1571–1574.

Muller, T. (1993). *Immigrants and the American city.* New York: New York University Press.

Muntaner, C., Eaton, W. W., Diala, C., Kessler, R. C., & Sorlie, P. D. (1998). Social class, assets, organizational control and the prevalence of common groups of psychiatric disorders. *Social Science and Medicine, 47,* 2043–2053.

Narikiyo, T. A., & Kameoka, V. A. (1992). Attributions of mental illness and judgments about help seeking among Japanese-American and white American students. *Journal of Counseling Psychology, 39,* 363–369.

National Institute of Mental Health. (1998). *Genetics and mental disorders: Report of the National Institute of Mental Health's Genetics Workgroup.* Rockville, MD: Author.

National Institutes of Health. (2000). *Strategic research plan to reduce and ultimately eliminate health disparities, fiscal years 2002–2006.* Draft, October 6, 2000.

National Institutes of Health. (2001). *ORMH Mission.* Retrieved June 21, 2001, from www1.od.nih.gov/ormh/mission.html.

Neal-Barnett, A. M., & Smith, J. (1997). African Americans. In S. Friedman (Ed.), *Cultural issues in the treatment of anxiety* (pp. 154–174). New York: Guilford Press.

Neighbors, H. W., & Jackson, J. S. (1984). The use of informal and formal help: Four patterns of illness behavior in the black community. *American Journal of Community Psychology, 12,* 629–644.

Neighbors, H. W., Musick, M. A., & Williams, D. R. (1998). The African American minister as a source of help for serious personal crises: Bridge or barrier to mental health care? *Health Education and Behavior, 25,* 759–777.

Ng, C. H. (1997). The stigma of mental illness in Asian cultures. *Australian and New Zealand Journal of Psychiatry, 31,* 382–390.

Noh, S., Beiser, M., Kaspar, V., Hou, F., & Rummens, J. (1999). Perceived racial discrimination, depression and coping: A study of Southeast Asian refugees in Canada. *Journal of Health and Social Behavior, 40,* 193–207.

OPEN MINDS. (1999). Over 72% of insured Americans are enrolled in MBHOs: Magellan Behavioral Health continues to dominate the market. *OPEN MINDS Behavioral Health and Social Service Industry Analyst, 11,* 9.

Optenberg, S. A., Thompson, I. M., Friedrichs, P., Wojcik, B., Stein, C. R., Kramer, B. (1995). Race, treatment, and long-term survival from prostate cancer in an equal-access medical care system. *Journal of the American Medical Association, 274,* 1599–1605.

Paabo, S. (2001). Genomics and society. The human genome and our view of ourselves. *Science, 291* (5507), 1219–1220.

Palmatier, M. A., Kang, A. M., & Kidd, K. K. (1999). Global variation in the frequencies of functionally different catechol-O-methyltransferase alleles. *Biological Psychiatry, 15,* 557–567.

Pedersen, P. B., & Ivey, A. (1993). *Culture-centered counseling and interviewing skills: A practical guide.* New York: Praeger.

Peifer, K. L., Hu, T. W., & Vega, W. (2000). Help seeking by persons of Mexican origin with functional impairments. *Psychiatric Services, 51,* 1293–1298.

Penn, D. L., & Martin, J. (1998). The stigma of severe mental illness: Some potential solutions for a recalcitrant problem. *Psychiatric Quarterly, 69,* 235–247.

Pescosolido, B. A., Monahan, J., Link, B. G., Stueve, A., & Kikuzawa, S. (1999). The public's view of the competence, dangerousness, and need for legal coercion of persons with mental health problems. *American Journal of Public Health, 89,* 1339–1345.

Peterson, J. L., Folkman, S., Bakeman, R. (1996). Stress, coping, HIV status, psychosocial resources, and depressive mood in African American gay, bisexual, and heterosexual men. *American Journal of Community Psychology, 24,* 461–487.

Porter, R. (1997). *The greatest benefit to mankind: A medical history of humanity.* New York: Norton.

Portes, A., & Rumbaut, R. G. (1990). *Immigrant America: A portrait.* Berkeley, CA: University of California Press.

Provan, K. G., & Carle, N. (2000). *A guide to behavioral health managed care for Native Americans.* Tucson, AZ: University of Arizona, Center for Native American Health.

Prudhomme, C., & Musto, D. F. (1973). Historical perspectives on mental health and racism in the United States. In C. V. Willie, B. M. Kramer, & B. S. Brown (Eds.), *Racism and mental health* (pp. 25–57). Pittsburgh, PA: University of Pittsburgh Press.

Ramirez, M. (1991). *Psychotherapy and counseling with minorities: A cognitive approach to individual and cultural differences.* New York: Pergamon Press.

Regier, D. A., Narrow, W. E., Rae, D. S., Manderscheid, R. W., Locke, B. Z., & Goodwin, F. K. (1993). The de facto U.S. mental and addictive disorders service system. Epidemiologic Catchment Area prospective 1-year prevalence rates of disorders and services. *Archives of General Psychiatry, 50,* 85–94.

Ren, X. S., Amick, B., & Williams, D. R. (1999). Racial/ethnic disparities in health: The interplay between discrimination and socioeconomic status. *Ethnicity & Disease, 9,* 151165.

Ridley, C. R., Mendoza, D. W., Kanitz, B. E., Angermeier, L., & Zenk, R. (1994). Cultural sensitivity in multicultural counseling: A perceptual schema model. *Journal of Counseling Psychology, 41,* 125–136.

Rogler, L. H., & Cortes, D. E. (1993). Help-seeking pathways: A unifying concept in mental health care. *American Journal of Psychiatry, 150,* 554–561.

Rogler, L. H., Malgady, R. G., Costantino, G., & Blumenthal, R. (1987). What do culturally sensitive mental health services mean? The case of Hispanics. *American Psychologist, 42,* 565–570.

Rost, K., Nutting, P., Smith, J., Coyne, J. C., Cooper-Patrick, L., & Rubenstein, L. (2000). The role of competing demands in the treatment provided primary care patients with major depression. *Archives of Family Medicine, 9,* 150–154.

Rumbaut, R. G. (1989). Portraits, patterns, and predictors of the refugee adaptation process. In D.W. Haines (Ed.), *Refugees as immigrants: Cambodians, Laotians and Vietnamese in America* (pp. 138–182). Totowa, NG: Rowman and Littlefield.

Rumbaut, R. G. (1994). The Crucible Within: Ethnic Identity, Self-Esteem, and Segmented Assimilation Among Children of Immigrants. *International Migration Review, 28,* 748–794.

Scadding, J. G. (1996). Essentialism and nominalism in medicine: Logic of diagnosis in disease terminology. *Lancet, 348* (9,027), 594–596.

Sclar, D. A., Robison, L. M., Skaer, T. L., & Galin, R. S. (1999). Ethnicity and the prescribing of antidepressant pharmacotherapy: 1992–1995. *Harvard Review of Psychiatry, 7,* 29–36.

Scholle, S., & Kelleher, K. (1998). *Managed care for seriously emotionally disturbed children.* Paper presented at a Substance Abuse and Mental Health Services Administration Managed Care Seminar, Washington, DC.

Schwab-Stone, M. E., Ayers, T. S., Kasprow, W., Voyce, C., Barone, C., Shriver, T., Weissberg, R. P. (1995). No safe haven: A study of violence exposure in an urban community. *Journal of the American Academy of Child and Adolescent Psychiatry, 34,* 1343–1352.

Schwartz, R. C. (2001). Racial profiling in medical research. *New England Journal of Medicine, 344,* 1392–1393.

Shiefer, S. E., Escarce, J. J., Schulman, K. A. (2000). Race and sex differences in the management of coronary artery disease. *American Heart Journal, 139,* 848–857.

Shorter, E. (1997). *A history of psychiatry.* New York: Wiley.

Snowden, L. R., & Cheung, F. K. (1990). Use of inpatient mental health services by members of ethnic minority groups. *American Psychologist, 45,* 347–355.

Snyder, H., & Sickmund, M. (1999). *Juvenile Offenders and Victims: 1999 National Report.* Washington, DC: Office of Juvenile Justice and Delinquency Prevention.

Starr, P. (1982). *The social transformation of American medicine.* New York: Basic Books.

Stolley, P. D. (1999). Race in epidemiology. *International Journal of Health Services, 29,* 905–909.

Stolley, P. D. (2000). Reply to commentaries by Drs. Krieger and LaVeist on "Race in epidemiology." *International Journal of Health Services, 30,* 221–222.

Sue, D. W., & Sue, D. (1999). *Counseling the culturally different: Theory and practice (3rd edition).* New York: Wiley.

Sue, S. (1998). In search of cultural competence in psychotherapy and counseling. *American Psychologist, 53,* 440–448.

Sue, S., Fujino, D., Hu, L. T., Takeuchi, D. T., & Zane, N. W. (1991). Community mental health services for ethnic minority groups: A test of the cultural responsiveness hypothesis. *Journal of Consulting and Clinical Psychology, 59,* 533–540.

Sue, S., Kurasaki, K. S., & Srinivasan, S. (1998). Ethnicity, gender, and cross-cultural issues in research. In P. C. Kendall, J. N. Butcher, & G. N. Holmbeck (Eds.). *Handbook of research methods in clinical psychology* (2nd ed., pp. 51–71). New York: Wiley.

Sue, S., & Morishima, J. K. (1982). *The mental health of Asian Americans.* San Francisco: Jossey-Bass.

Sue, S., & Zane, N. (1987). The role of culture and cultural techniques in psychotherapy: A critique and reformulation. *American Psychologist, 42,* 37–45.

Sussman, L. K., Robins, L. N., & Earls, F. (1987). Treatment-seeking for depression by black and white Americans. *Social Science and Medicine, 24,* 187–196.

Szapocznik, J., Kurtines, W., Santisteban, D. A., Pantin, H., Scopetta, M., Mancilla, Y., Aisenberg, S., McIntosh, S., Perez-Vidal, A., & Coatsworth, J. D. (1997). The evolution of structural ecosystemic theory for working with Latino families. In J. G. Garcia & M. C. Zea (Eds.), *Psychological interventions and research with Latino populations* (pp. 166–190). Boston: Allyn & Bacon.

Takaki, R. (1993). *A different mirror: A history of multicultural America.* Boston: Little, Brown.

Takeuchi, D. T., & Uehara, E. S. (1996) Ethnic minority mental health services: Current research and future conceptual directions. In. B. L. Levin & J. Petrila (Eds.), *Mental health services: A public health perspective* (pp. 63–80). New York: Oxford University Press.

Tambor, E. S., Bernhardt, B. A., Chase, G. A., Faden, R. R., Geller, G., Hofman, K. J., & Holtzman, N. A. (1994). Offering cystic fibrosis carrier screening to an HMO population: Factors associated with utilization. *American Journal of Human Genetics, 55,* 626–637.

Taylor, A. J., Meyer, G. S., Morse, R. W., & Pearson, C. E. (1997). Can characteristics of a health care system mitigate ethnic bias in access to cardiovascular procedures? Experience from the Military Health Services System. *Journal of the American College of Cardiology, 30,* 901–907

U.S. Census Bureau. (1999). *Statistical Abstract of the United States: The National Data Book.* Washington, DC: Author.

U.S. Census Bureau. (2001) *Census 2000 Redistricting [Public Law 94–171] Summary File.* Washington, DC: Author.

U.S. Center for Mental Health Services. (2000). *Cultural competence standards in managed care mental health services: Four underserved/underrepresented racial/ethnic groups.* Rockville, MD: Author.

U.S. Department of Health and Human Services. (1999). *Mental health: A report of the Surgeon General.* Rockville, MD: Author.

U.S. Department of Health and Human Services. (2000). *Healthy People 2010* (2nd ed.). With *Understanding and improving health and Objectives for improving health* (2 vols.). Washington, DC: Author.

U.S. Department of Health and Human Services. (2001). *Youth violence: A report of the Surgeon General.* Rockville, MD: Author.

U.S. Immigration and Naturalization Service. (1999). *1999 Statistical Yearbook.* Washington, DC: Government Printing Office.

van Heeringen, K., Hawton, K., & Williams, J. M. G. (2000). Pathways to suicide: An integrative approach. In K. Hawton & K. van Heeringen (Eds.), *The international handbook of suicide and attempted suicide* (pp. 223–234). New York: Wiley.

Vega, W. A., Kolody, B., Aguilar-Gaxiola, S., Alderate, E., Catalano, R., & Carveo-Anduaga, J. (1998). Lifetime prevalence of DSM–III–R psychiatric disorders among urban and rural Mexican Americans in California. *Archives of General Psychiatry, 55,* 771–778.

Vega, W. A., & Rumbaut, R. G. (1991). Ethnic minorities and mental health. *Annual Review of Sociology, 17,* 351–383.

Wahl, O. F. (1999). Mental health consumers' experience of stigma. *Schizophrenia Bulletin, 25,* 467–478.

Wahl, O. F., & Harman, C. R. (1989). Family views of stigma. *Schizophrenia Bulletin, 15,* 131–139.

Wang, P. S., Berglund, P., & Kessler, R. C. (2000). Recent care of common mental disorders in the United States. *Journal of General Internal Medicine, 15,* 284–292.

Weissman, M. M., Bland, R. C., Canino, G. J., Faravelli, C., Greenwald, S., Hwu, H. G., Joyce, P. R., Karam, E. G., Lee, C. K., Lellouch, J., Lepine, J. P., Newman, S. C., Rubio-Stipec, M., Wells, J. E., Wickramaratne, P. J., Wittchen, H., & Yeh, E. K. (1996a). Cross-national epidemiology of major depression and bipolar disorder. *Journal of the American Medical Association, 276,* 293–299.

Weissman, M. M., Bland, R. C., Canino, G. J., Faravelli, C., Greenwald, S., Hwu, H. G., Joyce, P. R., Karam, E. G., Lee, C. K., Lellouch, J., Lepine, J. P., Newman, S. C., Rubio-Stipec, M., Wells, J. E., Wickramaratne, P. J., Wittchen, H., & Yeh, E. K. (1997). The cross-national epidemiology of panic disorder. *Archives of General Psychiatry, 54,* 305–309.

Weissman, M. M., Bland, R. C., Canino, G. J., Greenwald, S., Hwu, H. G., Lee, C. K., Newman, S. C., Oakley-Browne, M. A., Rubio-Stipec, M., Wickramaratne, P. J., et al. (1994). The cross national epidemiology of obsessive compulsive disorder. The Cross National Collaborative Group. *Journal of Clinical Psychiatry, 55* (Suppl.), 5–10.

Weissman, M. M., Broadhead, W. E., Olfson, M., Sheehan, D. V., Hoven, C., Conolly, P., Fireman, B. H., Farber, L., Blacklow, R. S., Higgins, E. S., & Leon, A. C. (1998). A diagnostic aid for detecting (DSM–IV) mental disorders in primary care. *General Hospital Psychiatry, 20,* 1–11.

Weisz, J. R., McCarty, C. A., Eastman, K.L., Chaiyasit, W., Suwanlert, S. (1997). Developmental psychopathology and culture: Ten lessons from Thailand. In S. S. Luthar, J. A. Burack, D. Cicchetti, & J. R. Weisz (Eds.), *Developmental psychopathology: Perspectives on adjustment, risk, and disorder* (pp. 568–592). Cambridge, England: Cambridge University Press.

Whaley, A. L. (1997). Ethnic and racial differences in perceptions of dangerousness of persons with mental illness. *Psychiatric Services, 48,* 1328–1330.

Whaley, A. L. (1998). Issues of validity in empirical tests of stereotype threat theory. *American Psychologist, 5,* 679–680.

Williams, D. R. (1996). Race/ethnicity and socioeconomic status: Measurement and methodological issues. *International Journal of Health Services, 26,* 483–505.

Williams, D. R. (2000). Race, stress, and mental health. In C.Hogue, M. Hargraves, & K. Scott-Collins (Eds.). *Minority health in America* (pp. 209–243). Baltimore: Johns Hopkins University Press.

Williams, D. R. & Williams-Morris, R. (2000). Racism and mental health: The African American experience. *Ethnicity and Health, 5,* 243–268.

Williams, D. R., Yu, Y., Jackson, J. S., & Anderson, N.B. (1997). Racial Differences in Physical and Mental Health: Socio-Economic Status, Stress and Discrimination. *Journal of Health Psychology, 2,* 335–351.

Williams, J. W., Jr., Rost, K., Dietrich, A. J., Ciotti, M. C., Zyzanski, S. J., & Cornell, J. (1999). Primary care physicians' approach to depressive disorders: Effects of physician specialty and practice structure. *Archives of Family Medicine, 8,* 58–67.

World Health Organization. (1973). *Report of the International Pilot Study on Schizophrenia.* Geneva, Switzerland: Author.

World Health Organization. (1992). *International statistical classification of diseases and related health problems* (10th revision, ICD–10). Geneva: Author.

Yehuda, R. (2000). The biology of post traumatic stress disorder. *Journal of Clinical Psychiatry, 61* (Suppl. 7), 14–21.

Yen, I. H., & Syme, S. L. (1999). The Social Environment and Health: A Discussion of the Epidemiologic Literature. *Annual Review of Public Health, 20,* 287–308.

Ying, Y. (1988). Depressive symptomatology among Chinese-Americans as measured by the CES–D. *Journal of Clinical Psychology, 44,* 739–746.

Yinger, J. (1995). *Closed doors, opportunities lost: The continuing costs of housing discrimination.* New York: Russell Sage Foundation.

Young, A. S., Klap, R., Shebourne, C. D., Wells, K.B. (2001). The quality of care for depressive and anxiety disorders in the United States. *Archives of General Psychiatry, 58,* 55–61.

Zhang, A. Y., Snowden, L. R., & Sue, S. (1998). Differences between Asian- and White-Americans' help-seeking and utilization patterns in the Los Angeles area. *Journal of Community Psychology, 26,* 317–326

CHAPTER 3
MENTAL HEALTH CARE FOR AFRICAN AMERICANS

Contents

Contents, *continued*

MENTAL HEALTH CARE FOR AFRICAN AMERICANS

Introduction

African Americans occupy a unique niche in the history of America and in contemporary national life. The legacy of slavery and discrimination continues to influence their social and economic standing. The mental health of African Americans can be appreciated only within this wider historical context. Resilience and forging of social ties have enabled many African Americans to overcome adversity and to maintain a high degree of mental health.

Approximately 12 percent of people in the United States, or 34 million people, identify themselves as African American[1] (U.S. Census Bureau, 2001a). However, this figure may be lower than the actual number, because African Americans are overrepresented among people who are hard to reach through the census, such as those who are homeless or incarcerated (O'Hare et al., 1991). Census takers especially miss younger and middle-aged African American males because they are overrepresented in these vulnerable populations and because they often decline to participate in the census (Williams & Jackson, 2000).

The African American population is increasing in diversity as greater numbers of immigrants arrive from Africa and the Caribbean. Indeed, 6 percent of all blacks in the United States today are foreign-born. Most of them come from the Caribbean, especially the Dominican Republic, Haiti, and Jamaica; in 1998, nearly 1.5 million blacks residing in the United States were born in the Caribbean (U.S. Census, 1998). In addition, since 1983, over 100,000 refugees have come to the United States from African nations.

Historical Context

The overwhelming majority of today's African American population traces its ancestry to the slave trade from Africa. Over a period of about 200 years, millions of Africans are estimated to have been kidnapped or purchased and then brought to the Western Hemisphere.

Ships delivered them to the Colonies and later to the United States (Curtin, 1969). Legally, they were considered chattel—personal property of their owners. By the early 1800s, most Northern States had taken steps to end slavery, where it played only a limited economic role, but slavery continued in the South until the Emancipation Proclamation in 1863 and passage of the 13th Amendment to the U.S. Constitution in 1865 (Healey, 1995).

The 14th Amendment (1868) extended citizenship to African Americans and forbade the States from taking away civil rights; the 15th Amendment (1870) prohibited disfranchisement on the basis of race. However, these advances did not eliminate the subjugation of African Americans. The right to vote, supposedly assured by the 15th Amendment, was systematically denied through poll taxes, literacy tests, grandfather clauses, and other exclusionary practices. Racial segregation prevailed. Many Southern State governments passed laws that became known as Jim Crow laws or "black codes," which reinforced informal customs that separated the races in public places, and perpetuated an inferior status for African Americans.

The economy of the South remained heavily agricultural, and most people were poor. Exploited and consigned to the bottom of the economic ladder, most African Americans toiled as sharecroppers. They rented land and paid for it by forfeiting most, if not all, of their harvested crops. Some worked as agricultural laborers and were paid rock-bottom wages. With very low, irregular incomes and little opportunity for betterment, African Americans continued to live in poverty. They were kept dependent and uneducated, with limited horizons (Thernstrom & Thernstrom, 1997).

As late as 1910, 89 percent of all blacks lived in legalized subservience and deep poverty in the rural South. When World War I interrupted the supply of cheap labor provided by European immigrants, African Americans began to migrate to the industrialized cities of the North in the Great Migration. As Southern agriculture became mechanized, and as the need for indus-

---

[1] This figure includes individuals reporting Black or African American race alone. It does not include individuals who also identify as Hispanic or who indicate two or more races.

trial workers in Midwestern and Northeastern States increased, African Americans moved north in even greater numbers. Following World War II, blacks began to migrate to selected urban centers in the West, mostly in California.

Segregation continued until the early 1950s. Then in 1954, in *Brown v. Board of Education*, the Supreme Court declared racially segregated education unconstitutional. In the 1960s, a protest movement arose. Led by the 1964 Nobel laureate, the Rev. Dr. Martin Luther King, Jr., activists confronted and sought to overturn segregationist practices, often at considerable peril. New legislation followed. The Civil Rights Act of 1964 prohibited both segregation in public accommodations and discrimination in education and employment. The Voting Rights Act, passed in 1965, suspended the use of voter qualification tests.

While the African American experience in the United States is rife with episodes of subjugation and displacement, it is also characterized by extraordinary individual and collective strengths that have enabled many African Americans to survive and do well, often against enormous odds. Through mutual affiliation, loyalty, and resourcefulness, African Americans have developed adaptive beliefs, traditions, and practices. Today, their levels of religious commitment are striking: Almost 85 percent of African Americans have described themselves as "fairly religious" or "very religious" (Taylor & Chatters, 1991), and prayer is among their most common coping responses. Another preferred coping strategy is not to shrink from problems, but to confront them (Broman, 1996). Yet another successful coping strategy is the tradition of turning for aid to significant others in the community, especially family, friends, neighbors, voluntary associations, and religious figures. This strategy has evolved from the historical African American experience of having to rely on each other, often for their very survival (Milburn & Bowman, 1991; Hatchett & Jackson, 1993).

African Americans have also developed a capacity to downplay stereotypical negative judgments about their behavior and to rely on the beliefs and behavior of other African Americans as a frame of reference (Crocker & Major, 1989). For this reason, at least in part, most African Americans do not suffer from low self-esteem (Gray-Little & Hafdahl, 2000). African Americans have a collective identity and perceive themselves as having a significant sphere of collectively defined interests. Such psychological and social frameworks have enabled many African Americans to overcome adversity and sustain a high degree of mental health.

What it means to be African American, belonging to a certain race, can no longer be taken for granted. As noted in Chapter 1, racial classification based on genetic origins is of questionable scientific legitimacy and of limited utility as a basis for understanding complex social phenomena (Yee et al., 1993). Still, the category "African American" provides a basis for social classification. African Americans are recognized by their physical features and are treated accordingly. Many African Americans identify as African American; they share a social identity and outlook (Frable, 1997; Cooper & Denner, 1998). Scholars have defined and measured aspects of this sense of racial identity: its salience, its centrality to the sense of self, the regard others hold for African Americans, what African Americans believe about the regard others hold for them, and beliefs about the role and status of African Americans (Sellers et al., 1998).

Current Status

Geographic Distribution

In spite of the Great Migration to the North, a large African American population remained in the South, and in recent years, a significant return migration has taken place. Today, 53 percent of all blacks live in the South. Another 37 percent live in the Northeast and Midwest, mostly in metropolitan areas. About 10 percent of all blacks live in the West (U.S. Census Bureau, 2001; see Figure 3-1). Nationally, 15 percent live in rural areas, compared to 23 percent of whites and 25 percent of Americans overall (Rural Policy Research Institute, 1997).

Many African Americans still live in segregated neighborhoods (Massey & Denton, 1993), and poor African Americans tend to live among other African Americans who are poor. Poor neighborhoods have few resources, a disadvantage reflected in high unemployment rates, homelessness, crime, and substance abuse (Wilson, 1987). Children and youth in these environments are often exposed to violence, and they are more likely to suffer the loss of a loved one, to be victimized, to attend substandard schools, to suffer from abuse and neglect, and to encounter too few opportunities for safe, organized recreation and other constructive outlets (National Research Council, 1993). Personal vulnerabilities are exacerbated by problems at the community level, beyond the sphere of individual control.

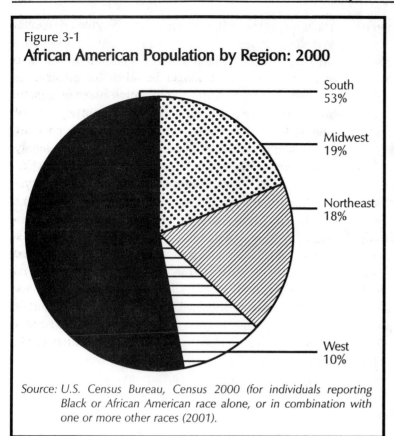

Figure 3-1
African American Population by Region: 2000

South
53%

Midwest
19%

Northeast
18%

West
10%

Source: U.S. Census Bureau, Census 2000 (for individuals reporting Black or African American race alone, or in combination with one or more other races (2001).

On the other hand, not all African American communities are distressed. Like other well functioning communities, stronger African American communities (both rich and poor) possess cohesion and informal mechanisms of social control, sometimes called *collective efficacy*. Evidence indicates that collective efficacy can counteract the effects of disabling social and economic conditions (Sampson et al., 1997). It also forms the foundation for community-building efforts (Bell & Fink, 2000).

Family Structure

In 2000, there were approximately 9 million African American families in the United States. On average, African American families are larger than white families; (65% versus 54% of families had three or more members), but smaller than families from other racial and ethnic minority groups (76% had three or more members). On the other hand, many African American children grow up in homes with only one parent. Only 38 percent were living in 2-parent families compared to 69% of all children in the United States. For children who lived with one parent, African Americans were more likely to live with their mothers than were U.S. children overall (92% versus 69%)(U.S. Census Bureau, 2001c).

Those who study African American life have argued that these trends are offset by an extended family orientation that calls for mutual material and emotional support (Hatchett & Jackson, 1993). This perspective has found wide acceptance and is reflected in policies such as family foster care, where children and youth removed from their homes are placed with relatives. African Americans participate extensively in family foster care in numbers proportional to their representation in foster care in general (Berrick et al., 1994; Landsverk et al., 1996; Altshuler, 1998).

Increasingly, however, researchers have discovered gaps and limitations in extended family support. Analyzing data from the National Survey of Families and Households, a large, community survey, Roschelle (1997) demonstrated that African American women were more likely than other women to provide assistance with child care and household tasks, but were less likely to receive such assistance in return. Respondents reported during in-depth interviews that levels of intergenerational support provided to teen mothers had waned (McDonald & Armstrong, 2001). They further indicated that several factors, including the youth of many grandmothers and the burden of problems brought on by urban poverty, had undermined supportive traditions.

Education

African Americans have shown an upward trend in educational attainment throughout the latter half of the 20th century. By 1997, there was no longer a gap in high school graduation rates between African Americans and whites. The number of African Americans enrolled in college in 1998 was 50 percent higher than the number enrolled a decade earlier. By 2000, 79 percent of Arican Americans age 25 and over had earned at least a high school diploma and 17 percent had attained a bachelor's or graduate degree. These rates are in comparsion to 84% and 26%, respectively, for Americans overall (U.S. Census Bureau, 2001c).

Income

When considered in aggregate, African Americans are relatively poor. In 1999, about 22 percent of African American families had incomes below the poverty line ($17,029 for a family of 4 in 1999) but only 10 percent of all U.S. families did (U.S. Census Bureau, 2001c). The difference in poverty rates has shrunk over the past decade, however, and the socioeconomic distribution of African Americans has become increasingly complex.

At one end of the income spectrum, the official poverty rate may understate the true extent of African American poverty. African Americans are more likely than whites to live in severe poverty, with incomes at or below 50 percent of the poverty threshold; the African American rate of severe poverty is more than three times the white rate. Children and youth are especially affected; while the national poverty rate for U.S. children is nearly 20 percent, almost 37 percent of African Americans 18 and younger live in poor families (U.S. Census Bureau, 1999b). There is considerable turnover in the poverty population. Most of the poor move out of poverty over time but are replaced by others. African Americans move in and out of poverty, but their periods of poverty tend to last longer, making African Americans more likely than whites to suffer from long-term poverty (O'Hare, 1996).

African American families fall well below white families on an important measure of aggregate financial resources: total wealth. Net worth, the value of assets minus liabilities, is a useful indicator. The median net worth of whites is about 10 times that of blacks (U.S. Census Bureau, 1999a). This wide disparity reflects limited African American family assets, lower rates of home ownership, limited savings, and few investments (O'Hare et al., 1991). Because most are descendants of deeply impoverished rural agricultural workers, many contemporary African Americans can expect to borrow only modest sums from relatives and can expect only small inheritances. Most African Americans have little financial cushion to absorb the impact of the social, legal, or health-related adversity that often accompanies mental illness.

African American poverty is associated with family structure. Despite historical patterns to the contrary and a slight reduction in recent years, African American children in particular, are especially likely to live in single-parent, mother-only families. This pattern reflects relatively low and declining marriage rates; the number of never-married African American adults almost equals the number of those who are married. Taking cohabitation into account reduces, but does not eliminate differences in the domestic partnership rates of African Americans versus other groups (*Statistical Abstract of the United States*, 1999).

The disparity in poverty rates affects older adults as well. Older African Americans are almost three times as likely as whites to be poor. The poverty rate among single African American women living alone or with non-relatives is very high (Ruiz, 1995). Older African American women are far more numerous than older African American men because of different mortality rates.

While many African Americans live in poverty, many others have joined the middle class. Between 1967 and 1997, African Americans benefited from a 31 percent boost in their real median household income, a raise that contrasts with an 18 percent increase for whites (U.S. Census Bureau, 1998). Nearly a quarter of all African Americans had incomes greater than $50,000 in 1997, and the median income of African Americans living in married-couple households was 87 percent that of comparable whites. Almost 32 percent of African Americans lived in the suburbs (Thernstrom & Thernstrom, 1997).

Thus, in socioeconomic terms, the African American population has become polarized. Many African Americans are very poor and sometimes suffer an added burden from living in impoverished communities. African Americans, poor and nonpoor alike, possess relatively few financial assets. However, a large and increasing number of African Americans—more than once expected—have taken up well-earned positions in the middle class.

Physical Health Status

As a group, African Americans bear a disproportionate burden of health problems (DHHS, 2000a). Mortality rates until age 85 are higher for blacks than for whites (National Center for Health Statistics, 1996). Disparities in morbidity, too, are pronounced. The African American rate of:

- diabetes is more than three times that of whites;

- heart disease is more than 40 percent higher than that of whites;

- prostate cancer is more than double that of whites;

- HIV/AIDS is more than seven times that of whites (In the past decade, deaths due to HIV/AIDS have increased dramatically in the African American population, and this disease is now one of the top five causes of death for this group.);

- breast cancer is higher than it is for whites, even though African American women are more likely to receive mammography screening than are white women (DHHS, 2000a);

- infant mortality is twice that of whites.

The disparity in infant mortality rates, which are considered sensitive indicators of a population's health status, is particularly stark. It is not entirely accounted for by socioeconomic factors. Although infant mortality tends to decrease with maternal education, the most educated black women have infant mortality rates that exceed those of the least educated white women (DHHS, 1998).

High rates of African American HIV/AIDS pose special challenges related to mental health. HIV infection can lead to mental impairment, from minor cognitive disorder to full-blown dementia, as well as precipitate the onset of mood disorders or psychosis. Opportunistic infections, use of psychoactive substances associated with HIV infection, and adverse effects from treatment can gravely compromise mental functioning (McDaniel et al., 1997).

Disparities in access to appropriate health care partially explain the differences in health status. In 1996, about 76 percent of whites had an office-based usual point of care, which facilitates preventive and primary care treatment. This compared to only 64 percent of African Americans (Kass et al., 1999). Only 10 percent of African Americans, versus 12 percent of other Americans, made a visit to an outpatient physician in 1997; African Americans made 26 percent fewer annual visits than whites. African Americans are especially likely to obtain health care from hospital outpatient and emergency departments. In 1997, African Americans made about 22 percent of emergency department visits (U.S. Census Bureau, 1999b). As will be shown in the next section, the pattern of mental health treatment for African Americans is characterized by low rates of outpatient care and high rates of emergency care.

The Need for Mental Health Care

Historical and Sociocultural Factors that Relate to Mental Health

Historical adversity, which included slavery, sharecropping, and race-based exclusion from health, educational, social, and economic resources, translates into the socioeconomic disparities experienced by African Americans today. Socioeconomic status, in turn, is linked to mental health: Poor mental health is more common among those who are impoverished than among those who are more affluent (Chapter 2). Also related to socioeconomic status is the increased likelihood of African Americans becoming members of high-need populations, such as people who are homeless, incarcer-

ated, or have substance abuse problems, and children who come to the attention of child welfare authorities and are placed in foster care. Members of these groups face special circumstances not fully explained by socioeconomic differences, however.

Racism is another aspect of the historical legacy of African Americans. Negative stereotypes and rejecting attitudes have decreased, but continue to occur with measurable, adverse consequences for the mental health of African Americans (Clark et al., 1999). Historical and contemporary negative treatment have led to mistrust of authorities, many of whom are not seen as having the best interests of African Americans in mind.

The overrepresentation of African Americans in the South, especially in impoverished rural areas, is another result of history. Hardship in these communities is notable, and a limited safety net provides relatively few services to address high levels of mental health need (Fox et al., 1995).

Key Issues for Understanding the Research

When seeking to explain differences between African Americans and whites, it is important that researchers first consider the impact of black-white demographic and socioeconomic differences. This is because disparities found in research sometimes are attributable to differences in poverty and marriage rates, regional distribution, and other population characteristics. However, investigators often continue to observe black-white differences after controlling for differences in social status and demographics and must look elsewhere to explain their findings. One of many possible explanations is racial bias: African Americans might, under the circumstances being investigated, be victims of adverse treatment because they are black.

Researchers must conceive and evaluate other explanations also. Differences in access to insurance and other mechanisms to defray costs, in levels of illness or patterns of symptom expression, in health-risk behaviors, and in beliefs, preferences, and help-seeking traditions can also explain disparities. Citing a large-scale study of Medicare beneficiaries (McBean & Gornick, 1994), Williams (1998) reported numerous black-white disparities in health care and mortality. The findings were consistent with the presence of race-based discrimination, but other possibilities were also noted: "A greater percentage of black Medicare beneficiaries made out-of-pocket payments;" "There may be higher levels of severity of illness among black patients;" "Blacks may be more likely than whites to refuse procedures recommended by their physicians;" and "Whites may be more aggressive in pursuing medical care" (p. 312).

Survey researchers face challenges when they attempt to generalize findings from household samples to the larger African American population. Because of African American overrepresentation in high-need populations, community surveys that do not include persons living in jails, shelters, foster care, or other institutional settings are likely to undercount the number of African Americans with mental illness. Furthermore, mistrust causes large segments of the African American population not to participate in the U.S. Census, making accurate accounting difficult and having what are estimated to be dramatic effects on population-based rates of health and social problems (Williams & Jackson, 2000).

The legitimacy accorded assessment procedures widely used to measure mental illness and mental health, when they are applied to African American and other minority groups, is sometimes questioned (Snowden, 1996). If African Americans do not disclose symptoms as readily as other groups, for example, or if they present their symptoms in a distinctive manner, then attempts to accurately assess African American mental illness will suffer. For many procedures, neither validity nor lack of validity among African Americans has been demonstrated; the issue has not yet been addressed. Variation in reliability and validity can be and should be assessed (Chow et al., in press).

Mental Disorders

Adults

The Epidemiologic Catchment Area study (ECA) of the 1980s sampled residents of Baltimore, St. Louis, Durham-Piedmont, Los Angeles, and New Haven and assessed samples from both the community at large and institutions such as mental hospitals, jails, residential drug or alcohol treatment facilities, and nursing homes (Robins & Regier, 1991). In total, it included 4,638 African Americans, 12,944 whites, and 1,600 Hispanics. A more recent study, the National Comorbidity Survey (NCS), included a representative sample of persons living in the community that included 666 African Americans, 4,498 whites, and 713 additional U.S. residents (Kessler et al., 1994). Participants of both studies reported whether or not they had experienced symptoms of frequently diagnosed mental disorders in the past month, the past year, or at any time during their lives.

Results for certain disorders are presented in Table 3-1. After taking into account demographic differences between African Americans and whites, the ECA found that African Americans were less likely to be depressed and more likely to suffer from phobia than were whites (Zhang & Snowden, 1999). The NCS findings also indicate that African Americans were less likely than whites to suffer from major depression.

The studies revealed gender differences in rates of mental illness. Prevalence rates of depression, anxiety disorder, and phobia were higher among African American women than African American men. These differentials paralleled those found for white women and men.

In light of the findings, whether African Americans differ from whites in rate of mental illness cannot be answered simply. On the ECA, African Americans had higher levels of any lifetime or current disorder than whites. This was true both over the respondent's lifetime (Robins & Regier, 1991) and over the past month (Regier et. al., 1993). Taking into account differences in age, gender, marital status, and socioeconomic status, however, the black-white difference was eliminated. From the ECA then, it appears that African Americans in the community suffer from higher rates of mental illness than whites, but that the difference is explained by differences in demographic composition of the groups and in their social positions.

Evidence from the NCS, on the other hand, indicated that even without controlling for demographic and socioeconomic differences, African Americans living in the community had lower lifetime prevalence of mental illness than did white Americans living in the community (Kessler et al., 1996). This difference existed for all of the disorders assessed.

The results from these major epidemiological surveys appear to converge on at least one point: The rates of mental illness among African Americans are similiar to those of whites. Yet this judgment, too, is open to challenge because of African American overrepresentation in high-need populations. Persons who live, for example, in psychiatric hospitals, prisons, the inner city, and poor rural areas are not readily accessible to researchers who conduct household surveys. By counting members of these high-need groups, higher rates of mental illness among African Americans might be detected.

Children and Youth

Mental health epidemiological research on children and youth provides little basis for conclusions about differences between African Americans and whites. Certain

Table 3-1

Results of the ECA and NCS Studies of Mental Health Care for African Americans

	ECA			NCS		
	Black n=4,638	White n=12,944	Total n=19,182	Black n=666	White n=4,498	Total n=5,877
12-month	% (se)	% (se)	% (se)	% (se)	% (se)	% (se)
Major Depression	2.2 (0.1)	2.8 (0.6)	2.7	8.2 (1.1)	9.9 (0.6)	10.0 (0.6)
Panic Disorder	1.0 (0.3)	0.9 (0.1)	0.9 (0.1)	1.1 (0.5)	2.4 (0.3)	2.2 (0.2)
Phobic Disorder	16.2 (1.5)	9.1 (0.4)	9.7 (0.4)	14.5 (1.8)	14.8 (0.6)	15.0 (0.6)
Lifetime						
Major Depression	3.1	5.1	4.9	11.6 (1.4)	17.7 (0.7)	16.9 (0.6)
Dysthymia	4.0	6.3	3.2	5.4 (1.0)	6.7 (0.4)	6.5 (0.4)
Panic Disorder	1.3 (0.4)	1.6 (0.1)	1.6 (0.1)	1.4 (0.5)	3.9 (0.3)	3.4 (0.2)
Phobic Disorder	23.4 (0.5)	9.7 (3.2)	14.3 (0.4)	19.2 (2.0)	22.3 (0.8)	21.9 (0.7)

The SE (Standard Error) is the average dispersion around the percentage.

studies suggest higher rates of symptoms or of certain types of full-blown mental illness among African American children and youth than among whites: functional enuresis (Costello et al., 1996), obsessive-compulsive disorder (Valleni-Basile et al., 1996), symptoms of conduct disorder (Costello et al., 1988), and symptoms of depression (Roberts et al., 1997). Other studies have reported no differences between rates for blacks and whites (Siegel et al., 1998). Underlying patterns are masked by differences in the regions from which the samples were drawn, in the age of respondents, in assessment methods, and in other methodological considerations.

A study discussed in the Surgeon General's report on mental health (DHHS, 1999b) included an assessment of

how much mental health care children in four geographic regions received. Children were identified as having unmet need if they were impaired because of mental illness and had had no mental health care in the preceding six months; African American children and youth were more likely to have unmet need than were white children and youth (Shaffer et al., 1996).

Older Adults

Little is known about rates of mental disorders among older African Americans. Older African American ECA respondents exhibited higher rates of cognitive impairment than did their counterparts from other groups. The rate of severe cognitive impairment continued to be high-

Box 3-1 A Child's Grief

John (age 10)

A 10-year-old African American male, "John," suffered from declining grades. Formerly a B and C student, he now received Ds. His mother could not explain his drop in academic achievement. John was unable to concentrate on homework and was sick to his stomach when studying. When questioned, John said that his father, now deceased, had formerly helped him carry out his assignments.

John told this story of his father's death: He and his father had been entering an elevator. They came upon two men arguing; one drew a gun and began to shoot. John's father, an innocent bystander, was shot in the stomach. He died on the moving elevator. The shooting and death produced a nauseating smell; John became sick and threw up.

Studying reminded John of his father's death and triggered nausea. This recognition helped to guide treatment. The focus was on providing a supportive relationship in which John could grieve his father's death. Overwhelmed, his mother had been unable to tolerate John's grief. Over time, John was able to transform his remorse into academic effort as a memorial to his father. His grades gradually improved. (Bell, 1997).

er for African Americans even after the researchers controlled for differences in demographic factors and socioeconomic status. Cognitive impairment is strongly related to education; simple measures may fail to assess fully the long-term impact of excluding African Americans from good schools.

Even less is known about the mental health of older African Americans whose physical health is poor. It appears that many living in nursing homes need psychiatric care (Class et al., 1996). In addition, 27 percent of older African Americans living in public housing needed mental health treatment (Black et al., 1997).

Several studies have examined rates of depressive symptoms in older African Americans living in the community. Three of the more rigorous research efforts reported few differences in depressive symptoms between African Americans and whites (Husaini, 1997, Blazer et al., 1998; Gallo et al., 1998). As with older whites, elevated symptoms of depression in African Americans have been related to health problems (Okwumabua et al., 1997; Mui & Burnette, 1994).

Mental Health Problems

Symptoms

Sometimes symptoms are considered not as markers of an underlying mental disorder but as mental health problems in their own right. Although much remains to be learned about symptom distress, it can pose significant problems. Symptoms of depression have been associated with considerable impairment in the performance of day-to-day tasks of living, comparable to that associated with common medical conditions (Wells et al., 1989). Among African Americans especially, symptoms of depression are associated with increased risk of hypertension (Pickering, 2000).

Before the advent of the epidemiological studies discussed above, parallel studies addressed symptoms of depression. Vega and Rumbaut (1991) conducted a comprehensive review of the research focusing on African American-white comparisons. Sometimes African Americans reported more distress than did whites, but investigators were often able to attribute the differences to socioeconomic and demographic differences (Neighbors, 1984).

Somatization

Somatization is an idiom of distress in which troubled persons report symptoms of physical illness that cannot be explained in medical terms. In some people, somatization is thought to mask psychiatric symptom distress or full-blown mental illness; somatic symptoms may be a more acceptable way of expressing suffering than psychiatric symptoms. Severe forms of somatization, which qualify as a disorder, are relatively rare; less severe forms are more common.

Somatization is not confined to African Americans, but somatic symptoms are more common among African Americans (15%) than among white Americans (9%) (Robins & Regier, 1991). Milder somatic symptoms, too, are expressed more often in African American communities (Heurtin-Roberts et al., 1997).

Culture-Bound Syndromes

Some distress idioms are more confined to particular racial and ethnic groups. Several are characterized in the *Diagnostic and Statistical Manual of Mental Disorders, Fourth Edition* (DSM–IV; American Psychiatric Association, 1994), in an Appendix devoted to culture-bound syndromes. One is *isolated sleep paralysis*, a state experienced while awaking or falling asleep and characterized by an inability to move (Bell et al., 1984, 1986). Another such syndrome, a sudden collapse sometimes preceded by dizziness, is known as *falling out*. (See DSM–IV, 1994, Appendix I, "Outline for Cultural Formulation" and "Glossary of Culture-Bound Syndromes," p. 846.) How widely these syndromes occur among African Americans is unknown.

These syndromes are examples of what anthropologists describe as a rich indigenous tradition of ways for African Americans to express psychiatric distress and other forms of emotion (Snow, 1993). Researchers have demonstrated that the symptoms reported in anthropological literature resemble those of certain established mental disorders, and that they are linked among African Americans to a tendency to seek assistance (Snowden, 1999a).

Suicide

Because most people who commit suicide have a mental disorder (DHHS, 1999b), suicide rates indicate potential need for mental health care. Official statistics indicate that whites are nearly twice as likely as African Americans to commit suicide (National Center for Health Statistics, 1996).

Suicide among African Americans has attracted significant scholarly interest (Baker, 1990; Gibbs & Hines, 1989; Griffith & Bell, 1989). Attempts to explain the disparity between African Americans and whites have brought to light several qualifying considerations. It has been noted that much of the difference is attributable to very high rates of suicide among older white males. When looking at other age groups, "the risk of suicide among young African American men is comparable to that of young white men" (Joe & Kaplan, 2001). Moreover, the disparity has shrunk appreciably over time (Griffith & Bell, 1989; Baker, 1990). The increasing convergence is associated with striking increases in suicide rates among African American youth. Between 1980 and 1995, for example, the suicide rate among African Americans ages 10 to 14 increased 233 percent; the suicide rate for comparable whites increased 120 percent (Centers for Disease Control and Prevention [CDC], 1998).

A coroner judges whether someone has died by suicide. The accuracy of suicide determinations, especially in the case of African Americans, has also been called into question (Phillips & Ruth, 1993). Mohler and Earls (2001) notably reduced the gap in suicide rates between African American and white youths and young adults after correcting for attribution to other causes.

High-Need Populations

Owing to a long history of oppression and the cumulative impact of economic hardship, African Americans are significantly overrepresented in the most vulnerable segments of the population. More African Americans than whites or members of other racial and ethnic minority groups are homeless, incarcerated, or are children in foster care or otherwise supervised by the child welfare system. African Americans are especially likely to be exposed to violence-related trauma, as were the large number of African American soldiers assigned to war zones in Vietnam. Exposure to trauma leads to increased vulnerability to mental disorders (Kessler et al., 1994).

Individuals Who Are Homeless

African Americans make up a large part of the homeless population. One attempt to consolidate the best scientific estimates reported that 44 percent of the people who are homeless were African American (Jencks, 1994). Other estimates concur, concluding that the African American proportion is no lower than 40 percent (Barrett et al., 1992; U.S. Conference of Mayors, 1996). Proportionally, 3.5 times as many African Americans as whites are homeless. This overrepresentation includes many African American women, children, and youth (Cauce et al., 1994; McCaskill et al., 1998).

People who are homeless suffer from mental illnesses at disturbingly high rates. The most serious disorders are the most common: schizophrenia (11 to 13% of the homeless versus 1% of the general population) and mood disorders (22 to 30% of homeless versus 8% of the general population) (Koegel et al., 1988; Vernez et al., 1988; Breakey et al., 1989). Homeless and runaway youth also suffer from mental disorders at high rates (Feitel et al., 1992; Mundy et al., 1989; McCaskill et al., 1998).

Individuals Who Are Incarcerated

Nearly half of all prisoners in State and Federal jurisdictions are African American (Bureau of Justice Statistics, 1999), as are nearly 40 percent of juveniles in legal custody (Bureau of Justice Statistics, 1998; Bureau of Justice Statistics, 1999). African Americans are also overrepresented in local jails (Bureau of Justice Statistics, 1999).

African American jail inmates and prisoners have somewhat lower rates of mental illness than comparable white American populations, but African American and white differences are overshadowed by the high rates of mental illness for incarcerated persons in general (Teplin,

1999; Teplin et al., 1996). A study conducted on women entering prison in North Carolina (Jordan et al., 1996) is illustrative. Investigators found that while lifetime rates of mental disorders among African American were slightly lower than those for whites, rates for both incarcerated groups typically were eight times greater than rates observed among African American and white American community residents. Incarcerated African Americans with mental illnesses are less likely than whites to receive mental health care (Bureau of Justice Statistics, 1998)

Children in Foster Care and the Child Welfare System

African American children make up about 45 percent of the children in public foster care and more than half of all children waiting to be adopted (DHHS, 1999a). Children come to the attention of child welfare authorities because they are suspected victims of abuse or neglect. Often they are removed from their homes and placed elsewhere—and then again placed elsewhere if an initial placement cannot be continued. These conditions carry a high risk of mental illness, as confirmed in epidemiological research. After investigating a large representative sample, Garland, and colleagues (1998) reported that around 42 percent of children and youth in child welfare programs met DSM-IV criteria for a mental disorder.

Individuals Exposed to Violence

Blacks of all ages are more likely to be the victims of serious violent crime than are whites (Griffith & Bell, 1989; Jenkins et al., 1989; Gladstein et al., 1992; Bureau of Justice Statistics, 1997; Jenkins & Bell, 1997). In one area, a community survey revealed that "nonwhites," many of whom were African American, were not only at greater risk of being victims of physical violence, but also at greater risk of knowing someone who had suffered violence (Breslau et al., 1998). The greater risk could not be attributed to socioeconomic differences or differences in area of residence.

The link between violence and psychiatric symptoms and illness is clear (Fitzpatrick & Boldizar, 1993; Breslau et. al, 1998; Schwab-Stone et al., 1999). One investigator reported that over one-fourth of African American youth who had been exposed to violence had symptoms severe enough to warrant a diagnosis of PTSD (Fitzpatrick & Boldizar, 1993).

Box 3-2: Fragmentation in the Foster Care System

Michael (age 17)

A 17-year-old African American male in foster care, "Michael," was referred for mental health care. He was described as "hostile"; he had recently dropped out of school.

Michael was surly and irritable initially, but ultimately began to cry. Eventually he spoke about his past.

His father lost his job when Michael was 9 and was unable to support Michael, his mother, and his three siblings. In desperation, Michael's father began to sell drugs. Michael's mother came to use the drugs being sold by his father. She became unable to care for her four children, resulting in their placement in foster care.

Michael reported living in five foster homes; lack of continuity undermined his educational success. He had seen none of his siblings for some time and knew nothing of their whereabouts or of his parents' well-being. He revealed that he had suffered crying spells for over a year (Bell, 1997).

Vietnam War Veterans

Although 10 percent of U.S. soldiers in Vietnam were black and 85 percent were white, more black (21%) than white (14%) veterans suffer from PTSD (Kulka et al., 1990). Investigators attribute this difference to the greater exposure of blacks to war-zone trauma, which increases risk not only for PTSD but also for many health-related and psychosocial adversities (Fairbank et al., 2001). African American and white veterans used Veterans' Administration (VA) mental health care equally, but African Americans proved less likely to use supplemental care outside the VA system (Rosenheck & Fontana, 1994).

Availability, Accessibility, and Utilization of Mental Health Services

Availability of Mental Health Services

The overrepresentation of African Americans in high-need populations implies great reliance on the programs and providers—public hospitals, community health centers, and local health departments—comprising the health care and mental health safety net (Lewin & Altman, 2000). State and local mental health authorities figure most prominently in the treatment of mental illness among African Americans. They may provide care either directly through the administration of mental health programs, or by contracting with not-for-profit providers or for-profit firms. The number, type, and distribution of safety net providers, as well as arrangements made for the provision of care, greatly influence the treatment options available to the most vulnerable populations of African Americans and others. Fortunately, the safety net includes programs and practitioners that specialize in treating African Americans. Several studies suggest that these care providers are especially adept at recruiting and retaining African Americans in outpatient treatment (Yeh et al., 1994; Snowden et al., 1995; Takeuchi et al., 1995).

The supply of African American clinicians is important. Studies of medical care reveal that African American physicians are five times more likely than white physicians to treat African American patients (Komaromy et al., 1996; Moy & Bartman, 1995) and that African American patients rate their physicians' styles of interaction as more participatory when they see African American physicians (Cooper-Patrick et al., 1999). *Mental Health United States* reported that, among clinically trained mental health professionals, only 2 percent of psychiatrists, 2 percent of psychologists, and 4 percent of social workers said they were African American (Holzer et al., 1998). African Americans seeking help-who would prefer an African American provider will have difficulty finding such a provider in these prominent mental health specialties.

The availability of mental health services also depends on where one lives. As discussed earlier, a relatively high proportion of African Americans live in the rural South. Evidence indicates that mental health professionals are concentrated in urban areas and are less likely to be found in the most rural counties of the United States (Holzer et al., 1998). Furthermore, African Americans living in urban areas are often concentrated in poor communities; urban practitioners who do not accept Medicaid or offer services to high-need clientele are not available to them.

Accessibility of Mental Health Services

Lack of health insurance is a barrier to seeking mental health care. Nearly one-fourth of African Americans are uninsured (Brown et al., 2000), a percentage 1.5 times greater than the white rate. In the United States, health insurance is typically provided as an employment benefit. Because African Americans are more often employed in marginal jobs, the rate of employer-based coverage among employed African Americans is substantially lower than the rate among employed whites (53% versus 73%; Hall et al., 1999).

Although insurance coverage is one of the most important determinants for deciding to seek treatment among both African Americans and whites, it is clear that insurance alone, at least when provided by private sector plans, fails to eliminate disparities in access between African Americans and whites (Scheffler & Miller, 1989; Snowden & Thomas, 2000). Provision of insurance benefits with more generous mental health coverage does not increase treatment seeking as much among African Americans as among whites (Padgett et al., 1995). Overcoming financial barriers is an important step in eliminating disparities in care; however, according to evidence currently available, it is not in itself sufficient.

Medicaid, a major public health insurance program subsidizing treatment for the poor, covers nearly 21 percent of African Americans. Medicaid payments are among the principal sources of financing for the services of safety net providers on which many African Americans depend. Medicaid-funded providers have been more successful than others in reducing disparities in access to mental health treatment (Snowden & Thomas, 2000).

African American attitudes toward mental illness are another barrier to seeking mental health care. Mental illness retains considerable stigma, and seeking treatment is not always encouraged. One study found that the proportion of African Americans who feared mental health treatment was 2.5 times greater than the proportion of whites (Sussman et al., 1987). Another study of parents of children meeting criteria for AD/HD discovered that African American parents were less likely than white parents to describe their child's difficulties using specific medical labels and more likely to expect a shorter term course (Bussing et al., 1998). Yet another study indicated that older African Americans were less knowledgeable about depression than elderly whites (Zylstra & Steitz, 1999).

Practitioners and administrators have sometimes failed to take into account African American preferences in formats and styles of receiving assistance. African Americans are affected especially by the amount of time spent with their providers, by a sense of trust, and by whether the provider is an African American (Keith, 2000). Among focus group participants, African Americans were more likely than whites to describe stigma and spirituality as affecting their willingness to seek help (Cooper-Patrick et al., 1997).

Utilization of Mental Health Services

Community Studies

Adults

Both the ECA and NCS investigated the use of mental health services by African Americans. Although only about 1 person in 3 of all respondents needing care received it, African Americans were distinguished by even lower levels of use (Robins & Regier, 1991). After eliminating the impact of sociodemographic differences and differences in need, the percentage of African Americans receiving treatment from any source was only about half that of whites (Swartz et al., 1998). Most African Americans who received care relied on the safety net public sector programs.

The more recent NCS also examined how many persons used mental health services. Results indicated that only 16 percent of African Americans with a diagnosable mood disorder saw a mental health specialist, and fewer than one-third consulted a health care provider of any kind. Table 3-2 shows that most African Americans suffering from mood and anxiety disorders did not receive care. The NCS also compared the use of mental health services by various ethnic groups and concluded that African Americans received less care than did white Americans.

Disparities between African Americans and whites also exist after initial barriers have been overcome. After entering care, African Americans are more likely than whites to terminate prematurely (Sue et al., 1994). They are also more likely to receive emergency care (Hu et al., 1991). These differences may come about because African Americans are relatively often coerced or otherwise legally obligated to have treatment (Akutsu et al., 1996; Takeuchi & Cheung, 1998).

Besides using fewer mental health services than do white Americans, African Americans appear to choose

Table 3-2

Use of Mental Health Services by African Americans

(*n*=1011)

12-month disorder	Mental Health Specialist* % (se)	Any Provider** % (se)
Mood disorder	15.6 (3.5)	28.7 (4.5)
Anxiety disorder	12.6 (2.4)	25.6 (5.3)

Data from the National Comorbidity Survey (Kessler et al., 1994)

The SE (Standard Error) is the average dispersion around the percentage.

* Psychologist, psychiatrist, or social worker

** Mental health specialist, general medical provider, other professional (nurse, occupational therapist, other health professional, minister, priest, rabbi, counselor), spiritualist, herbalist, natural therapist, or faith healer

different care providers. The National Ambulatory Medical Care Survey, which asked U.S. physicians about their patients, found that African Americans with mental health concerns were appreciably more likely to see their primary care physician than to see a psychiatrist (Pingitore et al., in press). Whites with mental health concerns, on the other hand, were only slightly more likely to see their primary care physician than to see a psychiatrist. Another study that included only private sector providers reported similar findings (Cooper-Patrick et al., 1994).

Research cited above documents a pervasive underrepresentation of African Americans in outpatient treatment. At the same time, it may be that African Americans have become willing to seek mental health care as much as, if not more than, other Americans. In a follow-up study at the Baltimore site of the ECA, Cooper-Patrick and colleagues (1999) discovered that all groups studied had increased their rates of mental health help-seeking. The increase among African Americans was such that the disparity between blacks and whites had been eliminated.

Notable differences between African Americans and white Americans have been documented in the use of inpatient psychiatric care. African Americans are significantly more likely than whites to be hospitalized in specialized psychiatric hospitals and beds (Snowden & Cheung, 1990; Breaux & Ryujin, 1999, Snowden, 1999b). Underlying the difference are a number of factors, such as delays in treatment seeking and a high African American rate of repeat admission. One study of clients discharged from State mental hospitals found that African Americans were substantially more likely than others to be hospitalized again during the ensuing year (Leginski et al., 1990). Researchers have not yet evaluated the impact of managed care rationing on hospitalization rates.

Children and Youth

African American and white American children receive outpatient mental health treatment at differing rates. Using the National Medical Expenditure Survey, a large, community survey, Cunningham and Freiman (1996) discovered that African American children were less likely than white children to have made a mental health outpatient visit. The difference could not be attributed to underlying socioeconomic, family-related, or regional differences between the groups. Among children who received outpatient mental health treatment, African Americans and whites had similar rates of receiving care from a mental health specialist.

A handful of smaller studies support this finding. One of them considered mental health care provided by specialists, by physicians and nurses, and in the schools (Zahner & Daskalakis, 1997). African American children and youth were less likely than whites to receive treatment, and their underrepresentation varied little, no matter which source of treatment was used. Other school-based studies have reported similar findings (Cuffe et al., 1995; Costello et al., 1997).

Perhaps because of lack of health insurance, few African American children are in psychiatric inpatient care (Chabra et al., 1999), but there are many black children in residential treatment centers (RTCs) for emotionally disturbed youth (Firestone, 1990). RTCs provide residential psychiatric treatment similar to that available in hospitals, but they are more likely to be funded from public sources.

In many cases, it is not parents, but child welfare authorities who initiate treatment for African American children. The child welfare system is a principal gatekeeper for African American mental health care (Halfon et al., 1992; Takayama et al., 1994). For this reason, several studies focusing on metropolitan areas have found an overrepresentation of African American children and youth in public mental health services (Bui & Takeuchi,

1992; McCabe et al., 1999). However, access via the child welfare system often does not result in beneficial treatment.

Older Adults

Little evidence is available documenting the use of mental health services by older black adults. However, one study found that these adults, like their younger counterparts, often do not obtain care (Black et al., 1997). In fact, this study reported that 58 percent of older African American adults with mental disorders were not receiving care. Another study indicated that older blacks in long-term care were less likely to use available community services than were older whites in long-term care (Mui & Burnette, 1994).

Complementary Therapies

African Americans are thought to make extensive use of alternative treatments for health and mental health problems. This preference is deemed to reflect African American cultural traditions developed partly when African Americans were systematically excluded from mainstream health care institutions (Smith Fahie, 1998).

Box 3-3: Complementary treatments are not always beneficial

Joan (age 50)

A 50-year-old African American woman, "Joan," was hospitalized following a suicide attempt. She cried and was nearly mute, reporting only her inability to sleep and having heard voices commanding her to kill herself. Her medical records indicated a previous admission for psychotic depression. Joan recovered after she took antidepressant medication.

In response to questioning, Joan indicated that she had been successfully treated before, but that she had discontinued psychiatric medication after responding to a letter from an itinerant minister. He had administered holy oil in exchange for payment and informed her to stop taking medication because she had been cured.

After relating this story, Joan was supported in her religious belief and in seeking spiritual uplift from one of many legitimate religious institutions in her community. She was warned, however, against opportunists and charlatans (Bell, 1997).

However, there is scant empirical data on the use of complementary therapies among African Americans suffering from mental health or other health problems (Koss-Chioino, 2000). Preliminary community- and clinic-based studies have found that complementary therapies are used to treat anxiety and depression (Elder et al., 1997; Davidson et al., 1998) and to treat health problems that occur in conjunction with mental health problems (Druss & Rosenheck, 2000). One nationally representative survey indicated that African Americans held more favorable views toward use of home remedies than did whites (Snowden et al., 1997).

It is important to realize that alternative therapies are popular in general: As many as 40 percent of Americans use them to complement standard medical care (Eisenberg et al., 1998). Nevertheless, research from rural Mississippi and from public housing in Los Angeles suggests that African Americans may turn to alternative therapies more than do whites (Becerra & Inlehart, 1995; Frate et al., 1995; Smith Fahie, 1998).

Appropriateness and Outcomes of Mental Health Services

Upon entering treatment, do African Americans receive effective care? That effective treatments do exist was documented in the Surgeon General's Report on Mental Health (DHHS, 1999b). The questions that remain are whether novel, standardized treatments and treatment-as-usual are equally effective when administered to African Americans, and whether in settings where African Americans receive care, clinicians diagnose their problems correctly and assign effective forms of treatment.

Studies on Treatment Outcomes

Clearly, an effective treatment is better than no treatment at all. However, for psychosocial interventions that might be sensitive to social and cultural circumstances, there is the question of whether interventions are as effective for African Americans as they are for whites. Few researchers have addressed this question when considering either novel, standardized treatments or treatment-as-usual. Among the handful of studies available for review, many included small samples of participants and lacked adequate controls.

One preliminary effort found that African Americans and white Americans responded similarly to treatment for PTSD (Rosenheck & Fontana, 1994; Zoellner et al., 1999). Cognitive-behavioral therapy, which focuses on altering demoralizing patterns of thought, has been shown to be equally effective in reducing anxiety among African American and white children and adults (Friedman et al., 1994; Treadwell et al., 1995). Similarly, behavioral treatment for older medical patients has been shown effective for African Americans (Lichtenberg et al., 1996). A study of persons suffering from severe and persistent mental illness found that a heavily African American sample, drawn from an intensive psychosocial rehabilitation program located in an urban, predominantly African American area, demonstrated increased levels of adaptive functioning in the community (Baker et al., 1999).

On the other hand, African Americans were found less responsive than white Americans in a pilot study of behavioral treatment for agoraphobia (Chambless & Williams, 1995). In another study of treatment for depression, African Americans proved similar to whites in response to psychotherapy and medication, except that African Americans had less improvement in their ability to function in the community (Brown et al., 1999). In a study of treatment as usually provided in the Los Angeles County mental health system, African Americans improved less than whites and members of other racial and ethnic minority groups (Sue et al., 1991). Exposure therapy, which involves overcoming fears in graduated steps, proved ineffective as a treatment for panic attacks among African Americans (Williams & Chambless, 1994).

Studies of children and youth have largely shown positive effects from treatment. African American and white juvenile offenders were assisted comparably by multisystemic therapy, which engages a network of supportive figures in a helping effort (Borduin et al., 1995). In addition, African Americans showed positive outcomes for medication for attention-deficit/hyperactivity disorder (Brown & Sexson, 1988).

Diagnostic Issues

Appropriate care depends on accurate diagnosis. Carefully gathered evidence indicates that African Americans are diagnosed accurately less often than white Americans when they are suffering from depression and seen in primary care (Borowsky et al., 2000), or when they are seen for psychiatric evaluation in an emergency room (Strakowski et al., 1997).

For many years, clinicians and researchers observed a pattern whereby African Americans in treatment presented higher than expected rates of diagnosed schizophrenia and lower rates of diagnosed affective disorders (Neighbors et al., 1989). When structured procedures were used for assessment, or when retrospective assessments were made via chart review, the disparities between African Americans and whites failed to emerge (Baker & Bell, 1999).

One explanation for the findings is clinician bias: Clinicians are predisposed to judge African Americans as schizophrenic, but not as suffering from an affective disorder. One careful study of psychiatric inpatients found that African Americans had higher rates of both clinical and research-based diagnoses of schizophrenia (Trierweiler et al., 2000). The clinicians in the study were well trained and included both African Americans and white Americans. However, it was found that they applied different decision rules to African American and white patients in judging the presence of schizophrenia. The role of clinician bias in accounting for this complex problem has not yet been ascertained.

Evidence-Based Treatments

In a nationally representative telephone and mail survey conducted in 1996, African Americans were found to be less likely than white Americans to receive appropriate care for depression or anxiety. Appropriate care was defined as care that adheres to official guidelines based on evidence from clinical trials. (Wang et al., 2000). Similar findings emerged in another large study that examined a representative national sample (Young et al., 2001). One large study of antidepressant medication use included all Medicaid recipients who had a diagnosis of depression at some time between 1989 and 1994 (Melfi et al., 2000). This study found that African Americans were less likely than whites to receive an antidepressant when their depression was first diagnosed (27% versus 44%). Of those who did receive antidepressant medications, African Americans were less likely to receive the newer selective serotonin reuptake inhibitor (SSRI) medications than were the white clients. This is important because the SSRIs have fewer troubling side effects than the older antidepressants; therefore, they tend to be more easily tolerated, and patients are less likely to discontinue taking them. Failure to treat with SSRI medications may be widespread and might help to explain African American overrepresentation in inpatient facilities and emergency rooms. Also, in a large study of older community residents followed from 1986 through 1996, whites in 1986 were nearly twice as likely, and in 1996, almost 4 times more likely, to use an antidepressant than were African Americans (Blazer et al., 2000).

Best Practices

Biological similarities between African Americans and whites are such that effective medications are suitable for treating mental illness in both groups. At the same time, recent evidence suggests that African Americans and white Americans sometimes have different dosage needs. For example, a greater percentage of African Americans than whites metabolize some antidepressants and antipsychotic medications slowly and might be more sensitive than whites (Ziegler & Biggs, 1977; Rudorfer & Robins, 1982; Bradford et al., 1998). This higher sensitivity is manifested in a faster and higher rate of response (Overall et al., 1969; Henry et al., 1971; Raskin & Crook, 1975; Ziegler & Biggs, 1977) and more severe side effects, including delirium (Livingston et al., 1983), when treated with doses commonly used for whites. However, clinicians in psychiatric emergency services prescribe both more and higher doses of oral and injectable antipsychotic medications to African Americans than to whites (Segel et al., 1996), as do other clinicians working in inpatient services (Chung et al., 1995). Other studies suggest that African Americans are also likely to receive higher overall doses of neuroleptics than are whites (Marcolin, 1991; Segel et al., 1996; Walkup et al., 2000).

The combination of slow metabolism and overmedication of antipsychotic drugs in African Americans can yield extra-pyramidal side effects, including stiffness, jitteriness, and muscle cramps (Lin et al., 1997), as well as increased risk of long-term severe side effects such as tardive dyskinesia, marked by abnormal muscular movements and gestures. Tardive dyskinesia has been shown in several studies to be significantly more prevalent among African Americans than among whites (Morgenstern & Glazer, 1993; Glazer et al., 1994; Eastham & Jeste, 1996; Jeste et al., 1996).

Conclusions

African Americans have made great strides in education, income, and other indicators of social well-being. Their improvement in social standing is marked, attesting to the resilience and adaptive traditions of African American communities in the face of slavery, racism, and discrimination. Contributions have come from diverse African American communities, including immigrants from Africa, the Caribbean, and elsewhere. Nevertheless, significant problems remain:

(1) African Americans living in the community appear to have overall rates of distress symptoms

and mental illness similar to those of whites, although some exceptions may exist. One major epidemiological study found that the rates of disorder for whites and blacks were similar *after* controlling for differences in income, education, and marital status. A later, population-based study found similar rates *before* accounting for such socioeconomic variables. Furthermore, the distribution of disorders may be different between groups, with African Americans having higher rates of some disorders and lower rates of others.

(2) The mental health of African Americans cannot be evaluated without considering the many African Americans found in high-need populations whose members have high levels of mental illness and are significantly in need of treatment. Proportionally, 3.5 times as many African Americans as white Americans are homeless. None of them are included in community surveys. Other inaccessible populations also compound the problem of making accurate measurements and providing effective services.

The mental health problems of persons in high-need populations are especially likely to occur jointly with substance abuse problems, as well as with HIV infection or AIDS (Lewin & Altman, 2000). Detection, treatment, and rehabilitation become particularly challenging in the presence of multiple and significant impediments to well-being.

(3) African Americans who are distressed or have a mental illness may present their symptoms according to certain idioms of distress. African American symptom presentation can differ from what most clinicians are trained to expect and may lead to diagnostic and treatment planning problems. The impact of culture on idioms of distress deserves more attention from researchers.

(4) African Americans may be more likely than white Americans to use alternative therapies, although differences have not yet been firmly established. When complementary therapies are used, their use may not be communicated to clinicians. A lack of provider knowledge of their use may interfere with delivery of appropriate treatment.

(5) Disparities in access to mental health services are partly attributable to financial barriers. Many of the working poor, among whom African Americans are overrepresented, do not qualify for public coverage and work in jobs that do not provide private coverage. Better access to private insurance is an important step, but is not in itself sufficient. African American reliance on public financing suggests that provisions of the Medicaid program are also important. Publicly financed safety net providers are a critical resource in the provision of care to African American communities.

(6) Disparities in access also come about for reasons other than financial ones. Few mental health specialists are available for those African Americans who prefer an African American provider. Furthermore, African Americans are overrepresented in areas where few providers choose to practice. They may not trust or feel welcomed by the providers who are available. Feelings of mistrust and stigma or perceptions of racism or discrimination may keep them away.

(7) African Americans with mental health needs are unlikely to receive treatment—even less likely than the undertreated mainstream population. If treated, they are likely to have sought help from primary care providers. African Americans frequently lack a usual source of health care as a focal point for treatment. African Americans receiving specialty care tend to leave treatment prematurely. Mental health care occurs relatively frequently in emergency rooms and psychiatric hospitals. These settings and patterns of treatment undermine delivery of high-quality mental health care.

(8) African Americans are more likely to be incorrectly diagnosed than white Americans. They are more likely to be diagnosed as suffering from schizophrenia and less likely to be diagnosed as suffering from an affective disorder. The pattern is longstanding but cannot yet be fully explained.

(9) Whether African Americans and whites benefit from mental health treatment in equal measure is still under investigation. The limited information available suggests African Americans respond favorably for the most part, but few clinical trials have evaluated the response of

African Americans to evidence-based treatments. Little research has examined the impact on African Americans of care delivered under usual conditions of community practice. More remains to be learned about when and how treatment must be modified to take into account African American needs and preferences.

Adaptive traditions have sustained African Americans through long periods of hardship imposed by the larger society. Their resilience is an important resource from which much can be learned. African American communities must be engaged, their traditions supported and built upon, and their trust gained in attempts to reduce mental illness and increase mental health. Mutual benefit will accrue to African Americans and to the society at large from a concerted effort to address the mental health needs of African Americans.

References

Akutsu, P. D., Snowden, L. R., & Organista, K. C. (1996). Referral patterns to ethnic-specific and mainstream mental health programs for Hispanics and non-Hispanic Whites. *Journal of Counseling Psychology, 43,* 56–64.

Altshuler, S. (1998). Child well-being in kinship foster care: Similar to, or different from, non-related foster care? *Children and Youth Services Review, 20,* 369–388.

American Psychiatric Association (1994). *Diagnostic and Statistical Manual of Mental Disorders* (4th ed.). Washington, DC: Author.

Baker, F. M. (1990). Black youth suicide: Literature review with a focus on prevention. *Journal of the National Medical Association, 82,* 495–507.

Baker, F. M., & Bell, C. C. (1999). Issues in the psychiatric treatment of African Americans. *Psychiatric Services, 50,* 362–368.

Baker, F. M., Stokes-Thompson, J., Davis, O. A., Gonzo, R., & Hishinuma, E. S. (1999). Two-year outcomes of psychosocial rehabilitation of black clients with chronic mental illness. *Psychiatric Services, 50,* 535–539.

Barrett, D. F., Anolik, I., & Abramson, F. H. (1992, August). *The 1990 Census shelter and street night enumeration.* Paper presented at the American Statistical Association Annual Meetings, Boston, MA.

Becerra, R. M., & Inlehart, A. P. (1995). Folk medicine use: Diverse populations in a metropolitan area. *Social Work in Health Care, 21,* 37–52.

Bell, C.C. (1997). Stress-related disorders in African American children. *Journal of the National Medical Association, 89,* 335–340

Bell, C.C., Dixie-Bell, D. D., & Thompson, B. (1986). Further studies on the prevalence of isolated sleep paralysis in black subjects. *Journal of the National Medical Association, 78,* 649–659.

Bell, C.C., & Fink, P. J. (2000). Prevention of violence. In C. Bell (Ed.), *Psychiatric aspects of violence: Issues in prevention and treatment (New Directions for Mental Health Services, 86).* San Francisco: Jossey Bass.

Bell, C.C., Shakoor, B., Thompson, B., Dew, D., Hughley, E., Mays, R., & Shorter-Gooden, K. (1984). Prevalence of isolated sleep paralysis in black subjects. *Journal of the National Medical Association, 76,* 501-508.

Berrick, J., Barth, R., & Needell, B. A. (1994). Comparison of kinship foster homes and foster family homes: Implications for kinship foster care as family preservation. *Children and Youth Services Review, 16,* 33–64.

Black, B. S., Rabins, P. V., German, P., McGuire, M., & Roca, R. (1997). Need and unmet need for mental health care among elderly public housing residents. *The Gerontologist, 37,* 717–728.

Blazer, D. G., Hybels, C. F., Simonsick, E. M., & Hanlon, J. T. (2000). Marked differences in antidepressant use by race in an elderly community sample: 1986–1996. *American Journal of Psychiatry, 157,* 1089–1094.

Blazer, D. G., Landerman, L. R., Hays, J. C., Simonsick, E. M., & Saunders, W. B. (1998). Symptoms of depression among community-dwelling elderly African-American adults. *Psychological Medicine, 28,* 1311–1320.

Borduin, C. M., Mann, B. J., Cone, L. T., Henggeler, S. W., Fucci, B. R., Blaske, D. M., & Williams, R. A. (1995). Multisystemic treatment of serious juvenile offenders: Long-term prevention of criminality and violence. *Journal of Consulting and Clinical Psychology, 63,* 569–578.

Borowsky, S. J., Rubenstein, L. V., Meredith, L. S., Camp, P., Jackson-Triche, M., & Wells, K. B. (2000). Who is at risk of nondetection of mental health problems in primary care? *Journal of General Internal Medicine, 15,* 381–388.

Bradford, L. D., Gaedigk, A., & Leeder, J. S. (1998). High frequency of CYP2D6 poor and "intermediate" metabolizers in black populations: A review and preliminary data. *Psychopharmacology Bulletin. 34,* 797-804.

Breakey, W. R., Fischer, P. J., Kramer, M., Nestadt, G., Romanoski, A. J., Ross, A., Royall, R. M., & Stine, O. (1989). Health and mental health problems of homeless men and women in Baltimore . *Journal of the American Medical Association, 262,* 1352–1357.

Breaux, C., & Ryujin, D. (1999). Use of mental health services by ethnically diverse groups within the United States. *The Clinical Psychologist, 52,* 4–15.

Breslau, N., Kessler, R. C., Howard, D. C., Schultz, L. R., Davis, G. C., & Andreski, M. A. (1998). Trauma and post-traumatic stress disorder in the community. *Archives of General Psychiatry, 55,* 626–632.

Broman, C. L. (1996). Coping with personal problems. In H. W. Neighbors & J. S. Jackson (Eds.), *Mental health in black America* (pp. 117–129). Thousand Oaks, CA: Sage.

Brown, C., Shear, M. K., Schulberg, H. C., & Madonia, M. J. (1999). Anxiety disorders among African-American and white primary medical care patients. *Psychiatric Services, 50,* 407–409.

Brown, E. R., Ojeda, V. D., Wyn, R., & Levan, R. (2000). *Racial and ethnic disparities in access to health insurance and health care.* Los Angeles: UCLA Center for Health Policy Research and The Henry J. Kaiser Family Foundation.

Brown, R. T., & Sexson, S. B. (1988). A controlled trial of methylphenidate in black adolescents. *Clinical Pediatrics, 27,* 74–81.

Bui, K. V., & Takeuchi, D. L. (1992). Ethnic minority adolescents and the use of community mental health care services. *American Journal of Community Psychology, 20,* 403–417.

Bureau of Justice Statistics. (1997). *Criminal victimization 1997: Changes 1996 97 with trends 1993 1997.* Washington, DC: Author.

Bureau of Justice Statistics. (1998). *Probation and parole populations, 1997.* Washington, DC: Author.

Bureau of Justice Statistics. (1999). *The sourcebook of criminal justice statistics.* Washington, DC: Author.

Bussing, R., Schoenberg, N. E., Rogers, K. M., Zima, B. T., & Angus, S. (1998). Explanatory Models of ADHD: Do they differ by ethnicity, child gender, or treatment status? *Journal of Emotional and Behavioral Disorders, 6,* 233–242.

Cauce, A. M., Morgan, C. J., Wagner, V., Moore, E., Sy, J., Wurzbacher, K., Weeden, K., Tomlin, S., & Blanchard, T. (1994). Effectiveness of intensive case management for homeless adolescents: Results of a 3-month follow-up. *Journal of Emotional and Behavioral Disorders, 2,* 219–227.

Centers for Disease Control and Prevention. (1998). Suicide among black youths—United States, 1980–1995. *Morbidity and Mortality Weekly Report, 47,* 193–195.

Chabra, A., Chavez, G. F., Harris, E. S., & Shah, R. (1999). Hospitalization for mental illness in adolescents: Risk groups and impact on the health care system. *Journal of Adolescent Health, 24,* 349–356.

Chambless, D. L., & Williams, K. E. (1995). A preliminary study of the effects of exposure in vivo for African Americans with agoraphobia. *Behavior Therapy, 26,* 501–515.

Chow, J., Snowden, L. R., & McConnell, W. (in press). A confirmatory factor analysis of the BASIS–32 in racial and ethnic samples. *Journal of Behavioral Health Services and Research.*

Chung, H., Mahler, J. C., & Kakuma, T. (1995). Racial differences in treatment of psychiatric in clients. *Psychiatric Services, 46,* 586–591.

Clark, R., Anderson, N. B., Clark, V. R., & Williams, D. R. (1999). Racism as a stressor for African Americans. *American Psychologist, 54,* 805–816.

Class, C. A., Unverzagt, F. W., Gao, S., Hall, K. S., Baiyewu, O., & Hendrie, H. C. (1996). Psychiatric disorders in African American nursing home residents. *American Journal of Psychiatry, 153,* 677–681.

Cooper, C. R., & Denner, J. (1998). Theories linking culture and psychopathology: Universal and community-specific processes. *Annual Review of Psychology, 49,* 559–584.

Cooper-Patrick, L., Crum, R. M., & Ford, D. E. (1994). Characteristics of patients with major depression who received care in general medical and specialty mental health settings. *Medical Care, 32,* 15–24.

Cooper-Patrick, L., Gallo, J. J., Gonzales, J J., Vu, H. T., Powe, N. R., Nelson, C., Ford, D .E. (1999). Race, gender, and partnership in the patient–physician relationship. *Journal of the American Medical Association, 282,* 583–589.

Cooper-Patrick, L., Gallo, J. J., Powe, N. R., Steinwachs, D. M., Eaton, W. W., & Ford, D. E. (1999). Mental health service utilization by African Americans and whites: The Baltimore Epidemiologic Catchment Area follow-up. *Medical Care, 37,* 1034–1045.

Cooper-Patrick, L., Powe, N. R., Jenckes, M. W., Gonzales, J. J., Levine, D. M., Ford, D. E. (1997). Identification of patient attitudes and preferences regarding treatment for depression. *Journal of General Internal Medicine, 12,* 431–438.

Costello, E. J., Angold, A., Burns, B. J., Stangl, D. K., Tweed, D. L., Erkanli, A., Worthman, C. M. (1996). The Great Smoky Mountains study of youth. *Archives of General Psychiatry, 53,* 1129–1136.

Costello, E. J., Costello, A. J., Edelbrock, C., Burns, B. J., Dulcan, M. K., Brent, D., & Janiszewski, S. (1988). Psychiatric disorders in primary care: Prevalence and risk factors. *Archives of General Psychiatry, 45*, 107–1116.

Costello, E. J., Farmer, E. M., Angold, A., Barns, B. J., & Erkanli, A. (1997). Psychiatric disorders among American Indian and white youth in Appalachian Mountains study. *American Journal of Public Health, 87*, 827–832.

Crocker, J., & Major, B. (1989). Social stigma and self esteem: The self protective properties of stigma. *Psychological Bulletin, 96*, 608–630.

Cuffe, S. P., Waller, J. L., Cuccaro, M. L., Pumariega, A. J., & Garrison, C. Z. (1995). Race and gender differences in the treatment of psychiatric disorders in young adolescents. *Journal of the American Academy of Child and Adolescent Psychiatry, 34*, 1536–1543.

Cunningham, P. J., Freiman, M. P. (1996). Determinants of ambulatory mental health service use for school-age children and adolescents. *Mental Health Services Research, 31*, 409–427.

Curtin, P. D. (1969). *The Atlantic Slave Trade.* Madison, WI: University of Wisconsin Press.

Davidson, J. R. T., Rampes, H., Eisen, M., Fisher, P., Smith, R. D., Malik, M. (1998). Psychiatric disorders in primary care patients receiving complementary medical treatments. *Comprehensive Psychiatry, 39*,16–20.

Druss, B. G., & Rosenheck, R. A. (2000). Use of practitioner-based complementary therapies by persons reporting mental conditions in the United States. *Archives of General Psychiatry, 57*, 708.

Eastham, J. H., & Jeste, D. V. (1996). Differentiating behavioral disturbances of dementia from drug side effects. *International Psychogeriatrics, 8*, (Suppl. 3), 429–434.

Eisenberg, D. M., Davis, R. B., Ettner, S. L., Appel, S., Wilkey, S., Van Rompay, M., & Kessler, R. C. (1998). Trends in alternative medicine use in the United States, 1990–1997: Results of a follow-up national survey. *Journal of the American Medical Association, 280*, 1569–1575.

Elder, N. C., Gillcrist, A., & Minz, R. (1997). Use of alternative health care by family practice patients. *Archives of Family Medicine, 6*, 181–184.

Fairbank, J. A., Friedman, M. J., & Southwick, S. (2001). Veterans of armed conflicts. In E. Gerrity, T. M. Keane, & F. Tuma (Eds.), *The mental health consequences of torture.* New York: Kluwer Academic/Plenum.

Feitel, B., Margetson, N., Chamas, R. & Lipman, C. (1992). Psychosocial background and behavioral and emotional disorders of homeless and runaway youth. Hospital and *Community Psychiatry, 43*, 155–159.

Firestone, B. (1990). *Information packet on use of mental health services by children and adolescents.* Rockville, MD: Center for Mental Health Services Survey and Analysis Branch.

Fitzpatrick, K. M., & Boldizar, J. P. (1993). The prevalence and consequences of exposure to violence among African-American youth. *Journal of the American Academy of Child and Adolescent Psychiatry, 32*, 424–430.

Fox, J., Merwin, E., & Blank, M. (1995). De facto mental health services in the rural south. *Journal of Health Care for the Poor and Underserved, 6*, 434–468.

Frable, D. E. S. (1997). Gender, racial, ethnic, sexual, and class identities. *Annual Review of Psychology, 48*, 139–162.

Frate, D. A., Croom, E. M., Frate, J. B., Jergens, J. P., & Meydrech, E. F. (1995). Self-treatment with herbal and other plant-derived remedies—rural Mississippi, 1993. *Morbidity and Mortality Weekly Report, 44*, 204–207.

Friedman, S., Paradis, C. M., & Hatch, M. (1994). Characteristics of African-American and white patients with panic disorder and agoraphobia. *Hospital and Community Psychiatry, 45*, 798–803.

Gallo, J. J., Cooper-Patrick, L., & Lesikar, S. (1998). Depressive symptoms of whites and African Americans aged 60 years and older. *Journal of Gerontology: Psychological Sciences, 53B*, P277–P286.

Garland, A. F., Hough, R. C., McCabe, K. M., Yeh, M., Wood, P. A., Aarons, G.A. (2001). Prevalence of psychiatric disorders in youths across five sectors of care. *Journal of the American Academy of Child and Adolescent Psychiatry, 40*, 409–418.

Gibbs, J. T., & Hines, A.M. (1989). Factors related to sex differences in suicidal behavior among black youth: Implications for intervention and research. *Journal of Adolescent Research, 4*, 152–172.

Gladstein, J., Rusonis, F. J., & Heald, F. P. (1992). A comparison of inner-city and upper-middle class youths' exposure to violence. *Journal of Adolescent Health, 13*, 275–280.

Glazer, W. M., Morgenstern, H., & Doucette, J. (1994). Race and tardive dyskinesia in a community mental health center outpatient population. *Hospital and Community Psychiatry, 45*, 38–42.

Gray-Little, B., & Hafdahl, A. R. (2000). Factors influencing racial comparisons of self-esteem: A quantitative review. *Psychological Bulletin, 126*, 26–54.

Griffith, E. E. H., & Bell, C. C. (1989). Recent trends in suicide and homicide among blacks. *Journal of the American Medical Association, 262*, 2265–2269.

Halfon, N., Berkowitz, G. & Klee, L. (1992). Mental health service utilization by children in foster care in California. *Pediatrics, 89,* 1238–1244.

Hall, M., Bromberger, J., & Matthews, K. (1999). Socio-economic status as a correlate of sleep in African-American and Caucasian women. *Annals of the New York Academy of Science, 896,* 427–430.

Hatchett, S. J., & Jackson, J. S. (1993). African American extended kin systems: An assessment. In H. P. McAdoo (Ed.), *Family ethnicity: strength in diversity* (pp. 90–108). Newbury Park, CA: Sage.

Healey, J. F. (1995). *Race, ethnicity, gender, and class.* Thousand Oaks, CA: Pine Forge Press.

Henry, B. W., Overall, J. E., & Markette, J. R. (1971). Comparison of major drug therapies for alleviation of anxiety and depression. *Diseases of the Nervous System, 32,* 655–667.

Heurtin-Roberts, S., Snowden, L., & Miller, L. (1997). Expressions of anxiety in African Americans: Ethnography and the Epidemiological Catchment Area studies. *Cultural Medical Psychiatry, 21,* 337–363.

Holzer, C. E., Goldsmith, H .F., & Ciarlo, J. A. (1998). Effects of rural-urban county type on the availability of health and mental health care providers. In R. W. Manderscheid & M. J. Henderson (Eds.), *Mental health, United States,* Rockville, MD: Center for Mental Health Services.

Hu, T. W., Snowden, L. R., Jerrell, J. M., & Nguyen, T. D. (1991). Ethnic populations in public mental health: Services choice and level of use. *American Journal of Public Health, 81,* 1429–1434.

Husaini, B. A. (1997). Predictors of depression among the elderly: Racial differences over time. *American Journal of Orthopsychiatry, 67,* 48–58.

Jencks, C. (1994). *The Homeless.* Cambridge, MA: Harvard University Press.

Jenkins, E. J., & Bell, C. C. (1997). Exposure and response to community violence among children and adolescents. In J. Osofsky (Ed.), *Children in a violent society.* New York: Guilford Press.

Jenkins, E. J., Bell, C. C., Taylor, J., & Walker, D. (1989). Circumstances of sexual and physical victimization of black psychiatric outpatients. *Journal of the National Medical Association, 81,* 246–252.

Jeste, D. V., Lindamer, L. A., Evans, J., & Lacro, J. P. (1996). Relationship of ethnicity and gender to schizophrenia and pharmacology of neuroleptics. *Psychopharmacology Bulletin, 32,* 243–251.

Joe, S., & Kaplan, M. S. (2001). Suicide among African American men. *Suicide and Life Threatening Behavior, 31,* 106–121.

Jordan, B. K., Schlenger, W. E., Fairbank, J. A., & Caddell, J. M. (1996). Prevalence of psychiatric disorders among incarcerated women II: Convicted felons entering prison. *Archives of General Psychiatry, 53,* 514–519.

Kass, B., Weinick, R., & Monheit, A. (1999, February). Racial and Ethnic Differences in Health, *MEPS Chartbook No. 2.* Medical Expenditure Survey of the Agency for Health Care Policy and Research. Rockville, MD: U.S. Department of Health and Human Services.

Keith, V. M. (2000). A profile of African Americans' health care. In C. Hogue, M.A. Hargreaves, & K. S. Collins (Eds.), *Minority health in America* (pp. 47–76). Baltimore: Johns Hopkins University Press.

Kessler, R. C., Berglund, P. A., Zhao, S., Leaf, P. J., Kouzis, A. C., Bruce, M. L., Freidman, R. L., Grosser, R. C., Kennedy, C., Narrow, W. E., Kuehnel, T. G., Laska, E. M., Manderscheid, R. W., Rosenheck, R. A., Santoni, T. W., & Schneier, M. (1996). The 12-month prevalence and correlates of serious mental illness (SMI). In R. W. Manderscheid & M. A. Sonnenschein (Eds.), *Mental health, United States.* Rockville, MD: Center for Mental Health Services.

Kessler, R. C., McGonagle, K. A., Zhao, S., Nelson, C. B., Hughes, M., Eshelman, S., Wittchen, H. U., & Kendler, K. S. (1994). Lifetime and 12-month prevalence of DSM–III–R disorders in the United States. *Archives of General Psychiatry, 51,* 8–19.

Koegel, P., Burnam, M. A., & Farr, R. K. (1988). The prevalence of specific psychiatric disorders among homeless individuals in the inner city of Los Angeles. *Archives of General Psychiatry, 45,* 1085–1092.

Komaromy, M., Grumbach, K., Drake, M., Vrazizan, K., & Lurie, N. (1996). The role of black and Hispanic physicians in providing health care for underserved populations. *New England Journal of Medicine, 334,* 305–310.

Koss-Chioino, J. D. (2000). Traditional and folk approaches among ethnic minorities. In J. F. Aponte & J. Wohl (Eds.), *Psychological Intervention and Cultural Diversity.* Needham Heights, MA: Allyn & Bacon.

Kulka, R. A., Schlenger, W. E., Fairbank, J. E., Hough, R. L., Jordan, B. K., Marmar, C. R., & Weiss, D. S. (1990). *Trauma and the Vietnam War generation: Report of findings from the National Vietnam Veterans Readjustment Study.* New York: Brunner/Mazel.

Landsverk, J., Davis, I, Ganger, W., Newton, R., & Johnson, I. (1996). Impact of child psychosocial functioning on reunification from out-of-home placement. *Children and Youth Services Review, 18,* 4–5.

Lewin, M. E., & Altman, S. (Eds.). (2000). *America's health care safety net: Intact but endangered.* Washington, DC: National Academy Press.

Leginski, W. A., Manderscheid, R. W., & Henderson, P. R. (1990). Clients served in State mental hospitals: Results from a longitudinal database. In R. W. Manderscheid & M. A. Sonnenheim (Eds.), *Mental health, United States.* Rockville, MD: Center for Mental Health Services.

Lichtenberg, P. A., Kimbarow, M. L., Morris, P., & Vangel, S. J. (1996). Behavioral treatment of depression in predominantly African-American medical clients. *Clinical Gerontologist, 17,* 15–33.

Lin, K. M., Cheung, F., Smith, M., & Poland, R. E. (1997). The use of psychotropic medications in working with Asian patients. In E. Lee (Ed.), *Working with Asian Americans: A guide for clinicians* (pp. 388–399). New York: Guilford Press.

Livingston, R. L., Zucker, D. K., Isenberg, K., & Wetzel, R. D. (1983). Tricyclic antidepressants and delirium. Journal of *Clinical Psychiatry, 44,* 173–176.

Marcolin, M. A. (1991). The prognosis of schizophrenia across cultures. *Ethnicity & Disease, 1,* 99–104.

Massey, D. S., & Denton, N. A. (1993). *American apartheid: Segregation and the making of the underclass.* Boston: Harvard University Press.

McBean, A. M., & Gornick, M. (1994). Differences by races in the rates of procedures performed in hospitals for Medicare beneficiaries. *Health Care Financing Review, 15,* 77–90.

McCabe, K. M., Clark, R., & Barnett, D. (1999). Family protective factors among urban African American youth. *Journal of Clinical Child Psychology, 28,* 137–150.

McCaskill, P. A., Toro, P. A., & Wolfe, S. M. (1998). Homeless and matched housed adolescents: A comparative study of psychopathology. *Journal of Clinical and Child Psychology, 27,* 306–319.

McDaniel, J. S., Purcell, D. W., & Farber, E. W. (1997). Severe mental illness and HIV-related medical and neuropsychiatric sequelae. *Clinical Psychology Review, 17,* 311–325.

McDonald, K. B., & Armstrong, K. B. (2001). De-romanticizing black intergenerational support: The questionable expectations of welfare reform. *Journal of Marriage and Family, 63,* 213–223.

Melfi, C., Croghan, T., Hanna, M., & Robinson, R. (2000). Racial variation in antidepressant treatment in a Medicaid population. *Journal of Clinical Psychiatry, 61,* 16–21.

Milburn, N. G., & Bowman, P. J. (1991). Neighborhood life. In J. S. Jackson (Ed.). Life in black America (pp. 31–45). Newbury Park CA: Sage.

Mohler, B., & Earls, F. (2001). Trends in adolescent suicide: Misclassification bias? *American Journal of Public Health, 91,* 150–153.

Morgenstern, H., & Glazer, W. M. (1993). Identifying risk factors for tardive dyskinesia among chronic outpatients maintained on neuroleptic medications: Results of the Yale tardive dyskinesia study. *Archives of General Psychiatry, 50,* 723–733.

Moy, E., & Bartman, B. A. (1995). Physician race and care of minority and medically indigent patients. *Journal of the American Medical Association, 273,* 1515-1520.

Mui, A.C., & Burnette, D. (1994). Long-term care service use by frail elders: Is ethnicity a factor? *The Gerontologist, 34,* 190–198.

Mundy, P., Robertson, J. M., Greenblatt, M., & Robertson, J. M. (1989). Residential instability in adolescent psychiatric inclients. *Journal of the American Academy of Adolescent and Child Psychiatry, 28,* 176–181.

National Center for Health Statistics. (1996). *Leading causes of death by age, sex, race, and Hispanic origin: United States, 1992.* (Vital and Health Statistics; PHS Report No. 96–1857). Washington, DC: Government Printing Office.

National Research Council. (1993). *Losing generations: Adolescents in high risk settings.* Washington DC: National Academy Press.

Neighbors, H. W. (1984). The distribution of psychiatric morbidity in African Americans: A review and suggestions for research. *Community Mental Health Journal, 20,* 5–18.

Neighbors, H. W., Jackson, J. S., Campbell, L., & Williams, D. R. (1989). The influence of racial factors on psychiatric diagnosis: A review and suggestions for research. *Community Mental Health Journal, 24,* 301–311.

O'Hare, W. P. (1996). A new look at poverty in America. *Population Bulletin, 51,* 1–48.

O'Hare, W. P., Pollard, K. M., Mann, T. L., & Kent, M. M. (1991). African Americans in the 1990s. *Population Bulletin, 46,* 1–40.

Okwumabua, J. O., Baker, F. M., Wong, S. P., & Pilgram, B. O. (1997). Characteristics of depressive symptoms in elderly urban and rural African American residents. *Journal of Gerontology: Medical Sciences, 52,* M241–M246.

Overall, J. E., Hollister, L. E., Kimbell, I., Jr., & Shelton, J. (1969). Extrinsic factors influencing responses to psychotherapeutic drugs. *Archives of General Psychiatry, 21,* 89–94.

Padgett, D., Struening, E. L., Andrews, H., & Pittman, J. (1995). Predictors of emergency room use by homeless adults in New York City: The predisposing, enabling and need factors. *Social Science & Medicine, 41,* 547–556.

Phillips, D. P., & Ruth, T. E. (1993). Adequacy of official suicide statistics for scientific research and public policy. *Suicide and Life Threatening Behavior, 23,* 307–319.

Pickering, T. (2000). Depression, race, hypertension, and the heart. *Journal of Clinical Hypertension, 2,* 410–412.

Pingitore, D., Snowden, L. R., Sansome, R., & Klinkman, M. (in press). Persons with depression and the treatments they receive: A comparison of primary care physicians and psychiatrists. *International Journal of Psychiatry in Medicine.*

Raskin, A., & Crook, I. (1975). The rater and rating instrument as sources of variance in evaluating drug efficiency. *Psychopharmacological Bulletin, 11,* 16–17.

Regier, D. A., Narrow, W. F., Rae, D. S., Manderscheid, R. W., Locke, B. Z., & Goodwin, F. K. (1993). The de facto US mental and addictive disorders service system. Epidemiological and prospective 1-year prevalence rates of disorders and services. *Archives of General Psychiatry, 50,* 85–94.

Robins, L., & Regier, D. A. (1991). *Psychiatric disorders in America: The Epidemiologic Catchment Area Study.* New York: The Free Press.

Roschelle, A. (1997). *No more kin: Exploring race, class, and gender in family networks.* Thousand Oaks, CA: Sage.

Rosenheck, R., & Fontana, A. (1994). Utilization of mental health services by minority veterans of the Vietnam era. *Journal of Nervous and Mental Disease, 182,* 685–691.

Ruiz, D. S. (1995). A demographic and epidemiologic profile of the African American elderly. In D. K. Padgett (Ed.), *Handbook of ethnicity, aging, and mental health.* Westport, CT: Greenwood Press.

Rural Policy Research Institute. (1997). *Mapping rural health: The geography of health care and health resources in rural America.* Chapel Hill, NC: University of North Carolina.

Sampson, R. J., Raudenbush, S. W., & Earls, P. (1997). Neighborhoods and violent crime: A multilevel study of collective efficacy. *Science, 277,* 918–924.

Scheffler, R. M., & Miller, A. B. (1989). Demand analysis of mental health service use among ethnic subpopulations. *Inquiry, 26,* 202–215.

Schwab-Stone, M., Chen, C., Greenberger, E., Silver, D., Lichtman, J., & Voyce, C. (1999). No safe haven II: The effects of violence exposure on urban youth. *Journal of the American Academy of Child and Adolescent Psychiatry, 38,* 359–367.

Segel, S. P., Bola, J. R., & Watson, M. A. (1996). Race, quality of care, and antipsychotic prescribing practices in psychiatric emergency services. *Psychiatric Services, 47,* 282–286.

Sellers, R. M., Smith, M. A., Shelton, J. N., Rowley, S. J., & Chavous, T. M. (1998). Multidimensional models of racial identity: A reconceptualization of African American racial identity. *Personality and Social Psychology Review, 2,* 18–39.

Shaffer, D., Fisher, P., Dulcan, M. K., Davies, M., Piacentini, J., Schwab-Stone, M. E., Lahey, B. B., Bourdon, K., Jensen, P. S., Bird, H. R., Canino, G., & Regier, D. A. (1996). The NIMH Diagnostic Interview Schedule for Children Version 2.3 (DISC-2.3): Description, acceptability, prevalence rates, and performance in the MECA Study. Methods for the Epidemiology of Child and Adolescent Mental Disorders Study. *Journal of the American Academy of Child and Adolescent Psychiatry, 35,* 865–877.

Siegel, J. M., Aneshensel, C. S., Taub, B., Cantwell, D. P., & Driscoll, A. K. (1998). Adolescent depressed mood in a multiethnic sample. *Journal of Youth and Adolescence, 27,* 413–427.

Smith Fahie, V. P. (1998). Utilization of folk/family remedies by community-residing African American elders. *Journal of Cultural Diversity, 5,* 19–22.

Snow, L. (1993). *Walkin' over medicine.* Boulder, CO: Westview Press.

Snowden, L. R. (1996). Ethnic minority populations and mental health outcomes. In D. M. Steinwachs, L. M. Flynn, G. S. Norquist, & E. A. Skinner (Eds.), *Using client information to improve mental health and substance abuse outcomes. New directions for mental health services, 71* (pp. 79–87). San Francisco: Jossey-Bass.

Snowden, L. R. (1999a). African American folk idiom and mental health services use. *Cultural Diversity and Ethnic Minority Psychology, 5,* 364–369.

Snowden, L. R. (1999b). African American service use for mental health problems. *Journal of Community Psychology, 27,* 303–313.

Snowden, L. R., & Cheung, F. K. (1990). Use of inpatient mental health services by members of ethnic minority groups. *American Psychologist, 45*, 347–355.

Snowden, L. R., Hu, T., & Jerrell, J. M. (1995). Emergency care avoidance: Ethnic matching and participation in minority-serving programs. *Community Mental Health Journal, 31*, 463–473.

Snowden, L. R., Libby, A., & Thomas, K. (1997). Health-care-related attitudes and utilization among African American women. *Women's Health, 3*, 301–314.

Snowden, L. R., & Thomas, K. (2000). Medicaid and African American outpatient treatment. *Mental Health Services Research, 2*, 115–120.

Strakowski, S. M., Hawkins, J. M., Keck, P. E., McElroy, S. L., West, S. A., Bourne, M. L., Sax, K. W., & Tugrul, K. C. (1997). The effects of race and information variance on disagreement between psychiatric emergency service and research diagnoses in first-episode psychosis. *Journal of Clinical Psychiatry, 58*, 457–463.

Sue, S., Fujino, D. C., Hu, L., Takeuchi, D., & Zane, N. (1991). Community mental health services for ethnic minority groups: A test of the cultural responsiveness hypothesis. *Journal of Consulting and Clinical Psychology, 59*, 616–624.

Sue, S., Zane, N., & Young, K. (1994). Research on psychotherapy on culturally diverse populations. In A. Bergin & S. Garfield (Eds.), *Handbook of psychotherapy and behavior change* (4th Ed., pp. 783–817). New York: Wiley.

Sussman, L. K., Robins, L. N., & Earls, F. (1987). Treatment-seeking for depression by black and White Americans. *Social Science and Medicine, 24*, 187–196.

Swartz, M. S., Wagner, H. R., Swanson, J. W., Burns, B. J., George, L. K., & Padgett, D. K. (1998). Comparing use of public and private mental health services: The enduring barriers of race and age. *Community Mental Health Journal, 34*, 133–144.

Takeuchi, D. T., & Cheung, M. K. (1998). Coercive and voluntary referrals: how ethnic minority adults get into mental health treatment. *Ethnicity and Health, 3*, 149–158.

Takeuchi, D. T., Sue, S., & Yeh, M. (1995). Return rates and outcomes from ethnic specific and outcomes from ethnic specific mental health programs in Los Angeles. *American Journal of Public Health, 85*, 638–643.

Takayama, J. I., Bergman, A. B., & Connell, F. A. (1994). Children in foster care in the State of Washington: Health care utilization and expenditures. *Journal of the American Medical Association, 271*, 1850–1855.

Taylor, R. J., & Chatters, L. M. (1991). Religious life. In J. S. Jackson (Ed.), *Life in black America*. Newbury Park, CA: Sage.

Teplin, L. A. (1990). The prevalence of severe mental disorder among male urban jail detainees: Comparison with the Epidemiologic Catchment Area Program. *American Journal of Public Health, 80*, 663–669.

Teplin, L. A., Abram, K. M., & McClelland, G. M. (1996). Prevalence of psychiatric disorders among incarcerated women. *Archives of General Psychiatry, 53*, 505–512.

Thernstrom, S., & Thernstrom, A. (1997). *America in black and white*. New York: Simon & Schuster.

Treadwell, K. R. H., Flannery-Schroeder, E. C., & Kendall, P. C. (1995). Ethnicity and gender in relation to adaptive functioning, diagnostic status, and treatment outcome in children from an anxiety clinic. *Journal of Anxiety Disorders, 9*, 373–384.

Trierweiler, S. J., Neighbors, H. W., Munday, C., Thompson, S. E., Binion, V. J., & Gomez, J. P. (2000). Clinician attributions associated with diagnosis of schizophrenia in African American and non-African American patients. *Journal of Consulting and Clinical Psychology, 68*, 171–175.

U.S. Census Bureau. (1998). *The black population in the United States: March 1998* (Update). Washington, DC: Author.

U.S. Census Bureau. (1999a). *The black population in the United States: March 1999* (Update). Washington, DC: Author.

U.S. Census Bureau. (1999b). *Statistical abstract of the United States*. Washington, DC: Author.

U.S. Census Bureau. (2001a). *Overview of race and Hispanic origin: Census 2000 brief*. Retrieved June 28, 2001, from http://www.census.gov/population/www/socdemo/race.html.

U.S. Census Bureau. (2001b). *Profiles of general demographic characteristics: 2000 Census of Population and Housing, United States*. Retrieved June 22, 2001, from http:// www2. census.gov/census_2000/datasets/demographic_profile/0_National_Summary/.

U.S. Census Bureau. (2001c). *The black population in the United States: March 2000 (Update)* (Report No. PPL-146). Retrieved June 28, 2001, from http://www.census.gov/population/www/ socdemo /race/ppl-142.html.

U.S. Conference of Mayors. (1998). *Summary: A status report on hunger and homelessness in American cities—1998*. Washington, DC: Author.

U.S. Department of Health and Human Services. (1998). *The initiative to eliminate racial and ethnic disparities in health.* Retrieved June 26, 2001, from http://raceand-health.hhs.gov.

U. S. Department of Health and Human Services. (2000a). *Healthy people 2010.* Rockville, MD: Author.

U. S. Department of Health and Human Services. (2000b). *National vital statistics reports, 48* (11). Rockville, MD: Author.

Valleni-Basile, L. A., Garrison, C. Z., Waller, J. L., Addy, C. L., McKeown, R. E., Jackson, K. L., & Cuffe, S. P. (1996). Incidence of obsessive-compulsive disorder in a community sample of young adolescents. *Journal of the American Academy of Child and Adolescent Psychiatry, 35,* 898–906.

Vega, W., & Rumbaut, R. (1991). Ethnic minorities and mental health. *Annual Review of Sociology, 17,* 351–383.

Vernez, G. M., Burnam, M. A., McGlynn, E. A., Trude, S., & Mittman, B. (1988). *Review of California's program for the homeless mentally ill disabled* (Report No. R3631–CDMH). Santa Monica, CA: RAND.

Walkup, J. T., McAlpine, D. D., Olfson, M., Labay, L. E., Boyer, C., & Hansell, S. (2000). Patients with schizophrenia at risk for excessive antipsychotic dosing. *Journal of Clinical Psychiatry, 61,* 344–348.

Wang, P. S., Berglund, P., & Kessler, R. C. (2000). Recent care of common mental disorders in the United States. *Journal of General Internal Medicine, 15,* 284–292.

Wells, K. B., Stewart, A., Hays, R. D., Burnam, M. A., Rogers, W., Daniels, M., Berry, S., Greenfield, S., & Ware, J. (1989). The functioning and well-being of depressed patients: Results from the Medical Outcomes Study. *Journal of the American Medical Association, 262,* 914–919.

Williams, D. R., & Jackson, J. S. (2000). Race/ethnicity and the 2000 census: Recommendations for African American and other black populations in the United States. *American Journal of Public Health, 90,* 1728–1730.

Williams, D. R. (1998). African American health: The role of the social environment. *Journal of Urban Health: Bulletin of the New York Academy of Sciences, 75,* 300–321.

Williams, K. E., & Chambless, D. L. (1994). The results of exposure-based treatment in agoraphobia. In S. Friedman (Ed.), *Anxiety disorders in African Americans* (pp. 149–165). New York: Springer

Wilson, W. J. (1987). *The truly disadvantaged: The inner city, the underclass, and public policy.* Chicago: University of Chicago Press.

Yee, A. H., Fairchild, H. H., Weizmann, F., & Wyatt, G. E. (1993). Addressing psychology's problem with race. *American Psychologist, 48,* 1132–1140.

Yeh, M., Takeuchi, D. T., & Sue, S. (1994). Asian American children seen in the mental health system: A comparison of parallel and mainstream outpatient service centers. *Journal of Clinical Child Psychology, 23,* 5–12.

Young, A. S., Klap, R., Sherbourne, C. D., & Wells, K. B. (2001). The quality of care for depressive and anxiety disorders in the United States. *Archives of General Psychiatry, 52,* 472–478.

Zhang, A. Y., & Snowden, L. R. (1999). Ethnic characteristics of mental disorders in five U.S. communities. *Cultural Diversity and Ethnic Minority Psychology, 5,* 134–146.

Ziegler, V. E., & Biggs, J. T. (1977). Tricyclic plasma levels. Effect of age, race, sex, and smoking. *Journal of the American Medical Association, 14,* (238), 2167–2169.

Zoellner, L. A., Feeny, N. C., Fitzgibbons, L. A., & Foa, E. B. (1999). Response of African American and Caucasian women to cognitive behavioral therapy for PTSD. *Behavior Therapy, 30,* 581–595.

Zylstra, R. G., & Steitz, J. A. (1999). Public knowledge of late-life depression and aging. *Journal of Applied Gerontology, 18,* 63–76.

CHAPTER 4

MENTAL HEALTH CARE FOR AMERICAN INDIANS AND ALASKA NATIVES

Contents

Contents, *continued*

CHAPTER 4

MENTAL HEALTH CARE FOR AMERICAN INDIANS AND ALASKA NATIVES

Introduction

American Indians and Alaska Natives (Indians, Eskimos, and Aleuts) were self-governing people who thrived in North America long before Western Europeans came to the continent and Russians to the land that is now Alaska. American Indians and Alaska Natives occupy a special place in the history of our Nation; their very existence stands as a testament to the resilience of their collective and individual spirit. This chapter first reviews history and the current social contexts in which American Indians and Alaska Natives live and then presents what is known about their mental health needs and the extent to which those needs are met by the mental health care system.

The U.S. Census Bureau estimates that 4.1 million American Indians and Alaska Natives lived in the United States in 2000[1]. This represented less than 1.5 percent of the total U.S. population (U.S. Census Bureau, 2001). However, between 1960 and 2000, the recorded population of this minority group increased by over 250 percent, largely due to better data collection by the Census Bureau, an increasing number of individuals who identify themselves as American Indians or Alaska Natives, and an increase in the birth rate of this population. Alaska Natives comprise approximately 4 percent of the combined population of American Indians and Alaska Natives (Population Reference Bureau, 2000). But numbers alone tell little of this population, for it is the social and political history of Native people[2] and their relationship to the U.S. Government that define their distinctive place in American life.

---

[1]This figure includes people identifying themselves as Hispanic and/or multiracial members of this group. Those identifying solely as American Indian or Alaska Native comprise just less than 1 percent of the U.S. population.

[2]In 1977, the National Congress of American Indians and the National Tribal Chairmen's Association issued a joint resolution indicating that in the absence of specific tribal designations, the preferred reference to people indigenous to North America is American Indian and/or Alaska Native. A variety of other referents are apparent in the professional literature, including Native Americans, First Americans, and Natives. In keeping with the 1977 resolution, this report adopts American Indian and/or Alaska Native except in limited instances where, editorially, Native people or Native American is used as a general term to refer to both American Indians and Alaska Natives.

Historical Context

American Indians

As members of federally recognized sovereign nations that exist within another country, American Indians are unique among minority groups in the United States. Ever since the European "discovery" and colonization of North America, the history of American Indians has been tied intimately to the influence of European settlers and to the policies of the U.S. Government.

Early European contact in the 17th century exposed Native people to infectious diseases from which their natural immunity could not protect them, and the population of American Indians plummeted. In 1820, as European settlers pushed westward, Congress passed the Indian Removal Act to force Native Americans west of the Mississippi River. Brutal marches of Native people, sometimes in the dead of winter, ensued. Later, as colonists moved farther westward to the Great Plains and beyond, the U.S. Government sent many tribes to live on reservations of marginal land where they had little chance of prospering. Treaties between the tribes and the U.S. Government were signed, then broken, and struggles for territory followed. The Plains Indian Wars raged until the end of the 19th century, punctuated by wholesale slaughter of American Indian men, women, and children. As the settlers migrated toward the Pacific Ocean, the U.S. Congress passed legislation that effectively made Native Americans wards of the state.

Even as American Indians were being killed or forced onto reservations, some Americans protested the destruction of entire Indian "nations" (tribes and tribal confederacies). In 1887, after the bloodiest of the Indian Wars ended, Congress passed the Dawes Severalty Act, which allotted portions of reservation land to Indian families and individuals. The government then sold the leftover reservation land at bargain prices. This Act, which intended to integrate American Indians into the rest of U.S. society, had disastrous consequences. In addition to losing surplus tribal lands, many Natives lost their allotted lands as well and had little left for survival. By the early 1900s, the population of American Indians reached its lowest point, an incredible 5 percent of the original population estimated at first European contact (Thornton, 1987).

The Federal Indian Boarding School Movement began in earnest in 1875. By 1899, there were 26 off-reservation schools scattered across 15 states. The emphasis within the Indian educational system later shifted to reservation schools and public schools, but boarding schools continued to have a major impact into the next century because they were perceived as "civilizing" influences on American Indians. During the 1930s and 1940s, nearly half of all Indian people who received formal education attended such schools.

American Indians experienced both setbacks and progress during the 20th century. In June 1924, Congress granted American Indians U.S. citizenship. The Indian Citizenship Act later was amended to include Alaska Natives (Deloria, 1985; Thornton, 1987). The subsequent passage of the Indian Reorganization Act (1934) placed great emphasis on civilizing Native people and teaching them Christianity. To this end, many more Native American children were sent to learn "American ways" at government- or church-run boarding schools that were often thousands of miles from the "detrimental influences" of their home reservations.

The era of American Indian educational reform began in the 1920s. Public criticism of Indian Bureau policies and practices culminated in an in-depth investigation of Indian affairs by the Brookings Institution in 1926. Its report, *The Problem of Indian Administration*, concluded:

> *The first and foremost need in Indian education is a change in point of view. Whatever may have been the official government attitude, education for the Indian in the past has proceeded on the theory that it is necessary to remove the Indian child as far as possible from his home environment; whereas the modern point of view in education and social work lays stress on upbringing in the natural setting of home and family life. Although some children did well in these settings, other did not. Reports of harsh discipline were widespread (Brookings, 1971).*

Even worse, the National Resource Center on Child Sexual Abuse (1990) cites evidence that many Native American children were sexually abused while attending boarding schools (Horejsi et al., 1992).

One positive result of the collective experience of boarding school students is that it gave rise to a shared social consciousness across previously disparate tribes, thereby fueling political change. One lesson from the boarding school era is that tribal peoples have encountered tremendous adversity yet survived—politically, culturally, linguistically, and spiritually (Hamley, 1994).

Near the end of World War II, Congress began to withdraw Federal support and to abdicate responsibility for American Indian affairs. Whereas earlier assimilationists had envisioned a time when tribes and reservations would vanish as Native Americans became integrated into U.S. society, the proponents of "termination" decided to legislate such entities out of existence. As a consequence, over the following two decades, many Federal services were withdrawn, and Federal trust protection was removed from tribal lands.

One policy from this era was an attempt by the U.S. Government to extinguish Native spiritual practices. A government prohibition on participation in traditional spiritual ceremonies continued until the American Indian Religious Freedom Act of (1978). Despite the prohibitions and the Christianizing efforts by various churches, indigenous culture and spirituality have survived and are widely practiced (Bryde, 1971). Even in areas where many Native people practice Christianity, traditional cultural views still heavily influence the way in which Native people understand life, health, illness, and healing (Todd-Bazemore, 1999).

In the 1970s, American Indians and Alaska Natives began to demand greater authority over their own lives and communities, encouraged by the 1969 publication of the report of the Congressional Committee on Labor and Public Welfare: *Indian Education: A National Tragedy—A National Challenge.* Current Federal policy encourages tribal administration of the government's health, education, welfare, law enforcement, and housing programs for Native Americans. Local communities have responded to this in a variety of ways that reflect the continuing diversity of their experiences and perspectives.

Alaska Natives

The history of Alaska Natives is similar to the history of their American Indian cousins to the south, yet differs in some important ways. Similar to American Indians, Alaska Natives are culturally diverse. Inupiats settled the Arctic coasts from the Chukchi Sea as far east as Greenland. In interior Alaska, along the Yukon and Tanana rivers, live Athabascan Indians; their link to the Navajo and Apache of Arizona and New Mexico is evident in the similarity of their languages. In southeast Alaska, Tlingit, Haida, Tsimshian, and Eyak Indians live by the sea; their arts and crafts have been well known for over 200 years. The coast of northeast Alaska and the deltas of the Yukon and Kuskokwim rivers are home to some 20,000 Yup'ik and Cup'ik Eskimos, the greatest concentration of Eskimos in the world. They still depend on hunting, fishing, and gathering. On the Pribilof Islands and the Aleutian chain, the Aleuts, kin to the Yup'ik, maintain their cultural identity even though decimated by a century and a half of Russian occupation (Berger, 1985). The Aleuts share with American Indians a history of devastation as a result of diseases introduced by white men. Their peak population, estimated at 80,000 just prior to European contact, dwindled to 25,000 by 1909. The early Russian invaders took control of the native Aleut and Inuit people and forced them to hunt for furs. In 1867, the United States bought Alaska from Russia, and the Treaty of Cession stated that the "uncivilized [Native] tribes will be subject to such laws and regulations as the United States may, from time to time, adopt in regard to aboriginal tribes of that country" (Treaty of Cession, Article III). Although the U.S. Government had legal control over Alaskan land from that point on, Alaska Natives were not forced to move to reservations. In fact, the Federal Government did not create reservations in Alaska until 1891, and, even then, it established only a few for a small percentage of the Alaska Native population.

In 1971, upon the discovery of huge oil deposits on Alaska's North Slope and the wish to clear the area for construction of the Alaska Pipeline, Congress passed the Alaska Native Claims Settlement Act (ANCSA). This Act organized Alaska Natives into regional and village corporations and gave them control over more than 44 million acres of land and almost $1 billion. In exchange, Alaska Natives waived all claims to many of their original lands.

In the 1970s, more and more Alaska Natives petitioned for the right to self-government, and traditional institutions such as tribal courts and councils re-emerged. The U.S. Census Bureau now recognizes 200 Native communities in Alaska; more than half have state-chartered municipal governments, and 69 have elected Native Councils (Douglas K. Mertz, personal communication). The sheer number of these governments and councils reflects a rich and diverse Alaskan heritage (Berger, 1985).

Current Status

Geographic Distribution

Most American Indians live in Western States, including California, Arizona, New Mexico, South Dakota, Alaska,

and Montana, with 42 percent residing in rural areas, compared to 23 percent of whites (Rural Policy Research Institute, 1999). The number of American Indians who live on reservations and trust lands (areas with boundaries established by treaty, statute, and executive or court order) has decreased substantially in the past few decades. For example, in 1980, most American Indians lived on reservations or trust lands; today, only 1 in 5 American Indians live in these areas, and more than half live in urban, suburban, or rural nonreservation areas.

Family Structure

Consistent with a national trend, the proportion of American Indian families maintained by a single female increased between 1980 and 1990. However, the Native American increase of 27 percent was considerably larger than the national figure of 17 percent. In 1990, 6 in 10 American Indian and Alaska Native families were headed by married couples; in contrast, about 8 in 10 of the Nation's other families were headed by married couples (U.S. Census Bureau, 1993). In 1993, American Indian families were slightly larger than the average size of all U.S. families (3.6 versus 3.2 persons per family) (U.S. Census Bureau, 1993). An even more telling insight into the family structure of American Indians follows from consideration of the dependency index, which compares the proportion of household members between the ages of 16 and 64 to those younger than 16 years of age combined with those 65 years of age and older. Here the assumption is that the former are more likely to contribute economically to a household, and the latter are not, thus the dependency of one on the other. In this regard, households in many American Indian communities exhibit much higher dependency indices than other segments of the U.S. population and are more comparable to impoverished Third World countries (Manson & Callaway, 1988).

Education

In 1990, 66 percent of American Indians and Alaska Natives 25 years old and over had graduated from high school or achieved a higher level of education; in contrast, only 56 percent had done so in 1980. Despite this advance, the figure was still below that for the U.S. population in general (75%). American Indians and Alaska Natives were not as likely as others in the United States to have completed a bachelor's degree or higher (U.S. Census Bureau, 1993). Data suggest that Indian students achieve on a par with or beyond the performance of non-Indian students in elementary school and show a crossover or decline in performance between fourth and seventh grades (Barlow & Walkup, 1998). Explanations for this crossover vary. Indian children may have a culturally rooted way of learning at odds with teaching methods currently used in public education. Several researchers cite differences between Indian cognitive styles and Western teaching styles. For example, Indian children are primarily visual learners, rather than auditory or verbal learners. Indian youngsters tend to excel at nonverbal performance scales of development and fall below national averages on verbal scales (Yates, 1987). Verbal learners are favored by modes of mainstream public education and testing (Yates, 1987). Linguistic experts have observed that Native languages stress keen descriptive observation and form rather than the verbal or conceptual abstractions that are common in English, which may make learning in English-language schools difficult (Basso, 1996).

Regardless of the reasons for lower academic achievement, negative consequences often ensue. The academic crossover is paralleled by a similar trend in mental health status, as extrapolated from rates of child and adolescent outpatient treatment. Specifically, one study noted that Indian youth enter mental health treatment at a sharply increased rate during the same period, fourth to seventh grades, and that the rate dramatically exceeds their non-Indian counterparts, with a continuously widening gap into late adolescence (Beiser & Attneave, 1982). Subsequent work by Beiser and colleagues clearly underscores the contribution of cultural dynamics in the classroom to these outcomes (Beiser et al., 1998).

Income

Following the devastation of these once-thriving Indian nations, the social environments of Native people have remained plagued by economic disadvantage. Many American Indians and Alaska Natives are unemployed or hold low-paying jobs. Both men and women in this population were roughly twice as likely as whites to be unemployed in 1998 (Population Reference Bureau, 2000). From 1997 to 1999, about 26 percent of American Indians and Alaska Natives lived in poverty; this percentage compares with 13 percent for the United States as a whole and 8 percent for white Americans (U.S. Census Bureau, 1999b).

Physical Health Status

With some exceptions, the health of this ethnic minority group has begun to improve, and the gap in life expectancy rates between Native Americans and others has begun to close. For instance, the infant mortality rate

of American Indians decreased from 22 per 1,000 live births in 1972–1974 to 13 in 1990 and 9 in 1997 (Indian Health Service, 1997). Still, American Indians and Alaska Natives have the second highest infant mortality rate in the Nation (National Center for Health Statistics, 1999) and the highest rate of sudden infant death syndrome (DHHS, 1998). The death rates among American Indians ages 15 to 24 are also higher than those for white persons in the same age group (Grant Makers in Health, 1998). American Indians and Alaska Natives are five times more likely to die of alcohol-related causes than are whites, but they are less likely to die from cancer and heart disease (Indian Health Service, 1997). The rate of diabetes for this population group is more than twice that for whites. In particular, the Pima tribe of Arizona has one of the highest rates of diabetes in the world. The incidence of end-stage renal disease, a known complication of diabetes, is higher among American Indians and Alaska Natives than for both whites and African Americans.

Nationally, one-third of American Indians and Alaska Natives do not have a usual source of health care, that is, a doctor or clinic that can provide regular preventive and medical care (Brown et al., 2000). In 1955, the U.S. Government established the Indian Health Service (IHS) within the Department of Health and Human Services (DHHS). The IHS mission is to provide a comprehensive health service delivery system for American Indians and Alaska Natives "... with opportunity for maximum Tribal involvement in developing and managing programs to meet their health needs" (IHS, 1996). The IHS is responsible for working to provide health delivery programs run by people who are cognizant of entitlements of Native people to all Federal, State, and local health programs, in addition to IHS and tribal services. The IHS also acts "as the principal Federal health advocate for the American Indian and Alaska Native people in the building of health coalitions, networks, and partnerships with Tribal nations and other government agencies as well as with non-Federal organizations [such as] academic medical centers and private foundations" (IHS, 1996).

Although the goal of the IHS is to provide health care for Native Americans, IHS clinics and hospitals are located mainly on reservations, giving only 20 percent of American Indians access to this care (Brown et al., 2000). Furthermore, IHS-eligible American Indians are less likely than others with private health insurance coverage to have obtained the minimum number of physician visits[3] for their age and health status.

More than half of American Indians and Alaska Natives live in urban areas (U.S. Census Bureau, 1990). Title V of Public Law 94–437 of the Indian Health Care Improvement Act authorizes the appropriation of funds for urban Indian health programs. Presently, there are 34 such programs across 41 sites, independently operated through grants and contracts offered by the IHS. Though there is little data available regarding the health needs and access to care among urban Native Americans, the constellation of problems is similar to that of rural communities and includes serious mental illness, alcohol and substance abuse, alcohol and substance dependence, and suicidal ideation (Novins, 1999). An Urban Indian Epidemiology Center was recently funded by the IHS to address this important knowledge gap (Indian Health Service, 2001).

Even where the IHS is active, health service systems in general fail to meet the wide-ranging needs of indigenous populations, especially in remote and isolated regions of the United States. This includes rural, "bush" Alaska, which is divided into 12 Native regions that encompass several villages whose languages, dialects, and cultural connections are only somewhat similar (Reimer, 1999). For example, ethnographic studies in two Pacific Northwest Indian tribal communities document the lack of trust between American Indians and the IHS. Many community members felt they were not receiving appropriate care. Furthermore, holistic education programs to address health needs across the lifespan were considered lacking. Overall, many community members reported that they felt unheard and trapped in a system of care over which they have no control (Strickland, 1999).

Today, the IHS remains the primary entity responsible for the mental health care of American Indians and Alaska Natives. Until 1965, the delivery of mental health services was sporadic. That year, the first Office of Mental Health was opened on the Navajo Reservation. It remained severely understaffed and underfunded until its dissolution in 1977. Legislation to authorize comprehensive mental health services for tribes has been enacted and amended several times, but Congress consistently failed to appropriate funds for such initiatives (Nelson & Manson, 2000). Financial inadequacies have resulted in four IHS service areas without child or adolescent mental health professionals. Fragmented Federal, State, trib-

al, private foundation, and national nonprofit attempts to meet such obvious needs have led to isolation, difficult work conditions, cultural differences, and high turnover rates that dilute efforts to provide mental health services (Barlow & Walkup 1998; Novins, Fleming, et al., 2000).

The Need for Mental Health Care

Historical and Sociocultural Factors That Relate to Mental Health

The history of American Indians and Alaska Natives sets the stage for understanding their mental health needs. Past governmental policies regarding this population have led to mistrust of many government services or care provided by white practitioners. Attempts to eradicate Native culture, including the forced separation of Indian and Native children from parents in order to send them to boarding schools, have been associated with negative mental health consequences (Kleinfeld, 1973; Kleinfeld & Bloom, 1977). Some argue that, as a consequence of past separation from their families, when these children become parents themselves, they are not able to draw on experiences of growing up in a family to guide their own parenting (Special Subcommittee on Indian Education, 1969). The effect of boarding school education on American Indian students remains controversial (Kunitz et al., 1999; Irwin & Roll, 1995).

The socioeconomic consequences of these historical policies are also telling. The removal of American Indians from their lands, as well as other policies summarized above, has resulted in the high rates of poverty that characterize this ethnic minority group. One of the most robust scientific findings has been the association of lower socioeconomic status with poor general health and mental health. Widespread recognition that many Native people live in stressful environments with potentially negative mental health consequences has led to increasing study and empirical documentation of this link (Manson, 1996b, 1997; Beals et al, under review; Jones et al., 1997).

Key Issues for Understanding the Research

Because American Indians and Alaska Natives comprise such a small percentage of U.S. citizens in general, nationally representative studies do not generate sufficiently large samples of this special population to draw accurate conclusions regarding their need for mental health care. Even when large samples are acquired, find-

---

[5]Minimum number of visits set by the Kaiser Commission are at least one physician visit in the past year for children ages 0-5 and in the past two years for children ages 6-17 (as recommended by the *American Academy of Pediatrics in Pediatrics, 96, 712*), and in the past year for adults in fair or poor health and in the past two years for adults in good or excellent health (Kaiser Commission on Medicaid and the Uninsured, 2000).

ings are constrained by the marked heterogeneity that characterizes the social and cultural ecologies of Native people. There are 561 federally recognized tribes, with over 200 indigenous languages spoken (Fleming, 1992). Differences between some of these languages are as distinct as those between English and Chinese (Chafe, 1962). Similar differences abound among Native customs, family structures, religions, and social relationships. The magnitude of this diversity among Indian people has important implications for research observations. Novins and colleagues provide an excellent illustration of this point in a paper that shows that the dynamics underlying suicidal ideation among Indian youth vary significantly with the cultural contexts of the tribes of which they are members (Novins, et al., 1999). A tension arises, then, between the frequently conflicting objectives of comparability and cultural specificity—a tension not easily resolved in research pursued among this special population.

As widely noted, language is important when assessing the mental health needs of individuals and the communities in which they reside. Approximately 280,000 American Indians and Alaska Natives speak a language other than English at home; more than half of Alaska Natives who are Eskimos speak either Inuit or Yup'ik. Consequently, evaluations of need for mental health care often have to be conducted in a language other than English. Yet the challenge can be more subtle than that implied by stark differences in language. Cultural differences in the expression and reporting of distress are well established among American Indians and Alaska Natives. These often compromise the ability of assessment tools to capture the key signs and symptoms of mental illness (Kinzie & Manson, 1987; Manson, 1994, 1996a). Words such as "depressed" and "anxious" are absent from some American Indian and Alaska Native languages (Manson et al., 1985). Other research has demonstrated that certain DSM diagnoses, such as major depressive disorder, do not correspond directly to the categories of illness recognized by some American Indians. Thus, evaluating the need for mental health care among American Indians and Alaska Natives requires careful clinical inquiry that attends closely to culture.

Census 2000 reports a significant increase in the number of individuals who identify, at least in part, as American Indian or Alaska Native. This finding resurrects longstanding debates about definition and identification (Passel, 1996). The relationship of those who have recently asserted their Indian ancestry to other, tribally defined individuals is unknown and poses a difficult challenge. It suggests a newly emergent need to consider the mental health status and requirements of individuals who live primarily within mainstream society, while continuing to build the body of knowledge on groups already defined.

Mental Disorders

Although not all mental disorders are disabling, these disorders always manifest some level of psychological discomfort and associated impairment. Such symptoms often improve with treatment. Therefore, the presence of a mental disorder is one reasonable indicator of need for mental health care. As noted in previous chapters, in the United States such disorders are identified according to the *Diagnostic and Statistical Manual of Mental Disorders* (DSM) diagnostic categories established by the American Psychiatric Association (1994).

Adults

Unfortunately, no large-scale studies of the rates of mental disorders among American Indian and Alaska Native adults have yet been published. The discussion at this point must rely on smaller, suggestive studies that await future confirmation.

The most recently published information regarding the mental health needs of adult American Indians living in the community comes from a study conducted in 1988 (Kinzie et al., 1992). The 131 respondents were inhabitants of a small Northwest Coast village who had participated in a previous community-based epidemiological study (Shore et al., 1973). They were followed up 20 years later using a well accepted method for diagnosing mental disorders, the Schedule for Affective Disorders and Schizophrenia-Lifetime Version. Nearly 70 percent of the sample had experienced a mental disorder in their lifetimes. About 30 percent were experiencing a disorder at the time of the follow-up.

The American Indian Vietnam Veterans Project (AIVVP) is the most recent community-based, diagnostically oriented psychiatric epidemiological study among American Indian adults to be reported within the last 25 years (Beals et al., under review; Gurley et al., 2001; National Center for Post-Traumatic Stress Disorder and the National Center for American Indian and Alaska Native Mental Health Research [NCPTSD/NCAIAN-MHR], 1996). It was part of a congressionally mandated effort to replicate the National Vietnam Veterans Readjustment Study that had been conducted in other ethnic groups (Kulka et al., 1990).

The AIVVP found that rates of PTSD among the Northern Plains and Southwestern Vietnam veterans, respectively, were 31 percent and 27 percent, current; 57 percent and 45 percent, lifetime. These figures were significantly higher than the rates for their white, black, and Japanese American counterparts. Likewise, current and lifetime prevalence of alcohol abuse and/or dependence among the Indian veterans (more than 70% current; more than 80% lifetime) was far greater than that observed for the others, which ranged from 11 to 32 percent current and 33 to 50 percent lifetime (NCPTSD/NCAIANMHR, 1997).

There are no recent, scientifically rigorous studies that could shed light on the need for mental health care among Alaska Natives. The only systematic studies of Alaska Natives are outdated (Murphy & Hughes, 1965; Foulks & Katz, 1973; Sampath, 1974) and not based on the current DSM system of disorders. One study of Alaska Natives seen in a community mental health center indicated that substance abuse is a common reason for men (85% of those seen) and women (65% of those seen) to seek mental health care (Aoun & Gregory, 1998).

Children and Youth

Two recent studies examined the need for mental health care among American Indian youth. The Great Smoky Mountain Study assessed psychiatric disorders among 431 youth ages 9 to 13 (Costello et al., 1997). Children were defined as American Indian if they were enrolled in a recognized tribe or were first- or second-generation descendants of an enrolled member. Overall, American Indian children were found to have fairly similar rates of disorder (17%) in comparison to white children from surrounding counties (19%). Lower rates of tics (2 vs. 4%) and higher rates of substance abuse or dependence (1 vs. 0.1%) were found in American Indian children as compared with white children. The difference in substance abuse is almost totally accounted for by alcohol use among 13-year-old Indian children (Costello et al., 1997). Rates of anxiety disorders, depressive disorders, conduct disorders, and attention-deficit/hyperactivity disorder (AD/HD) were not significantly different for American Indian and white children. Yet, for white children, poverty doubled the risk of mental disorders, whereas poverty was not associated with increased risk of mental disorders among the American Indian children. Overall, these American Indian children appeared to experience rates of mental disorders similar to those for white children.

The second study reported a followup of a school-based psychiatric epidemiological study involving Northern Plains youth, 13 to 17 years of age (Beals et al., 1997). Of 109 adolescents, 29 percent received a diagno-sis of at least one psychiatric disorder. Altogether, more than 15 percent of the students qualified for a single diagnosis; 13 percent met criteria for multiple diagnoses. In terms of the broad diagnostic categories, 6 percent of the sample met criteria for an anxiety disorder, 5 percent for a mood disorder (either major depressive disorder or dysthymia), 14 for one or more of the disruptive behavior disorders, and 18 percent for substance abuse disorders. Only 1 percent was diagnosed with an eating disorder. The five most common specific disorders were alcohol dependence or abuse (11%), attention- deficit/hyperactivity disorder (11%), marijuana dependence or abuse (9%), major depressive disorder (5%), and other substance dependence or abuse (4%). Considerable comorbidity among disorders was observed. More than half of those with a disruptive behavior disorder also qualified for a substance use disorder. Similarly, 60 percent of those youth diagnosed with any depressive disorder had a substance use disorder as well.

Beals and colleagues compared their findings with those reported for nonminority children drawn from the population at large (Lewinsohn et al., 1993; Shaffer et al., 1996). The American Indian youth were diagnosed with fewer anxiety disorders than the nonminority children in the Shaffer sample. However, American Indian adolescents were much more likely to be diagnosed with AD/HD and substance abuse or substance dependence disorders. The rates of conduct disorder and oppositional defiant disorder were also elevated in the American Indian sample. Rates of depressive disorders were essentially equivalent. This latter finding was consistent with a study published in 1994 (Sack et al., 1994) that reported clinical depression among youth from several reservations below 1 percent, "a prevalence rate compatible with other studies in white populations, which typically varies from 1 to 3 percent" (Fleming & Offord, 1990). When compared with the Lewinsohn sample, American Indian adolescents in the study by Beals and colleagues demonstrated statistically significant higher 6-month prevalence rates than did the nonminority children for lifetime prevalence of ADHD and alcohol abuse/dependence. In addition, the American Indian youth had higher 6-month rates of simple phobias, social phobias, overanxious disorder, and oppositional defiant and conduct disorders than the nonminority children's lifetime rates for those disorders.

At present, there are no published estimates of the rates of mental disorders among Alaska Native youth. One study of Eskimo children seen in a community mental health center in Nome, Alaska, indicated that substance abuse, including alcohol and inhalant use, and previous suicide attempts are the most common types of

Box 4–1:

Charlie (age 9); Mike (father, age 29)

Charlie frequently argued with teachers and started fights with other children. Charlie's schoolteacher recommended him for counseling because of his acting out in school.

Charlie had lived all his life with his mother and two younger siblings on their Southwestern reservation. Charlie's father, Mike, lived in the home until Charlie was 3 years old, when he was sent to prison for attempted murder of Charlie's mother. Mike was a chronic alcoholic who frequently battered his wife when their arguments became heated. Charlie often witnessed violence between his mother and father and was aware of the circumstances leading to his father's imprisonment. During Mike's incarceration, Charlie visited him in prison and maintained regular contact by mail and phone. At the time of Charlie's referral, Mike had been out of prison for one year and had just returned home from a 30-day alcohol rehabilitation program.

Mike had been the youngest of eight children; his mother, the primary caretaker, sent Mike away to boarding school because she was unable to care for him. Mike never had contact with his father, whom he described as "an alcoholic and a womanizer." Although Mike recognized the economic hardship his mother faced after his father left, he nonetheless felt abandoned by her and frequently wondered why she had had him in the first place.

Mike described boarding school as a constant struggle. On the weekends and holidays, Mike rarely went home; his family did not visit him. Over the years, Mike felt great sadness over his childhood loss and great anger toward his mother for her complete abandonment of him.

In addition to being physically abusive toward his wife, Mike frequently fought other men. He often felt great rage and was easily provoked into violence, especially during times of drunkenness.

Mike was a talented artist who created pottery and woodwork designs that were derived from traditional practices within his tribe. He was a full-blooded member of his tribe. Though raised on the reservation, he spent most of his life shuttling between it and various institutions, such as boarding school, prison, and alcohol rehabilitation facilities.

In talking about his childhood, Mike was confused and incoherent, especially about his parents. He sometimes needed to leave the therapeutic setting because he had become so agitated by these feelings. Mike was preoccupied with the sense that he had been dealt a bad lot in life. This contributed to his quickness to see that others were betraying him and thus needed to be dealt with swiftly and harshly without forgiveness.

At the time of Charlie's referral, Mike was newly committed to being a parent. Mike wanted to teach his children about his art and culture, to play sports with them, and to guide them in ways that he had not been guided. Mike acknowledged that the problems Charlie was having were not unlike the problems he had as a child. He had not appreciated the impact that the rage rooted in his own childhood experience of abandonment had on Charlie's development. In witnessing the violence that his father let explode on his mother, Charlie had learned to fear his father and to feel powerless to protect his mother. Charlie appears to be making up for this powerlessness at home by dominating his peers through his own acts of violence. (*Adapted from Christensen & Manson, 2001*)

problems for which these children receive mental health care (Aoun & Gregory, 1998). An earlier study found a high need for mental health care among Yup'ik and Cup'ik adolescents who were in boarding schools (Kleinfeld & Bloom, 1977), but current DSM diagnostic categories were not used.

Older Adults

Although large-scale studies of mental disorders among older American Indians are lacking, Manson (1992) found that over 30 percent of older American Indian adults visiting one urban IHS outpatient medical facility reported significant depressive symptoms; this rate is higher than most published estimates of the prevalence of depression among older whites with chronic illnesses (9 to 31%) (Berkman et al., 1986). In another clinic-based investigation, nearly 20 percent of American Indian elders who received primary care reported significant psychiatric symptoms (Goldwasser & Badger, 1989), with rates increasing as a function of age. These findings are consistent with a survey of older, community-dwelling, urban Natives in Los Angeles, among whom more than 10 percent reported depression, and an additional 20 percent reported sadness and grieving (Kramer, 1991).

A recent study of 309 Great Lakes American Indian elders revealed that 18 percent of the sample scored above a traditional cutoff for depression on the Center for Epidemiology Studies Depression Scale (CES–D) (Curyto et al., 1998, 1999). However, upon further examination of that data, the factor structure of the CES–D was found to be different in this population as compared to available norms (Chapleski, Lamphere, et al., 1997). Therefore, the concern remains that the CES–D may not accurately measure depressive symptoms in this population. Nonetheless, depressive symptoms were strongly associated with impaired functioning (Chapleski, Lichtenberg, et al., 1997), which is in keeping with past findings (Baron et al., 1990) and underscores the burden posed by such distress, as well as the need for intervention (Manson & Brenneman, 1995).

Mental Health Problems

Symptoms

Although little is known about rates of psychiatric disorders among American Indians and Alaska Natives in the United States, one recent, nationally representative study looked at mental distress among a large sample of adults (Centers for Disease Control and Prevention, 1998). Overall, American Indians and Alaska Natives reported much higher rates of frequent distress—nearly 13 percent compared to nearly 9 percent in the general population. The findings of this study suggest that American Indians and Alaska Natives experience greater psychological distress than the overall population.

Somatization

The distinction between mind and body common among individuals in industrialized Western nations is not shared throughout the world (Manson & Kleinman, 1998; Manson, 2000). Many ethnic minorities do not discriminate bodily from psychic distress and may express emotional distress in somatic terms or bodily symptoms. Relatively little empirical research is available concerning this tendency among American Indians and Alaska Natives. However, a sample of 120 adult American Indians belonging to a single Northwest Coast tribe was screened using the Center for Epidemiologic Studies Depression Scale, which includes both psychological and somatic symptoms. Analyses showed that somatic com-

plaints and emotional distress were not well differentiated from each other in this population (Somervell et al., 1993). Other inquiries into the psychometric properties of the CES–D and other measures of depressive symptoms among American Indians have yielded similar findings, providing some evidence of the lack of such distinctions within this population (Ackerson et al., 1990; Manson et al., 1990).

Culture-Bound Syndromes

A large body of ethnographic work reveals that some American Indians and Alaska Natives, who may express emotional distress in ways that are inconsistent with the diagnostic categories of the DSM, may conceptualize mental health differently. Many unique expressions of distress shown by American Indians and Alaska Natives have been described (Trimble et al., 1984; Manson et al., 1985; Manson 1994; Nelson & Manson, 2000). Prominent examples include *ghost sickness* and *heartbreak syndrome* (Manson et al., 1985). The question becomes how to elicit, understand, and incorporate such expressions of distress and suffering within the assessment and treatment process of the DSM–IV.

Suicide

Given the lack of information about rates of mental disorders among American Indian and Alaska Native populations, the prevalence of suicide often serves as an important indicator of need. The Surgeon General's 1999 *Call to Action to Prevent Suicide* indicates that from 1979 to 1992, the suicide rate for this ethnic minority group was 1.5 times the national rate. The suicide rate is particularly high among young Native American males ages 15 to 24. Accounting for 64 percent of all suicides by American Indians and Alaska Natives, the suicide rate of this group is 2 to 3 times higher than the general U.S. rate (May, 1990; Kettle & Bixler, 1991; Mock et al., 1996). In another survey of American Indian adolescents (n = 13,000), 22 percent of females and 12 percent of males reported having attempted suicide at some time; 67 percent who had made an attempt had done so within the past year (Blum et al., 1992). Furthermore, an analysis of Bureau of Vital Statistics death certificate data from 1979 to 1993 found that "Alaska Native males had one of the highest documented suicide rates in the world" (1997). Alaska Natives, in general, were more likely to commit suicide than non-Natives living in Alaska (Gessner, 1997). It is important to note that violent deaths (unintentional injuries, homicide, and suicide) account for 75 percent of all mortality in the second decade of life for

American Indians and Alaska Natives (Resnick et al., 1997).

High-Need Populations

American Indians and Alaska Natives are the most impoverished ethnic minority group in the United States. Although no causal links have yet been demonstrated, there is good reason to suspect that the history of oppression, discrimination, and removal from traditional lands experienced by Native people has contributed to their current lack of educational and economic opportunities and their significant representation among populations with high need for mental health care.

Individuals Who Are Homeless

American Indians and Alaska Natives are overrepresented among people who are homeless. Although they comprise less than 1 percent of the general population, American Indians and Alaska Natives constitute 8 percent of the U.S. homeless population (U.S. Census Bureau, 1999a). It is not clear that homeless American Indians and Alaska Natives are at greater risk of mental disorder than their non-Native counterparts. In one study, American Indian veterans who were homeless had fewer psychiatric diagnoses than did white veterans who were homeless (Kasprow & Rosenheck, 1998), although these differences were relatively small. Nevertheless, because there are more individuals with mental disorders among the homeless population than among the general population (Koegel et al., 1988), this finding likely points to a substantial number of Native people with a high need for mental health care.

Individuals Who Are Incarcerated

In 1997, an estimated 4 percent of racially identified American Indian and Alaska Native adults were under the care, custody, or control of the criminal justice system. Also, 16,000 adults in this group were held in local jails (Bureau of Justice Statistics, 1999). Although research specific to rates of mental disorders among American Indian and Alaska Native adults in jails is not available, a recent study has evaluated disorders among incarcerated adolescents. Rates of mental disorders among those held in a Northern Plains reservation juvenile detention facility were examined (Duclos et al., 1998). Among the 150 youth evaluated, nearly half (49%) had at least one alcohol, drug, or mental health disorder. The most common problems detected were substance abuse, conduct disorder, and depression.

These rates were higher than those found in Indian adolescents in the community, indicating that incarcerated American Indians are likely to be at high need for mental health and substance abuse interventions.

Individuals with Alcohol and Drug Problems

Actual rates of alcohol abuse among American Indian adults are difficult to estimate, yet indirect evidence suggests that a substantial proportion of this population suffers from this problem. For example, the estimated rate of alcohol-related deaths for Indian men is 27 percent and for Indian women 13 percent (May & Moran, 1995). Rates appear to vary widely among different tribes. Although the topic of substance abuse is beyond the scope of this Supplement, alcohol problems and mental disorders often occur together in American Indian and Alaska Native populations (Westermeyer, 1982; Whittaker, 1982; Westermeyer & Peake, 1983; Kinzie et al., 1992; Beals et al., 2001). A recent study, which sought to understand the link between alcohol problems and psychiatric disorders in American Indians, included over 600 members of three large families (Robin et al., 1997a). More than 70 percent qualified for a lifetime diagnosis of alcohol disorders. Among both men and women, those who were alcohol-dependent were also more likely to have psychiatric disorders, as were those who engaged in binge-drinking behavior. This finding underscores the likelihood that American Indians with alcohol disorders are at high risk for concomitant mental health problems.

Given the high rates of alcohol abuse among some American Indians and Alaska Natives, fetal alcohol syndrome is an important influence on mental health needs (May et al., 1983). The Centers for Disease Control and Prevention (1998) monitored the rate of fetal alcohol syndrome (FAS), identifying cases based on hospital discharge diagnoses collected from more than 1,500 hospitals across the United States between 1980 and 1986. The overall rate of FAS was 2.97 per 1,000 for Native Americans, 0.6 per 1,000 for African Americans, 0.09 for Caucasians, 0.08 for Hispanics, and 0.03 for Asians (Chavez et al., 1988). As might be expected given the fact that physicians often do not identify this disease, these rates are much lower than those found in clinic-based investigations (Stratton et al., 1996). Fetal alcohol syndrome now is recognized as the leading known cause of mental retardation in the United States (Streissguth et al., 1991), surpassing Down's syndrome and spina bifida. Fetal alcohol syndrome is not just a childhood disorder; predictable long-term progression of the disorder into adulthood includes maladaptive behaviors such as poor judgment, distractibility, and difficulty perceiving social cues. Consequently, American Indians and Alaska Natives with fetal alcohol syndrome are likely to have high need for intervention to facilitate the management of their disabilities.

Drinking by American Indian youth has been more thoroughly studied than drinking by American Indian adults. Ongoing school-based surveys have shown that, although about the same proportion of Indian and non-Indian youth in grades 7 to 12 have tried alcohol, Indian youth who drink appear to drink more heavily than do youth of other ethnicities (Plunkett & Mitchell, 2000; Novins et al., under review). They also experience more negative social consequences from their drinking than do their non-Indian counterparts (Oetting et al., 1989; Mitchell et al., 1995). Although drinking and mental disorders may be less linked for youth than for adults, those adolescents with serious drinking problems are likely to be at risk for mental health problems as well (Beals et al., 2001).

Individuals Exposed to Trauma

Lower socioeconomic status is associated with an increased likelihood of experiencing undesirable life events (McLeod & Kessler, 1990). As a result of lower socioeconomic status, American Indians and Alaska Natives are also more likely to be exposed to trauma than members of more economically advantaged groups. Exposure to trauma is related to the development of subsequent mental disorders in general and of post-traumatic stress disorder (PTSD) in particular (Kessler et al., 1995). Recent evidence suggests that American Indians may be at high risk for exposure to trauma.

An investigation of Northern Plains youth ages 8 to 11 found that 61 percent of them had been exposed to some kind of traumatic event. These children were reported to have more trauma-related symptoms, but not substantially higher rates of diagnosable PTSD (3%) (Jones et. al., 1997). According to the Bureau of Justice Statistics (1999), the rate of violent victimization of American Indians is more than twice as high as the national average. Indeed, the data regarding reported child abuse in Native communities indicate that this phenomenon has increased 18 percent in the last 10 years (Bureau of Justice Statistics, 1999). Another study noted a high prevalence of trauma exposure (e.g., car accidents, deaths, shootings, beatings) and PTSD within those in the family study mentioned above (Robin et al., 1997c). Of those studied, 82 percent had been exposed to one trau-

matic event, and the prevalence of PTSD was 22 percent. Because American Indians probably are similar to non-Indians in their likelihood of developing PTSD after a traumatic exposure (Kessler et al., 1995), the substantially higher prevalence of the disorder (22% for AI/AN vs. 8% in the general community) does not signal greater vulnerability to PTSD, but rather higher rates of traumatic exposure.

Maltreatment and neglect have been shown to be relatively common among older urban American Indian and Alaska Native patients in primary care. A chart review of 550 Native adults 50 years of age or older seen at one of the country's largest, most comprehensive, urban Indian health programs during one calendar year revealed that 10 percent met criteria for definite and probable physical abuse or neglect (Buchwald et al., 2000). After controlling for other factors in a logistic regression model, patient age, female gender, alcohol abuse, domestic violence, and current depression remained significant correlates of physical abuse or neglect of these Native elders.

The previously mentioned American Indian Vietnam Veterans Project (AIVVP) replicated the National Vietnam Veterans Readjustment Study that examined psychiatric disorders among African American, Latino, and white veterans (Kulka et al., 1990). Between 1992 and 1995, researchers evaluated random samples of Vietnam combat veterans drawn from three Northern Plains reservations (n = 305) and one Southwest reservation (n = 316). Approximately one-third of the Northern Plains (31%) and Southwestern (27%) American Indian participants had PTSD at the time of the study. Approximately half had experienced the disorder in their lifetimes (57% and 45%, respectively). This rate is far in excess of rates of current PTSD for white veterans (14%) and for black veterans (21%) (Kulka et al., 1990). The excess rates, however, were largely attributable to the fact that American Indian veterans had been exposed to more combat-related traumas than their non-Indian peers (National Center for Post-Traumatic Stress Disorder and the National Center for American Indian and Alaska Native Mental Health Research, 1996; Beals et al., under review).

Children in Foster Care

Studies have consistently indicated that children who are removed from their homes are at increased risk for mental health problems (e.g., Courtney & Barth, 1996), as well as for serious subsequent adult problems such as homelessness (Koegel et al., 1995). By the mid-1970s, many American Indian children were experiencing out-of-home placements. In Oklahoma, four times as many

---

Box 4–2

John : Vietnam Combat Veteran (age 45)

John is a 45-year-old, full-blood Indian, who is married and has 7 children. The family lives in a small, rural community on a large reservation in Arizona. John served as a Marine Corps infantry squad leader in Vietnam during 1968–1969. He most recently was treated through a VA medical program, where he participates in a post-traumatic stress disorder (PTSD) support group. John suffers from alcoholism, which began soon after his initial patrols in Vietnam. These involved heavy combat and, ultimately, physical injury. He exhibits the hallmark symptoms of PTSD, including flashbacks, nightmares, intrusive thoughts on an almost daily basis, marked hypervigilance, irritability, and avoidant behavior.

Some 10 years after his return from Vietnam, John began cycling through several periods of treatment for his alcoholism in tribal residential programs. It wasn't until one month after he began treatment for his alcoholism at a local VA facility that a provisional diagnosis of PTSD was made. Upon completing that treatment, he transferred to an inpatient unit specializing in combat-related trauma. John left the unit against medical advice, sober but still experiencing significant symptoms.

John speaks and understands English well; he also is fluent in his native language, which is spoken in his home. John is the descendant of a family of traditional healers. Consequently, the community expected him to assume a leadership role in its cultural and spiritual life. However, boarding school interrupted his early participation in important aspects of local ceremonial life. His participation was further delayed by military service and then forestalled by his alcoholism. During boarding school, John was frequently harassed by non-Indian staff for speaking his native language, for wearing his hair long, and for running away. Afraid of similar ridicule while in the service, he seldom shared his personal background with fellow infantrymen. Yet John was the target of racism, from being selected to act as point on patrol because he was an Indian to being called "Chief" and "blanket ass."

Until recently, tribal members had never heard of PTSD, but now frequently refer to it as the "wounded spirit." His community has long recognized the consequences of being a warrior, and indeed, a ceremony has evolved over many generations to prevent as well as treat the underlying causes of these symptoms. Within this tribal worldview, combat-related trauma upsets the balance that underpins someone's personal, physical, mental, emotional, and spiritual health. The events in John's life (the Vietnam war, his father's death, and his impairment due to PTSD and alcoholism) conspired to prevent his participation in this and other tribal ceremonies.

John attends a VA-sponsored support group, comprised of all Indian Vietnam veterans, which serves as an important substitute for the circle of "Indian drinking buddies" from whom he eventually separated as part of his successful alcohol treatment. John reports having left the VA's larger PTSD inpatient program because of his discomfort with its non-Native styles of disclosure and expectations regarding personal reflection. Through the VA's Indian support group, he joined a local gourd society that honors warriors and dances prominently at pow-wows. His sobriety has been aided by involvement in the Native American Church, with its reinforcement of his decision to remain sober and its support for positive life changes.

Though John has a great deal of work ahead of him, he feels that he is now ready to participate in the tribe's major ceremonial intended to bless and purify its warriors. His family, once alienated but now reunited, is busily preparing for that event. (*Adapted from Manson, 1996*).

Indian children were either adopted or in foster care as non-Indian children. In New Mexico, twice as many Indian children were in foster care than any other minority group. Estimates suggest that as many as 25 to 30 percent of American Indian children have been removed from their families (Cross, et al., 2000). As a result, Congress passed the Indian Child Welfare Act in 1978 to protect American Indian children. The Congressional investigation that led to the passage of the act concluded that "a pattern of discrimination against American Indians is evident in the area of child welfare, and it is the responsibility of Congress to take whatever action is within its power to see that Indian communities and their families are not destroyed" (Fischler, 1985). Accordingly, in 1999, the number of American Indian and Alaska Native children in foster care had decreased to 1 percent of all children in foster care in the United States (DHHS, 1999). Yet the mental health consequences for the children, now adults, who were placed out of their homes, especially those placed in non-Indian homes, during this lengthy period of mass cultural dislocation is not known (Nelson et al., 1996; Roll, 1998).

Availability, Accessibility, and Utilization of Mental Health Services

The historical and current socioeconomic factors presented highlight several elements that may affect the use of mental health services by American Indians and Alaska Natives. Foremost, given the history of this ethnic group's relationship with the U.S. Government, many American Indian and Alaska Native people may not trust institutional sources of care and may be unwilling to seek help from them. Second, mental health services are quite limited in the rural and isolated communities where many Indian and Native peoples live. Alaska Natives, in particular, have little mental health care available to them, as is the case of Alaskans generally (Rodenhauser, 1994). Although little is known about the role of mental health care within American Indian and Alaska Native life, there is some evidence regarding their use of such services.

Availability of Mental Health Services

There is little information to indicate whether American Indians and Alaska Natives are more likely to seek care if it is available from ethnically similar, as opposed to dissimilar providers. Although there is likely to be great variability regarding this preference, given the historical relationships between Native people and white authorities, a proportion of the population is likely to prefer ethnically matched providers (Haviland et al., 1983). However, the fact is that few American Indian and Alaska Native mental health professionals are available. Approximately 101 American Indian and Alaska Native mental health providers (psychiatrists, psychologists, social workers, psychiatric nurses, and counselors) are available per 100,000 members of this ethnic group; this compares with 173 per 100,000 for whites (Manderscheid & Henderson, United States, 1998). The scarcity of American Indian and Alaska Native psychiatrists is particularly striking. In 1996, only an estimated 29 psychiatrists in the United States were of Indian or Native heritage. The same scarcity exists among other physicians as well, whereas American Indians and Alaska Natives make up close to 1 percent of the population, only .0003 percent of physicians in the United States identify themselves as American Indians or Alaska Natives.

Accessibility of Mental Health Services

As noted earlier, the Federal Government has responsibility for providing health care to the members of over 500 federally recognized tribes through the Indian Health Service (IHS). However, only 1 in 5 American Indians reports access to IHS services (Brown et al., 2000). IHS services are provided largely on reservations; consequently, Native people living elsewhere have quite limited access to this care. Furthermore, American Indian tribes that are recognized by their State, but not by the Federal Bureau of Indian Affairs, are ineligible for IHS funding (Brown et al., 2000).

In addition, according to a recent report based on national data, only about half of American Indians and Alaska Natives have employer-based insurance coverage; this is in contrast to 72 percent of whites. Medicaid is the primary source of coverage for 25 percent of American Indians and Alaska Natives, particularly for the poor and near poor; 24 percent of American Indians and Alaska Natives do not have health insurance (Brown et al., 2000).

These circumstances are compounded by the dramatic change which the IHS is undergoing as a consequence of tribal options to self-administer Federal functions under the contracting or compacting provisions of P. L. 93–638. The attendant downsizing of Federal participation in Indian health care has diminished local ability to recover Medicaid, Medicare, and private reimbursement, leading to fewer resources to support health care delivery to Native people.

Recent policy changes enable tribes to apply directly for substance abuse block-grant funds, independent of the states in which they reside. No such provision is available with respect to mental health block grants, but it is the subject of increasing discussion. It is not known, however, if these changes in policy have or will have increased Federal support of relevant programs at the local level.

Utilization of Mental Health Services

Community Studies

Representative community studies of American Indians and Alaska Natives have not been published, so little is known about the use of mental health services among

91

those with established need. A previously mentioned study that examined the relationship of substance abuse and psychiatric disorders among family members (Robin et al., 1997b) also considered their use of mental health services. Of those with a mental disorder, only 32 percent had received mental health or substance abuse services. Although the special design of this study does not permit generalization of its findings to the community at large, it is noteworthy that very low rates of service use were observed among those most in need of care.

The use of mental health services by American Indian children with mental disorders has been the subject of several recent studies. For instance, the Great Smoky Mountain Study examined mental health service use among Cherokee and non-Indian youth living in adjacent western North Carolina communities (Costello et al., 1997). Among Cherokee children with a diagnosable DSM–III–R psychiatric disorder, 1 in 7 received professional mental health treatment. This rate is similar to that for the non-Indian sample. However, Cherokee children were more likely to receive this treatment through the juvenile justice system and inpatient facilities than were the non-Indian children. Similarly, in a small study of Plains Indian students in the north-central United States, more than one-third (39%) of those with psychiatric disorders (21%) used services at some time during their lives (Novins, et al., 2000). Two-thirds of those who received services were seen through school; just one adolescent was treated in the specialty mental health system. Among those youth with a psychiatric disorder who did not receive services, over half were recognized as having a problem by a parent, teacher, or employer.

Finally, the use of mental health services by incarcerated American Indian youth also has been considered in the literature (Novins, et al., 1999). The previously described study in a Northern Plains reservation juvenile detention facility found that about one-third of the youth suffering from a mental disorder reported having received treatment at some point in their lives, and 40 percent of those with a substance abuse disorder had done so. Overall, service use was greater among these detained youth than among their counterparts in the community. However, substantial unmet need was still evident. While services for substance-related problems were most commonly provided in residential settings, services for emotional problems typically were delivered through outpatient settings. Traditional healers and pastoral counselors provided more than one-quarter of the services received by these youth.

Mental Health Systems Studies

When data regarding the use of services by individuals who suffer from mental disorders is as limited as it is for American Indians and Alaska Natives, data generated by the overall health system may provide insight into how effective the mental health sector is in meeting the needs. However, in the case of Native people, there are two problems with this approach. First, rates of service use are related to the prevalence of mental illness in the target group. Given that American Indians and Alaska Natives may differ from white Americans in their respective rates of mental disorder, comparisons of this nature may not accurately identify differences in unmet need for care. Second, as noted in the initial SGR, less than one-third of adults with a diagnosable mental disorder receive care within a year. Therefore, disparities in care received must be interpreted in light of differences in the use of services by those in need, which appears to vary by ethnicity. With these cautions in mind, what does the available evidence suggest?

An evaluation of national data from 1980 to 1981 found that American Indians and Alaska Natives were admitted to state and county hospitals at higher rates than whites (Snowden & Cheung, 1990). This pattern was true for psychiatric services at non-Federal hospitals and at Veterans Administration (VA) medical centers. At private psychiatric hospitals, however, American Indians and Alaska Natives were admitted at a lower rate than whites. With all the rates combined, there were more American Indian and Alaska Natives than whites in inpatient psychiatric units, with even greater rates of admission if IHS hospitals were included (Snowden & Cheung, 1990). Conversely, data from 1983 (Cheung & Snowden, 1990) and again from 1986 (Breaux & Ryujin, 1999) suggested that American Indians used inpatient facilities at rates equal to their proportion in the general population.

These same studies also looked at use of outpatient mental health services (Cheung & Snowden, 1990; Breaux & Ryujin, 1999). In both, American Indians and Alaska Natives were found to use outpatient mental health services at a rate similar to their representation in the U.S. population. Yet, two smaller studies of use of outpatient care in Seattle found greater than expected use by American Indians and Alaska Natives (Sue, 1977; O'Sullivan et al., 1989). Just as important, fewer than half of the American Indian clients who were seen returned after the initial contact, which was a significantly higher nonreturn rate than was observed for African American, Asian, Hispanic, and white clients.

The picture with respect to mental health service use by American Indians and Alaska Natives is inconsistent and puzzling. But there is a clear indication of significant need equal to, if not greater than, the need of the general population.

Complementary Therapies

Several targeted studies suggest that in many cases American Indians and Alaska Natives use alternative therapies at rates that are equal to or greater than the rates for whites. For example, 62 percent of Navajo patients interviewed at a rural IHS clinic in New Mexico had used native healers, and 39 percent reported using native healers on a regular basis (Kim & Kwok, 1998). In another study, 38 percent of the individuals interviewed in an urban clinic in Wisconsin (representing at least 30 tribal affiliations) reported concurrent use of a native healer. Of those who were not currently seeing a native healer, 9 out of 10 would consider seeing one in the future (Marbella et al., 1998). A third study at one of the country's largest, most comprehensive urban primary care programs for Indians in Seattle, Washington, revealed that two-thirds of the 871 patients sampled employed traditional healing practices regularly and felt that such practices significantly improved their health status (Buchwald, et al., 2000). Use was strongly associated with cultural affiliation, poor functional status, alcohol abuse, dysphoria, and trauma, but not with specific medical problems (except for musculoskeletal pain). In all these studies, alternative therapies and healers were generally used to complement care received by mainstream sources, rather than as a substitute for such care.

In a study of mental health service utilization by American Indian veterans in two tribes, use of both traditional Native American and mainstream medical services was markedly apparent (Gurley et al., 2001). Overall, they used services much less for mental health problems than for physical health problems. IHS facilities were equally available to both tribes, but VA services were available more readily to one of them. Within the tribe with less access to VA services, more traditional healing services were used, so that similar amounts of care were received. This demonstrates that need drives service utilization, although local availability of care dictates the forms that such service may assume.

Appropriateness and Outcomes of Mental Health Services

During the past decade, many guidelines for treating mental disorders have been offered to ensure the provision of evidence-based care. Even though few American Indians or Alaska Natives were included in the studies that led to their development, such professional practice guidelines offer the clearest, most carefully considered recommendations available regarding appropriate treatment for this population. They therefore warrant special attention.

The DSM–IV, both within the main text and in its "Outline for Cultural Formulation," does provide clear guidelines for addressing cultural matters, including those specific to this population, in the assessment and treatment of mental health problems (Manson & Kleinman, 1998; Mezzich et al., 1999). A growing body of case material demonstrates the utility of applying these guidelines to American Indian children (Novins et al., 1997), as well as to adults (Fleming, 1996; Manson, 1996; O'Nell, 1998).

Novins and colleagues (1997) critically analyzed the extension of the "Outline for Cultural Formulation" to American Indian children. Drawing upon rich clinical material, they demonstrated the merits and utility of this approach for understanding the emotional, psychological, and social forces that often buffet Native children. However, Novins and his colleagues underscored the importance of obtaining the perspectives of adult family members and teachers, as well as the children themselves, which is not explicitly considered in the formulation.

No studies have been published regarding the outcomes associated with standard psychiatric care for American Indians and Alaska Natives. Hence, it is not known if practitioners accurately diagnose the mental health needs of American Indians and Alaska Natives, nor whether they receive the same benefits from guideline-based psychiatric care as do whites. For this we must await related studies of treatment outcome, studies that venture beyond the limitations of current thinking with respect to intervention technology and best practices.

Mental Illness Prevention and Mental Health Promotion

Up to this point, the chapter has focused on the prevalence, risk, assessment, and treatment of mental illness

93

among American Indian and Alaska Native youth and adults. The public health model that guides this Supplement stresses the importance of preventive and promotive interventions as well. Indeed, virtually any serious dialogue at both local and national levels about mental health and well-being among American Indians and Alaska Natives underscores the central place of preventive and promotive efforts in the programmatic landscape (Manson, 1982).

Preventing Mental Illness

Among Indian and Native people, efforts to prevent mental illness have been overshadowed by a much more aggressive agenda in regard to preventing alcohol and drug abuse (May & Moran, 1995). The research literature mirrors a similar emphasis on interventions intended to prevent or ameliorate developmental situations of risk, with special emphasis on family, school, and community (Manson, 1982; Beiser & Manson, 1987; U.S. Congress, 1990).

As discussed earlier, poverty and demoralization combine with rapid cultural change to threaten effective parenting in many Native families. This can lead to increased neglect and abuse and ultimately to the removal of children into foster care and adoption (Piasecki et al., 1989). Poverty, demoralization, and rapid culture change also increase the risk for domestic violence, spousal abuse, and family instability, with their attendant negative mental health effects (Norton & Manson, 1995; Christensen & Manson, 2001). The preventive interventions that have emerged in response to such deleterious circumstances in American Indian communities are particularly creative, in form as well as in reliance upon cultural tradition. One example is the introduction of the indigenous concept of the Whipper Man, a nonparental disciplinarian, into a Northwest tribe's group home for youth in foster care (Shore & Nicholls, 1975). This unique mechanism of social control, coupled with placement counseling and intensive family outreach, significantly enhanced self-esteem, decreased delinquent behavior, and reduced off-reservation referrals (Shore & Keepers, 1982). Another example is a developmental intervention that targeted Navajo family mental health (Dinges et al., 1974). This effort sought to improve stress resistance in Navajo families whose social survival was threatened and to prepare their children to cope with a rapidly changing world. It focused on culturally relevant developmental tasks and the caregiver-child interactions thought to support or increase mastery of these tasks. Delivered through home visits by Navajo staff, the intervention promoted cultur-

al identification, strengthened family ties, and enhanced child and caregiver self-images (Dinges, 1982).

Fueled by longstanding concern regarding the disruptive nature of boarding schools for the emotional development of Indian youth, early prevention programs focused largely on social and cultural enrichment. The most widely known of these early efforts is the Toyei Model Dormitory Project, which improved the ratio of adult dormitory aides to students, replaced non-Navajo houseparents with tribal members, and trained them to be both caretakers and surrogate parents (Goldstein, 1974). As a result, youth in the Toyei model dormitory showed accelerated intellectual development, better emotional adjustment, and superior performance on psychomotor tests. The promise of this approach was slow to be realized, however, in part because of a change in Federal policy away from boarding school education for American Indians and Alaska Natives, and in part because local control over educational settings in Indian communities was rare until recently (Kleinfeld, 1982). Schoolwide interventions only now are emerging in Native communities, as successful litigation and legislative change in funding mechanisms transfer to tribes the authority to manage health and human services, including education (Dorpat, 1994).

Targeted prevention efforts have flourished in tribal and public schools. Most have centered on alcohol and drug use, but a growing number of programs are being designed and implemented with a specific mental health focus, typically suicide prevention (Manson et al., 1989; Duclos & Manson, 1994; Middlebrook et al., 2001). These preventive interventions take into account culture-specific risk factors: lack of cultural and spiritual development, loss of ethnic identity, cultural confusion, and acculturation. Careful evaluation of their effects, though still the exception, illustrates, as in the case of the Zuni Life Skills Development Curriculum, the significant gains that can accompany such investments (LaFromboise & Howard-Pitney, 1994).

With increasing frequency, entire Indian and Native communities have become both the setting and the agent of change in attempts to ameliorate situations of risk and to prevent mental illness. Among the earliest examples is the Tiospaye Project on the Rosebud Sioux Reservation in South Dakota, which entailed organizing a series of community development activities that were cast as the revitalization of the *tiospaye*, an expression of traditional Lakota lifestyle based on extended family, shared responsibility, and reciprocity (Mohatt & Blue, 1982). More recent ones include the Blue Bay Healing Project among the Salish-Kootenai of the Flathead Reservation

(Fleming, 1994) and the Western Athabaskan "Natural Helpers" Program (Serna et al., 1998). Both of these community-based interventions marshaled local cultural resources consistent with long-held tribal traditions, albeit in quite different ways that reflected their distinct orientations. Other nationwide initiatives, such as those mentioned earlier in this chapter, are likewise deeply steeped in the emphasis on community solutions to community problems.

Promoting Mental Health

Indian and Native people are quick to observe that the prevention of mental illness—with its goals of decreasing risk and increasing protection—is defined by a disease-oriented model of care. Although this approach is valued, professionals are encouraged by Indian and Native people to move beyond the exclusive concern with disease models and the separation of mind, body, and spirit, to consider individual as well as collective strengths and means in the promotion of mental health.

There is less clarity about and little common nomenclature for such strengths, their relationship to mental health, and technologies for promoting them than there is for risk, mental illness, and prevention. Even less data exist upon which to base empirical discussions about targets for promotion and outcomes, but there are relevant intellectual histories that suggest this is no quixotic quest. For example, the contemporary literature on psychological well-being has its roots in past work on dimensions of positive mental health and the related concept of happiness (Jahoda, 1958; Bradburn, 1969), which have evolved into the closely related constructs of competence, self-efficacy, mastery, empowerment, and communal coping (David, 1979; Swift & Levin, 1987; Sternberg & Kolligian, 1990; Bandura, 1991). Clear parallels exist between these ideas and central themes for organizing life in Native communities. Consider, for example, the concept of *hozhq* in the Navajo worldview:

> *Kluckhohn identified hozhq as the central idea in Navajo religious thinking. But it is not something that occurs only in ritual song and prayer; it is referred to frequently in everyday speech. A Navajo uses this concept to express his happiness, health, the beauty of his land, and the harmony of his relations with others. It is used in reminding people to be careful and deliberate, and when he says good-bye to someone leaving, he will say hozhqqgo naninaa doo "may you walk or go about according to hozhq." (Witherspoon, 1977)*

Hozhq encompasses the notions of connectedness, reciprocity, balance, and completeness that underpin contextually oriented views of health and well-being (Stokols, 1991). Although the terms of reference vary, this orientation is commonly held across Indian and Native communities. The American Indian and Alaska Native experience may lead to the rediscovery of the fundamental aspects of psychological and social well-being and the mechanisms for their maintenance.

In this regard, as noted in Chapter 1, recent years have seen the development of sophisticated theoretical formulations of the relationships among spirituality, religion, and health. Most work in this area has focused on populations raised in Judeo-Christian traditions and, consequently, measurement approaches generally remain contained within this cultural horizon (The Fetzer Institute & National Institute on Aging, 1999). American Indian and Alaska Native populations, on the other hand, often participate in very different spiritual and religious traditions, which require expanded notions of spirituality and religious practice (Reichard, 1950; Gill, 1982; Hultkrantz, 1990; Vecsey, 1991 Beauvais, 1992; Harrod, 1995; Tafoya & Roeder, 1995; Csordas, 1999). Especially notable here are the importance in many Native traditions of private religious and spiritual practice, an emphasis on individual vision and revelation, ritual action in a world inhabited by multiple spiritual entities, and complex ceremonies that are explicitly oriented to healing. Moreover, many American Indian and Alaska Native people participate in multiple traditions. Traditional tribal and pan-Indian beliefs and practices continue to be influential, especially in help-seeking (Kim & Kwok, 1998; Csordas, 1999; Buchwald et al., 2000; Gurley et al., 2001). Christian religions are also quite important in many Indian communities (Spangler et al., 1997). There is mounting evidence that many Indian people do not see Christianity and traditional practices as incompatible (Csordas, 1999). This dynamic is probably most evident in the Native American Church (NAC), where Christian and Native beliefs coexist (Aberle, 1966; Pascarosa et al., 1976; Vecsey, 1991).

More explicit attention to the connections between spirituality and mental health in Native communities is especially warranted given the nature and type of problems described previously.

Conclusions

As evidenced through history and current socioeconomic realities, American Indian and Alaska Native nations have withstood the consequences of colonialism and of subsequent subjugation by the U.S. Government. Many members of this minority population are regaining control of their lives and rebuilding the health of their communities.

(1) Although relatively little evidence is available, the existing data suggest that American Indian and Alaska Native youth and adults suffer a disproportionate burden of mental health problems compared with other Americans. Because of the unique and painful history of this minority group, many of its members are quite vulnerable. Given the high rates of suicide documented among some segments of this population, they are likely to experience increased need for mental health care as compared with white Americans. Yet, in sharp contrast to other minority groups and the general population, there is a lack of epidemiology and surveillance. This information is needed to understand the nature, extent, and sources of burden to mental health, as well as concomitant disparities. This is true across the developmental lifespan.

(2) Those who are homeless, incarcerated, and victims of trauma are particularly likely to need mental health care. Indian and Native people are overrepresented in these vulnerable groups. It is not known whether they receive mental health care within the institutions intended to serve them, but there appears to be considerable unmet need. Research is needed to understand the paths by which American Indians and Alaska Natives reach these points. Just as important, methods for detecting and managing their mental health are needed in related institutional settings through culturally appropriate ways that both ameliorate their present burden and protect them from the future consequences of adversity.

(3) There is significant comorbidity in regard to mental and substance abuse disorders, notably alcoholism, among both Native youth and adults. There is some indication that disorders occurring together are unlikely to be addressed by most mental health or substance abuse treatment settings. This underscores an important unmet need. Neither philosophies of treatment nor funding streams should preclude the timely and culturally appropriate treatment of such comorbidities, which otherwise threaten successful, lasting intervention.

(4) Little is known about either the use of mental health services by American Indians and Alaska Natives, or whether those who need treatment actually obtain it. However, the available research has important implications. First, practical considerations, such as availability of culturally sensitive providers and accessibility of services through insurance or geographic location, are extremely important for this ethnic group. Second, services for those in greatest need of care may best be provided within targeted settings, such as those serving the homeless, incarcerated, or alcohol dependent. Medical services that provide care for victims of trauma or older primary care patients also hold promise for meeting the needs of a significant portion of this population.

(5) Major changes in the financing and organization of mental health care are underway in American Indian and Alaska Native communities as a consequence of relatively recent policies regarding self-determination. There is limited understanding of these changes, their implications for resources, the resulting continuum of care, or the quality of services. Thus, it is imperative that organizational and financing changes be closely examined with an eye toward the best interests of Native people. It would be a sad legacy to conclude 20 years from now that the assimilationist pressures that proved so devastating in the past have been unwittingly repeated.

(6) The knowledge base underpinning treatment guidelines for mental health care have been built with little specific analysis of their benefit to ethnic minority groups. The evidence behind them is an extrapolation from largely majority clinical populations. This is in spite of the fact that cultural forces are known to be at work in virtually every aspect of psychopathology, from risk to onset, presentation, assessment, treatment response, and relative burden. Moreover, the efficacy of treatment alternatives that may be especially relevant to this population has not yet been examined. Accordingly, clinical research needs to be undertaken to shed light on the applicability and outcomes of treatment recommendations for American Indians and Alaska Natives.

(7) Though long-suppressed by social and political forces, traditional healing practices and spirituality are strongly evident in the lives of American Indians and Alaska Natives. They usually complement, rather than compete with, medical care. The challenge is to find ways to support and strengthen their respective contributions to the health and well-being of those in need. How well this is accomplished depends on advances in the science by which healing practices and spirituality are conceptualized and examined.

(8) Despite the mental health problems that plague Indian and Native people, the majority, though at risk, are free of mental illness. Thus, prevention should remain a high priority. Native voices are clear and unequivocal in this regard; preventive and promotive approaches strike a resonant chord in the hearts of these individuals and their communities. Abundant evidence attests to the creativity of intervention strategies mounted in an attempt to ameliorate situations of developmental risk for mental health problems among American Indians and Alaska Natives. Unfortunately, the current limits of science, notably the conceptualization and measurement of both the culturally defined and relevant points of intervention as well as outcomes, impede the evaluation of these strategies. Here the challenge is to understand how preventive interventions developed in other populations work for the American Indian and Alaska Native population in order to determine what adaptations must be made to improve their cultural fit and effectiveness. Conversely, the country as a whole has a great deal to gain by attending to advances in prevention among American Indians and Alaska Natives, for the lessons learned in these instances may have broader application to all Americans.

(9) Lastly, the individual and collective strengths of Native communities warrant closer, systematic attention. Interventions are needed to promote the strengths, resiliencies, and other psychosocial resources that characterize full, productive, meaningful lives and contribute to their maintenance. New perspectives need to be explored, bending our scientific tools to the task.

American Indian and Alaska Native people speak about a journey as beginning with its initial steps. With respect to mental health, this journey already has begun. Some paths have been well traveled and feel familiar; some paths are new and intriguing; some paths have yet to be marked. It is clear that the Nation can serve as a guide for hastening this journey along certain paths. It is equally clear that the Nation would also do well to watch carefully and follow Native people along the paths that they have emblazoned.

References

Aberle, D. F. (1966). *The Peyote Religion among the Navajo.* Chicago: Aldine.

Ackerson, L. M., Dick, R. W., Manson, S. M., & Baron, A. E. (1990). Depression among American Indian adolescents: Psychometric characteristics of the Inventory to Diagnose Depression. *Journal of the American Academy of Child and Adolescent Psychiatry, 29*, 601–607.

American Psychiatric Association. (1994). *Diagnostic and statistical manual of mental disorders* (4th ed.). Washington, DC: Author.

Aoun, S. L., & Gregory, R. J. (1998). Mental disorders of Eskimos who were seen at a community mental health center in western Alaska. *Psychiatric Services, 49*, 1485–1487.

Bandura, A. (1991). Self-efficacy in physiological activation and health-promoting behavior. In J. Madden (Ed.), *Neurobiology of learning, emotion and affect* (pp. 229–269). New York: Raven Press.

Barlow, A., & Walkup, J. T. (1998). Developing mental health services for Native American children. *Child and Adolescent Psychiatry Clinic of North America, 7*, 555–577.

Baron, A. E., Manson, S. M., & Ackerson, L. M. (1990). Depressive symptomatology in older American Indians with chronic disease. In C. Attkisson & J. Zitch (Eds.), *Screening for depression in primary care* (pp. 217–231) New York: Routledge, Kane.

Basso, K. H. (1996). *Wisdom sits in places: Landscape and language among the Western Apache.* Albuquerque, NM: University of New Mexico Press.

Beals, J., Holmes, T., Ashcraft, M., Fairbank, J., Friedman, M., Jones, M., Schlenger, W., Shore, J., & Manson, S. M. (under review). A comparison of the prevalence of posttraumatic stress disorder across five racially and ethnically distinct samples of Vietnam theater veterans. *Journal of Traumatic Stress.*

Beals, J., Novins, D. K., Mitchell, C., Shore, J. H., & Manson, S. M. (2001). Comorbidity between alcohol abuse/dependence and psychiatric disorders: Prevalence, treatment implications, and new directions among American Indian populations. In P. Mail (Ed.), National Institute on Alcohol Abuse and Alcoholism Monograph. Washington, DC: U. S. Government Printing Office.

Beals, J., Piasecki, J., Nelson, S., Jones, M., Keane, E., Dauphinais, P., Red Shirt, R., Sack, W., & Manson, S. M. (1997). Psychiatric disorder among American Indian adolescents: Prevalence in Northern Plains youth. *Journal of the American Academy of Child and Adolescent Psychiatry, 36*, 1252–1259.

Beauvais, F. (1992). Characteristics of Indian youth and drug use. *American Indian and Alaska Native Mental Health Research, 5*, 50–67.

Beiser, M., & Manson, S. M. (1987). Prevention of emotional and behavioral disorders in North American native children. *Journal of Preventive Psychiatry, 3*, 225–240.

Beiser, M., & Attneave, C. L. (1982). Mental disorder among Native American children: Rates and risk periods for entering treatment. *American Journal of Psychiatry, 139*, 193–198.

Beiser, M., Sack, W., Manson, S. M., Redshirt, R., & Dion, R. (1998). Mental health and the academic performance of First Nations and minority culture children. *American Journal of Orthopsychiatry, 68*, 455–467.

Berger, T. R. (1985). *Village journey: The report of the Alaska Native Review Commission.* Anchorage, AK: The Inuit Circumpolar Conference.

Berkman, L. F., Berkman, C. S., Kasl, S., Freeman, D. H., Jr., Leo, L., Ostfeld, A. M., Cornoni-Huntley, J., & Brody, J. A. (1986). Depressive symptoms in relation to physical health and functioning in the elderly. *American Journal of Epidemiology, 124*, 372–388.

Blum, R. W., Harmon, B., Harris, L., Bergeisen, L., & Resnick, M. D. (1992). American Indian-Alaska Native youth health. *Journal of the American Medical Association, 267*, 1637–1644.

Bradburn, N. M. (1969). *The structure of psychological well-being.* Chicago: Aldine.

Breaux, C., & Ryujin, D. (1999). Use of mental health services by ethnically diverse groups within the United States. *The Clinical Psychologist, 52*, 4–15.

Brookings Institution. (1971). *The problem of Indian administration.* Institute for Government Research. New York: Johnson Reprint.

Brown, E. R., Ojeda, V. D., Wyn, R., & Levan, R. (2000). *Racial and ethnic disparities in access to health insurance and health care.* Los Angeles: UCLA Center for Health Policy Research and The Henry J. Kaiser Family Foundation.

Bryde, J. F. (1971). *Indian students and guidance.* Boston: Houghton Mifflin.

Buchwald, D. S., Beals, J., & Manson, S. M. (2000). Use of traditional healing among Native Americans in a primary care setting. *Medical Care, 38*, 1191–1199.

Buchwald, D. S., Tomita, S., Ashton, S., Furman, R., & Manson, S. M. (2000). Physical abuse of urban Native Americans. *Journal of General Internal Medicine, 15*, 562–564.

Bureau of Justice Statistics. (1999). *American Indians and Crime.* Washington, DC: U. S. Government Printing Office.

Centers for Disease Control and Prevention. (1998). Self-reported frequent mental distress among adults—United States, 1993–1996. *Morbidity and Mortality Weekly Report, 47*, 326–331.

Chafe, W. (1962). Estimates regarding the present speakers of North American Indian languages. *International Journal of American Linguistics, 28*, 162–171.

Chapleski, E. E., Lamphere, J. K., Kaczynski, R., Lichtenberg, P. A., & Dwyer, J. W. (1997). Structure of a depression measure among American Indian elders: Confirmatory factor analysis of the CES–D Scale. *Research on Aging, 19*, 462–485.

Chapleski, E. E., Lichtenberg, P. A., Dwyer, J. W., Youngblade, L. M., & Tsai, P. F. (1997). Morbidity and comorbidity among Great Lakes American Indians: Predictors of functional ability. *Gerontologist, 37*, 588–597.

Chavez, G. F., Cordero, J. F., & Becerra, J. E. (1988). Leading major congenital malformations among minority groups in the United States, 1981–1986. *Morbidity and Mortality Weekly Report*, Centers of Disease Control and Prevention Surveillance Summary, 37, 17–24.

Cheung, F. K., & Snowden, L. R. (1990). Community mental health and ethnic minority populations. *Community Mental Health Journal, 26*, 277–291.

Christensen, M., & Manson, S. M. (2001). Adult attachment as a framework for understanding mental health and American Indian families: A study of three family cases. *American Behavioral Scientist, 44*, 1447-1465.

Costello, E. J., Farmer, E. M., Angold, A., Burns, B. J., & Erkanli, A. (1997). Psychiatric disorders among American Indian and white youth in Appalachia: The Great Smoky Mountains Study. *American Journal of Public Health, 87*, 827–832.

Courtney, M. E., & Barth, R. P. (1996). Pathways of older adolescents out of foster care: Implications for independent living services. *Social Work, 41*, 75–83.

Cross, T. A., Earle, K. A., & Simmons, D. (2000). Child abuse and neglect in Indian country: Policy issues. *Families in Society, 81*, 49–58.

Csordas, T. J. (1999). Ritual healing and the politics of identity in contemporary Navajo society. *American Ethnologist, 26*, 3–23.

Curyto, K. J., Chapleski, E. E., & Lichtenberg, P. A. (1999). Prediction of the presence and stability of depression in the Great Lakes Native American elderly. *Journal of Mental Health & Aging, 5*, 323–340.

Curyto, K. J., Chapleski, E. E., Lichtenberg, P. A., Hodges, E., Kaczynski, R., & Sobeck, J. (1998). Prevalence and prediction of depression in American Indian elderly. *Clinical Gerontologist, 18*, 19–37.

David, H. P. (1979). Healthy family functioning: Cross-cultural perspectives. In P. Ahmed & G. Coelho (Eds.), *Toward a new definition of health: Psychosocial dimensions* (pp. 251–320). New York: Plenum Press.

Deloria, V. (1985). *American Indian Policy in the 20th Century*. Norman, OK: University of Oklahoma Press.

Dinges, N. (1982). Mental health promotion with Navajo families. In S. M. Manson (Ed.), *New directions in prevention among American Indian and Alaska Native communities* (pp. 119–141). Portland, OR: Oregon Health Sciences University.

Dinges, N., Yazzie, M., & Tollefson, G. (1974). Developmental intervention for Navajo family mental health. *Journal of Personnel and Guidance Psychology, 52*, 390–395.

Dorpat, N. (1994). PRIDE: Substance abuse education/intervention program. In C. W. Duclos & S. M. Manson (Eds.), *Calling from the rim: Suicidal behavior among American Indian and Alaska Native adolescents* (pp. 122–133). Boulder, CO: University Press of Colorado.

Duclos, C. W., Beals, J., Novins, D. K., Martin, C., Jewett, C. S., & Manson, S. M. (1998). Prevalence of common psychiatric disorders among American Indian adolescent detainees. *Journal of the American Academy of Child and Adolescent Psychiatry, 37*, 866–873.

Duclos, C. W., & Manson, S. M. (Eds.) (1994). *Calling from the rim: Suicidal behavior among American Indian and Alaska Native adolescents*. Boulder, CO: University Press of Colorado.

Fetzer Institute and the National Institute on Aging. (1999). *Measurement of religiousness and spirituality*. Kalamazoo, MI: Author.

Fischler, R. S. (1985). Child abuse and neglect in American Indian communities. *Child Abuse and Neglect, 9*, 95–106.

Fleming, C. M. (1992). American Indians and Alaska Natives: Changing societies past and present. In M. A. Orlandi, R. Weston, & L. G. Epstein. (Eds.), *Cultural competence for evaluators: A guide for alcohol and other drug abuse prevention practitioners working with ethnic/racial communities* (OSAP cultural competence series 1, pp. 147–171). Rockville, MD: U. S. Department of Health & Human Services.

Fleming, C. M. (1994). The Blue Bay Healing Center: Community development and healing as prevention. In C. W. Duclos & S. M. Manson (Eds.), *Calling from the rim: Suicidal behavior among American Indian and Alaska Native adolescents* (pp. 134–166). Boulder, CO: University Press of Colorado.

Fleming, C. M. (1996). Cultural formulation of psychiatric diagnosis. Case No. 01. An American Indian woman suffering from depression, alcoholism and childhood trauma. *Culture, Medicine & Psychiatry, 20*, 145–154.

Fleming, J. E., & Offord, D. R. (1990). Epidemiology of childhood depressive disorders: A critical review. *Journal of the American Academy of Child and Adolescent Psychiatry, 29*, 571–580.

Foulks, E. F., & Katz, S. (1973). The mental health of Alaskan natives. *Acta Psychiatrica Scandinavica, 49*, 91–96.

Gessner, B. D. (1997). Temporal trends and geographic patterns of teen suicide in Alaska, 1979–1993. *Suicide and Life Threatening Behavior, 27*, 264–273.

Gill, S. D. (1982). *Native American religions: An introduction*. Belmont, CA: Wadsworth.

Goldstein, G. (1974). The model dormitory project. *Psychiatric Annals, 4* (9), 85–92.

Goldwasser, H. D., & Badger, L. W. (1989). Utility of the psychiatric screen among the Navajo of Chinle: A fourth-year clerkship experience. *American Indian Alaska Native Mental Health Research, 3*, 6–15.

Grant Makers in Health. (1998). *Eliminating racial and ethnic disparities in health*. Washington, DC: Author.

Gurley, D., Novins, D. K., Jones, M. C., Beals, J., Shore, J. H., & Manson, S. M. (2001). Comparative use of biomedical services and traditional health options by American Indian veterans. *Psychiatric Services, 52,* 68–74.

Hamley, J. L. (1994). *Cultural genocide in the classroom: A History of the federal boarding school movement in American Indian education, 1875–1920.* Unpublished doctoral dissertation, Harvard Graduate School of Education, Cambridge, MA.

Haviland, M. G., Horswell, R. K., O'Connell, J. J., & Dynneson, V. V. (1983). Native American college students' preference for counselor race and sex and the likelihood of their use of a counseling center. *Journal of Counseling Psychology, 30,* 267–270.

Harrod, H. L. (1995). *Becoming and remaining a people: Native American religions on the Northern Plains.* Tucson, AZ: University of Arizona Press.

Horejsi, C., Craig, B. H. R., & Pablo, J. (1992). Reactions by Native American parents to child protection agencies: Cultural and community factors. *Child Welfare, 71,* 329–342.

Hultkrantz, A. (1990). A decade of progress: Works on North American Indian religions in the 1980s. In C. Vecsey (Ed.), *Religion in Native North America* (pp. 167–201). Moscow, ID: University of Idaho Press.

Indian Health Service. (1996). *Appendix I: HHS Department Organization.* Retrieved June 26, 2001, from http://hhs.gov/hhsplan/apol.html.

Indian Health Service. (1997). 1997 *Trends in Indian Health.* Rockville, MD: Author.

Indian Health Service. (2001). *Urban Indian health.* Rockville, MD: Author.

Institute of Medicine. (1994). Reducing risks for mental disorders: *Frontiers for preventive intervention research.* Washington, DC: National Academy Press.

Irwin, M. H., & Roll, S. (1995). The psychological impact of sexual abuse of Native American boarding-school children. *Journal of the American Academy of Psychoanalysis, 23,* 461–473.

Jahoda, M. (1958). *Current concepts of positive mental health.* New York: Basic Books.

Johnson, R., Manson, S., Shore, J. H., Heinz, J., & Williams, M. (1992). Psychiatric epidemiology of an Indian village. A 19-year replication study. Journal of Nervous Mental Disorders, 180, 33–39.

Jones, M. C., Dauphinais, P., Sack, W. H., & Somervell, P. D. (1997). Trauma-related symptomatology among American Indian adolescents. *Journal of Traumatic Stress, 10,* 163–173.

Kaiser Commission on Medicaid and the Uninsured. (2000). *Health insurance coverage and access to care among American Indians and Alaska Natives.* Washington, DC: The Henry J. Kaiser Family Foundation.

Kasprow, W. J., & Rosenheck, R. (1998). Substance use and psychiatric problems of homeless Native American veterans. *Psychiatric Services, 49,* 345–350.

Kessler, R. C., Sonnega, A., Bromet, E., Hughes, M., & Nelson, C. B. (1995). Posttraumatic stress disorder in the National Comorbidity Survey. *Archives of General Psychiatry, 52,* 1048–1060.

Kettle, P. A., & Bixler, E. O. (1991). Suicide in Alaskan Natives, 1979–1984. *Psychiatry, 54,* 55–63.

Kim, C., & Kwok, Y. S. (1998). Navajo use of native healers. *Archives of Internal Medicine, 158,* 2245–2249.

Kinzie, J. D., & Manson, S. M. (1987). Self-rating scales in cross-cultural psychiatry. *Hospital and Community Psychiatry, 38,* 190–196.

Kleinfeld, J. (1973). *A long way from home: Effects of public high schools on village children away from home.* Fairbanks, Alaska: Center for Northern Educational Research and Institute of Social, Economic, and Government Research.

Kleinfeld, J. (1982). Getting it together at adolescence: Case studies of positive socializing environments for Eskimo youth. In S. M. Manson (Ed.), *New directions in prevention among American Indian and Alaska Native communities* (pp. 341–364). Portland, OR: Oregon Health Sciences University.

Kleinfeld, J., & Bloom, J. (1977). Boarding schools: Effects on the mental health of Eskimo adolescents. *American Journal of Psychiatry, 134,* 411–417.

Kluckhohn. (1968).

Koegel, P., Burnam, M. A., & Farr, R. K. (1988). The prevalence of specific psychiatric disorders among homeless individuals in the inner city of Los Angeles. *Archives of General Psychiatry, 45,* 1085–1092.

Koegel, P., Melamid, E., & Burnam, M. A. (1995). Childhood risk factors for homelessness among homeless adults. *American Journal of Public Health, 85,* 1642–1649.

Kramer, B. J. (1991). Urban American Indian aging. *Journal of Cross Cultural Gerontology, 6,* 205–217.

Kulka, R. A., Fairbank, J. A., Jordan, B. K., Weiss, D., & Cranston, A. (1990). *Trauma and the Vietnam War generation: Report of findings from the National Vietnam Veterans Readjustment Study.* New York: Brunner/Mazel.

Kunitz, S. J., Gabriel, K. R., Levy, J. E., Henderson, E., Lampert, K., McCloskey, J., Quintero, G., Russell, S., & Vince, A. (1999). Risk factors for conduct disorder among Navajo Indian men and women. *Social Psychiatry and Psychiatric Epidemiology, 34,* 180–189.

LaFromboise, T. D., & Howard-Pitney, B. (1994). The Zuni Life Skills Development curriculum: A collaborative approach to curriculum development. In C. W. Duclos & S. M. Manson (Eds.), *Calling from the rim: Suicidal behavior among American Indian and Alaska Native adolescents* (pp. 98–121). Boulder, CO: University Press of Colorado.

Lewinsohn, P. M., Hops, H., Roberts, R. E., Seeley, J. R., & Andrews, J. A. (1993). Adolescent psychopathology: Prevalence and incidence of depression and other DSM–III–R disorders in high school students. *Journal of Abnormal Psychology, 102,*133–144.

Manderscheid, R. W., & Henderson, M. J., (Eds.). (1998). *Mental Health, United States, 1998.* Rockville, MD: Center for Mental Health Services.

Manson, S. M. (Ed.). (1982). *New directions in prevention among American Indian and Alaska Native communities.* Portland, OR: Oregon Health Sciences University.

Manson, S. M. (1992). Long-term care of older American Indians: Challenges in the development of institutional services. In C. Barresi & D. E. Stull (Eds.), *Ethnicity and long-term care* (pp. 130–143). New York: Springer.

Manson, S. M. (1994). Culture and depression: Discovering variations in the experience of illness. In W. J. Lonner & R. S. Malpass (Eds.), *Psychology and culture* (pp. 285–290). Needham, MA: Allyn and Bacon.

Manson, S. M. (1996a). Cross-cultural and multi-ethnic assessment of trauma. In J. P. Wilson & T. M. Keane (Eds.), *Assessing psychological trauma and PTSD: A handbook for practitioners* (pp. 239–266). New York: Guilford Press.

Manson, S. M. (1996b). The wounded spirit: A cultural formulation of post-traumatic stress disorder. *Culture, Medicine and Psychiatry, 20,* 489–498.

Manson, S. M. (1997) Ethnographic methods, cultural context, and mental illness: Bridging different ways of knowing and experience. *Ethos, 25,* 249–258.

Manson, S. M. (2000). Mental health services for American Indians: Need, use, and barriers to effective care. *Canadian Journal of Psychiatry, 45,* 617–626.

Manson, S. M., Ackerson, L. M., Dick, R. W., Baron, A. E., & Fleming, C. M. (1990). Depressive symptoms among American Indian adolescents: Psychometric characteristics of the Center for Epidemiologic Studies Depression Scale (CES–D). *Psychological Assessment, 2,* 231–237.

Manson, S. M., Beals, J., Dick, R., & Duclos, C. (1989). Risk factors for suicide among Indian adolescents at a boarding school. *Public Health Reports, 104,* 609–614.

Manson, S. M., & Brenneman, D. L. (1995). Chronic disease among older American Indians: Preventing depression and related problems of coping. In D. Padgett (Ed.), *Handbook on ethnicity, aging, and mental health* (pp. 284–303). Westport, CT: Greenwood Press.

Manson, S. M., & Callaway, D. (1988). Health and aging among American Indians: Issues and challenges for the biobehavioral sciences. In S. M. Manson & N. Dinges (Eds.), *Behavioral health issues among American Indians and Alaska Natives* (pp. 160–210). Denver, CO: University of Colorado Health Sciences Center.

Manson, S. M., & Kleinman, A. (1998). DSM–IV, culture, and mood disorders: A critical reflection on recent progress. *Transcultural Psychiatry, 35,* 377–386.

Manson, S. M., Shore, J. H., & Bloom, J. D. (1985). The depressive experience in American Indian communities: A challenge for psychiatric theory and diagnosis. In A. Kleinman & B. Good (Eds.), *Culture and depression* (pp. 331–368). Berkeley, CA: University of California Press.

Marbella, A. M., Harris, M. C., Diehr, S., Ignace, G., & Ignace, G. (1998). Use of Native American healers among Native American patients in an urban Native American health center. *Archives of Family Medicine, 7,* 182–185.

May, P. A. (1990). A bibliography on suicide and suicide attempts among American Indians and Alaska Natives. *Omega, 21,* 199–214.

May, P. A., Hymbaugh, K. J., Aase, J. M., & Samet, J. M. (1983). Epidemiology of fetal alcohol syndrome among American Indians of the Southwest. *Social Biology, 30,* 374–387.

May, P. A, & Moran, J. R. (1995). Prevention of alcohol misuse: A review of health promotion efforts among American Indians. *American Journal of Health Promotion, 9,* 288–299.

McLeod, J. D., & Kessler, R. C. (1990). Socioeconomic status differences in vulnerabilty to undesirable life events. *Journal of Health and Social Behavior, 31,* 162–172.

Mezzich, J. E., Kirmayer, L. J., Kleinman, A., Fabrega, H., Parron, D. L., Good, B. J., Lin, K., & Manson, S. M. (1999). The place of culture in DSM–IV. *Journal of Nervous and Mental Disease, 187,* 457–464.

Middlebrook, D., LeMaster, P., Beals, J., Novins, D., Manson, S. (2001). Suicide prevention in American Indian and Alaska Native communities: A critical review of programs. *Suicide and Life-Threatening Behavior, 31* (Suppl.), 132–139.

Mitchell, C. M., O'Nell, T. D., Beals, J., Dick, R., Keane, E., & Manson, S. M. (1995). Dimensionality of alcohol use among American Indian adolescents: Latent structure, construct validity, and implications for development research. *Journal of Research on Adolescence, 6,* 151–180.

Mock, C. N., Grossman, D. C., Mulder, D., Stewart, C., & Koepsell, T. S. (1996). Health care utilization as a marker for suicidal behavior on an American Indian reservation. *Journal of General Internal Medicine, 11,* 519–524.

Mohatt, G., & Blue, A. W. (1982). Primary prevention as it relates to traditionality and empirical measures of social deviance. In S. M. Manson (Ed.), *New directions in prevention among American Indian and Alaska Native communities* (pp. 91–116). Portland, OR: Oregon Health Sciences University.

Murphy, J., & Hughes, C. (1965). The use of psychophysiological symptoms as indicators of disorder among Eskimos. In J. Murphy & A. Leighton (Eds.), *Approaches to Cross-Cultural Psychiatry.* (pp. 108–160). Ithaca, NY: Cornell University Press.

National Center for Health Statistics. (1999). Infant mortality rates vary by race and ethnicity. Retrieved May 10, 2001, from http://www.cdc.gov/nchs/releases/99facts/99sheets/infmort.htm.

National Center for Post-Traumatic Stress Disorder & the National Center for American Indian and Alaska Native Mental Health Research. (1996). *Matsunaga Vietnam Veterans Project.* White River Junction, VT: Author.

National Resource Center on Child Sexual Abuse. (1990). *Enhancing child sexual abuse services to minority cultures.* Huntsville, AL: Author.

Nelson, K., Cross, T., Landsman, M., & Tyler, M. (1996). Native American families and child neglect. Children and *Youth Services Review, 18,* 505–522.

Nelson, S., & Manson, S. M. (2000). Mental health and mental disorder. In E. R. Rhoades, (Ed.), *The Health of American Indians and Alaska Natives* (pp. 311–327). Baltimore: Johns Hopkins University Press.

Norton, I. M., & Manson, S. M. (1995). The silent minority: Battered American Indian women. *Journal of Family Violence, 10,* 307–318

Novins, D. K. (1999). Results of mental health needs assessments performed by four urban American Indian organizations. *American Indian and Alaska Native Mental Health Research, 8* (3), vi–iv.

Novins, D. K., Beals, J., Roberts, R., & Manson, S. M. (1999). Factors associated with suicidal ideation among American Indian adolescents: Does culture matter? *Journal of Suicide and Life-Threatening Behavior, 29,* 332–345.

Novins, D. K., Beals, J., Sack, W. H., & Manson, S. M. (2000). Unmet needs for substance abuse and mental health services among Northern Plains American Indian adolescents. *Psychiatric Services, 51,* 1045–1047.

Novins, D. K., Bechtold, D. W., Sack, W. H., Thompson, J., Carter, D. R., & Manson, S. M. (1997). The DSM–IV Outline for Cultural Formulation: A critical demonstration with American Indian children. *Journal of the American Academy of Child and Adolescent Psychiatry, 36,* 1244–1251.

Novins, D. K., Duclos, C. W., Martin, C., Jewett, C. S., & Manson, S. M. (1999). Utilization of alcohol, drug, and mental health treatment services among American Indian adolescent detainees. *Journal of the American Academy of Child and Adolescent Psychiatry, 38,* 1102–1108.

Novins, D. K., Fleming, C. M., Beals, J., & Manson, S. M. (2000). Quality of alcohol, drug, and mental health services for *American Indian children and adolescents. American Journal of Medical Quality, 15,* 148–156.

Novins, D. K., Plunkett, M., & Beals, J. (under review). Sequences of substance use among American Indian adolescents. *Journal of the American Academy of Child and Adolescent Psychiatry.*

Oetting, E. R., Swaim, R. C., Edwards, W. R., & Beauvais, F. (1989). Indian and Anglo adolescent alcohol use and emotional distress: Path models. *American Journal of Drug and Alcohol Abuse, 15,* 153–172.

O'Nell, T. D. (1998). Cultural formulation of psychiatric diagnosis. Psychotic depression and alcoholism in an American Indian man. *Culture, Medicine & Psychiatry, 22,* 123–136.

O'Sullivan, M. J., Peterson, P. D., Cox, G. B., & Kirkeby, J. (1989). Ethnic populations: Community mental health services ten years later. *American Journal of Community Psychology, 17,* 17–30.

Pascarosa, P., Futterman, S., & Halsweig, M. (1976). Observations of alcoholics in the peyote ritual: A pilot study. *Annals of the New York Academy of Sciences, 273,* 518–524.

Passel, J. S. (1996). The growing American Indian population, 1960–1990: Beyond demography. In G. Sandefur, R. R. Rindfuss, & B. Cohen (Eds.), *Changing numbers, changing needs: American Indian demography and public health* (pp. 79–102). Washington, DC: National Academy Press.

Piasecki, J. M., Manson, S. M., Biernoff, M. P., Hiat, A. B., Taylor, S. S., & Bechtold, D. W. (1989). Abuse and neglect of American Indian children: Findings from a survey of federal providers. *American Indian and Alaska Native Mental Health Research, 3,* 43–62.

Plunkett, M., & Mitchell, C. M. (2000). Substance use among American Indian adolescents: Regional comparisons with monitoring the future high school seniors. *Journal of Drug Issues, 30,* 575–591.

Population Reference Bureau. (2000). *2000 United States Population Data Sheet* [Wall chart]. Washington, DC: Author.

Reichard, G. A. (1950). Navaho religion: *A study of symbolism.* Princeton, NJ: Princeton University Press.

Reimer, C. S. (1999). *Counseling the Inupiat Eskimos.* Westport, CT: Greenwood Press.

Resnick, M. D., Bearman, P. S., Blum, R. W., Bauman, K. E., Harris, K. M., Jones, J., Tabor, J., Beuhring, T., Sieving, R. E., Shew, M., Ireland, M., Bearinger, L. H., & Udry, J. R. (1997). Protecting adolescents from harm: Findings from the National Longitudinal Study on Adolescent Health. *Journal of the American Medical Association, 278,* 823–832.

Robin, R. W., Chester, B., Rasmussen, J. K., Jaranson, J. M., & Goldman, D. (1997a). *Prevalence, characteristics, and impact of childhood sexual abuse in a Southwestern American Indian tribe. Child Abuse and Neglect, 21,* 769–787.

Robin, R. W., Chester, B., Rasmussen, J. K., Jaranson, J. M., Goldman, D. (1997b). Prevalence and characteristics of trauma and posttraumatic stress disorder in a southwestern American Indian community. *American Journal of Psychiatry, 154,* 1582–1588.

Rodenhauser, P. (1994). Cultural barriers to mental health care delivery in Alaska. *Journal of Mental Health Administration, 21,* 60–70.

Roll, S. (1998). Cross-cultural considerations in custody and parenting plans. *Child & Adolescent Psychiatric Clinics of North America, 7,* 445–54.

Rural Policy Research Institute. (1999). Retrieved July 12, 2001, from http://www.rupri.org/policyres/rnumbers/demopop/demo.html.

Sack, W. H., Beiser, M., Baker-Brown, G., & Redshirt, R. (1994). Depressive and suicidal symptoms in Indian school children: Findings from the Flower of Two Soils. American Indian Alaska Native Mental Health Research Monograph Series, 4 (4), 81–96.

Sampath, H. M. (1974). Prevalence of psychiatric disorders in a Southern Baffin Island Eskimo settlement. *Canadian Psychiatric Association Journal, 19,* 363–367.

Serna, P., May, P. A., Sitaker, M., Indian Health Service, Centers for Disease Control and Prevention. (1998). Suicide prevention evaluation in a Western Athabaskan American Indian tribe—New Mexico, 1988–1997. *Morbidity and Mortality Weekly, 47,* 257–261.

Shaffer, D., Fisher, P., Dulcan, M. K., Davies, M., Piacentini, J., Schwab-Stone, M. E., Lahey, B. B., Bourdon, K., Jensen, P. S., Bird, H. R., Canino, G., & Regier, D. A. (1996). The NIMH Diagnostic Interview Schedule for Children Version 2.3 (DISC–2.3): Description, acceptability, prevalence rates, and performance in the MECA study. *Journal of American Academy of Child Adolescent Psychiatry, 35,* 865–877.

Shore, J. H., & Keepers, G. (1982). Examples of evaluation research in delivering preventive mental health services to Indian youth. In S.M. Manson (Ed.), *New directions in prevention among American Indian and Alaska Native communities* (pp. 325–337). Portland, OR: Oregon Health Sciences University.

Shore, J. H., Kinzie, J. D., Hampson, J. L., & Pattison, E. M. (1973). Psychiatric epidemiology of an Indian village. *Psychiatry, 36,* 70–81.

Shore, J. H., & Nicholls, W. M. (1975). Indian children and tribal group homes: New interpretations of the Whipper Man. *American Journal of Psychiatry, 132,* 454–456.

Snowden, L. R., & Cheung, F. K. (1990). Use of inpatient mental health services by members of ethnic minority groups. *American Psychologist, 45,* 347–355.

Somervell, P. D., Beals, J., Kinzie, J. D., Leung, P., Boehnlein, J., Matsunaga, D., & Manson, S. M. (1993). Use of the CES-D in an American Indian village. *Culture, Medicine and Psychiatry, 16,* 503–517.

Spangler, J. G., Bell, R. A., Dignan, M. B., & Michielutte, R. (1997). Prevalence and predictors of tobacco use among Lumbee Indian women in Robeson County, North Carolina. *Journal of Community Health, 22,* 115–125.

Special Subcommittee on Indian Education, Senate Committee on Labor and Public Welfare. (1969). *Indian education: A national tragedy, a national challenge* (Senate report 91–501). Washington, DC: U.S. Senate.

Sternberg, R. J., & Kolligian, J., Jr. (1990). *Competence considered.* New Haven, CT: Yale University Press.

Stokols, D. (1991). *Establishing and maintaining healthy environments: Toward a social ecology of health promotion*. Wellness Lecture Series. Berkeley, CA: University of California Press.

Stratton, K., Howe, C., & Battaglia, F. C. (1996). *Fetal alcohol syndrome: Diagnosis, epidemiology, prevention, and treatment*. Washington, DC: Institute of Medicine.

Streissguth, A. P., Aase, J. M., Clarren, S. K., Randels, S. P., LaDue, R. A., & Smith, D. F. (1991). Fetal alcohol syndrome in adolescents and adults. *Journal of the American Medical Association, 265*, 1961–1967.

Strickland, C. J. (1999). Conducting focus groups cross-culturally: Experiences with Pacific Northwest Indian people. *Public Health Nursing, 16*, 190–197.

Sue, S. (1977). Community mental health services to minority mroups: Some optimism, some pessimism. *American Psychologist, 32*, 616–624.

Swift, C., & Levin, G. (1987). Empowerment: An emerging mental health technology. *Journal of Primary Prevention, 8*, 71–94.

Tafoya, T., & Roeder, K. R. (1995). Spiritual exiles in their own homelands: Gays, lesbians and Native Americans. *Journal of Chemical Dependency Treatment, 5*, 179–197.

Thornton, R. (1987). *American Indian holocaust and survival: A population history since 1492*. Norman, OK: University of Oklahoma Press.

Todd-Bazemore, E. (1999). Cultural issues in psychopharmacology: Integrating medication treatment with Lakota Sioux traditions. *Journal of Clinical Psychology in Medical Settings, 6*, 139–150.

Trimble, J. E., Manson, S. M., Dinges, N. G., & Medicine, B. (1984). Towards an understanding of American Indian concepts of mental health: Some reflections and directions. In P. Pederson, N. Sartorius, & A. Marsala (Eds.), *Mental Health Services: The cross cultural context*. (pp. 199–220). Beverly Hills, CA: Sage.

U.S. Census Bureau. (1993). We, the First Americans. Retrieved July 25, 2001, from http://minneapolisfed.org/pubs/cd/98-sum/WeFirst.html.

U.S. Census Bureau. (1999a). *National Survey of Homeless Assistance Providers and Clients*. Retrieved June 26, 2001, from http://www.census.gov/prod/www/nshapc/nshapc4.html.

U.S. Census Bureau. (1999b). *Statistical Abstract of the United States:* The National Data Book. Washington, DC: Author.

U.S. Census Bureau (2001). *Overview of race and Hispanic origin* (Census 2000 Brief No. C2KBR/01-1). Washington, DC: Author.

U.S. Department of Health and Human Services. (1999). *The AFCARS Report: Current estimates as of January 1999*. Rockville, MD: Author.

U.S. Congress. (1990). *Indian adolescent mental health*. Washington, DC: Office of Technology Assessment.

U.S. Department of Health and Human Services. (1999). T*he Surgeon General's Call to Action to Prevent Suicide*. Rockville, MD: Author.

U. S. Bureau of Justice Statistics. (1999). *American Indians and crime*. Washington, DC: United States Government Printing Office.

Vecsey, C. (1991). Imagine ourselves richly: *Mythic narratives of North American Indians*. New York: Harper Collins.

Westermeyer, J. (1982). Alcoholism and services for ethnic populations. In E. Pattison & E. Kaufman (Eds.), *Encyclopedic Handbook of Alcoholism* (pp. 709–717). New York: Gardner Press.

Westermeyer, J., & Peake, E. (1983). A ten year follow-up of alcoholic Native Americans in Minnesota. *American Journal of Psychiatry, 140*, 189–194.

Whittaker, J. O. (1982). Alcohol and the Standing Rock Sioux tribe: A twenty-year follow up study. *Journal of the Study of Alcohol, 43*, 191–200.

Witherspoon, G. (1977). *Language and art in the Navajo universe* (p. 47). Ann Arbor, MI: University of Michigan Press.

Yates, A. (1987). Current status and future directions of research on the American Indian child. *American Journal of Psychiatry, 144*, 1135–1142.

CHAPTER 5
MENTAL HEALTH CARE FOR
ASIAN AMERICANS AND PACIFIC ISLANDERS

Contents

Contents, *continued*

MENTAL HEALTH CARE FOR ASIAN AMERICANS AND PACIFIC ISLANDERS

Introduction

Asian Americans and Pacific Islanders (AA/PIs) are diverse in ethnicity (See Figure 5-1) and in their historical experiences in the United States. As many as 43 different ethnic groups (Lee, 1998) have struggled as immigrants, refugees, or American-born Asian Americans to overcome prejudice and discrimination on the path to achievements ranging from the building of the first transcontinental railroad to innovations in medicine and technology. Asian immigrants now account for about 4 percent of the U. S. population. The majority of AA/PIs were born overseas (See Figure 5-2), and Asian Americans constitute more than one-quarter of the foreign-born population in the United States.

AA/PIs are a fast-growing racial group in the United States. The population grew 95 percent from 3.7 in 1980 to 7.2 in 1990. From 1990 to 2000[1], the number of people identifying as Asian American, or Native Hawaiian or Other Pacific Islander grew another 44 percent to 10 million for Asian Americans and 350,000 for Native Hawaiian or Other Pacific Islander (U.S. Census Bureau, 2001b). It is projected that by the year 2020, the combined AA/PI population will reach approximately 20 million, or about 6 percent of the total U.S. population. American-born Asian and Pacific Island Americans will outnumber the foreign-born ones by 2020 (U.S. Census Bureau, 2000).

Given the high proportion of recent immigrants, Asian Americans and Pacific Islanders in the United States have, as a group, great linguistic diversity. They speak over 100 languages and dialects. Estimates from reports covering the 1990s indicate that 35 percent of Asian Americans and Pacific Islanders live in linguistically isolated households, where no one age 14 or older speaks English "very well." For some Asian American ethnic groups, this rate is much higher. For example, 61 percent of Hmong American, 56 percent of Cambodian American, 52 percent of Laotian American, 44 percent of Vietnamese American, 41 percent of Korean American, and 40 percent of Chinese American households are linguistically isolated (President's Advisory Commission on Asian Americans and Pacific Islanders, 2001).

Historical Context

Asian Americans

The Chinese were among the first Asians to come to the United States. Small numbers came as early as the late 1700s on trade and educational missions, but the discovery of gold in California brought 300,000 more Chinese immigrants between 1848 and 1882 (Huang, 1991). Most were indentured to work in the mining and railroad industries. Later in the 1800s, Japanese immigrants filled the need for cheap contract laborers on Hawaiian sugar plantations. Many left Hawaii and settled in California, where they contributed substantially to the state's agricultural success. Then the U.S. Government began passing various laws to strictly control the flow of Asian immigrants and restrict their rights. For example, the Chinese Exclusion Act of 1882 limited the admission of unskilled Chinese workers. In 1907 and 1908, a Gentlemen's Agreement placed similar limits on Japanese and Koreans, and in 1917, another Immigration Act restricted the entry of Asian Indians. In response to a growing population of Filipino immigrants who worked as daily wage laborers in California agriculture, the Tydings-McDuffie Act of 1934 denied entry to Filipinos. During World War II, President Franklin Roosevelt signed Executive Order 9066, which incarcerated over 120,000 people of Japanese heritage, including more than 70,000 U.S.-born citizens, in internment camps and Federal prisons. This order was a reaction to the public's strong anti-Japanese sentiment and to mistaken beliefs that Japanese Americans presented a threat to national security during the War.

With the passage of the 1965 Immigration Act, which favored family reunification and discouraged systematic discrimination against Asians, Asian immigra-

---

[1] Because the Office of Management and Budget has separated Asian Americans from Native Hawaiians and Other Pacific Islanders (OMB, 2000), Census 2000 lists "Asian" and "Native Hawaiian and Other Pacific Islander" as separate racial categories.

Figure 5-1

Percent Distribution of the Asian American and Pacific Islander Population by Subgroup: 2000

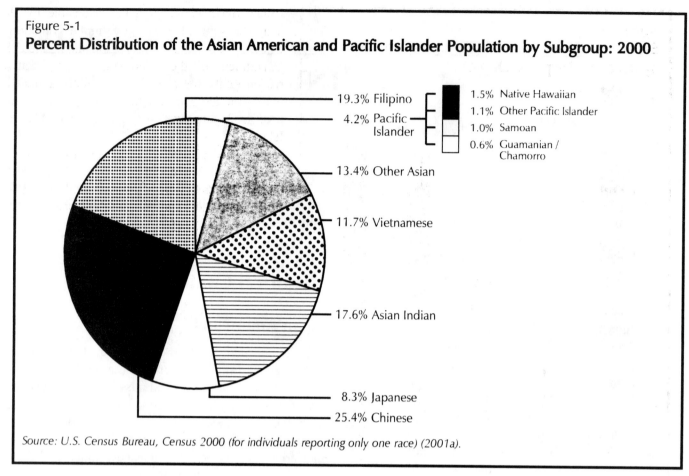

19.3% Filipino

4.2% Pacific Islander

13.4% Other Asian

11.7% Vietnamese

17.6% Asian Indian

8.3% Japanese

25.4% Chinese

1.5% Native Hawaiian

1.1% Other Pacific Islander

1.0% Samoan

0.6% Guamanian / Chamorro

Source: U.S. Census Bureau, Census 2000 (for individuals reporting only one race) (2001a).

tion to the United States grew rapidly. While Asians comprised less than 7 percent of total immigrants to the United States in 1965, they accounted for nearly 25 percent in 1970. In 1971, new legislation eliminated all quotas on countries of origin and replaced them with a general limit of 290,000 immigrants a year. Although the proportion of Asian immigration to the United States is now relatively large, it must be noted that Asians comprise about 60 percent of the world's population.

Today immigrants come from China, India, the Philippines, Vietnam, Korea, and other Asian countries in search of better educational and economic opportunities. For example, most Korean Americans are not American-born descendants of the first wave of immigration from the early 1900s. Rather, they are part of the tens of thousands of immigrants that have entered the United States every year since 1965. Similar numbers of Filipinos have immigrated annually since 1965, so most Korean and Filipino Americans today are first or second generation. Because of the U.S. military presence in the Philippines until 1992, Filipino immigrants are more likely than other Asian immigrants to be acculturated to American ways and to speak English. During the late 1970s and 1980s, many Southeast Asian refugees from

Vietnam, Cambodia, and Laos were accepted by the United States for political and humanitarian reasons. This brief history of Asian immigration reveals the heterogeneity of the Asian American population in the United States.

Pacific Islanders

Unlike Asian Americans, most Pacific Islanders are not immigrants, but are descendants of the original inhabitants of land claimed by the United States. Thus, Pacific Islanders share the history of American Indians and Alaska Natives, whose lives dramatically changed upon contact with various European explorers. In the late 1760s, for example, Captain James Cook and his crew arrived in Hawaii and brought with them formerly unknown diseases that devastated much of the indigenous population. By the late 1840s, after colonists had taken and redistributed the land in Hawaii, American missionaries and businessmen controlled most of the land and trade of these islands. A similar fate befell the Tongans. When Cook discovered the Tonga islands in 1773, English missionaries followed. Tonga became a British protectorate in 1900 and gained its independence in 1970.

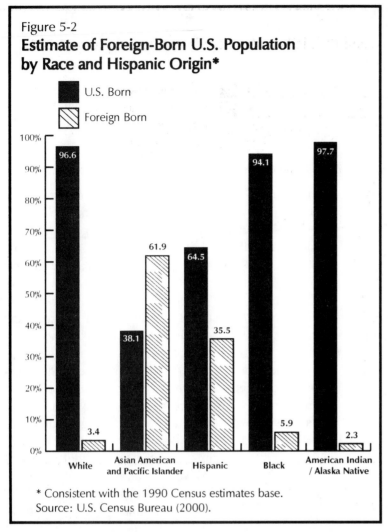

Figure 5-2

Estimate of Foreign-Born U.S. Population by Race and Hispanic Origin*

* Consistent with the 1990 Census estimates base.
Source: U.S. Census Bureau (2000).

United States. Each area is responsible for the administration of local government functions. Under the Compacts of Free Association, the U.S. Department of the Interior has administrative responsibility for coordinating Federal policy in the Pacific territories of American Samoa, Guam, and the Commonwealth of the Northern Mariana Islands, where most residents have U.S. citizenship. The Department of Interior also has oversight of Federal programs and funds in the freely associated states of the Federated States of Micronesia, the Republic of the Marshall Islands, and the Republic of Palau.

Current Status

Asian Americans and Pacific Islanders represent very diverse populations in terms of ethnicity, language, culture, education, income level, English proficiency, and sociopolitical experience. Although cultural ties exist among the different AA/PI communities, it is important to recognize the differences among the groups.

Geographic Distribution

Asian Americans and Pacific Islanders are heavily concentrated in the western United States; more than half of this group (54%) lived in the West in 2000 (U.S Census Bureau, 2001b). However, a good number of AA/PIs also live in the South (17%) and Northeast (18%). A growing number of AA/PIs live in the Midwest (11%). One reason for this distribution is that some Asian Americans are descendants of the Chinese laborers who came in the mid-1800s to work on the transcontinental railroad. Other Asian Americans are descendants of the Japanese immigrants who came to California in the late 19th and early 20th centuries. Since 1965, when Asians began arriving in greater numbers, more entered the United States through New York as well as California. According to 1997 data, 37 percent of all Asian Americans and Pacific Islanders lived in California, 10 percent lived in New York, and 7 percent lived in Hawaii (Population Reference Bureau, 1999).

The largest proportion of nearly every major Asian American ethnic group lives in California. The 1990 census showed that three-fifths of Chinese Americans lived in California or New York, while about two-thirds of Filipinos and Japanese lived in California and Hawaii. Asian Indian (or South Asians) and Korean populations are somewhat less concentrated geographically, although

Guam was under U.S. Navy control from the time it was acquired during the Spanish American War in 1898 until its transfer to the Office of Insular Affairs in 1950. American Samoa was ceded to the United States in 1900 and transferred to the Office of Insular Affairs in 1951. In 1947, the United Nations grouped the Northern Mariana Islands, the Marshall Islands, and the Caroline Islands into the Trust Territory of the Pacific Islands. Authority over these islands was given to the U.S. Secretary of the Interior in 1951. The Northern Mariana Islands became a U.S. Commonwealth in 1976. In 1986, the Republic of the Marshall Islands and the Federated States of Micronesia became sovereign states and now maintain relations with the United States through the Department of State. In 1994, Palau joined the freely associated States.

Until recently, the Secretary of the Interior held broad authority over these islands, but the people living there now have their own elected legislatures and governors. Today the U.S.- Associated Pacific Basin jurisdictions remain as freely associated States affiliated with the large communities have emerged in a handful of States, including Illinois, New Jersey, and Texas, as well as California and New York. Approximately 75 percent of Pacific Islanders lived in Hawaii and California. Southeast Asians are distributed in a different pattern because of Federal resettlement programs that created pockets of Southeast Asian refugees in a few States. Nearly two-fifths of the Hmong population, for example, lived in Minnesota and Wisconsin in 1990. One-tenth of Vietnamese Americans live in Texas—the largest concentration of Vietnamese Americans outside of California (Population Reference Bureau, 1999). The overwhelming majority (96%) of Asian Americans and Pacific Islanders live in metropolitan areas (U.S. Census Bureau, 2001b).

Family Structure

Compared with white Americans and African Americans, AA/PIs are more likely to live in households that are comprised exclusively of family members, an arrangement referred to as "family households." In 2000, family households made up 75 percent of Asian American households, compared to 67 percent of non-Hispanic white and African American households (U.S. Census Bureau, 2001b). Asian Americans also have a relatively low percentage of female-headed households (13%), which is comparable to the rate for white Americans but much lower than the rates for other groups. Asian Indian, Chinese, Korean, and Japanese Americans all tend to have lower percentages of female-headed households, from 7 to 13 percent, while Vietnamese, Filipinos, and other Southeast Asians each have a rate of 18 percent (Lee, 1998). Pacific Islanders have larger families than most Asian Americans and other Americans. Pacific Islander family size averages 4.1 persons, compared to 3.8 for Asian American families and 3.2 for all American families (U.S. Census Bureau, 1990).

While subgroup differences exist, Asian Americans tend to wait longer to have children and to have fewer children than other major ethnic groups. Only 6 percent of all live births occur to Asian American women under the age of 20 years. This is strikingly different from the percentages for white Americans (10%), African Americans (23%), and Latinos (18%) (Lee, 1998). Fertility rate data suggest that the AA/PI population will change, and that some ethnic group numbers will decrease over time. The fertility rates of Chinese American women (1.4 children per woman) and Japanese American women (1.1) are lower than the replacement level of 2.1 (the number of children needed

for a generation to replace itself). Among Southeast Asian Americans, however, women have high fertility rates and tend to have children at earlier ages than Chinese and Japanese Americans (Lee, 1998). If fertility becomes a more dominant factor than immigration, the proportion of Southeast Asian Americans can be expected to rise compared to that of Chinese and Japanese Americans.

Education

On average, Asian Americans have attained more education than any other ethnic group in the United States. In 2000, 44 percent of Asian Americans age 25 years or older had a college or professional degree, whereas only 28 percent of the white population had achieved that level of education (U.S. Census Bureau, 2001b). According to 1997 data, 58 percent of Americans who descended from natives of the Indian subcontinent (India, Pakistan, Bangladesh, and Sri Lanka) had undergraduate, graduate, or professional degrees.

Some groups of AA/PIs did not have high educational attainment, however. In 1990, only 12 percent of Hawaiians and 10 percent of non-Hawaiian Pacific Islanders had achieved a bachelor's degree or more. Furthermore, almost two-thirds of Cambodians, Hmong, and Laotians had not completed high school. Many of these Southeast Asians were not able to complete school, but their offspring are clearly taking advantage of the academic opportunities in the United States. In 1990, 49 percent of Vietnamese, 45 percent of Cambodian, 32 percent of Hmong, and 26 percent of Laotians between the ages of 18 and 24 years were enrolled in college.

Income

Three factors are important to note when examining the income characteristics of AA/PIs. First, there are substantial ethnic group differences in average income. Second, it is important to control for family size because AA/PIs tend to have large extended families. Finally, in some groups, income averages may disguise the bimodal income distribution within a population.

In 1998, the per capita income of AA/PIs was $18,709, compared to $22,952 for non-Hispanic whites. The average family income for AA/PIs tends to be higher than the national average. About one-third of Asian American and Pacific Islander families had incomes of $75,000 or more, compared with 29 percent for non-Hispanic white families. However, because Asian families often include extended family members, per capita income (i.e., income per each member of the family) is highest for whites, followed by Asian Americans.

Approximately 25 percent of the Asian Indian population had household incomes that exceeded $75,000, while less than 5 percent of the Cambodian, Hmong, and Laotian populations had similar household incomes.

In 1990, for which detailed information on specific AA/PI groups is available, approximately 14 percent of all Asian Americans were living in poverty. Again, variations in poverty rates were evident when specific Asian ethnic groups were compared. The rates of poverty were Chinese Americans (14%), Korean Americans (14%), Thai Americans (13%), Asian Indian Americans (10%), Japanese Americans (7%), and Filipino Americans (6%). Southeast Asians experienced much higher rates of poverty: Vietnamese (26%), Laotian (35%), Cambodian (43%), and Hmong (64%). Rates of poverty were also high among Pacific Islanders. In 1990, approximately 17 percent of Pacific Islanders were living in poverty, with Samoans (26%) and Tongans (23%) reporting the highest levels of poverty.

Physical Health Status

The small number of studies that report health status by different subgroups limits an examination of overall physical health among Asian Americans and Pacific Islanders. While administrative data and health surveys include AA/PIs as a category, more often than not they do not have adequate comparable data for specific ethnic subgroups. Accordingly, an overall assessment of the AA/PI ethnic category leads to simple but misleading conclusions.

When it is reported that Asian Americans and Pacific Islanders have lower death rates attributable to cancer and heart disease than other minority groups, some might be misled and conclude that AA/PIs enjoy better health than other groups in the United States. However, when subgroup data are available, more accurate statements about the health profile of AA/PIs can be made (Zane, et al., 1994). For example, Native Hawaiian men have higher rates of lung cancer than white men do, and the incidence of cervical cancer among Vietnamese women in the United States is more than five times greater than that among white women (Kuo & Porter, 1998). While coronary heart disease and stroke kill nearly as many Americans as all other diseases combined, mortality from heart disease for Asian Americans and Pacific Islanders is 40 percent lower than that for whites.

The Need For Mental Health Care

Historical and Sociocultural Factors That Relate to Mental Health

Historical events and circumstances shape the mental health profile of any racial and ethnic group. For example, refugees from Cambodia were exposed to trauma before migrating to the United States because of persecution by the Khmer Rouge Communists under Pol Pot. During the four years of Pol Pot's regime (1975–1979), between 1 and 3 million of the 7 million people in Cambodia died through starvation, disease, or mass executions. This national trauma, as well as the stressors associated with relocation, including English language difficulties and cultural conflicts, continues to affect the emotional health of many Cambodian refugees and other immigrants.

Somatization

Another important factor related to mental health is culture. Culture shapes the expression and recognition of psychiatric problems. Western culture makes a distinction between the mind and body, but many Asian cultures do not (Lin, 1996). Therefore, it has long been hypothesized that Asians express more somatic symptoms of distress than white Americans. The influence of the teachings and philosophies of a Confucian, collectivist tradition discourages open displays of emotions, in order to maintain social and familial harmony or to avoid exposure of personal weakness. Mental illness is highly stigmatizing in many Asian cultures. In these societies, mental illness reflects poorly on one's family lineage and can influence others' beliefs about how suitable someone is for marriage if he or she comes from a family with a history of mental illness. Thus, either consciously or unconsciously, Asians are thought to deny the experience and expression of emotions. These factors make it more acceptable for psychological distress to be expressed through the body rather than the mind (Tseng, 1975; Kleinman, 1977; Nguyen, 1982; Gaw, 1993; Chun et al., 1996). It has been found that Chinese Americans are more likely to exhibit somatic complaints of depression than are African Americans or whites (Chang, 1985), and Chinese Americans with mood disorders exhibit more somatic symptoms than do white Americans (Hsu & Folstein, 1997).

Hsu and Folstein (1997) and Leff (1988) also suggest that psychological expression of distress is a relatively recent Western phenomenon, and that physical expression of psychological distress is normal in many cultures. Others have argued that somatization is often under the control of display rules that dictate when, where, and what symptoms are shown (Cheung, 1982). In this view, it is not so much that Chinese suppress or repress affective symptoms, but that the context of the situation influences what is presented. Chinese may display somatic symptoms to mental health workers but show depressive symptoms to others. Mental health professionals who rely solely on the standard psychiatric diagnoses used in the United States may not identify these somatic expressions of distress.

Key Issues for Understanding the Research

Methodology

The history of AA/PI groups reveals the tremendous diversity within the population. Unfortunately, in the past, research studies have typically classified Asian and Pacific Islander Americans as belonging to a homogenous ethnic category. Chapter 1 outlined some of the serious methodological problems (e.g., the high cost of screening rare populations) that partially explain why AA/PIs are often lumped together or into an "other" category. Despite the practical basis for creating a single racial designation for AA/PIs, using it has had real scientific and policy consequences. One consequence, as demonstrated later in this chapter, is that very little is known about the rates of mental illness, access to care, quality of care, and outcomes of treatment for different groups of Asian Americans and Pacific Islanders. The AA/PI category is a social and political convenience because the use of the term allows researchers, service providers, and policymakers to easily describe and discuss groups who seemingly share similar backgrounds. Unfortunately, this classification masks the social, cultural, and psychological variations that exist among AA/PI ethnic groups and constrains analyses of the interethnic differences in mental illness, help-seeking, and service use. The conclusions drawn from analyses using AA/PIs as a single racial category may be substantively different than ones made when specific AA/PI ethnic groups are examined (Uehara et al., 1994).

A second consequence of using a single ethnic category in research analyses is that it can lead to the conclusion that AA/PIs are a model minority. On average, AA/PIs have relatively high levels of educational, occupational, and economic achievement, and low rates of certain health problems. A simple interpretation of these types of data has resulted in portrayals of AA/PIs as extraordinarily successful, which justifies the lack of research attention and resources allocated to this popula-

tion. However, recognition of the diverse ethnic groups that comprise the AA/PI category helps to cast doubt on the model minority image. It should be noted that occasionally research on an aggregate group (e.g., Asian Americans) might be appropriate, particularly when the characteristic under observation is common to many Asian American groups. Nevertheless, care must be exercised to avoid stereotyping this population. The needs of specific AA/PI ethnic groups must be considered in order to fully understand the mental health of Asian Americans and Pacific Islanders.

Diagnosis

Establishing the rates of psychiatric disorders among AA/PIs is important in determining the need for mental health care in this population. As mentioned earlier, a common standard in setting the criteria for different mental disorders is the American Psychiatric Association's (APA) *Diagnostic and Statistical Manual of Mental Disorders* (1994). A critical issue is whether or not AA/PIs manifest symptoms similar to those found in Western societies as defined by the DSM–IV. Marsella and colleagues (1985) note that there is a tendency in the mental health field to overlook cultural variations in the expression of mental disorder when developing nosological categories. Groups vary in how they define such constructs as "distress," "normality," and "abnormality." These variations affect definitions of mental health and mental illness, expressions of psychopathology, and coping mechanisms (Marsella, 1982).

In addition, ethnic and cultural groups may have unique ways of expressing distress. As discussed later, neurasthenia, a condition often characterized by fatigue, weakness, poor concentration, memory loss, irritability, aches and pains, and sleep disturbances, is recognized in China. It is an official category in the International Classification of Diseases (Version 10) but not in the DSM–IV. Neurasthenia is a common diagnosis in China (Yamamoto, 1992), although it is not an official category in the DSM–IV. It is sometimes classified as undifferentiated somatoform disorder (if symptoms last at least six months) or as a rheumatological disorder. Some of the symptoms found in neurasthenia (loss of energy, inability to concentrate, sleep disturbances, etc.) overlap with those in depressive disorders. However, in neurasthenia, the somatic symptoms rather than depressed moods are critical, and any depressive symptoms are not sufficiently persistent and severe to warrant a diagnosis of a mood disorder.

Acculturation

An important factor in understanding the symptom expression, rates of illness, and use of services by immigrants and refugees is their *acculturation*, or adoption of the worldviews and living patterns of a new culture. Asian Americans differ in how they are integrated within the dominant U.S. culture, how they remain tied to the cultures of their ethnic origins, or how they are able to negotiate life in multiple cultures. Although many advances have been made in measuring acculturation, this area of research still has unresolved conceptual and methodological problems. Many factors affect the way and extent to which immigrants become involved in a new culture and remain connected with their earlier heritage. For example, age at time of immigration, presence of similar immigrants, and interaction with others from the new environment all influence adaptation. The influence of acculturation on mental health has not been clearly identified, in part because of problems with measuring acculturation. Nonetheless, the level of exposure to and involvement in U.S. culture is important when examining mental health factors for Asian Americans.

Mental Disorders

Adults

Less is known about the rates of psychiatric disorders using DSM categories for AA/PIs than for most of the other major ethnic groups. Even when AA/PIs are included as part of the sample of large-scale studies, it is not often possible to make estimates of mental disorders for this population. Two major studies, the Epidemiologic Catchment Area (ECA) study and the National Comorbidity Study (NCS), examined the need for mental health care in the U.S. population. In the 1980s, researchers who were conducting the Epidemiologic Catchment Area study (Regier et al., 1993) included residents of Baltimore, St. Louis, Durham, Los Angeles, and New Haven in their sample. English-speaking Asian Americans, who were classified in a single ethnic category, comprised less than 2 percent of the total sample (N 242). Because of the limited sample size and the unclear composition of the AA/PI category, accurate conclusions could not be drawn about this population's need for mental health care (Zhang & Snowden, 1999).

While the ECA study was limited to samples from five U.S. cities, the NCS (Kessler et al., 1994) estimated the rates of psychiatric disorders in a representative sample of the entire U.S. population. Just as in the ECA study, the NCS included a small sample of English-speaking Asian Americans and classified all ethnic groups into a single AA/PI category. Again, the group of Asian American respondents in the NCS was small, extremely diverse, and not representative of any particular Asian American subgroup.

The Chinese American Psychiatric Epidemiological Study (CAPES), was a large-scale investigation of the prevalence of selected disorders using DSM–IIIR (APA, 1987) criteria. This study, conducted in 1993 and 1994, examined rates of depression among more than 1,700 Chinese Americans in Los Angeles County (Sue et al., 1995; Takeuchi et al., 1998). The CAPES sample was comprised predominantly of Chinese immigrants; 90 percent of the sample was born outside the United States. Researchers conducted interviews in Cantonese, Mandarin, and English, and they used a multistage sampling procedure to select respondents. CAPES was similar in some ways to the ECA and NCS. Like the ECA, CAPES used one geographic site rather than a national sample. To measure depression, CAPES used the Composite International Diagnostic Interview Schedule—the University of Michigan version (UM–CIDI)—which is similar to the diagnostic instrument used in the NCS.

CAPES results showed that Chinese Americans had moderate levels of depressive disorders (Table 5–1). About 7 percent of the respondents reported experiencing depression in their lifetimes, and a little over 3 percent had been depressed during the past year. These rates were lower than those found in the NCS (Kessler et al., 1994). On the other hand, the rate for dysthymia more nearly matched the NCS estimates. It should be noted that the rates of lifetime and 12-month depression and dysthymia were very similar to the prevalence rates found in the Los Angeles site for the ECA. The implications of these find-

---

Table 5-1

Results of the Chinese American Psychiatric Epidemiological Study (CAPES) and the National Comorbidity Survey (NCS)

Mental Disorder		Rate in Chinese-American adults (CAPES)	Rate in national sample of adults (NCS)
Major Depressive Episode	Lifetime	6.9%	16.9%
	12-month	3.4%	10.0%
Dysthymia	Lifetime	5.2%	6.4%
	12-month	0.9%	2.5%

---

ings are reviewed at the end of the discussion of other studies using symptom scales.

No study has addressed the rates of mental disorders for Pacific Islander American ethnic groups.

Children and Youth

Very little is known about the mental health needs of the diverse populations of Asian American and Pacific Islander children and adolescents. No large studies documenting rates of psychiatric disorders in these youth have been conducted. However, several studies of symptoms of emotional distress have been conducted in small group samples of Asian American and Pacific Islander youth. Most of these studies find few differences between Asian American and Pacific Islander youth and white youth. For example, Filipino youth (Edman et al., 1998) and Hawaiian youth (Makini et al., 1996) attending high schools in Hawaii were found to have rates of depressive symptoms similar to those of white youth in the same schools. On the other hand, Chinese immigrant students have reported high rates of anxiety (Sue & Zane, 1985).

Older Adults

Little information is available on the prevalence of psychiatric disorders among older Asian Americans. Yamamoto and colleagues (1994) found a relatively low lifetime prevalence of most psychiatric disorders according to DSM–III (APA, 1980) criteria among a sample (N 100) of older Koreans drawn from the Korean Senior Citizens Association in Los Angeles (Yamamoto et al., 1994). Researchers also compared older Koreans in Los Angeles with community epidemiological studies conducted in Korea. The prevalence of almost all psychiatric disorders was similar for older Koreans in Los Angeles and those in Korea (Yamamoto et al., 1994).

Four other studies have examined the psychological well-being of older Asian Americans. These studies are weak from a methodological standpoint because they involve small, non-random samples and use general measures of distress rather than measures of psychiatric disorders. Three studies used the translated version of the Geriatric Depression Scale (GDS). A convenience sample of Japanese American older adults in Los Angeles (N 86) was found to be relatively healthy and not depressed (Iwamasa et al., 1998). In a sample of older Chinese American adults in Minneapolis–St. Paul (N 45) between the ages of 59 and 89 years, 20 percent were found to have significant depressive symptoms. A study of older, community-dwelling Chinese immigrants

(N 50) in a Northeast urban area revealed that 18 percent of respondents were mildly to severely depressed (Mui, 1996). These rates are similar to those found in other community samples of older people. Raskin and colleagues (1992) compared Chinese and white Americans between the ages of 60 and 99 from senior citizen housing complexes, senior citizen centers, senior citizen clubs at churches, and other community locations. Chinese Americans reported somatic psychiatric distress similar to what their white American counterparts reported. Finally, White and colleagues (1996) found a 9 percent prevalence for dementia among Japanese American men living in institutions or in the community in Honolulu, a rate lower than that for Japanese men in Japan, but similar to that for other American men in their age group.

In sum, researchers must be cautious about generalizations based on the limited findings on the mental health of older Asian Americans. Subjects for these studies are often recruited through Asian American senior organizations; the extent to which these findings can be generalized to less active older adults is limited. However, these results do not reveal high rates of psychopathology among older Asian adults.

Mental Health Problems

Symptoms

Much more is known about mental health problems measured by symptom scales as opposed to DSM criteria. In these studies, AA/PIs do appear to have an increased risk for symptoms of depression. Diagnoses of psychiatric disorders rely both on the presence of symptoms and on additional strict guidelines about the intensity and duration of symptoms. In studies of depressive symptoms, individuals are often asked to indicate whether or not they have specific depressive symptoms and how many days in the past week they experienced these symptoms. In several studies, Chinese Americans, Japanese Americans, Filipino Americans, and Korean Americans in Seattle (Kuo, 1984; Kuo & Tsai, 1986), Korean immigrants in Chicago (Hurh & Kim, 1990), and Chinese Americans in San Francisco (Ying, 1988) reported more depressive symptoms than did whites in those cities. One interpretation of the findings suggests that AA/PIs show high rates of depression, or simply have more symptoms but not necessarily higher rates of depression. Few studies exist on the mental health needs of other large ethnic groups such as Indian, Hmong, and Pacific Islander Americans.

Culture-Bound Syndromes

Even if Asian Americans are not at high risk for a few of the psychiatric disorders that are common in the United States, they may experience so-called culture-bound syndromes (APA, 1994). Two such syndromes are neurasthenia and *hwa-byung*.

As described earlier, Chinese societies recognize a disorder called neurasthenia. In a study of Chinese Americans in Los Angeles, Zheng and his colleagues (1997) found that nearly 7 percent of a random sample of respondents reported that they had experienced neurasthenia. The neurasthenic symptoms often occurred in the absence of symptoms of other disorders, which raises doubt that neurasthenia is simply another disorder (e.g., depression) in disguise. Furthermore, more than half of those with this syndrome did not have a concomitant Western psychiatric diagnosis from the DSM–III–R. Thus, although Chinese Americans are likely to experience neurasthenia, mental health professionals using the standard U.S. diagnostic system may not identify their need for mental health care.

Koreans may experience *hwa-byung*, a culture-bound disorder with both somatic and psychological symptoms. *Hwa-byung*, or "suppressed anger syndrome," is characterized by sensations of constriction in the chest, palpitations, sensations of heat, flushing, headache, dysphoria, anxiety, irritability, and problems with concentration (Lin, 1983; Prince, 1989). A community survey in Los Angeles found that 12 percent of Korean Americans (total *N* 109), the majority of whom were recent immigrants, suffered from this disorder (Lin, 1983; Lin et al., 1992); this rate is higher than that found in Korea (4%) (Min, 1990).

Suicide

Little research is available to shed light on the mental health needs of Asian Americans, but some information may be obtained by looking at suicide rates (Table 5-2). It is thought that Asian Americans are generally less likely to commit suicide than whites. A study by Lester (1994) compared suicide rates (per 100,000 per year) in the United States for various groups. Chinese (8.3), Japanese (9.1), and Filipino (3.5) Americans had lower suicide rates than whites (12.8). However, other subgroups of Asian Americans and Pacific Islanders may be at higher risk for suicide. For example, Native Hawaiian adolescents have a higher risk of suicide than other adolescents in Hawaii.

Concerns have been raised regarding high rates of suicide among young women who immigrate to the United States from the Indian subcontinent (Patel & Gaw, 1996) and among Micronesian adolescents (Rubinstein, 1983), but these groups have not been well studied. Finally, older Asian American women have the highest suicide rate of all women over the age of 65 in the United States (DHHS, 1999). Clearly, more information is needed on suicide among subgroups of Asian Americans.

Table 5-2
Suicide Rates

POPULATION	SUICIDES PER 100,000 PEOPLE PER YEAR
Asian Americans	7
White Americans	12.8
Native Hawaiian adolescents	12.9
Non-native Hawaiian adolescents in Hawaii	9.6

Source: Lester, 1994.

High-Need Populations

Refugees

The mental health needs of a population may be indicated by rates of mental disorders in the population as a whole, or by the existence of smaller subpopulations that have a particularly high need for mental health care. The relationship between poverty, poor health, and mental health is very consistent in the mental health literature. Given the relative economic status of Asian Americans and Pacific Islanders, it is not surprising that they are not present in large numbers among the Nation's homeless (U.S. Census Bureau, 1996). Furthermore, they make up less than 1 percent of the national incarcerated population (Bureau of Justice Statistics, 1999). Although there are inadequate data to draw conclusions about how often Asian American and Pacific Islander children are exposed to violence, this exposure is often related to socioeconomic deprivation. Most studies indicate that Asian Americans are less likely to have substance abuse problems than are other Americans (Makimoto, 1998). In sum, Asian Americans and Pacific Islanders are not heavily represented in many of the groups known to have high need for mental health care. However, many do experience difficulties, such as the lack of English proficiency, acculturative stress, prejudice, discrimination, and racial hate crimes, which place them at risk for emotional and behavioral problems. Southeast Asian refugees, in particular, are considered to be at high risk.

Many Southeast Asian refugees are at risk for post-traumatic stress disorder (PTSD) associated with the trauma they experienced before they immigrated to the United States. Refugees who fled Vietnam after the fall of Saigon in 1975 were mainly well-educated Vietnamese who were often able to speak some English and prosper financially. Although subsequent Vietnamese refugees were less educated and less financially secure, they were able to join established communities of other Vietnamese in the United States. Cambodians and Laotians became the second wave of refugees from Indochina. The Cambodians were survivors of Pol Pot's holocaust of killing fields. Several groups of Laotians, including the Mien and Hmong, had cooperated with American forces and left Laos after the war from fear of retribution. One-third of the Laotian population had been killed during the war, and many others fled to escape the devastation.

Studies document high rates of mental disorders among these refugees. A large community sample of Southeast Asian refugees in the United States (Chung & Kagawa-Singer, 1993) found that premigration trauma events and refugee camp experiences were significant predictors of psychological distress even five years or more after migration. Significant subgroup differences were also found. Cambodians reported the highest levels of distress, Laotians were next, then Vietnamese. Studies of Southeast Asian refugees receiving mental health care uniformly find high rates of PTSD. One study found 70 percent met diagnostic criterion for the disorder, with Mien from the highlands of Laos and Cambodians having the highest rates (Kinzie et al., 1990; Carlson & Rosser-Hogan, 1991; Moore & Boehnlein, 1991).

Another study examined the mental health of 404 Southeast Asian refugees during an initial clinical evaluation of patients seen for psychiatric assessment at a Southeast Asian mental health clinic in Minnesota. The sample was Hmong, Laotian, Cambodian, and Vietnamese. Clinical diagnoses were made according to DSM-III by two psychiatrists, who also used information from a symptom checklist. In this sample, 73 percent had major depression, 14 percent had post-traumatic stress disorder, and 6 percent had anxiety and somatoform disorders (Kroll et al., 1989). Blair (2000) found that a random, community sample of Cambodian adults

(N 124) had high rates of trauma-related stress and depression. This study, which used a standard diagnostic interview, found that 45 percent had PTSD, and 81 percent experienced five or more symptoms. Furthermore, 51 percent suffered from depression. Most of these individuals (85%) had experienced horrible traumas prior to immigrating to the United States, including starvation, torture, and losing family members to the war. On average, individuals in the sample experienced 20 war traumas (Blair, 2000). Similarly, 168 adults, recruited from a community of resettled Cambodian refugees in Massachusetts, were interviewed for a study of trauma, physical and emotional health, and functioning. Of the 161 participants who had ever had children, 70 parents (43%) reported the death of between 1 and 6 of their children. Child loss was positively associated with health-related concerns, a variety of somatic symptoms, and culture-bound conditions of emotional distress such as "a deep worrying sadness not visible to others" (Caspi et al., 1998).

Some subgroups of Vietnamese refugees may also be at high risk for mental health problems. Hinton and colleagues (1997) compared Vietnamese and Chinese refugees from Vietnam 6 months after their arrival in the United States and 12 to 18 months later. The ethnic Vietnamese had higher depression at the second assessment than did the Chinese immigrants.

Two studies have found high rates of distress among refugee youth. Cambodian high school students had symptoms of PTSD and mild, but prolonged, depressive symptoms (Kinzie et al. 1986). Researchers also have noted high levels of anxiety among unaccompanied minors, adolescents, and young adult refugees from Vietnam (Felsman et al., 1990). Likewise, in a study of Cambodian adolescents who survived Pol Pot's concentration camps, Kinzie and colleagues (1989) found that nearly half suffered from PTSD, and 41 percent experienced depression approximately 10 years after this traumatic period. Clearly, because many Southeast Asian refugees experienced significant trauma prior to immigration, rates of PTSD and depression are extraordinarily high among both adult and youth refugees.

Researchers conducting the next generation of studies need not only to derive accurate estimates of psychopathology among AA/PIs, but also to identify the specific ways that social and cultural factors influence the expression of mental disorders among AA/PIs. The results might then prove or disprove several of the general hypotheses that are currently made about the prevalence of mental disorders among Asian Americans.

Box 5–1:

The Plight of Southeast Asian Refugees

A Khmer woman (mid-40's)

Because of premigration traumas and the adjustment to relocation in the United States, many Southeast Asian refugees are experiencing great stress. The following excerpts were elicited in a mental health interview of a mid-40-year-old, Khmer woman from Cambodia by Rumbaut (1985).

"I lost my husband, I lost my country, I lost every property/fortune we owned. And coming over here, I can't learn to speak English and the way of life here is different; my mother and oldest son are very sick; I feel crippled, I can do nothing, I can't control what's going on. I don't know what I'm going to do once my public assistance expires. I may feel safe in a way—there is no war here, no Communist to kill or to torture you—but deep down inside me, I still don't feel safe or secure. I feel scared. I get scared so easily." (p. 475)

The first hypothesis suggests that rates of disorders will be high because many Asian Americans are immigrants who undergo difficult transitions in their adjustment to American society, and many have experienced prejudice, discrimination, and major trauma in their homelands. Indeed, as reported earlier, studies have found that some Asian American ethnic groups do have higher symptom scores than whites. A second hypothesis argues that the rates of mood disorders will be low because Asian Americans, like Asians in other countries, are likely to express their problems in behavioral or somatic terms rather than in emotional terms. Available evidence, for example, does suggest that the rates of mood disorders are low in Taiwan, Hong Kong, and China (Hwu et al., 1989). A third hypothesis maintains that the rates of mental disorders will be lowest for recent immigrants and highest for native-born residents. Low rates of mental disorders have been found among recent Mexican immigrants, for whom culture may be protective against mental health problems at first; but these low rates erode over time as Mexican immigrants acculturate. With Asian Americans, however, the preliminary evidence suggests that acculturation is directly related to well-being, at least in the case of Asian American students (Abe & Zane, 1990; Sue et al., 1996)

Availability, Accessibility, and Utilization of Mental Health Services

Disparities exist in the provision of adequate and effective mental health care to Asian Americans. Culturally competent and effective services are often unavailable or inaccessible.

Availability of Mental Health Services

Nearly half of the Asian American and Pacific Islander population's ability to use the mental health care system is limited due to lack of English proficiency, as well as to the shortage of providers who possess appropriate language skills. No reliable information is available regarding the Asian language capabilities of providers. Of the mental health care professionals who were practicing in the late 1990s, approximately 70 Asian American providers were available for every 100,000 Asian Americans in the United States; this is about half the ratio for whites (Manderscheid & Henderson, 1998).

Accessibility of Mental Health Services

Access to mental health care often depends on health insurance coverage. About 21 percent of Asian Americans and Pacific Islanders lack health insurance. However, within Asian American subgroups, the rate varies significantly. For instance, 34 percent of Korean Americans have no health insurance, whereas 20 percent of Chinese Americans and Filipino Americans lack such insurance. Furthermore, the rate of Medicaid coverage for most Asian American and Pacific Islander subgroups is well below that of whites. It has been suggested that lower Medicaid participation rates are, in part, due to widespread but mistaken concerns[2] among immigrants that enrolling themselves or their children in Medicaid would jeopardize their applications for citizenship (Brown et al., 2000). Nevertheless, even among U.S. citizens who live in families with children and have family incomes below 200 percent of the Federal poverty level (i.e., those who are most likely to be eligible for Medicaid), only 13 percent of Chinese Americans have

---

[2]These concerns originate from, among other things, confusion on the part of immigrants and providers about who is eligible for benefits and in fears relating to the application of the public charge doctrine. "Public charge" is a term used by the Federal Government to describe someone who is, or is likely to become, dependent on public benefits (Fix & Passel, 1999). The Immigration and Naturalization Service does not include Medicaid or other public health benefits in public charge determinations. Furthermore, the public charge doctrine applies to admission and deportation, but not to the naturalization of immigrants (Edwards, 2001).

Medicaid coverage, compared to 24 percent of whites in the same income bracket (Brown et al., 2000). These findings are important to consider because there is evidence that the lack of insurance coverage is associated with lower access to and utilization of health care (Chin et al., 2000).

Utilization of Mental Health Services

Community Studies

The Chinese American Psychiatric Epidemiological Study (CAPES) did not include a large enough sample of Asian Americans and Pacific Islanders to determine an accurate percentage of how many use care. In the study, participants with and without mental disorders indicated whether or not they had sought help for problems with emotions, anxiety, drugs, alcohol, or mental health in the past six months. Unfortunately, few of those experiencing problems (17%) sought care. Less than 6 percent of those who did seek care saw a mental health professional; 4 percent saw a medical doctor; and 8 percent saw a minister or priest (Young, 1998). Likewise, in the small sample of Asian Americans who participated in the National Comorbidity Study (NCS), less than 25 percent of those who had experienced a mood or anxiety disorder had sought care.

Zhang and colleagues (1998) compared Asian Americans and whites from a randomly selected sample based on the first wave of the Epidemiologic Catchment Area study on help seeking for psychological problems. Asian Americans were significantly less likely than whites to mention their mental health problems to a friend or relative (12 versus 25%), psychiatrist or mental health specialist (4 versus 26%), or physician (3 versus 13%). Asian Americans used health services less frequently in the past 6 months than whites (36 versus 56%). Compared with white Americans, Asian Americans less frequently visited a mental health center, a psychiatric outpatient clinic in a general hospital, an emergency unit, or a community mental health program, natural therapist, or self-help group. However, Asian Americans and whites did not differ in their use of outpatient clinics located in psychiatric or Veterans' Administration hospitals (Zhang et al., 1998).

Mental Health Systems Studies

Another way to determine whether Asian Americans and Pacific Islanders are using mental health care is to look at mental health systems of care. What must be determined is whether individuals from different groups served by the same system use care in proportion to their representation in the community. A problem with this approach is that it assumes, perhaps incorrectly, that groups have identical needs for mental health care. Three comprehensive studies that examined the entire formal mental health system found that Asian Americans used fewer services per capita than did other groups (Snowden & Cheung, 1990; Cheung & Snowden, 1990; Matsuoka et al., 1997).

Results consistent with the findings of these national studies were found in studies of many local mental health systems, such as Los Angeles County. The pro-

---

Box 5–2:

Avoidance of Mental Health Service

An (age 30)

Gee and Ishii (1997) describe a case that illustrates the difficulties that some Asian Americans have in using mental health services. An was a 30-year-old bilingual, Vietnamese male who was placed in involuntary psychiatric hold for psychotic disorganization. After neighbors found him screaming and smelling of urine and feces, they called the police, who escorted him to a psychiatric emergency room. An had been hospitalized several previous times for psychotic episodes. He was the oldest of five children and was living at home while attending college.

His parents had a poor understanding of schizophrenia and were extremely distrustful of mental health providers. They thought that his psychosis was caused by mental weakness and poor tolerance of the recent heat wave. They believed that they themselves could help An by providing him with their own food and making him return to school. Furthermore, the family incorrectly attributed An's facial injury, sustained while in the locked facility, to beatings from the mental health staff.

These misconceptions and differences in beliefs caused the parents to avoid the use of mental health services.

portion of Asian Americans among those who use psychiatric clinics and hospitals was found to be lower than their proportion of the general population (Kitano, 1969; Brown et al., 1973; Sue, 1977; Los Angeles County Department of Mental Health, 1984; Cheung, 1989; Snowden & Cheung, 1990; Sue et al., 1991; Uba, 1994; Durvasula & Sue, 1996; Snowden & Hu, 1997; Shiang et al., 1998). This disparity occurred whether the Asian American groups considered were students or nonstudents, inpatients or outpatients, children or adults, or whether they were living in neighborhoods with many or few other Asians. One exception to this finding has been published (O'Sullivan et al., 1989). Asian Americans in Seattle were found to use services at rates similar to their representation in the community. However, representation in the community was based on earlier census data, and the Asian American population grew rapidly during the subsequent period.

Another large-scale study focused on use of mental health services by Asian Americans and Pacific Islanders in Hawaii (Leong, 1994). This study examined outpatient and inpatient utilization rates from 1971 to 1981. Consistent with the findings of mainland studies, all Asian American and Pacific Islander groups used fewer inpatient services than would be expected given their representation in the population. However, lower utilization of outpatient care was not consistent across different groups of Asian Americans. Although both Chinese and Japanese Americans used less outpatient care than would be expected, Filipino Americans used these services at rates similar to their proportion in the population.

Many studies demonstrate that Asian Americans who use mental health services are more severely ill than white Americans who use the same services. This pattern is true in many community mental health centers (Brown et al., 1973; Sue, 1977), county mental health systems (Durvasula & Sue, 1996, for adults; Bui & Takeuchi, 1992, for adolescents), and student psychiatric clinics (Sue & Sue, 1974). Two explanations for this finding are that (1) Asian Americans are reluctant to use mental health care, so they seek care only when they have severe illness, and (2) families tend to discourage the use of mental health facilities among family members until disturbed members become unmanageable. Sue and Sue have found evidence that the reluctance to use services is attributable to factors such as the shame and stigma accompanying use of mental health services, cultural conceptions of mental health and treatment that may be inconsistent with Western forms of treatment, and the cultural or linguistic inappropriateness of services (Sue & Sue, 1999).

Complementary Therapies

Asian Americans and Pacific Islanders are not represented in the national studies that report on use of alternative or complementary health care sources (both home-based and alternative providers) to supplement or substitute for care received from mainstream sources (Eisenberg et al., 1998; Astin, 1998; Druss & Rosenheck, 2000). Nevertheless, some smaller studies conducted within subgroups of Asian Americans and Pacific Islanders suggest use of complementary therapies at rates equal to or higher than those used by white Americans. For example, one study of first- and second-generation Chinese Americans seeking care in an emergency department near New York City's Chinatown found that 43 percent had used Chinese therapies within one week of the visit (Pearl et al., 1995). Another study found that 95 percent of Chinese immigrants in Houston and Los Angeles used home remedies and self-treatments, including dietary and other approaches. Of this group, a substantial number of immigrants consulted traditional healers (Ma, 1999). Similarly, 90 percent of Vietnamese immigrants in the San Francisco Bay area used indigenous health practices (Jenkins et al., 1996). Almost half of the older Korean immigrant participants in Los Angeles County reported seeing a traditional healer (Pourat et al., 1999). Like members of other ethnic groups, these individuals generally use traditional therapies and healers to complement care from mainstream sources.

Asian Americans use a range of healing methods. For example, traditional Chinese medicine has existed for almost 3,000 years, and traditional Vietnamese healing derives from these historical roots. However, the healing practices of Laotians and Cambodians are influenced more by India and South Asia and have origins in ayurvedic medicine. Polynesian culture and healing practices are influential in Hawaii and other Pacific Islands.

Little is known about how Asian Americans and Pacific Islanders use indigenous therapies specifically for mental illness. Nevertheless, medications prescribed by mainstream health care providers can interact with herbal remedies or other forms of traditional medicine, so an awareness of the potential use of complementary methods of healing is essential.

Appropriateness and Outcomes of Mental Health Services

Limited evidence is available regarding the response of Asian Americans to mental health treatment. One study of outpatient individual psychotherapy in a San Francisco clinic found that Asian American clients had poorer short-term outcomes and less satisfaction with care than white Americans (Zane et al., 1994). In a recent pilot study using cognitive-behavioral therapy to treat depressive symptoms (Dai et al., 1999), older Chinese Americans appeared to respond in the same manner as a previously studied multiethnic population had. In two large-scale studies of mental health systems, there was evidence that the treatment outcomes for Asian American clients were either similar to, or poorer than those for whites (Sue, 1977; Sue et al., 1991).

Researchers have not compared the relative likelihood of Asian Americans and others to receive appropriate psychiatric care. One study suggested that primary care doctors may not identify depression in their Asian American clients as often as they identify depression in white clients (Borowsky et al., 2000). However, the study sample was too small to draw strong conclusions.

The fact that further research is needed on treatment outcomes for AA/PIs is especially evident in the use of psychotropic medicines. Recent research indicates that Asian Americans may respond clinically to psychotropic medicines in a manner similar to white Americans but at lower dosages (Lin & Cheung, 1999). These studies are based on very small samples and should be considered preliminary. However, consistent findings are appearing with regard to Asian Americans' response to neuroleptics, tricyclic antidepressants, lithium, and benzodiazepines (Chin, 1998; Lin et al., 1997). These findings suggest that, in the treatment of mental disorders among Asian Americans, care must be taken not to overmedicate. Initial doses of medication for these individuals should be as low as is appropriate, with gradual increases in order to obtain therapeutic effects (Du & Lu, 1997).

Under the assumption that AA/PI clients may respond better to therapists of the same ethnicity because of a better cultural match, Sue and colleagues (1991) examined whether treatment outcomes were better with ethnically matched versus unmatched therapists. They found that Asian American clients who are matched with Asian American therapists are less likely to leave treatment prematurely than Asian American clients who are not matched ethnically with their therapists (Sue et al., 1991). Ethnic match also increased length of treatment, even after other sociodemographic and clinical variables were controlled. Not surprisingly, an ethnic and linguistic match between the client and provider was more important for clients who were relatively less acculturated to U.S. society than for those clients who were more immersed in American society.

Hu and colleagues found that Asian Americans used services at a higher rate in Santa Clara County and San Francisco County where community mental health outpatient service centers specifically oriented to Asian Americans and Latinos had been established (Hu et al., 1991). Likewise, Yeh and colleagues found that Asian American children who attended Asian-oriented mental health centers in Los Angeles received more care and functioned better at the end of care than Asian American children who attended mainstream centers (Yeh et al., 1994).

These Asian-oriented or ethnic-specific services provide cultural elements that may welcome AA/PIs, such as notices or announcements written in Asian or pacific Island languages, tea served to clients in addition to coffee, and bilingual and bicultural therapists. Thus, matching the ethnicity of the client and the mental health care provider and providing care within settings specifically developed to treat this group may be important aspects of providing appropriate care for Asian Americans. Speaking the Asian language of patients whose English is limited, understanding the cultural experiences of clients, and having bicultural skills (i.e., being proficient in working with Asians who have different levels of acculturation) are also important.

Finally, in view of the shame and stigma felt by AA/PIs over mental health problems, and the lack of health care coverage that many AA/PIs experience, it is important to intervene at other levels. For example, community education about the nature of mental disorders may help to reduce shame and stereotypes about the mentally ill. Increasing health insurance coverage for mental disorders is important to increase the accessibility of services. Also, the introduction of prevention efforts in AA/PI communities is beneficial. A number of newer programs are working to promote mental health. For example, parent training programs, bicultural adjustment strategies, and culturally oriented self-help groups have been initiated to promote mental health and well-being in AA/PI communities.

Conclusions

Asian Americans and Pacific Islanders can be characterized in *four* important ways. First, their population in the United States is increasing rapidly, primarily due to the recent large influx of immigrants. Second, they are diverse, with some subgroups experiencing higher rates of social, health, and mental health problems than others. For example, poverty rates are higher among Southeast Asians and Pacific Islanders than among AA/PIs as a whole. Third, AA/PIs may collectively exhibit a wide range of strengths (e.g., family cohesion, educational achievements, motivation for upward mobility, and willingness to work hard) and risk factors (e.g., premigration traumas, English language difficulties, minority group status, and culture conflict), which again point to the diversity within the population. Fourth, very little national data are available that describe the prevalence of mental disorders using standardized DSM criteria.

In terms of what is known about mental health issues among AA/PIs, several conclusions are warranted:

(1) Our knowledge of the mental health needs of Asian Americans is very limited. Two of the most prominent psychiatric epidemiological studies, the ECA and the NCS, included extremely small samples of AA/PIs and were not conducted in any of the Asian languages. The only contemporary study of AA/PIs using DSM criteria is CAPES, but it is limited to one Asian ethnic group and focuses primarily on mood disorders. No study has addressed the rates of mental disorders for Pacific Islander American ethnic groups. When symptom scales are used, Asian Americans do show an elevated level of depressive symptoms compared to white Americans. Although these studies have been informative, most of them have focused on Chinese Americans, Japanese Americans, and Southeast Asians. Few studies exist on the mental health needs of other large ethnic groups such as Filipino Americans, Hmong Americans, and Pacific Islanders.

(2) Available mental health studies suggest that the overall prevalence of mental health problems and disorders does not significantly differ from the prevalence rates for other Americans, although the distribution of disorders may be different. This means that AA/PIs are not "mentally healthier" than other populations. For example, they may have lower rates of some disorders but higher rates of others, such as neurasthenia. Types of mental health problems appear to depend on level of acculturation. Those who are less Westernized appear to exhibit culture- bound syndromes more frequently than those who are more acculturated. The acculturated population shows more Western types of disorders. Furthermore, the rates of disorders vary according to within-group differences. Rates tend to be higher among Southeast Asian refugees, for instance.

(3) Without greater knowledge of the rate and distribution of particular disorders and the factors associated with mental health, care providers have a difficult time devising optimal intervention to treat mental disorders and promote well-being.

(4) AA/PIs have the lowest rates of utilization of mental health services among ethnic populations. This underrepresentation is characteristic of most AA/PI groups, regardless of gender, age, and geographic location. Among those who use services, severity of disturbance is high. The explanation for this seems to be that individuals delay using services until problems are very serious. The unmet need for services among AA/PIs is unfortunate, because mental health treatment can be very beneficial.

(5) The low utilization of mental health services is attributable to stigma and shame over using services, lack of financial resources, conceptions of health and treatment that differ from those underlying Western mental health services, cultural inappropriateness of services (e.g., lack of providers who speak the same languages as limited english proficiency clients), and the use of alternative resources within the AA/PI communities.

(6) Attention to ethnic or culture-specific forms of intervention and to racial or ethnic differences in treatment response is warranted to effect greater service utilization and more positive mental health outcomes. The ethnic matching of therapists with clients and the services of ethnic-specific programs have been found to be associated with increased use of services and favorable treatment outcomes. The development of culturally and linguistically competent services should be of the highest priority in providing mental health care for Asian Americans and Pacific Islanders. Attention must also be paid to differences in responses to medication because effective dosage levels of psychotropic medication may vary considerably among Asian Americans, with many people requiring lower than average doses to achieve therapeutic effects.

(7) It is imperative that more research be conducted on the AA/PI population. Priority should be given to investigations that focus on particular AA/PI groups, the rate and distribution of mental

health problems (including culture-bound syndromes), culturally competent forms of intervention, and preventive strategies that can promote mental health.

References

Abe, J. S., & Zane, N. (1990). Psychological maladjustment among Asian and Caucasian American college students. Controlling for confounds. *Journal of Counseling Psychology, 37*, 437–444.

American Psychiatric Association. (1980). *Diagnostic and statistical manual of mental disorders* (3rd ed.). Washington, DC: Author.

American Psychiatric Association. (1987). *Diagnostic and statistical manual of mental disorders* (3rd ed., rev.). Washington, DC: Author.

American Psychiatric Association. (1994). *Diagnostic and statistical manual of mental disorders* (4th ed.). Washington, DC: Author.

Astin, J. A. (1998). Why patients use alternative medicine: Results of a national study. *Journal of the American Medical Association, 279*, 1548–1553.

Blair, R. G. (2000). Risk factors associated with PTSD and major depression among Cambodian refugees. *Health and Social Work, 25*, 23–30.

Borowsky, S. J., Rubenstein, L. V., Meredith, L. S., Camp, P., Jackson-Triche, M., & Wells, K. B. (2000). Who is at risk of nondetection of mental health problems in primary care? *Journal of General Internal Medicine, 15*, 381–388.

Brown, E. R., Ojeda, V. D., Wyn, R., & Levan, R. (2000). *Racial and ethnic disparities in access to health insurance and health care.* Los Angeles, CA: UCLA Center for Health Policy and Research and The Henry J. Kaiser Family Foundation.

Brown, T. R., Huang, K., Harris, D. E., & Stein, K. M. (1973). Mental illness and the role of mental health facilities in Chinatown. In S. Sue & N. Wagner (Eds.), *Asian-American: Psychological perspectives* (pp. 212–231). Palo Alto, CA: Science and Behavior Books.

Bui, K. V., & Takeuchi, D. T. (1992). Ethnic minority adolescents and the use of community mental health care services. *American Journal of Community Psychology, 20* (4), 403–417.

Bureau of Justice Statistics. (1999). *The sourcebook of criminal justice statistics.* Washington, DC: Author.

Carlson, E. B., & Rosser-Hogan, R. (1991). Trauma experiences, post-traumatic stress, dissociation, and depression in Cambodian refugees. *American Journal of Psychiatry, 148*, 1548–1551.

Caspi, Y., Poole, C., Mollica, R. F., & Frankel, M. (1998) Relationship of child loss to psychiatric and functional impairment in resettlements. *Journal of Nervous and Mental Disease, 186*, 484–491.

Chang, W. (1985). A cross-cultural study of depressive symptomatology. *Culture, Medicine, and Psychiatry, 9*, 295–317.

Cheung, F. K. (1989, May). *Culture and mental health care for Asian Americans in the United States.* Paper presented at the Annual Meeting of the American Psychiatric Association, San Francisco.

Cheung, F. K., & Snowden, L. R. (1990). Community mental health and ethnic minority populations. *Community Mental Health Journal. 26*, 277–291.

Cheung, F. M. (1982). Psychological symptoms among Chinese in urban Hong Kong. *Social Science and Medicine, 16*, 1339–1344.

Chin, D., Takeuchi, D. T., & Suh, D. (2000). Access to health care among Chinese, Korean, and Vietnamese Americans. In C. Hogue, M. A. Hargraves, & K. S. Collins (Eds.), *Minority health in America* (pp. 77–98). Baltimore: Johns Hopkins University Press.

Chin, J. L. (1998). Mental health services and treatment. In L. C. Lee & N. W. S. Zane (Eds.), *Handbook of Asian American Psychology* (pp. 485–504). Thousand Oaks, CA: Sage.

Chun, C., Enomoto, K., & Sue, S. (1996). Health care issues among Asian Americans: Implications of somatization. In P. M. Kato & T. Mann (Eds.), *Handbook of diversity issues in health psychology* (pp. 347–366). New York: Plenum.

Chung, R. C., & Kagawa-Singer, M. (1993). Predictors of psychological distress among Southeast Asian refugees. *Social Science and Medicine, 36*, 631–639.

Dai, Y., Zhang, S., Yamamoto, J., Ao, M., Belin, T. R., Cheung, F., & Hifumi, S. S. (1999). Cognitive behavioral therapy of depressive symptoms in early Chinese Americans: A pilot study. *Community Mental Health Journal, 35*, 537–542.

Druss, B. G., & Rosenheck, R. A. (2000). Use of practitioner based complementary therapies by persons reporting mental conditions in the United States. *Archives of General Psychiatry, 57*, 708–714.

Du, N., & Lu, F. L. (1997). Assessment and treatment of post-traumatic stress disorder among Asian Americans. In E. Lee (Ed.), *Working with Asian Americans: A guide for clinicians* (pp. 275–294). New York: Guilford Press.

Durvasula, R. S., & Sue, S. (1996). Severity of disturbance among Asian American outpatients. *Cultural Diversity and Mental Health, 2,* 43–52.

Edman, J. L., Andrade, N. N., Glipa, J., Foster, J., Danko, G. P., Yates, A., Johnson, R.C., McDermott, J.F., & Waldron, J.A. (1998). Depressive symptoms among Filipino American adolescents. *Cultural Diversity and Mental Health, 4,* 45–54.

Edwards, J. R., Jr. (2001). *Public charge doctrine: A fundamental principle of American immigration policy.* Washington, DC: Center for Immigration Studies.

Eisenberg, D. M., Davis, R. B., Ettner, S. L., Appel, S., Wilkey, S., Van Rompay, M., & Kessler, R. C. (1998). Trends in alternative medicine use in the United States, 1990–1997: Results of a national survey. *Journal of the American Medical Association, 280,* 1459–1475.

Felsman, J. K., Leong, F. T. L., Johnson, M. C., & Felsman, I. C. (1990). Estimates of psychological distress among Vietnamese refugees: Adolescents, unaccompanied minors and young adults. *Social Science and Medicine, 31,* 1251–1256.

Fix, M., & Passel, J. S. (1999). *Trends in noncitizens' and citizens' use of public benefits following welfare reform: 1994–97.* Washington, DC: The Urban Institute.

Gaw, A. C. (1993). Psychiatric care of Chinese Americans. In A. C. Gaw (Ed.), *Culture, ethnicity and mental illness* (pp. 245–280). Washington, DC: American Psychiatric Association.

Gee, K. K., & Ishii, M. M. (1997). Assessment and treatment of schizophrenia among Asian Americans. In E. Lee (Ed.), *Working with Asian Americans: A guide for clinicians* (pp. 227–251). New York: Guilford Press.

Hinton, W. L., Tiet, Q., Tran, C. G., & Chesney, M. (1997) Predictors of depression among refugees from Vietnam: A longitudinal study. *Journal of Nervous and Mental Disease, 185,* 39–45.

Hsu, L. K. G., & Folstein, M. F. (1997). Somatoform disorders in Caucasian and Chinese Americans. *Journal of Nervous and Mental Disease, 185,* 382–387.

Hu, T. W., Snowden, L. R., Jerrell, J. M., & Nguyen, T. D. (1991). Ethnic populations in public mental health: Services choice and level of use. *American Journal of Public Health, 81,* 1429–1434.

Huang, K. (1991). Chinese Americans. In N. Mokuau (Ed.), *Handbook of social services for Asian and Pacific Islanders* (pp. 79–96). Westport, CT: Greenwood Press.

Hurh, W. M., & Kim, K. C. (1990). Correlates of Korean immigrants' mental health. *Journal of Nervous and Mental Disease, 178,* 703–711.

Hwu, H. G., Yeh, E. K., & Chang, L. Y. (1989). Prevalence of psychiatric disorders in Taiwan defined by the Chinese Diagnostic. *Acta Psychiatrica Scandinavia, 79,* 136–147.

Iwamasa, G. Y., Hilliard, K. M., & Kost, C. (1998). The Geriatric Depression Scale and older Japanese American adults. *Clinical Gerontologist, 19,* 13–26.

Jenkins, C. N. H., Le, T., McPhee, S. J., Stewart, S., & Ha, N. T. (1996) Health care access and preventive care among Vietnamese immigrants: Do traditional beliefs and practices pose barriers? *Social Science and Medicine, 43,* 1049–1056.

Kessler, R. C., McGonagle, K. A., Zhao, S., Nelson, C. B., Hughes, M., Eshleman, S., Wittchen, H., & Kendler, K. S. (1994). Lifetime and 12-month prevalence of DSM–III–R psychiatric disorders in the United States. *Archives of General Psychiatry, 51,* 8–19.

Kinzie, J. D., Boehnlein, J. K., Leung, P. K., Moore, L. J., Riley, C., & Smith, D. (1990). The prevalence of post-traumatic stress disorder and its clinical significance among Southeast Asian refugees. *American Journal of Psychiatry, 147,* 913–917.

Kinzie, J. D., Sack, W. H., Angell, R. H., Clarke, G., & Rath, B. (1989). A three-year follow-up on Cambodian young people traumatized as children. *Journal of American Academy of Child and Adolescent Psychiatry, 28,* 501–504.

Kinzie, J. D., Sack, W. H., Angell, R. H., Manson, S., & Ben, R. (1986). The psychiatric effects of massive trauma on Cambodian children: I. The children. *Journal of the American Academy of Child and Adolescent Psychiatry, 25,* 370–376.

Kitano, H. H. (1969). Japanese-American mental illness. In S. C. Plog & R.B. Edgerton (Ed.), *Changing perspectives in mental illness* (pp. 256–284). New York: Holt, Rinehart & Winston.

Kleinman, A. (1977). Depression, somatization and the "new cross-cultural psychiatry." *Social Science and Medicine, 11,* 3–10.

Kroll, J., Habenicht, M., Mackenzie, T., Yang, M., Chan, S., Vang, T., Nguyen, T., Ly, M., Phommasouvanh, B., Nguyen, H., Vang, Y., Souvannasoth, L., & Cuagao, R. (1989). Depression and post-traumatic stress disorder in Southeast Asian refugees. *American Journal of Psychiatry, 146,* 1592–1597.

Kuo, J. A., & Porter, K. (1998). Health status of Asian Americans: United States, 1992–1994. *Advance Data, No. 298*. Hyattsville, MD: National Center for Health Statistics.

Kuo, W. H. (1984). Prevalence of depression among Asian Americans. *Journal of Nervous and Mental Disease, 172*, 449–457.

Kuo, W., & Tsai, Y. (1986). Social networking hardiness and immigrant's mental health. *Journal of Health and Social Behavior, 27*, 133–149.

Lee, S. M. (1998). Asian Americans: Diverse and growing. *Population Bulletin, 53(2)*. Washington, DC: Population Reference Bureau.

Leff, J. (1988). *Psychiatry around the globe*. London: Gaskell/Royal College of Psychiatrists.

Leong, F. T. L. (1994). Asian Americans' differential patterns of utilization of inpatient and outpatient public mental health services in Hawaii. *Journal of Community Psychology, 22*, 82–89.

Lester, D. (1994) Gender equality and the sex differential in suicide rates. *Psychological Reports, 75*, 1162.

Lin, K. M. (1983). Hwa-byung: A Korean culture-bound syndrome? *American Journal of Psychiatry, 140*, 105–107.

Lin, K. M. (1996). Cultural influences on the diagnosis of psychotic and organic disorders. In J. E. Mezzich, A. Kleinman, H. Fabrega, & D. L. Parron (Eds.), *Culture and psychiatric diagnosis: A DSM–IV perspective*. Washington, DC: American Psychiatric Press.

Lin, K. M., & Cheung, F. (1999). Mental health issues for Asian Americans. *Psychiatric Services, 50*, 774–780.

Lin, K. M., Cheung, F., Smith, M., & Poland, R. E. (1997). The use of psychotropic medications in working with Asian patients. In E. Lee (Ed.), *Working with Asian Americans: A guide for clinicians* (pp. 388–399). New York: Guilford Press.

Lin, K. M., Lau, J. K. C., Yamamoto, J., Zheng, Y. P., Kim, H. S., Cho, K. H., & Nagasaki, G. (1992). *Hwa-byung*: A community study of Korean Americans. *Journal of Nervous and Mental Disease, 180*, 386–391.

Los Angeles County Department of Mental Health. (1984). *Report on ethnic utilization of mental health services*. Unpublished manuscript.

Ma, G. X. (1999) Between two worlds: The use of traditional and Western health services by Chinese immigrants. *Journal of Community Health, 24*, 421–443.

Makimoto, K. (1998). Drinking patterns and drinking problems among Asian-American and Pacific Islanders. *Alcohol Health and Research World, 22*, 270–275.

Makini, G. K., Jr., Andrade, N. N., Nahulu, L. B., Yuen, N., Yates, A., McDermott, J. F., Jr., Danko, G. P., Nordquist, C. R., Johnson, R., & Waldron, J. A. (1996). Psychiatric symptoms of Hawaiian adolescents. *Cultural Diversity and Mental Health, 2*, 183–191.

Manderscheid, R. W., & Henderson, M. J. (Eds.). (1998). *Mental health, United States: 1998*. Rockville, MD: Center for Mental Health Services.

Marsella, A. J. (1982). Culture and mental health: An overview. In A. J. Marsella & G. M. White (Eds.), *Cultural conceptions of mental health and therapy* (pp. 359–388). Boston: Reidel.

Marsella, A. J., Sartoriu, N., Jablensky, A., & Fenton, F. R. (1985). Cross-cultural studies of depressive disorders: An overview. In A. Kleinman & B. Good (Eds.), *Culture and depression* (pp. 299–324). Berkeley, CA: University of California Press.

Matsuoka, J. K., Breaux, C., & Ryujin, D. H. (1997). National utilization of mental health services by Asian Americans/Pacific Islanders. *Journal of Community Psychology, 25* (2), 141–146.

Min, P. G. (1990). Problems of Korean immigrant entrepreneurs. *International Migration Review, 24*, 436–455.

Moore, L. J., & Boehnlein, J. K. (1991). Post-traumatic stress disorder, depression, and somatic symptoms in U.S. Mien patients. *Journal of Nervous and Mental Disease, 179*, 728–733.

Mui, A. C. (1996). Depression among elderly Chinese immigrants: An exploratory study. *Social Work, 41*, 633–645.

Nguyen, S. D. (1982). Psychiatric and psychosomatic problems among Southeast Asian refugees. *Psychiatric Journal of the University of Ottawa, 7*, 163–172.

O'Sullivan, M. J., Peterson, P. D., Cox, G. B., & Kirkeby, J. (1989). Ethnic populations: Community mental health services ten years later. *American Journal of Community Psychology, 17*, 17–30.

Patel, S. P., & Gaw, A. C. (1996). Suicide among immigrants from the Indian subcontinent: A review. *Psychiatric Services, 47*, 517–521.

Pearl, W. S., Leo, P., & Tsang, W. O. (1995) Use of Chinese therapies among Chinese patients seeking emergency department care. *Annals of Emergency Medicine, 26*, 735–738.

Population Reference Bureau, (1999). America's racial and ethnic minorities. Population Bulletin, 54. Retrieved July 25, 2001, from http://www.prb.org/pubs/population_bulletin /bu54-3/54_3_intro.htm.

Pourat, N., Lubben, J., Wallace, S. P., & Moon, A. (1999). Predictors of use of traditional Korean healers among elderly Koreans in Los Angeles. *The Gerontologist, 39,* 711–719.

President's Advisory Commission on Asian Americans and *Pacific Islanders.* (2001). *A people looking forward: Action for access and partnerships in the 21st Century. An interim report to the President.* Washington, DC: Government Printing Office.

Prince, R. (1989) Somatic complaint syndromes and depression: The problem of cultural effects on symptomatology. *Mental Health Research, 8,* 104–117.

Raskin, A., Chien, C., & Lin, K. (1992). Elderly Chinese-Americans compared on measures of psychic distress, somatic complaints and social competence. *International Journal of Geriatric Psychiatry, 7,* 191–198.

Regier, D. A., Narrow, W. E., Rae, D. S., Manderscheid, R. W., Locke, B. Z., & Goodwin, F. K. (1993). The de facto U.S. mental and addictive disorders service system. Epidemiologic Catchment Area prospective 1-year prevalence rates of disorders and services. *Archives of General Psychiatry, 50,* 85–94.

Rubinstein, D. H. (1983). Epidemic suicide among Micronesian adolescents. *Social Science and Medicine, 17,* 657–665.

Rumbaut, R. (1985). Mental health and the refugee experience: A comparative study of Southeast Asian refugees. *In T. C. Owan (Ed.), Southeast Asian mental health: Treatment, prevention, services, training, and research* (pp. 433–486). Washington, DC: National Institute of Mental Health.

Shiang, J., Kjellander, C., Huang, K., & Bogumill, S. (1998). Developing cultural competency in clinical practice: Treatment considerations for Chinese cultural groups in the United States. *Clinical Psychology, 5,* 182–210.

Snowden, L. R., & Cheung, F. K. (1990). Use of inpatient mental health services by members of ethnic minority groups. *American Psychologist, 45,* 347-355.

Snowden, L. R., & Hu, T. W. (1997). Ethnic differences in mental health services use among the severely mentally ill. *Journal of Community Psychology, 25,* 235–247.

Sue, D. W., & Sue, D. (1999). *Counseling the culturally different.* New York: Wiley.

Sue, S. (1977). Community mental health services to minority groups: Some optimism, some pessimism. *American Psychologist, 32,* 616–624.

Sue, S., Fujino, D., Hu, L. T., Takeuchi, D. T., & Zane, N. W. (1991). Community mental health services for ethnic minority groups: A test of the cultural responsiveness hypothesis. *Journal of Consulting and Clinical Psychology, 59* (4), 533–540.

Sue, S., Keefe, K., Enomoto, K., Durvasula, R., & Chao, R. (1996). Asian American and White college students' performance on the MMPI–2. In J. N. Butcher (Ed.), *International adaptations of the MMPI: Research and clinical applications* (pp. 206–220). Minneapolis: University of Minnesota.

Sue, S., & Sue, D. W. (1974). MMPI comparisons between Asian- and non-Asian-American students utilizing a university psychiatric clinic. *Journal of Counseling Psychology, 21,* 423–427.

Sue, S., Sue, D. W., Sue, L., & Takeuchi, D. T. (1995). Psychopathology among Asian Americans: A model minority? *Cultural Diversity and Mental Health, 1* (1), 39–54.

Sue, S., & Zane, N. (1985). Academic achievement and socioemotional adjustment among Chinese university students. *Journal of Counseling Psychology, 32,* 570–579.

Takeuchi, D. T., Chun, C. & Shen, H. (1997, August). *Stress exposure and cultural expressions of distress.* Paper presented at the 91st meeting of the American Sociological Association, New York.

Takeuchi, D. T., Chung, R. C., Lin, K. M., Shen, H., Kurasaki, K., Chun, C., & Sue, S. (1998). Lifetime and twelve-month prevalence rates of major depressive episodes and dysthymia among Chinese Americans in Los Angeles. *American Journal of Psychiatry, 155,* 1407–1414.

Tseng, W. (1975). The nature of somatic complaints among psychiatric patients: The Chinese case. *Comprehensive Psychiatry, 16,* 237–245.

Uba, L. (1994). Asian Americans: *Personality patterns, identity, and mental health.* New York: Guilford Press.

Uehara, E. S., Takeuchi, D. T., & Smukler, M. (1994). Effects of combining disparate groups in the analysis of ethnic differences: Variations among Asian American mental health service consumers in level of community functioning. *American Journal of Community Psychology, 22,* 83–99.

U.S. Census Bureau. (1990). *1990 profiles of Asians and Pacific Islanders: Selected characteristics.* (CPH–L–151). Washington, DC: U.S. Government Printing Office.

U.S. Census Bureau. (1996). *National survey of homeless assistance providers and clients.* Washington, DC: U.S. Government Printing Office.

U.S. Census Bureau. (2000). *Projections of the resident population by race, Hispanic origin, and nativity: Middle series, 2001 to 2005.* Washington, DC: U.S. Government Printing Office.

U.S. Census Bureau. (2001a). *Profiles of general demographic characteristics: 2000 Census of Population and Housing, United States.* Retrieved June 22, 2001, from http://www2.census.gov/census_2000/datasets/demographic_profile/0_National_Summary/.

U.S. Census Bureau. (2001b). *The Asian and Pacific Islander Population in the United States: March 2000 (Update)* (PPL-146). Retrieved June 28, 2001 from http://www.census.gov /population/www/ socdemo/race/ api.html.

U.S. Department of Health and Human Services. (1999). *The Surgeon General's Call to Action to Prevent Suicide.* Rockville, MD: Author.

U.S. Office of Management and Budget. (2000). *Guidance on aggregation and allocation of data on race for use in civil rights monitoring and enforcement* (OMB Bulletin No. 00–02). Retrieved July 20, 2001, from http://www.whitehouse.gov/omb/bulletins/b00-02.html.

White, L., Petrovitch, H., Ross, G. W., Masaki, K. H., Abbott, R. D., Teng, E. L., Rodriguez, B. L., Blanchette, P. L., Havlik, R. J., Wergowske, G., Chiu, D., Foley, D. J., Murdaugh, & Curb, J. D. (1996). Prevalence of dementia in older Japanese-American men in Hawaii: The Honolulu–Asia Aging Study. *Journal of the American Medical Association, 276,* 955–960.

Yamamoto, J. (1992). Psychiatric diagnoses and neurasthenia. *Psychiatric Annals, 22* (4), 171–172.

Yamamoto, J., Rhee, S., & Chang, D. S. (1994). Psychiatric disorders among elderly Koreans in the United States. *Community Mental Health Journal, 30,* 17–27.

Yeh, M., Takeuchi, D. T., & Sue, S. (1994). Asian-American children treated in the mental health system: A comparison of parallel and mainstream outpatient service centers. *Journal of Clinical Child Psychology, 23,* 5–12.

Ying, Y. (1988). Depressive symptomatology among Chinese-Americans as measured by the CES-D. *Journal of Clinical Psychology, 44,* 739–746.

Young, K. (1998). *Help seeking for emotional/psychological problems among Chinese Americans in the Los Angeles area: An examination of the effects of acculturation.* Unpublished doctoral dissertation, University of California, Los Angeles.

Zane, N., Enomoto, K., & Chun, C. (1994). Treatment outcomes of Asian- and White-American clients in outpatient therapy. *Journal of Community Psychology, 22,* 177–191.

Zane, N., Takeuchi, D. T., &. Young, K. (Eds.). (1994). *Confronting critical health issues of Asian and Pacific Islander Americans.* Newbury Park, CA: Sage.

Zhang, A. Y., & Snowden, L. R. (1999). Ethnic characteristics of mental disorders in five U.S. communities. *Cultural Diversity and Ethnic Minority Psychology, 5* (2), 134–146.

Zhang, A. Y., Snowden, L. R., & Sue, S. (1998). Differences between Asian- and White-Americans' help-seeking and utilization patterns in the Los Angeles area. *Journal of Community Psychology, 26,* 317–326.

Zheng, Y. P, Lin, K. M., Takeuchi, D., Kurasaki, K. S., Wang, Y. X., & Cheung, F. (1997). An epidemiological study of neurasthenia in Chinese-Americans in Los Angeles. *Comprehensive Psychiatry, 38,* 249–259.

CHAPTER 6

MENTAL HEALTH CARE FOR HISPANIC AMERICANS

Contents

Contents, *continued*

MENTAL HEALTH CARE FOR HISPANIC AMERICANS

Introduction

The Spanish language and culture are common bonds for many Hispanic Americans, regardless of whether they trace their ancestry to Africa, Asia, Europe, or the Americas. The immigrant experience is another common bond. Nevertheless, Hispanic Americans are very heterogeneous in the circumstances of their migration and in other characteristics. To understand their mental health needs, it is important to examine both the shared and unique experiences of different groups of Hispanic Americans.

One of the most distinguishing characteristics of the Hispanic-American population is its rapid growth. In the 2000 census, sooner than forecast, the number of Hispanics counted rose to 35.3 million, roughly equal to the number of African Americans (U.S. Census Bureau, 2001a). In fact, census projections indicate that by 2050, the number of Latinos will increase to 97 million; this number will constitute nearly one-fourth of the U.S. pop-

ulation. Projections for the proportion of Hispanic youth are even higher. It is predicted that nearly one-third of those under 19 years of age will be Hispanic by 2050 (Spencer & Hollmann, 1998). Persons of Mexican origin comprise the largest proportion of Latinos (almost two-thirds), with the remaining third distributed primarily among persons of Puerto Rican, Cuban, and Central American origin, as shown in Figure 6–1 (U.S. Census Bureau, 2001b). It is noteworthy that nearly two-thirds of Hispanics (64 %) were born in the United States (U.S. Census Bureau, 2000c).

Historical Context

To place the growth of the Latino population in context, it is important to review some of the historical events that have brought Latinos to the United States. Although the Spanish language and cultural influence form a bond among most Hispanics, many key differences among the

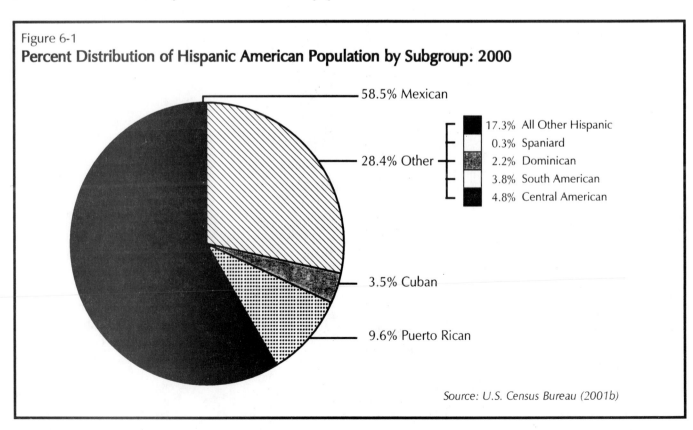

Figure 6-1

Percent Distribution of Hispanic American Population by Subgroup: 2000

58.5% Mexican

28.4% Other

17.3% All Other Hispanic
0.3% Spaniard
2.2% Dominican
3.8% South American
4.8% Central American

3.5% Cuban

9.6% Puerto Rican

Source: U.S. Census Bureau (2001b)

four main Latino groups are related to the circumstances of their migration.

Mexicans have been U.S. residents longer than any other Hispanic subgroup. After the Mexican War (1846–1848), when the United States took over large territories from Texas to California, the country gained many Mexican citizens who chose to remain in their "new" U.S. communities. The considerable economic, social, and political instability during the Mexican Revolution (1910–1917) contributed to the growth of the Mexican population in the United States. Economic pressures and wars have propelled subsequent waves of migration. Both push factors (economic hardships in Mexico) and pull factors (the need for laborers in the United States) have affected the flow. The sheer numbers of people who have come to the United States—well over 7 million—as well as the fact that many arrive "unauthorized" (without documentation) distinguishes Mexican immigration (U.S. Census Bureau, 2000d).

Puerto Ricans began arriving in large numbers on the U.S. mainland after World War II as Puerto Rico's population increased. High unemployment among displaced agricultural workers on the island also led to large-scale emigration to the mainland United States that continued through the 1950s and 1960s. In the 1980s, the migration pattern became more circular as many Puerto Ricans chose to return to the island. One distinctive characteristic of Puerto Rican migration is that the second Organic Act, or Jones Act, of 1917 granted Puerto Ricans U.S. citizenship.

Although **Cubans** came to the United States in the second half of the 19th century and in the early part of the 20th century, the greatest influx of Cuban immigrants began after Fidel Castro overthrew the Fulgencio Batista government in 1959. First, an elite group of Cubans came, but emigration continued with *balseros*, people who make the dangerous crossing to the United States by makeshift watercraft (Bernal & Shapiro, 1996). Some of these immigrants, such as the educated professionals who came to the United States during the early phase of Cuban migration, have become well established, whereas others who arrived with few economic resources are less so. Unlike immigrants from several other countries, many Cubans have gained access to citizenship and Federal support through their status as political refugees (Cattan, 1993).

Central Americans are the newest Latino subgroup in the United States. Many Central Americans fled their countries *por la situacion*, a phrase that refers to the political terror and atrocities in their homelands (Farias, 1994; Jenkins, 1991; Suarez-Orozco, 1990). Although the specific social, historical, and political contexts differ in El Salvador, Guatemala, and Nicaragua, conflicts in those countries led to a significant emigration of their citizens. About 21 percent of foreign-born Central Americans arrived in the United States between 1970 and 1979, and the bulk (about 70 %) arrived between 1980 and 1990 (Farias, 1994).

The circumstances that caused various Hispanic groups to migrate greatly influence their experience in the United States. Cubans fled a Communist government, and, as a result, the U.S. Government has provided support through refugee or entrant status, work permits (Gil & Vega, 1996), and citizenship. More than half (51 %) of Cuban immigrants have become U.S. citizens, compared to only 15 percent of Mexican immigrants (U.S. Census Bureau, 1998). Puerto Ricans, whether born on the mainland or in Puerto Rico, are by definition U.S. citizens and, as a result, have access to government-sponsored support services.

In contrast, many Central American immigrants are not recognized as political refugees, despite the fact that the war-related trauma and terror that preceded their immigration may place them at high risk for post-traumatic stress disorder (PTSD) and may make adjustment to their new home more difficult. Many Latinos who arrive without proper documentation have difficulty obtaining jobs or advancing in them and live with the chronic fear of deportation. Finally, many Mexicans, Puerto Ricans, Central Americans, and recent Cuban immigrants come as unskilled laborers or displaced agricultural workers who lack the social and economic resources to ease their adjustment.

Current Status

Geographic Distribution

Hispanics are highly concentrated in the U.S. Southwest (see Table 6–1). In 2000, 60 percent lived in five Southwestern States (California, Arizona, New Mexico, Colorado, and Texas). Approximately half of all Hispanic Americans live in two States, California and Texas (U.S. Census Bureau, 2001b). While many Southwestern Latinos are recent immigrants, others are descendants of Mexican and Spanish settlers who lived in the territory before it belonged to the United States. Some of these descendants, particularly those in New Mexico and Colorado, refer to themselves as "Hispanos." More recent immigrants from Mexico and Central America are drawn to the Southwest because of its proximity to their home countries, its employment

Table 6-1
Percentage of Hispanic Americans in State Populations: 2000

	Hispanic Population		Percent Hispanic of State Population	
	Number	Rank	Percent	Rank
New Mexico	765,386	8	42.1	1
California	10,966,556	1	32.4	2
Texas	6,669,666	2	32.0	3
Arizona	1,295,617	6	25.3	4
Nevada	393,970	14	19.7	5
Colorado	735,601	9	17.1	6
Florida	2,682,715	4	16.8	7
New York	2,867,583	3	15.1	8
New Jersey	1,117,191	7	13.3	9
Illinois	1,530,262	5	12.3	10

Source: U.S. Census Bureau, (2001b)

opportunities, and its established Latino communities, which can help them find jobs.

Outside the Southwest, New York, Florida, and Illinois are home to the largest concentrations of Hispanics. New York has 8.1 percent, Florida, 7.6 percent, and Illinois, 4.3 percent of all the Latinos estimated to reside in the United States in 2000 (U.S. Census Bureau, 2001b). Two-thirds of Puerto Ricans on the mainland live in New York and New Jersey, and two-thirds of Cuban Americans live in Florida (Population Reference Bureau, 2000).

Although specific subgroups of Latinos are associated with specific geographical regions, important demographic shifts have resulted in the increased visibility of Latinos throughout the United States. From 1990 to 2000, Latinos more than doubled in number in the following six states: Arkansas (170 %), Nevada (145 %), North Carolina (129 %), Georgia (120 %), Nebraska (108 %), and Tennessee (105 %) (U.S. Census Bureau, 2000c). Of the six States, Nevada is the only one located in a region with traditionally high concentrations of Latinos. Thus, in addition to growing in numbers, Hispanic Americans are spreading throughout the United States.

Family Structure

Latinos are often referred to as family oriented (Sabogal et al., 1987). It is important to note that familism is as much a reflection of social processes as of cultural practice (Lopez & Guarnaccia, 2000). Specifically, the shared experience of immigrating to a new land or of experiencing difficult social conditions in one's homeland can promote adherence to family ties. In many cases, family connections facilitate survival and adjustment.

The importance of family can be seen in Hispanic living arrangements. Although family characteristics vary by Latino subgroups, as a whole, Latinos, like Asian Americans and Pacific Islanders, are most likely to live in family households and least likely to live alone. In addition, children (especially the females) tend to remain in the family until they marry. Nearly 30 percent of both white and black households consisted of a single person in 1998, compared to just 14 percent of Hispanic households (Riche, 2000). Almost two-thirds (63 %) of Hispanic family households included children under age 18 in 1999, while fewer white families (47 %) and black families (56 %) included children (U.S. Census Bureau, 2001).

Education

Overall, Hispanics have less formal education than the national average. Of Latinos over 25 years of age, only 56 percent have graduated from high school, and only 11 percent have graduated from college. Nationally, 83 percent and 25 percent of the same age group have graduated from high school and college respectively (U.S. Census Bureau, 2000b). Hispanics' educational attainment is related to their place of birth. In 1999, only 44 percent of foreign-born Hispanic adults 25 years and older were high school graduates, compared to 70 percent of U.S.-born Hispanic adults (U.S. Census Bureau, 2000b). The dropout rate for foreign-born Hispanics ages 16 to 24 is more than twice the dropout rate for U.S.-born Hispanics in the same age range (Kaufman et al., 1999).

A recent study of middle school Latino students questions why foreign-born adolescents and adults have the worst educational outcomes (C. Suarez-Orozco & M. Suarez-Orozco, 1995). The study concluded that recent immigrants from Mexico and El Salvador had at least the same, or in some cases greater motivation to achieve than white or U.S.-born Mexican American students. (See also M. Suarez-Orozco, 1989.)

It is not clear how to reconcile these data on motivation with the national picture of poor educational outcomes for many Latino immigrants. One explanation may be that the high dropout rate reflects a large number of youth and young adults with little education who come to the United States to work, not to attend school (National Center for Education Statistics, 2000). Another explanation may be that many Latino immigrants who attend school lose their motivation over time, given the social, linguistic, and economic difficulties they face. Some may even turn to involvement in urban gangs (Vigil, 1988).

The educational achievement of three of the main Hispanic subgroups reveals further variability. Cubans have the highest percentage of formally educated people. Of persons over 25 years of age, 70 percent of Cuban Americans have graduated from high school, whereas 64 percent of Puerto Ricans and 50 percent of Mexican Americans have graduated from high school (U.S. Census Bureau, 2000d). Moreover, one-fourth of Cuban Americans have graduated from college, which is identical to the college graduation rate of Americans overall. In contrast, Puerto Rican and Mexican-origin adults have lower college graduation rates, 11 percent and 7 percent respectively. Although Latinos as a group have poorer educational outcomes than other ethnic groups, there is sufficient variability to offer hope for improving Latinos' educational success.

Income

The economic status of three of the main subgroups parallels their educational status. Cuban Americans are more affluent in standing than Puerto Ricans and Mexican Americans, as reflected in median family incomes (Cubans, $39,530; Puerto Ricans, $28,953; Mexicans, $27,883), the percentage of persons below the poverty line (Puerto Ricans, 31 %; Mexicans, 27 %; Cubans, 14 %) and the unemployment rates of persons 16 years and older (Puerto Ricans, 7 %; Mexicans, 7 %;

Cubans, 5 %) (U.S. Census Bureau, 2000d). The current income levels of the Latino subgroups are also related to the political and historical circumstances of their immigration. Elite Cuban immigrants have contributed in part to the relatively strong economic status of Cuban Americans. Their experience, however, stands in stark contrast to that of Mexican Americans, Puerto Ricans, and Central Americans, most of whom came to the United States as unskilled laborers.

Physical Health Status

Infant mortality is one sensitive indicator of a population's health. Hispanic Americans have lower infant mortality rates than do white Americans. For most groups, infant mortality tends to be related to the educational level of mothers. For example, white infants born to mothers with fewer than 12 years of education are 2.4 times as likely to die as those born to mothers with 16 or more years of education. Although Cubans and Puerto Ricans show this general pattern, the pattern is not so prominent for Mexican Americans or immigrants from Central America. Furthermore, although Mexican Americans and African Americans have similar socioeconomic profiles, infant mortality among Mexican Americans is less than half that of African Americans. Mexican American women who were born in Mexico are less likely to give birth to a baby of low birthweight than are U.S.-born Mexican American women (Becerra et al., 1991). This difference is partially explained by the fact that Mexican-born women are less likely to use cigarettes and alcohol than Mexican American women who were born in the United States (Scribner & Dwyer, 1989).

Other statistics show that Latinos in the United States suffer from more health disorders than white Americans. Latinos are twice as likely as whites to die from diabetes (Department of Health and Human Services, [DHHS], 2000). Although they comprised only 11 percent of the total U.S. population in 1996, Latinos had 20 percent of the new cases of tuberculosis in the United States that year. Latinos also exceed whites in rates of high blood pressure and obesity.

Health indicators for Puerto Rican Americans are worse than such indicators for other Latinos. According to the results of a nationally representative interview conducted in English and Spanish, Puerto Rican Americans reported more days in which they had to restrict their activities due to health disability, more days spent in bed, and more hospitalizations than did Mexican Americans and Cuban Americans (National Health Interview Survey, 1992–1995, see Hajat, 2000).

The Need for Mental Health Care

Historical and Sociocultural Factors That Relate to Mental Health

Historical and sociocultural factors suggest that, as a group, Latinos are in great need of mental health services. Latinos, on average, have relatively low educational and economic status. In addition, historical and social subgroup differences create differential needs within Latino groups. Central Americans may be in particular need of mental health services given the trauma experienced in their home countries. Puerto Rican and Mexican American children and adults may be at a higher risk than Cuban Americans for mental health problems, given their lower educational and economic resources. Recent immigrants of all backgrounds, who are adapting to the United States, are likely to experience a different set of stressors than long-term Hispanic residents.

Key Issues for Understanding the Research

Much of our current understanding of the mental health status of Latinos, particularly among adult populations, is derived from epidemiological studies of prevalence rates of mental disorders, diagnostic entities established by the *Diagnostic and Statistical Manual of Mental Disorders* (DSM; American Psychiatric Association, 1994). The advantage of focusing on rates of disorders is that such findings can be compared with and contrasted to findings from studies in other domains (e.g., clinical studies) using the same diagnostic criteria. In addition, diagnostic entities are now often associated with specific pharmacological and psychosocial treatments.

Although there are several advantages to examining DSM-based clinical entities, there are at least three disadvantages. One limitation is that individuals may experience considerable distress—a level of distress that disrupts their daily functioning—but the symptoms associated with the distress fall short of a given diagnostic threshold. Thus, if only disorder criteria are used, some individuals' need for mental health care may not be recognized. A second disadvantage is that the current definitions of the diagnostic entities have little flexibility to take into account culturally patterned forms of distress and disorder. As a result, disorders in need of treatment may not be recognized or may be mislabeled. A third limitation is that most of the epidemiological studies using the disorder-based definitions are conducted in community household surveys. They fail to include nonhousehold members, such as persons without homes or those who reside in institutions. Because of these limitations, it is important to broaden the review of research on mental health needs to include not only studies that report on disorders, but also studies that report on symptoms, symptom clusters, culturally patterned expressions of distress and disorder, and high-need populations not usually included in household-based surveys.

Mental Disorders

Adults

As noted in previous chapters, researchers have conducted two large-scale studies to identify the rates of psychiatric disorders among adults in the United States. The first, the Epidemiologic Catchment Area Study (ECA) (Robins & Regier, 1991), examined rates of psychiatric disorders in five communities ($N = 19,182$): New Haven, Baltimore, St Louis, Durham, and Los Angeles. Investigators at the Los Angeles site conducted interviews in English and Spanish and oversampled Mexican Americans ($N = 1,243$), so that rates of psychiatric disorders in this subpopulation could be estimated (Karno et al., 1987). The second study, the National Comorbidity Study (NCS) (Kessler et al., 1994), examined psychiatric disorders in a representative sample of individuals living throughout the United States ($N = 8,098$), excluding Alaska and Hawaii. This survey included Hispanics ($N = 719$), but was conducted only in English; thus, Spanish-speaking Hispanics were not represented (Ortega et al., 2000).

The ECA study found that Mexican Americans and white Americans had very similar rates of psychiatric disorders (Robins & Regier, 1991). However, when the Mexican American group was separated into two subgroups, those born in Mexico and those born in the United States, it was found that those born in the United States had higher rates of depression and phobias than those born in Mexico (Burnam et al., 1987). The NCS found that relative to whites, Mexican Americans had fewer lifetime disorders overall and fewer anxiety and substance use disorders. Like the Los Angeles ECA findings, Mexican Americans born outside the United States were found to have lower prevalence rates of any lifetime disorders than Mexican Americans born in the United States. Relative to whites, the lifetime prevalence rates did not differ for Puerto Ricans, nor for "Other Hispanics." However, the sample sizes of the latter two subgroups were quite small, thus limiting the statistical power to detect group differences (Ortega et al., 2000).

133

A third study examined rates of psychiatric disorders in a large sample of Mexican Americans residing in Fresno County, California (Vega et al., 1998). This study found that the lifetime rates of mental disorders among Mexican American immigrants born in Mexico were remarkably lower than the rates of mental disorders among Mexican Americans born in the United States. Overall, approximately 25 percent of the Mexican immigrants had some disorder (including both mental disorders and substance abuse), whereas 48 percent of the U.S.-born Mexican Americans had a disorder (Vega et al., 1998). Furthermore, the length of time that these Latinos had spent in the United States appeared to be an important factor in the development of mental disorders. Immigrants who had lived in the United States for at least 13 years had higher prevalence rates of disorders than those who had lived in the United States fewer than 13 years (Vega et al., 1998).

It is interesting to note that the mental disorder prevalence rates of U.S.-born Mexican Americans closely resembled the rates among the general U.S. population. In contrast, the Mexican-born Fresno residents' lower prevalence rates were similar to those found in a Mexico City study (e.g., for any affective disorder: Fresno, 8 %, Mexico City, 9 %) (Caraveo-Anduaga et al., 1999). Together, the results from the ECA, the NCS, and the Fresno studies suggest that Mexican-born Latinos have better mental health than do U.S.-born Mexican Americans and the national sample overall.

A similar pattern has been found in other sets of studies. One study examined the mental health of Mexicans and Mexican Americans who were seen in family practice settings in two towns equidistant from the Mexican border (Hoppe et al., 1991). This investigation found that 8 percent of the Mexican American participants had experienced a lifetime episode of depression, whereas only 4 percent of Mexican participants had. A group of earlier studies conducted in the mid-1980s also examined rates of depression in English- and Spanish-speaking Latinos, including Cuban Americans ($N = 857$) in Miami (Narrow et al., 1990); Mexican Americans ($N = 3,118$) in the Southwest (Moscicki et al., 1987); Puerto Ricans ($N = 1,140$) in New York City (Moscicki et al., 1987); and Puerto Ricans ($N = 1,513$) on the island (Canino et al., 1987). One of the most salient findings is that Puerto Ricans from the island had lower rates of lifetime depression (4.6 %) than those from New York City (9 %) (Canino et al., 1987; Moscicki et al., 1987).

The most striking finding from the set of adult epidemiological studies using diagnostic measures is that Mexican immigrants, Mexican immigrants who lived fewer than 13 years in the United States, or Puerto Ricans who resided on the island of Puerto Rico had lower prevalence rates of depression and other disorders than did Mexican Americans who were born in the United States, Mexican immigrants who lived in the United States 13 years or more, or Puerto Ricans who lived on the mainland. This consistent pattern of findings across independent investigators, different sites, and two Latino subgroups (Mexican Americans and Puerto Ricans) suggests that factors associated with living in the United States are related to an increased risk of mental disorders.

Some authors have interpreted these findings as suggesting that acculturation may lead to an increased risk of mental disorders (e.g., Vega et al., 1998; Escobar et al., 2000; Ortega et al., 2000). The limitation of this explanation is that none of the noted epidemiological studies directly tested whether acculturation and prevalence

Figure 6-2

Lifetime Prevalence of CIDI Disorders in Fresno and National Comorbidity Study (NCS)

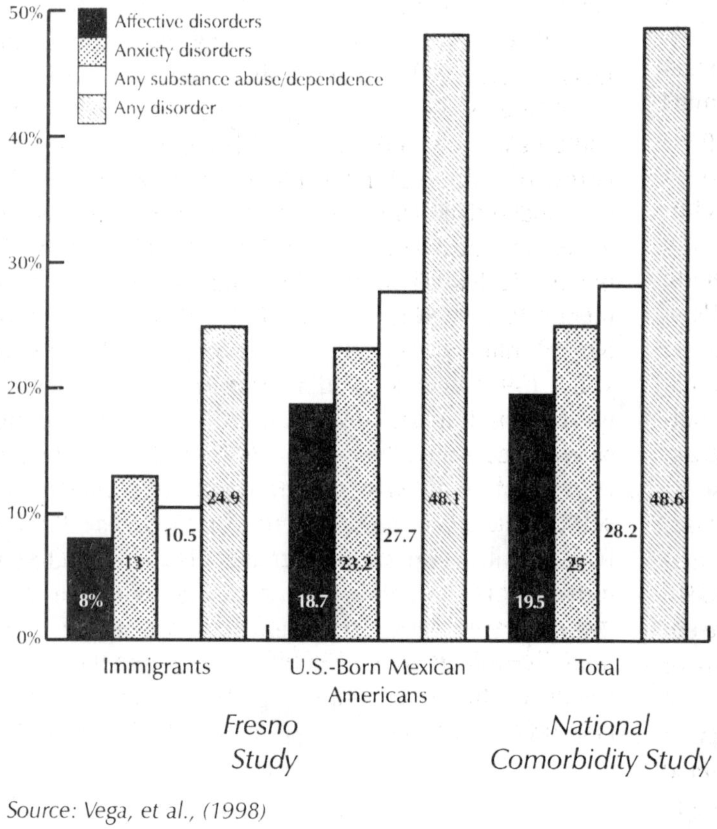

Legend:
- Affective disorders
- Anxiety disorders
- Any substance abuse/dependence
- Any disorder

Immigrants (Fresno Study): 8%, 13, 10.5, 24.9
U.S.-Born Mexican Americans (Fresno Study): 18.7, 23.2, 27.7, 48.1
Total (National Comorbidity Study): 19.5, 25, 28.2, 48.6

Source: Vega, et al., (1998)

rates are indeed related. At best, place of birth and number of years living in the United States are proxy measures of acculturation. Moreover, acculturation is a complex process (LaFromboise et al., 1993); it is not clear what aspect or aspects of acculturation could be related to higher rates of disorders. Is it the changing cultural values and practices, the stressors associated with such changes, or negative encounters with American institutions (e.g., schools or employers) that underlie some of the different prevalence rates (Betancourt & Lopez, 1993)? Before acculturation can be accepted as an explanation for this observed pattern of findings, it is important that direct tests of specific acculturation processes be carried out and that alternative explanations for these findings be ruled out. Longitudinal research would be especially helpful in identifying the key predictors of Latinos' mental health and mental illness.

Children and Youth

Most epidemiological studies of Latino children and adolescents have been conducted with symptom indices and problem behavior checklists, not diagnostic instruments. Efforts to study diagnostic entities among Latino children in community samples have been limited. In one study carried out in Puerto Rico, psychiatrists administered a standard diagnostic instrument, the Diagnostic Interview Schedule for Children (DISC), and found high rates of mental disorders (49 %) among Puerto Rican children who had previously been identified as having significant behavioral problems. However, the rate dropped to 18 percent when a diagnosis with some associated impairment was required (Bird et al., 1988). The importance of including impairment as a criterion for disorders in children was established in another recent study. Children living in Georgia, Connecticut, New York, and Puerto Rico were assessed to establish rates of mental disorders; the Puerto Rican children had rates comparable to the multiethnic sample from the U.S mainland (Shaffer et al., 1996). For all groups, rates of disorders dropped dramatically when impairment was required as part of the diagnosis.

An examination of studies of mental health problems reveals a generally consistent pattern: Latino youth experience a significant number of mental health problems, and in most cases, more problems than whites. Studies of child mental health problems typically used versions or portions of a popular screening instrument, the Childhood Behavior Checklist (CBCL, Achenbach & Edelbrock, 1983). Glover and colleagues (1999) found that Hispanic children in middle schools, specifically Mexican-origin youth from Texas, reported more anxi-

ety-related problem behaviors than white students. In addition, Hispanic sixth- and seventh-graders from a Southwestern city reported more delinquency-type problem behaviors than white students (Vazsonyi & Flannery, 1997). Youth in Puerto Rico were also found to have a significantly higher total problem score (35% versus 20%) and prevalence rate of "cases" (36% versus 9 %) than a three-State sample comprised primarily of whites (Achenbach et al., 1990). A study of Hispanic 10- to 16-year-old boys in Dade County, Florida, was the only exception. This investigation did not reveal any differences in total problem behaviors when comparing Hispanic, non-Hispanic white, and African American boys (Vega et al., 1995).

Studies of depressive symptoms and disorders also revealed more distress among Hispanic children and adolescents, particularly among Mexican-origin youth. This was evident in a community study in Las Cruces, New Mexico (Roberts & Chen, 1995), as well as in a national study within the 48 coterminous States (Roberts & Sobhan, 1992). In both these investigations, Mexican American adolescents reported more depressive symptoms than did white adolescents. In a recent study that used a self-report measure of major depression among middle school (grades 6–8) students in Houston, Texas, Mexican American youth were found to have a significantly higher rate of depression than white youth (12 % versus 6 %) (Roberts et al., 1997). These findings held even when level of impairment and sociodemographic factors were taken into account.

A large-scale survey of primarily Mexican American adolescents in schools on both sides of the Texas-Mexico border revealed high rates of depressive symptoms, drug use, and suicide (Swanson et al., 1992). Like the adult epidemiological studies, this investigation found that living in the United States is related to elevated risk for mental health problems. More Texas youth (48 %) reported high rates of depressive symptoms than did Mexican youth (39 %). Also, youth residing in Texas reported more illicit drug use in the last 30 days (21 %) and more suicidal ideation (23 %) than youth residing in Mexico.

Together the data indicate that Latino children and adolescents are at significant risk for mental health problems, and in many cases at greater risk than white children. At this time, it is not clear why a differential rate of mental health problems exists for Latino and white children. Special attention should be directed to the study of Latino youth, as they may be both the most vulnerable and the most amenable to prevention and intervention.

Older Adults

Few studies have examined the mental health status of older Hispanic American adults. A study of 703 Los Angeles area Hispanics age 60 or above found over 26 percent had major depression or dysphoria. Depression was related to physical health; only 5.5 percent of those without physical health complications reported depression (Kemp et al., 1987). Similar findings associated chronic health conditions and disability with depressive symptoms in a sample of 2,823 older community-dwelling Mexican Americans (Black et al., 1998). The findings from in-home interviews of 2,723 Mexican Americans age 65 or older in Southwestern communities revealed a relationship between low blood pressure and higher levels of depressive symptomatology (Stroup-Benham et al., 2000). These data are somewhat difficult to interpret. Given the fact that somatic symptoms (e.g., difficulty sleeping and loss of appetite) are related to poor health, these studies could simply document that these somatic symptoms are elevated among older Hispanics who are ill. (See Box 6–1, an illustration of the importance of considering the physical problems of older Latinos. This is one of many cases that Celia Falicov, 1998, uses to illustrate how the social and cultural world of Latino families expresses itself in clinical domains.) On the other hand, presence of physical illness is also related to depression. Taken together, these findings indicate that older Hispanics who have health problems may be at risk for depression. Furthermore, a recent study suggests that the risk for Alzheimer's disease may be higher among Hispanic Americans than among white Americans (Tang et al., 1998).

Mental Health Problems

Symptoms

The early epidemiological studies of Latinos examined the number of symptoms, not the number of mental disorders, reported by groups of Hispanic Americans, and in some cases compared them to the number of symptoms reported by white Americans. Much of this research found that Latinos had higher rates of depression or distress than whites (Frerichs et al., 1981; Roberts, 1981; Vernon & Roberts, 1982; Vega et al., 1984). In a large-scale study of Hispanics, Cuban Americans (Narrow et al., 1990) and Mexican Americans (Moscicki et al., 1989) were found to have lower rates of depressive symptoms than Puerto Ricans from the New York City metropolitan area (Moscicki et al., 1987; Potter et al., 1995). In another line of inquiry, Latina mothers who have children with mental retardation were found to report high levels of depressive symptomatology (Blacher et al., 1997a, 1997b).

It is important to note that measures of symptoms may reflect actual disorders that may not be measured in a given study, as well as general distress associated with social stressors but not necessarily associated with disorders. Two studies provide evidence that depressive symptom indices used with Latinos tend to measure distress more than disorder. In one study, rates of depressive

---

Box 6-1

Emotional or physical problems?

Mrs. Corrales (age 70)

Mrs. Corrales, a 70-year-old Puerto Rican, was referred to a mental health clinic by her local priest. Mrs. Corrales had no friends within the urban barrio. She had migrated from Puerto Rico eight years earlier to live with her two sons and her 45-year-old single and mildly developmentally impaired daughter. Two years before she came to the clinic, her sons had moved to a nearby city in search of better jobs. Mrs. Corrales remained behind with her daughter, who spoke no English and did not work. Among other questions, the Latin American therapist asked her if she was losing weight because she had lost her appetite, to which she quipped: "No, I've lost my teeth, not my appetite! That's what irks me!" Indeed, Mrs. Corrales had almost no teeth left in her mouth. Apparently, her conversations with the priest (an American who had learned to speak Spanish during a Latin American mission and was sensitive to the losses of migration) had centered on the emotional losses she had suffered with her sons' departure. The priest thought this was the cause of her "anxious depression." Though well meaning, he had failed to consider practical issues. Mrs. Corrales had no dental insurance, did not know any dentists, and had no financial resources.

Source: Falicov (1998), p. 255

Box 6-2: Rebellious teenager and father's *mal trato*

Javier (age 16)

Javier Reyes Balan, a 16-year-old boy, was referred by his school for persistent truancy. Nine years ago, his mother, father, and four younger siblings moved from Michoacan, Mexico, to San Diego, California, to better their economic situation. Javier was bilingual and served as the family interpreter in their dealings with outside institutions. He preferred to speak English and was clearly more savvy about American values and ways than his parents.

Mr. Reyes began the session by complaining bitterly about Javier's unruly behavior, lack of cooperation with his mother, and lack of respect toward his parents. Mrs. Reyes appeared to agree with her husband's view of Javier, although she protested that she didn't need much help around the house.

An inquiry about Mr. Reyes's occupation revealed that he had hoped to start his own small business as a car mechanic after moving from Mexico. He had not succeeded and was supporting the family precariously with occasional small jobs. He was proud of his competence and honesty as an automobile mechanic. But now he refused to work in a company under an Anglo-American foreman who would subject him to *mal trato*. In his view, "they [Americans] don't respect us Mexicans, and when you turn around they exploit you." The father's position in the family appeared to be debilitated by his unemployment.

Source: Falicov (1998), pp. 128-129.

symptoms were found to be similar among poor Puerto Ricans living in New York City and in Puerto Rico (Vera et al., 1991), even though earlier analyses indicated different rates of major depression for the two samples (Canino et al., 1987; Moscicki et al., 1987). In the second study, symptoms of depression were less related to diagnosis of depression for those Hispanics who were economically disadvantaged than for those Hispanics more socially advantaged (Cho et al., 1993). If an index of depressive symptoms were an indicator of both general distress and disorder, then that index would have been related to a diagnosis of depression for both economically advantaged and disadvantaged samples. An understanding of the interrelation of psychological distress, specific mental disorders, and social conditions would help shed light on how distress and disorder are moderated by social factors. (See Box 6–2 as an example of how the social world relates to family mental health problems.)

Somatization

The expression of distress through somatic symptoms has been observed in many groups, including Latinos (Escobar et al., 1987). Early research, influenced by psychodynamic theory, suggested that the expression of psychic distress via bodily complaints reflected limited psychological development. Current perspectives, however, accept somatic and psychological forms of expressing distress as equally valid. The two modes of expression are thought to mirror the sociocultural context; they do not necessarily reflect a lack of insight or psychological

sophistication. The critical questions today concern how social and cultural processes shape the expression of distress that emphasizes the soma, the psyche, or both (Kirmayer & Young, 1998).

Some research has examined the extent to which Latinos express physical symptoms, particularly in comparison to whites. Many of these studies have used symptom indices derived from the diagnostic interview used in the ECA studies. According to these studies, Mexican American women, particularly those over age 40, are more likely to report somatic symptoms; however, no differences were found between Mexican American and white men (Escobar et al., 1987). In an additional study, Puerto Rican men and women had higher rates of somatic symptoms than Mexican American and non-Hispanic men and women (Escobar et al., 1989).

A group of primary care patients that included Central American immigrants, Mexican immigrants, U.S.-born Mexican Americans, and whites were assessed for psychiatric disorders and somatization. After controlling for education and income differences, the immigrants reported fewer psychiatric disorders but higher rates of somatic symptoms when compared with the U.S.-born sample (Escobar et al., 2000). However, a more recent study questions the validity of those findings (Villasenor & Waitzkin, 1999), arguing that differences in use of health care services, different cultural understandings of the questions, and differences in socioeconomic status lead to spurious reports of somatic symptoms. For example, symptoms could have been considered "medically unexplained" because Latinos failed to receive adequate medical care and did not receive a diagnosis from a physician. Because high levels of somatic symptoms are related to disability (Escobar et al., 1987), research in this area is most important. Of particular significance are service factors (accessibility to care) and cultural factors (the meaning of physical and mental health) as they relate to somatization and distress.

Culture-Bound Syndromes

DSM-IV recognizes the existence of culturally related syndromes, referred to in the appendix of DSM as culture-bound syndromes. Relevant examples of these syndromes for Latinos are *susto* (fright), *nervios* (nerves), and *mal de ojo* (evil eye). One expression of distress that is most commonly associated with Caribbean Latinos but has been recognized in other Latinos as well is *ataques de nervios* (Guarnaccia et al., 1989). Symptoms of an *ataque de nervios* include screaming uncontrollably, crying, trembling, and verbal or physical aggression. Dissociative experiences, seizure-like or fainting episodes, and suicidal gestures are also prominent in some *ataques*. In one study carried out in Puerto Rico, researchers found that 14 percent of the population reported having had *ataques* (Guarnaccia et al., 1993). Furthermore, in detailed interviews of 121 individuals living in Puerto Rico (78 of whom had had an *ataque*), experiencing these symptoms was related to major life problems and subsequent psychological suffering (Guarnaccia et al., 1996). Clinical and ethnographic studies of individuals living in Boston and New York City also report observations of *ataques,* which in some instances required treatment (Guarnaccia et al., 1989; Liebowitz et al., 1994).

There is value in identifying specific culture-bound syndromes such as *ataques de nervios* because it is critical to recognize the existence of conceptions of distress and illness outside traditional psychiatric classification systems. These are often referred to as popular, lay, or common sense conceptions of illness or illness behavior (Koss-Chioino & Canive, 1993). Some of these popular conceptions may have what appear to be definable boundaries, while others are more fluid and cut across a wide range of symptom clusters. For example, many people of Mexican origin apply the more general concept of *nervios* to distress that is not associated with DSM disorders, as well as to distress that is associated with anxiety disorders, depressive disorders (Salgado de Snyder et al., 2000), and schizophrenia (Jenkins, 1988). Though it is valuable for researchers and clinicians alike to learn about specific culture-bound syndromes, it is

more important that they assess variable local representations of illness and distress. The latter approach casts a wider net around understanding the role of culture in illness and distress.

In the following quote, Koss-Chioino (1992) points out that a given presenting problem can have multiple levels of interpretation: the mental health view, the folk healing view (in this case, spiritist), and the patient's view.

The same woman, during one episode of illness, may experience "depression" in terms of hallucinations, poor or excessive appetite, memory problems, and feelings of sadness or depression, if she presents to a mental health clinic; or, alternatively, in terms of "backaches," "leg aches," and "fear," if she attends a Spiritist session. However, she will probably experience headaches, sleep disturbances, and nervousness regardless of the resource she uses. If we encounter her at the mental health clinic, she may explain her distress as due to disordered or out-of-control mind, behavior, or lifestyle. In the Spiritist session she will probably have her distress explained as an "obsession." And if we encounter her before she seeks help from either of these treatment resources, she may describe her problems as due to difficulties with her husband or children (or to their having abandoned her). (p. 198)

In the treatment setting, integrating consumers' popular or common sense notions of health and illness with biomedical notions has the potential to enhance treatment alliances and, in turn, treatment outcomes (Leventhal et al., 1997; Lopez, 1997).

Suicide

According to national statistics, Latinos had a suicide rate of approximately 6 percent in 1997 compared to a rate of 13 percent for the white population (DHHS, 1990). Overall, this lower rate suggests that Hispanic Americans are not demonstrating excess psychopathology through high rates of suicide. However, a national survey of 16,262 high school students in grades 9 through 12 found that Hispanics, both young women and young men, reported more suicidal ideation and specific suicidal attempts proportionally than whites and blacks. Over 10 percent of the Hispanics had attempted suicide, and 23 percent had considered the possibility of suicide (Centers for Disease Control and Prevention, 1998). Although this survey provided no data on actual suicides, these data suggest significant distress among Hispanic youth and are consistent with the several studies that found greater distress among Latinos than among largely white American youth.

High-Need Populations

Given that poverty is associated with homelessness and that many Hispanic American subgroups experience high rates of poverty, high rates of homelessness might be anticipated. However, the fact is that Hispanics are underrepresented among those without shelter (National Survey of Homeless Assistance Providers and Clients, 1996). Likewise, the need to place children in foster care is related to socioeconomic factors. Again, few Hispanic children are in the foster care system (DHHS, 1999). The fact that Hispanics are more likely to live with extended family members and with unrelated individuals suggests that family or friends may be taking care of those in need. Although Hispanics are relatively underrepresented among persons who are homeless or in foster care, they are present in high numbers within other vulnerable, high-need populations, such as incarcerated individuals, war veterans, survivors of trauma, and persons who abuse drugs or alcohol.

Individuals Who are Incarcerated

Low family socioeconomic status is associated with rates of chronic delinquency and crime (Wadsworth, 1979; Farrington, 1987; Tracy et al., 1990; Werner & Smith, 1992). The socioeconomic status of a neighborhood also predicts delinquency; that is, neighborhoods with high rates of adult unemployment, overcrowding, poor housing, low-achieving students, and high rates of mobility are all associated with high rates of delinquency (Rutter, 1979; Byrne & Sampson, 1986; McGahey, 1986; Schuerman & Kobrin, 1986). Given that many Latinos are poor and live within impoverished inner cities, relatively high rates of criminal involvement might be expected.

A larger proportion of Hispanic Americans (9 %) compared to white Americans (3 %) is incarcerated (Bureau of Justice Statistics, 1999). Among men, Hispanics are nearly four times as likely as whites to be in prison at some point during their lifetimes. Among women, less than 2 percent of Hispanics will enter prison compared to less than 1 percent of white women (Bureau of Justice Statistics, 1999). In addition, Hispanic youth make up 18 percent of juvenile offenders in residential placement (Bureau of Justice Statistics, 1999). Current epidemiological studies of incarcerated men and women include Hispanics and, in general, find that the rates of mental disorders among incarcerated individuals are higher than among community residents (Teplin, 1994; Teplin et al., 1996). Few ethnic differences among Hispanic Americans, white Americans, and African Americans were found. For those that were found, the small subsample of Latinos raises questions about the reliability of the findings.

Vietnam War Veterans

High rates of post-traumatic stress disorder (PTSD) exist among Vietnam War veterans. In a national study of Vietnam veterans (Kulka et al.,1990), Hispanics were found to be at higher risk for war-related PTSD than their white counterparts. In a further examination of Kulka's work, Ruef and her colleagues (2000) found the risk for Hispanics also higher than that for black veterans, suggesting that the risk is not just related to minority status. In another recent reexamination of the Kulka study, Puerto Rican veterans in particular were found to have a higher probability of experiencing PTSD than were others with similar levels of war zone stress exposure (Ortega & Rosenheck, 2000). Because these differences in prevalence were not explained by exposure to stressors or acculturation and were not accompanied by substantial reductions in functioning, the authors suggest that differences in symptom reporting may reflect features of expressive style rather than different levels of illness. Another plausible factor in explaining the higher likelihood of experiencing PTSD is greater exposure to violence and trauma prior to entering the military (Bremmer et al., 1993).

Refugees

Many Hispanics, particularly Central Americans, have come to the United States as refugees, and only a small number of them were granted refugee status as defined by the U.S. Government. During the period of civil wars in Nicaragua, El Salvador, and Guatemala, an estimated 2 million Central Americans migrated to Mexico, the United States, and Canada. From 1990 to 1997, from 4 to 8 percent of the refugees who entered the United States legally were from Central America. Many others are believed to have entered the country through unauthorized channels. Although self-help groups and assistance centers were set up by religious organizations, these refugees did not have official U.S. Government sanction and thus received no U.S. Government resettlement benefits (Carillo, 1990).

Because Central American refugees often experienced the systematic violation of human rights in their own countries (Farias, 1994), they are at high risk for mental disorders such as PTSD and depression. Adults attending three schools in Los Angeles were examined for symptoms of PTSD and depression (Cervantes et al., 1989). Half of the Central American participants reported symptoms that were consistent with a diagnosis of PTSD. In comparison with recent Mexican immigrants, a greater proportion of Central American refugees reported symptom clusters of PTSD (50% versus 25%) (Cervantes et al., 1989). In another study, 60 percent of adult Central American refugee patients were diagnosed with PTSD (Michultka et al., 1998). Central American immigrant children seeking care at refugee service centers also had high rates of PTSD (33 %) (Arroyo & Eth, 1984). Thus, Central American refugees who have been exposed to trauma have a high need for mental health care.

Individuals with Alcohol and Drug Problems

Studies have consistently shown that rates of substance abuse are linked with rates of mental disorders (Kessler et al., 1996; Ross et al., 1988; Rounsaville et al., 1991). Most studies of alcohol use among Hispanics indicate that rates of use are either similar to or slightly below those of whites (Kessler et al., 1994). However, two factors influence these rates. First, gender differences in rates of Latinos' use are often greater than the gender differences observed between whites. Latinas are particularly unlikely to use alcohol or drugs (Gilbert, 1987). In some cases, Latino men are more likely to use substances than white men. For example, in the Los Angeles ECA study, Mexican American men (31 %) had significantly higher rates of alcohol abuse and dependence than non-Hispanic white men (21 %). In addition, more alcohol-related problems have been found among Mexican American men than among white men (Cunradi et al., 1999).

A second factor associated with Latinos' rates of substance abuse is place of birth. In the Fresno study (Vega et al., 1998), rates of substance abuse were much higher among U.S.-born Mexican Americans compared to Mexican immigrants. Specifically, substance abuse rates were seven times higher among U.S.-born women compared to immigrant women. For men, the ratio was 2 to 1. U.S.-born Mexican American youth also had higher rates of substance abuse than Mexican-born youth (Swanson et al., 1992).

Strengths

The study of mental disorders and substance abuse among Latinos suggests two specific types of strengths that Latinos may have. First, as noted, Latino adults who are immigrants have lower prevalence rates of mental disorders than those born in the United States. Among the competing explanations of these findings is that Latino immigrants may be particularly resilient in the face of the hardships they encounter in settling in a new country. If this is the case, then the identification of what these immigrants do to reduce the likelihood of mental disorders could be of value for all Americans. One of many possible factors that might contribute to their resilience is what Suarez-Orozco and Suarez-Orozco (1995) refer to as a "dual frame of reference." Investigators found that Latino immigrants in middle-school frequently used their families back home as reference points in assessing their lives in the United States. Given that the social and economic conditions are often much worse in their homelands than in the United States, they may experience less distress in handling the stressors of their daily lives than those who lack such a basis of comparison. U.S.-born Latinos are more likely to compare themselves with their peers in the United States. Suarez-Orozco and Suarez-Orozco argue that these Latino children are more aware of what they do not have and thus may experience more distress.

A second factor noted by the Suarez-Orozcos that might be related to the resilience of Latino immigrants is their high aspiration to succeed. Particularly noteworthy is that many Latinos want to succeed in order to help their families, rather than for their own personal benefit. Because the Suarez-Orozcos did not include measures of mental health, it is not certain whether their observations about school achievement apply to mental health. Nevertheless, a dual frame of reference and collective achievement goals are part of a complex set of psychological, cultural, and social factors that may explain why some Latino immigrants function better than Latinos of later generations.

A second type of strength noted in the literature is how Latino families cope with mental illness. Guarnaccia and colleagues (1992) found that some families draw on their spirituality to cope with a relative's serious mental illness. Strong beliefs in God give some family members a sense of hope. For example, in reference to her brother's mental illness, one of the informants commented:

We all have an invisible doctor that we do not see, no? This doctor is God. Always when we go in search of a medicine, we go to a doctor, but we must keep in mind that this doctor is inspired by God and that he will give us something that will help us. We must also keep in mind that who really does the curing is God, and that God can cure us of anything that we have, material or spiritual. (p. 206)

Jenkins (1988) found that many Mexican Americans attributed their relatives' schizophrenia to *nervios,* a combination of both physical and emotional ailments. An important point here is that *nervios* implies that the patient is not blameworthy, and thus family members are less likely to be critical. Previous studies from largely non-Hispanic samples have found that both family criticism (for a review see Bebbington & Kuipers, 1994) and family blame and criticism together (Lopez et al., 1999) are associated with relapse in patients with schizophrenia. Mexican American families living with a relative who has schizophrenia are not only less likely to be critical, but also those who are Spanish-speaking immigrants have been found to be high in warmth. This is important because those patients who returned from a hospital stay to a family high in warmth were less likely to relapse than those who returned to families low in warmth (Lopez et al., 1998). Thus, Mexican American families' warmth may help protect the relative with schizophrenia from relapse. The spirituality of Latino families, their conceptions of mental illness, and their warmth all contribute to the support they give in coping with serious mental illness.

Although limited, the attention given to Latinos' possible strengths is an important contribution to the study of Latino mental health. Strengths are protective factors against distress and disorder and can be used to develop interventions to prevent mental disorders and to promote well-being. Such interventions could be used to inform interventions for all Americans, not just Latinos. In addition, redirecting attention to strengths helps point out the overemphasis researchers and practitioners give to pathology, clinical entities, and treatment, rather than to health, well-being, and prevention.

Availability, Accessibility, and Utilization of Mental Health Services

Availability of Mental Health Services

Finding mental health treatment from Spanish-speaking providers is likely to be a problem for many Spanish-speaking Hispanics. In the 1990 census, about 40 percent of Latinos reported that they either didn't speak English or didn't speak English well. Thus, a significant proportion of Latinos need Spanish-speaking mental health care providers. Presently there are no national data to indicate the language skills of the Nation's mental health professionals. However, a few studies reveal that there are few Spanish-speaking and Latino providers. One survey of 1,507 school psychologists who carry out psychoeducational assessments of bilingual children in the eight States with the highest percentages of Latinos found that 43 percent of the psychologists identified themselves as English-speaking monolinguals (Ochoa et al., 1996). In other words, a large number of English-speaking-only psychologists are evaluating bilingual children; this becomes a problem when these children's English language skills are limited.

Available clinical psychology human resources data indicate that Latinos comprise an extremely small portion of practicing psychologists. In fact, in a recent national survey of 596 licensed psychologists with active clinical practices who are members of the American Psychological Association, only 1 percent of the randomly selected sample identified themselves as Hispanic, whereas 96 percent identified themselves as white (Williams & Kohut, 1999). Another survey found that there were 29 Latino mental health professionals for every 100,000 Latinos in the U.S. population. For whites, the rate was 173 white providers per 100,000 (Center for Mental Health Service [CMHS], 1999). Clearly, Latino consumers have limited access to ethnically and linguistically similar providers.

Accessibility of Mental Health Services

The lack of health insurance is a significant barrier to mental health care for many Latinos. Although Hispanics comprise 12 percent of the U.S. population, they represent nearly one out of every four uninsured Americans (Brown et al., 2000; Kaiser Commission, 2000). Nationally, 37 percent of Latinos are uninsured; this is more than double the percent for whites. These high numbers are driven mostly by Latinos' lack of employer-based coverage: Only 43 percent of Latinos are covered through the workplace, compared to 73 percent of whites. Medicaid and other public coverage reaches 18 percent of Latinos. Citizenship and immigration status are other important factors that affect health insurance (Brown et al., 1999; Hanson, 2001). For example, among Latino youth ages 0 to 17 years in immigrant families, only 47 percent of noncitizens were insured compared to 71 percent of citizens. Of children born to U.S.-born parents, 84 percent were insured. Compared to Asian Americans, African Americans, and white Americans children, Latino children were the least likely to be insured, regardless of citizenship. For example, noncitizen Latino children had a significantly lower percentage of being insured (47 %) than noncitizen Asian children (80 %). Thus, the lower rate of insurance coverage for Latinos is a function of ethnicity, immigration status, and citizenship status.

Utilization of Mental Health Services

Community Studies

The available studies consistently indicate that Hispanic community residents with diagnosable mental disorders are receiving insufficient mental health care. In the Los Angeles Epidemiologic Catchment Area (ECA) study, for example, Mexican Americans who had experienced mental disorders within the past six months were less likely to use health or mental health services than whites (11 % versus 22 %) (Hough et al., 1987). The study of Mexican Americans residing in Fresno County revealed similar results. Only 9 percent of those with mental disorders during the 12 months prior to the interview sought services from a mental health specialist. This rate was even lower for those born in Mexico (5 %) compared to those born in the United States (12 %) (Vega et al., 1999). Furthermore, Latinos are twice as likely to seek treatment for mental disorders in general health care settings as opposed to mental health specialty settings.

These studies suggest that among Hispanic Americans with mental disorders, fewer than 1 in 11 contact mental health care specialists, while fewer than 1 in 5 contact general health care providers. Among Hispanic American immigrants with mental disorders, fewer than 1 in 20 use services from mental health specialists, while fewer than 1 in 10 use services from general health care providers.

The National Comorbidity Study also found that Latinos used few mental health services, even though all those surveyed were fluent in English. For example, only

11 percent of those with a mood disorder and 10 percent of those with an anxiety disorder used mental health specialists for care.

Reports on the use of mental health services in Puerto Rico are much different. In one community survey ($N = 1,551$ adults), 85 percent of those with diagnosable disorders reported using mental health care specialists or health care providers (Martinez et al., 1991). In a second large survey focused on poor Puerto Ricans, 32 percent of those identified as needing mental health care received services in the previous year (Alegria et al., 1991). Like mainland Latinos, Puerto Ricans obtained mental health care from the general medical sector more often than from mental health specialists.

Whereas most studies of Latinos' use of mental health services have been largely descriptive in nature, there have been some studies to identify the processes that lead to accessing mental health care. One study carried out in Puerto Rico, for example, found that low economic strain was related to the use of specialty mental health care, suggesting that economic barriers may contribute to low use of mental health services (Vera et al., 1998). In addition, these investigators pointed out that predictors vary with regard to the specific aspect of help seeking under study, from recognizing a mental health problem to seeking care from health care providers in general and mental health care providers in particular (See Box 6-3). Another important process that may be associated with Hispanics' use of mental health services is stigma. Research is needed to examine the role of stigma as it relates to their accessing mental health care.

Mental Health Systems Studies

Several evaluations of Latinos' use of services in care systems during the 1980s have been published. Two were based on national data (Snowden & Cheung, 1990, for 1980–1981; Cheung & Snowden, 1990, for 1983; Breaux & Ryujin, 1999, for 1986), and two examined insured populations (Scheffler & Miller, 1989, for 1979–1981; Padgett et al., 1994, for 1983). Most show low use of inpatient services. The results for outpatient care were equivocal. Differences between studies of inpatient and outpatient service use could have resulted from the study of different Latino subgroups in each sample.

Complementary Therapies

Several national studies show that Americans from all ethnocultural backgrounds turn to alternative sources of health care, either self-administered or given by alternative providers, to complement the general health and mental health care that they receive from mainstream sources (Astin, 1998; Eisenberg et al., 1998; Druss & Rosenheck, 2000). However, these studies have not included large enough samples of Latinos to give precise estimates of the use of complementary therapies by this group. The Hispanic Health and Nutrition Examination Survey (HHANES) found that only 4 percent of the

---

Box 6-3

Increasing use of services: Learning from the past

La Frontera Center

With the growing number and increasing spread of Latinos throughout the United States, some mental health systems are addressing for the first time how to reach Latinos in need of mental health care. To guide current efforts, there is some value in reflecting on how mental health centers in the 1960s first began to reach out to Latino communities. La Frontera Center, a mental health center located in South Tucson, Arizona, is well known for its success in making services available to Latinos (Preciado Martin, 1979).

When [La Frontera] first opened its doors, bilingual and bicultural social workers walked through the community introducing themselves and their services. In addition, service providers established collaborative working relations with other community organizations such as public health agencies, juvenile justice, public libraries, and the local Spanish-language radio station. For example, a depression prevention program was implemented in a public health well baby clinic where young mothers would bring their children for a free physical exam. A Spanish-speaking mental health worker would meet briefly with mothers and provide both educational and assessment services. When necessary, the mental health worker would refer the mother for an evaluation at the mental health center. The main point is that the center developed creative approaches to engage persons in need within their community context; clinic staff did not wait for potential consumers to walk through the clinic doors. Evidence of the same philosophy can be seen in more contemporary services as well, specifically those provided to caregivers of Latinos with Alzheimer's disease (Henderson et al., 1993).

Mexican American sample in five Southwestern States had reported consulting a *curandero, herbalista,* or other folk medicine practitioner within the prior 12 months (Higginbotham et al., 1990). However, some believe that the HHANES may not truly represent the extent of use among all Mexican Americans, because the methods the HHANES used tend to include individuals with higher education, higher income, and telephone access, while they tend to miss subgroups that are harder to reach (Skaer et al., 1996). In fact, studies of smaller subgroups of Mexican Americans have found that proportions ranging from 7 percent to 44 percent of the sample use *curanderos* and other traditional healers (Risser & Mazur, 1995; Keegan, 1996; Skaer et al., 1996; Macias & Morales, 2000).

Use of folk remedies is more common than consultation with a folk healer, however, and these remedies are generally used to complement mainstream care. A study of folk remedies for asthma in a mainland Puerto Rican community found that these remedies are well known and commonly used, even though the importance of receiving timely mainstream treatment was recognized (Pachter et al., 1995).

Integrating complementary care with traditional mental health care was an objective of a unique training project carried out in Puerto Rico (Koss-Chioino, 1992). Both *espiritistas* (Puerto Rican folk healers) and mental health providers participated in a program to enhance mutual understanding and communication. This model program included lectures and case presentations by experts representing both therapeutic perspectives, as well as visits to the healers' facility, or *centro*. The available evidence suggested that this program was most successful in helping both groups understand their differences, as well as in occasionally coordinating their treatments. Although mental health providers and folk healers do not often communicate with one another, this program demonstrated that the two systems of care have the potential to complement one another. Also, mental health service providers should be aware that in many places these complementary sources of care have been stigmatized by the church and by traditional medical practices. Therefore, some Latinos may be reluctant to disclose their participation in folk healing practices.

Children and Youth

Very few studies have addressed the use of mental health services by Latino children and youth. One exception is the Methods for the Epidemiology of Child and Adolescent Mental Disorders (MECA) study (Lahey et al., 1996). Researchers obtained community-based probability samples of parent and youth pairs ($N = 1,285$) in four sites: New Haven, Connecticut; Atlanta, Georgia; Westchester County, New York; and San Juan, Puerto Rico. They also administered a structured diagnostic instrument to assess these children and adolescents. These investigators found that Puerto Rican youth used mental health services significantly less than children from the other sites did. Of those Puerto Rican youth with a diagnosable mental disorder, only 20 percent reported using mental health-related services (Leaf et al., 1996). This percentage is markedly lower than the percentages of youth receiving care at the other sites; they range from 37 to 44 percent.

This study made a unique contribution to the understanding of children's use of mental health services because it obtained a measure of unmet need that was based both on a diagnosis and on a significant degree of impairment, where impairment was related to key symptoms of the diagnosis (Flisher et al., 1997). Including a level of impairment in identifying need for mental health care is likely to reduce the risk of overestimating need. Using this measure, 13 percent of Hispanic children, compared to 16 percent of white children, were rated as having unmet need for care.

Researchers conducted another study of children's use of mental health care in two communities in Texas: Galveston and the lower Rio Grande Valley (Pumariega et al., 1998). Hispanics reported significantly fewer lifetime counseling visits than white youth (2 versus 4). Bui and Takeuchi (1992) also found evidence that Hispanics were underrepresented in the use of outpatient mental health facilities in Los Angeles County from 1983 to 1988. Specifically, they reported that although Hispanics under 18 years of age in Los Angeles County were 42 percent of the under-18-year-old population, only 36 percent of the adolescent caseload was Hispanic. Together these studies indicate that Latino youth use mental health facilities less than they might.

Appropriateness and Outcomes of Mental Health Services

Studies on Treatment Outcomes

Few studies on the response of Latinos to mental health care are available. Only three small studies of depression have been published. They investigated the care for depression given to unmarried Puerto Rican mothers with depressive symptoms (Comas-Diaz, 1981), to Mexican American women (Alonso et al., 1997), and to Puerto Rican adolescents (Rossello & Bernal, 1999). Although all found that those who were treated had favorable results, the sample sizes are far too small to establish the response of Latinos to care for depression.

Another study examined interventions for schizophrenia among Latinos. In this randomized study, members of low-income, Spanish-speaking families were more likely to suffer a significant exacerbation of symptoms in highly structured family therapy than in the less structured case management (Telles et al., 1995). The authors of this study speculated that these individuals may have found this highly structured treatment too intrusive.

Several preventive intervention studies have focused on Latino children and families (Costantino et al., 1986, 1988; Szapocznik et al., 1989; Malgady et al., 1990; Lieberman et al., 1991). In these studies, mental health professionals provided culturally adapted preventive care to immigrant mothers and infants in San Francisco (Lieberman et al., 1991), Puerto Rican children and parents in New York City (Costantino et al., 1986), and families in Miami (Szapocznik et al., 1989). In general, the interventions resulted in short-term gains, but long-term follow-up evaluations to determine whether they actually prevented later mental disorders were not reported.

Two effectiveness studies examined treatment for depression among ethnically mixed samples of primary care patients with significant proportions of Latinos. In the first study, Miranda and Munoz (1994) investigated the effectiveness of group cognitive treatment for minor depression. Although analyses were not run separately for Latinos, who comprised 24 percent of the sample, the findings indicated that patients receiving the cognitive treatment improved significantly more than those who received no intervention or who watched a 40-minute videotape.

The second study was more ambitious. It was carried out in 46 primary care clinics across six managed systems of care (Wells et al., 2000). Two of the cities in the study, San Luis, Colorado, and San Antonio, Texas, have large Mexican American communities. Latinos comprised nearly a third (30 %) of the enrolled sample ($N = 1,356$). The purpose of the study was to assess the effects of programs to improve the quality of care for depression. Specifically, usual care was compared with two interventions, one for which medication was administered and closely followed for 6 or 12 months and the other for which local psychotherapists provided cognitive-behavior treatment ranging from 4 sessions for minor depression and related problems to 10–16 sessions for major depression. Although results broken down by ethnicity have yet to be published, the initial findings indicate that, relative to usual care, the quality improvement programs had significant effects on treatment process, clinical outcome, and even social outcomes such as employment.

Diagnostic and Testing Issues

Quality care requires valid diagnostic and clinical assessment. Several studies have found that bilingual patients are evaluated differently when interviewed in English as opposed to Spanish (Del Castillo, 1970; Marcos et al., 1973; Price & Cuellar, 1981; Malgady & Costantino, 1998); however, the extent to which these factors result in misdiagnoses is not known. One small study examining records of patients with bipolar disorder (manic depressive illness) found that in the past, both African American and Latino patients were more likely to have been misdiagnosed as schizophrenic than whites (Mukherjee et al., 1983). Further research is needed to clarify how cultural and linguistic factors influence diagnoses (Malgady et al., 1987; Lopez, 1988).

Psychological testing can also be affected by language and cultural factors. Of particular interest is testing that contributes to the diagnosis of mental retardation (e.g., cognitive intelligence tests), dementia (neuropsychological testing), and mental disorders (psychological tests such as the MMPI-2). The two main positions on testing are that (1) tests are biased against minority group members (e.g., Guthrie, 1998), and (2) there is no evidence of ethnic or cultural bias (Gottfredson, 1997). Cole (1981) refers to these positions as those of the reformers and the defenders. Most of the literature involves African Americans (e.g., Helms, 1992), and when Latinos are included, they are mostly English-speaking Latinos (e.g., Sandoval, 1979). However, the literature concerning Latinos and the particular challenge of assessing bilingual persons and those with limited English proficiency is growing (e.g., Jacobs et al., 1997).

The lack of reliable and valid tests normed on contemporary samples of Latinos, both Spanish-speaking and English-speaking, is a significant obstacle to carrying out the appropriate assessment of Latinos (Bird et al., 1987; Loewenstein et al., 1994; Velasquez et al., 1998). Two of the most widely used tests for diagnostic purposes are the Wechsler scales of intelligence and the MMPI-2. The available Wechsler test for Spanish-speaking adults, Escala Inteligencia de Wechsler para Adultos (EIWA), was published in 1968 and was based on a standardization sample of Puerto Rican islanders (Wechsler, 1968). Since then, two English language versions have been standardized and published (Wechsler, 1981, 1998).

The current Spanish language norms are significantly outdated, and available research has demonstrated their overestimating the level of functioning of some Spanish-speaking adults (e.g., Lopez & Taussig, 1991). The children's version of the WAIS, however, has been developed and standardized on a more contemporary sample of Puerto Rican island children (Wechsler, 1989). In the restandardization of the MMPI (MMPI–2; Butcher et al., 1989), little consideration was given to Latinos. Of the 2,600 who comprised the standardization sample, only 73, or 2.8 percent, were identified as Hispanic. This percentage reflected only one-third of the actual Hispanic representation in the Nation at that time. Both the EIWA and MMPI-2 demonstrate that some test publishers assign little importance to providing contemporary and representative norms of Latinos in the United States. This statement does not apply to all tests, since recent advances have been made in the development of language skills tests in Spanish and English (e.g., Woodcock & Munoz, 1993) and nonverbal tests (e.g., Bracken & McCallum, 1998, Naglieri & Bardos, 1999). At the very least, tests based on normative samples of U.S. adults or children should include subsamples of Latinos that accurately reflect their representation in the Nation. At best, Latinos should be oversampled so that tests of fairness can be carried out that attend to differences among subgroups within the Hispanic American population as well as differences between Hispanic Americans and other racial and ethnic groups.

Evidence-Based Treatment

To determine whether there are disparities in mental health care, it is important to discover whether Latinos are as likely as white Americans to receive care that is consistent with guidelines established by recognized psychiatric and psychological organizations. Recent data suggest that Latinos are less likely than whites to receive treatment according to evidence-based guidelines. Evidence from a representative national sample suggests that many individuals with depression and anxiety do not receive appropriate care (Young et al., 2001); fewer Hispanics receive appropriate care (24 %) than do whites (34 %).

Another study examined the use of antidepressants among clients who had visited a general medical doctor (National Ambulatory Medical Care Surveys of 1992–1993 and 1994–1995). During the two time periods in the early 1990s that were evaluated, Latinos were less than half as likely as whites to have received either a diagnosis of depression or antidepressant medication (Sclar et al., 1999).

A few small preliminary studies have examined pharmacologic responses in Latino populations. In the research that does exist, data are often drawn from aggregate samples of several different Hispanic groups in attempts to characterize a typical Hispanic response (Mendoza & Smith, 2000). However, evidence of important genetic variation among subgroups (i.e., Mexican Americans, Puerto Ricans, and Colombians) implies that disaggregated data are needed before any ethnopsychopharmacological findings should be considered conclusive (Hanis et al., 1991; Mendoza & Smith, 2000).

Cultural Competence

Sue and colleagues (1991) studied community mental health centers in Los Angeles in order to examine ethnically matched provider services versus nonmatched provider services. Ethnic match resulted in longer duration of treatment for Mexican Americans, as well as better patient response to treatment based on a global indicator of functioning. This suggests that ethnic match of provider and consumer can be important in providing services for some Latinos.

One limitation of ethnic match research is that there is no direct assessment of clinicians' cultural understanding or skills. Therefore, it is not clear if the cultural competence of practitioners is related to the positive findings of ethnic match. Direct study of cultural competence for Latinos is needed. Although there have been efforts to develop specific cultural competence guidelines for Latinos (Western Interstate Commission for Higher Education, 1996), most models that have been developed apply across ethnic groups.

Cultural competence has received widespread attention across the Nation. Some State and local policymakers now require cultural competence training for their practitioners. Federal agencies are supporting the development and implementation of guidelines (e.g., CMHS, 2000). Despite the several models and the growing interest in cultural competence, much work needs to be done before cultural competence will positively impact mental health service delivery for Latinos and other ethnic groups. Currently, cultural competence is largely a set of guiding principles that lack empirical validation. Thus, an essential step in advancing culturally competent services for Latinos is to carry out research to test the guidelines, standards, or models proposed by these expert clinicians and administrators. Bernal et al. (1995) and Lopez et al. (in press) discuss multiple strategies to develop culturally informed interventions.

Conclusions

(1) The system of mental health services currently in place fails to provide for the vast majority of Latinos in need of care. This failure is especially pronounced for immigrant Latinos, who make the least use of mental health services. Latinos within known vulnerable groups are also of concern. Incarcerated Latinos, those who use excessive amounts of alcohol or drugs, and those exposed to violence, such as Central American refugees, are most likely to be in need of mental health care. There are many ways to improve services for Latinos, from reducing systemic barriers—especially financial barriers—to increasing the number of mental health professionals who are linguistically and culturally skilled. Also, because Latinos are more likely to seek mental health services in primary care settings, improving detection and care within the general health care sector is important.

(2) Latino youth are at a significantly high risk for poor mental health outcomes. Evidence suggests that they are more likely to drop out of school, to report depression and anxiety, and to consider suicide than white youth. Prevention and treatment are needed to address their mental health problems. Given the rapid expansion of this young population of Latinos, these interventions could have major implications for the ongoing health of the Nation's youth.

(3) Sociohistorical data suggest that there should be mental health differences among Latino subgroups. Although the data are limited, there is some evidence that Central Americans do have greater problems than other Latino subgroups, especially with post-traumatic stress disorder. However, there is little evidence of Cuban Americans having lower rates of disorder than other Latino subgroups. The National Latino Asian American Study (NLAAS) now being conducted will be the first psychiatric epidemiological study to use a representative sample of the Nation's Latinos, which will enable researchers to test subgroup differences more systematically.

(4) In addition to the findings emphasizing the need for mental health care, a pattern of evidence for the strengths of Latino immigrants also emerges.

Resilience is indicated by the lower rates of mental disorders for Mexican-born adults and children and island-born Puerto Rican adults compared with the rates for those born in the United States. Some of the ways in which Latinos cope with mental illness suggest strengths as well. The factors underlying these observed strengths are not clear, but they hold promise for identifying social and cultural patterns that promote mental health. These patterns could be particularly helpful in developing culturally sensitive interventions to prevent and treat the mental health problems that Latinos face.

(5) Mental disorders and distress can be interpreted on many levels, from the molecular aspects of neuroscience to the social world of consumers and families. Psychosis can be understood as the result of dysfunctions in neurotransmitters as well as the result of a deeply felt personal loss. To provide culturally responsive therapy for Latinos, it is critical that providers access the local world of their patients and their families. Doing so will suggest ways practitioners can integrate effectively the social and cultural context of their Latino patients with their own worlds to provide effective care.

References

Achenbach, T. M., & Edelbrock, C. (1983). *Manual for the Child Behavior Checklist and Revised Child Behavior Profile.* Burlington, VT: University of Vermont, Department of Psychiatry.

Achenbach, T. M., Bird, H. R., Canino, G., Phares, V., Gould, M. S., & Rubio-Stipec, M. (1990). Epidemiological comparisons of Puerto Rican and U.S. mainland children: Parent, teacher, and self-reports. *Journal of the American Child and Adolescent Psychiatry, 29,* 84–93.

Alegria, M., Robles, R., Freeman, D. H., Vera, M., Jimenez, A. L., Rios, C., & Rios, R. (1991). Patterns of mental health utilization among island Puerto Rican poor. *American Journal of Public Health, 81,* 875–879.

Alonso, M., Val, E., & Rapaport, M. M. (1997). An open-label study of SSRI treatment in depressed Hispanic and non-Hispanic women. *Journal of Clinical Psychiatry, 58,* 31.

American Psychiatric Association. (1994). *Diagnostic and statistical manual of mental disorders* (4th ed.). Washington, DC: Author.

Arroyo, W., & Eth, S. (1984). Children traumatized by Central American warfare. In S. Eth & R. Pynoos (Eds.), *Post-traumatic stress disorder in children* (pp. 101–120). Washington, DC: American Psychiatric Press.

Astin, J.A. (1998). Why patients use alternative medicine: Results of a national study. *Journal of the American Medical Association, 279,* 1548–1553.

Bebbington, P., & Kuipers, L. (1994). The predictive utility of expressed emotion in schizophrenia: An aggregate analysis. *Psychological Medicine, 24,* 707–718.

Becerra, J. E., Hogue, C. J., Atrash, H. K., & Perez, N. (1991). Infant mortality among Hispanics. A portrait of heterogeneity. *Journal of the American Medical Association, 265,* 217–221.

Bernal, G., Bonilla, J., & Bellido, C. (1995). Ecological validity and cultural sensitivity for outcome research: Issues for the cultural adaptation and development of psychosocial treatments with Hispanics. *Journal of Abnormal Child Psychology, 23,* 67–82.

Bernal, G., & Shapiro, E. (1996). Cuban families. In M. McGoldrick, J. Giordano, & J. K. Pierce (Eds.), *Ethnicity and family therapy* (2nd ed., pp. 155–168). New York: Guilford Press.

Betancourt, H., & Lopez, S. R. (1993). The study of culture, ethnicity and race in American psychology. *American Psychologist, 48,* 629–637.

Bird, H. R., Canino, G., Rubio-Stipec, M., Gould, M. S., Ribera, J., Sesman, M., Woodbury, M., Huertas-Goldman, S., Pagan, A., Sanchez-Lacay, A., & Moscoso, M. (1988). Estimates of the prevalence of childhood maladjustment in a community survey in Puerto Rico: The use of combined measures. *Archives of General Psychiatry, 45,* 1120–1126.

Bird, H. R., Canino, G., Rubio-Stipec, M., & Shrout, P. (1987). Use of the Mini-Mental State Examination in a probability sample of a Hispanic population. *Journal of Nervous and Mental Disease, 175,* 731–737.

Black, S. A., Goodwin, J. S., & Markides, K. S. (1998). The association between chronic diseases and depressive symptomatology in older Mexican Americans. *Journals of Gerontology: Medical Sciences, 53A,* M188–M194.

Bracken, B. A., & McCallum, R. S. (1998). *Universal nonverbal intelligence test: Examiner's manual.* Chicago: Riverside.

Breaux, C., & Ryujin, D. (1999). Use of mental health services by ethnically diverse groups within the United States. *The Clinical Psychologist, 52* (3), 4.

Bremmer, J. D., Southwick, S. M., Johnson, D. R., Yehuda, R., & Charney, D. S. (1993). Childhood physical abuse and combat-related posttraumatic stress disorder in Vietnam veterans. *American Journal of Psychiatry, 150,* 235–239.

Brown, E. R., Ojeda, V. D., Wyn, R., & Levan, R. (2000). *Racial and ethnic disparities in access to health insurance and health care.* Los Angeles: UCLA Center for Health Policy Research and The Henry J. Kaiser Family Foundation.

Brown, E. R., Wyn, R., Hongjian, W., Valenzuela, A., & Dong, L. (1999). Access to health insurance and health care for children in immigrant families. In D. J. Hernandez (Ed.), *Children of immigrants.* Washington, DC: National Academy of Sciences.

Bui, K. T., & Takeuchi, D. T. (1992). Ethnic minority adolescents and the use of community mental health care services. *American Journal of Community Psychology, 20,* 403–417.

Bureau of Justice Statistics. (1999). *Correctional populations in the United States, 1996.* Washington, DC: Author.

Burnam, M., Hough, R., Escobar, J., Karno, M., Timbers, D. M., Telles, C. A., & Locke, B. Z. (1987a). Six-month prevalence of specific psychiatric disorders among Mexican American and non-Hispanic Whites in Los Angeles. *Archives of General Psychiatry, 44,* 687–694.

Burnam, M. Hough, R., Karno, M., Escobar, J., & Telles, C. A. (1987b). Acculturation and lifetime prevalence of psychiatric disorders among Mexican Americans in Los Angeles. *Journal of Health & Social Behavior, 28,* 89–102.

Butcher, J. N., Dahlstrom, W. G., Graham, J. R., Tellegen, A., & Kaemmer, B. (1989). *Minnesota Multiphasic Personality Inventory (MMPI-2).* Minneapolis: University of Minnesota Press.

Byrne, J., & Sampson, R. J. (1986). Key issues in the social ecology of crime. In J. Byrne & R. J. Sampson (Eds.), *The sociology of crime.* New York: Springer-Verlag.

Canino, G. J., Bird, H. R., Shrout, P. E., Rubio-Stipec, M., Bravo, M., Martinez, R., Sesman, M., & Guevara, L. M. (1987). The prevalence of specific psychiatric disorders in Puerto Rico. *Archives of General Psychiatry, 44,* 727–735.

Caraveo-Anduaga, J. J., Colmenares Bermúdez, E., Saldívar Hernández, G. J. (1999). Morbilidad psiquiátrica en la ciudad de México: Prevalencia y comorbilidad en la vida. (Psychiatric morbidity in Mexico City: Lifetime prevalence and cormorbity). *Salud Mental, 22* (Special Issue), 62–67.

Carillo, C. (1990). Application of refugee laws to Central Americans in the United States. In W. H. Holtzman & T. Bornemann (Eds.), *Mental health of immigrants and refugees* (pp. 143–154). Austin, TX: Hogg Foundation.

Cattan, P. (1993). The diversity of Hispanics in the U.S. work force. *Monthly Labor Review, 116* (8), 3–15.

Center for Mental Health Services. (2000). *Cultural competence standards in managed care mental health services: Four underserved/underrepresented racial/ethnic groups.* Retrieved July 26, 2001, from http://www.mentalhealth.org/publications/allpubs/SMA00–3457/.

Centers for Disease Control and Prevention. (1998). CDC surveillance summaries: Youth risk behavior surveillance: United States, 1997. *Morbidity and Mortality Weekly Report, 47,* 1–89.

Cervantes, R. C., Salgado de Snyder, V. N., & Padilla, A. M. (1989). Posttraumatic stress in immigrants from Cental America and Mexico. *Hospital and Community Psychiatry, 40,* 615–619.

Cheung, F. K., & Snowden, L. R. (1990). Community mental health and ethnic minority populations. *Community Mental Health Journal, 26,* 277–291.

Cho, M. J., Moscicki, E. K., Narrow, W. E., Rae, D. S., Locke, B. Z., & Regier, D. A. (1993). Concordance between two measures of depression in the Hispanic Health and Nutrition Examination Survey. *Social Psychiatry and Psychiatric Epidemiology, 28,* 156–163.

Cole, N. (1981). Bias in testing. *American Psychologist, 36,* 1067–1077.

Comas-Diaz, L. (1981). Effects of cognitive and behavioral group treatment on the dpressive symptoms of Puerto Rican women. *Journal of Consulting and Clinical Psychology, 49,* 627–632.

Costantino, G., Malgady, R., & Rogler, L. (1986). Cuento therapy: A culturally sensitive modality for Puerto Rican children. *Journal of Consulting and Clinical Psychology, 54,* 639–645.

Costantino, G., Malgady, R., & Rogler, L. (1988). Folk hero modeling therapy for Puerto Rican adolescents. *Journal of Adolescence, 11,* 155–166.

Cunradi, C. B., Caetano, R., Clark, C. L., & Schafer, J. (1999). Alcohol-related problems and intimate partner violence among white, black, and Hispanic couples in the U.S. *Alcoholism: Clinical and Experimental Research, 23,* 1492–1501.

Del Castillo, J. C. (1970). The influences of language upon symptomatology in foreign-born patients. *American Journal of Psychiatry, 127,* 160–162.

Druss, B. G., & Rosenheck, R. A. (2000). Use of practitioner-based complementary therapies by persons reporting mental conditions in the United States. *Archives of General Psychiatry, 57,* 708–714.

Eisenberg, D. M., Davis, R. B., Ettner, S. L., Appel, S., Wilkey, S., Van Rompay, M., & Kessler, R. C. (1998). Trends in alternative medicine use in the United States, 1990–1997: Results of a follow-up national survey. *Journal of the American Medical Association, 280*, 1569–1575.

Escobar, J. I., Burnam, M. A., Karno, M., Forsythe, A. & Golding, J. M. (1987). Somatization in the community: Relationship to disability and use of services. *Archives of General Psychiatry, 44*, 713–718.

Escobar, J. I., Rubio-Stipec, M., Canino, G., & Karno, M. (1989). Somatic Symptom Index (SSI): A new and abridged somatization construct: Prevalence and epidemiological correlates in two large community samples. *Journal of Nervous and Mental Disease, 177*, 140–146.

Escobar, J. I., Hoyos Nervi, C., & Gara, M. A. (2000). Immigration and mental health: Mexican Americans in the United States. *Harvard Review of Psychiatry, 8*, 64–72.

Falicov, C. J. (1998). *Latino families in therapy: A guide to multicultural practice.* New York: Guilford Press.

Farias, P. (1994). Central and South American refugees: Some mental health challenges. In A. J. Marsella, T. Bornemann, S. Ekblad, & J. Orley (Eds.), *Amidst peril and pain: The mental health and well being of the world's refugees* (pp. 101–113). Washington, DC: American Psychological Association.

Farrington, K. (1987). Taking the community into account. *The Health Service Journal, 97* (Suppl. 12, 14), 5072.

Flisher, A. J., Kramer, R. A., Gorsser, R. C., Alegria, M., Bird, H. R., Bourdon, K. H., Goodman, S. H., Greenwald, S., Horwitz, S. M., Moore, R. E., Narrow, W. E., & Hoven, C. W. (1997). Correlates of unmet need for mental health services by children and adolescents. *Psychological Medicine, 27*, 1145–1154.

Frerichs, R. R., Aneshensel, C. S., & Clark, V. A. (1981). Prevalence of depression in Los Angeles County. *American Journal of Epidemiology, 113*, 691–699.

Gil, A., & Vega, W. A. (1996). Two different worlds: Acculturation stress and adaptation among Cuban and Nicaraguan families in Miami. *Journal of Social and Personal Relations, 13*, 437–458.

Gilbert, M. J. (1987). Alcohol consumption patterns in immigrant and later generation Mexican American women. *Hispanic Journal of Behavioral Science, 9*, 299–313.

Glover, S. H., Pumariega, A. J., Holzer, C. E., Wise, B. K., & Rodriguez, M. (1999). Anxiety symptomatology in Mexican American adolescents. *Journal of Child and Family Studies, 8*, 47–57.

Gottfredson, L. S. (1997). Mainstream science on intelligence: An editorial with 52 signatories, history, and bibliography. *Intelligence, 24*, 13–23.

Guarnaccia, P. J., Canino, G., Rubio-Stipec, M., & Bravo, M. (1993). The prevalence of ataques de nervios in the Puerto Rico study: The role of culture in psychiatric epidemiology. *Journal of Nervous and Mental Disease, 181*, 157–165.

Guarnaccia, P. J., De La Cancela, V., & Carrillo, E. (1989). The multiple meanings of ataques de nervios in the Latino community. *Medical Anthropology, 11*, 47–62.

Guarnaccia, P. J., Parra, P., Deschamps, A., Milstein, G., & Argiles, N. (1992). Si Dios quiere: Hispanic families' experiences of caring for a seriously mentally ill family member. *Culture, Medicine and Psychiatry, 16*, 187–215.

Guarnaccia, P. J., Rivera, M., Franco, F., & Neighbors, C. (1996). The experiences of ataques de nervios: Towards an anthropology of emotions in Puerto Rico. *Culture, Medicine and Psychiatry, 20*, 343–367.

Guthrie, R. V. (1998). *Even the rat was white* (2nd ed.). Boston: Allyn & Bacon.

Hajat, A. (2000). Health outcomes among Hispanic subgroups: Data from the National Health Interview Survey, 1992–1995. Advance Data No. 310 from *Vital and Health Statistics.* Atlanta, GA: National Center for Health Statistics.

Hanis, C. L., Hewett-Emmett, D., Bertin, T. K., & Schull, W. J. (1991). Origins of U.S. Hispanics. Implications for diabetes. *Diabetes Care, 14*, 618–627.

Hanson, K. L. (2001). Patterns of insurance coverage within families with children. *Health Affairs, 20*, 240–246.

Helms, J. E. (1992). Why is there no study of cultural equivalence in standardized cognitive ability testing? *American Psychologist, 47*, 1083–1101.

Henderson, J. N., Gutierrez-Mayka, M., Garcia, J., & Boyd, S. (1993). A model for Alzheimer's disease support group development in African-American and Hispanic populations. *The Gerontologist, 33*, 409–414.

Higginbotham, J. C., Trevino, F. M., & Ray, L. A. (1990). Utilization of curanderos by Mexican Americans: Prevalence and predictors. Findings from the HHANES 1982–1984. *American Journal of Public Health, 80* (Suppl.), 32–35.

Hoppe, S. K., Garza-Elizondo, T., Leal-Isla, C., & Leon, R. I. (1991). Mental disorders among family practice patients in the United States–Mexico border region. *Social Psychiatry and Psychiatric Epidemiology, 26* (4), 178–182.

Hough, R. L., Landsverk, J. A., Karno, M., Burnam, M. A., Timbers, D. M., Escobar, J. I., & Regier, D. A. (1987). Utilization of health and mental health services by Los Angeles Mexican Americans and non-Hispanic whites. *Archives of General Psychiatry, 44*, 702–709.

Jacobs, D. M., Sano, M., Albert, S., Schofield, P., Dooneief, G., & Stern, Y. (1997). Cross-cultural neuropsychological assessment: A comparison of randomly selected, demographically matched cohorts of English- and Spanish-speaking older adults. *Journal of Clinical and Experimental Neuropsychology, 19,* 331–339.

Jenkins, J. H. (1988). Conceptions of schizophrenia as a problem of nerves: A cross-cultural comparison of Mexican Americans and Anglo-Americans. *Social Science and Medicine, 26,* 1233-1243.

Jenkins, J. H. (1991). The state construction of affect: Political ethos and mental health among Salvadoran refugees. *Culture, Medicine and Psychiatry, 15,* 139–165.

Kaiser Commission on Medicaid and the Uninsured. (2000). *Health centers' role as safety net providers for Medicaid patients and the uninsured.* Washington, DC: Author.

Karno, M., Hough, R. L., Burnam, M. A., Ecsobar, J. I., Timbers, D. M., Santana, F., & Boyd, J. (1987). Lifetime prevalence of specific psychiatry disorders among Mexican Americans and non-Hispanic whites in Los Angeles. *Archives of General Psychiatry, 44,* 695–701.

Kaufman, P., Kwon, J. Y., Klein, S., & Chapman, C. D. (1999). Dropout rates in the United States: 1998. *Statistical Analysis Report* (NCES Report No. 2000–022). Retrieved July 25, 2001, from http://nces.ed.gov/pubs2000/2000022.pdf.

Keegan L. (1996) Use of alternative therapies among Mexican Americans in the Texas Rio Grande Valley. *Journal of Holistic Nursing, 14,* 277–294.

Kemp, B. J., Staples, F., & Lopez-Aqueres, W. (1987). Epidemiology of depression and dysphoria in an elderly Hispanic population: Prevalence and correlates. *Journal of the American Geriatrics Society, 35,* 920–926.

Kessler, R. C., Nelson, C. B., McGonagle, K. A., Edlund, M. J., Frank, R. G., & Leaf, P. J. (1996). The epidemiology of co-occurring addictive and mental disorders: Implications for prevention and service utilization. *American Journal of Orthopsychiatry, 66,* 17-31.

Kessler, R. C., McGonagle, K. A., Zhao, S., Nelson, C. B., Hughes, M., Eshleman, S., Wittchen, H., & Kendler, K. (1994). Lifetime and 12-month prevalence of DSM-III-R psychiatric disorders in the United States. *Archives of General Psychiatry, 51,* 8–19.

Kirmayer, L. J., & Young, A. (1998). Culture and somatization: Clinical, epidemiological, and ethnographic perspectives. *Psychosomatic Medicine, 60,* 420–430.

Koss-Chioino, J. (1992). *Women as healers, women as patients: Mental health care and traditional healing in Puerto Rico.* Boulder, CO: Westview Press.

Koss-Chioino, J. D., & Canive, J. M. (1993). The interaction of popular and clinical diagnostic labeling: The case of embrujado. *Medical Anthropology, 15,* 171–188.

Kulka, R. A., Schlenger, W. E., Fairbank, J. A., Hough, R. L., Jordan, B. K., Marmar, C. R., & Weiss, D. S. (1990). *Trauma and the Vietnam war generation: Report of findings from the National Vietnam Veterans Readjustment Study.* Philadelphia: Brunner/Mazel.

Lahey, B. B., Flagg, E. W., Bird, H. R., Schwab-Stone, M. E., Canino, G., Dulcan, M. K., Leaf, P. J., Davies, M., Brogan, D., Bourdon, K., Horwitz, S. M., Rubio-Stipec, M., Freeman, D. H., Lichtman, J. H., Shaffer, D., Goodman, S. H., Narrow, W. E., Weissman, M. M., Kandel, D. B., Jensen, P. S., Richters, J. E., & Regier, D. A. (1996). The NIMH methods for the epidemiology of child and adolescent mental disorders (MECA) study: Background and methodology. *Journal of the American Academy of Child and Adolescent Psychiatry, 35,* 855–864.

LaFromboise, T., Coleman, H. L. K., & Gerton, J. (1993). Psychological impact of biculturalism: Evidence and theory. *Psychological Bulletin, 114,* 395–412.

Leaf, P. J., Alegria, M., Cohen, P., Goodman, S., Horwitz, S. M., Hoven, C. W., Narrow, W. E., Vaden-Kiernan, M., & Regier, D. (1996). Mental health service use in the community and schools: Results from the four-community MECA study. *Journal of the American Academy of Child & Adolescent Psychiatry, 35,* 889–897.

Leventhal, H., Lambert, J. F., Diefenbach, M., & Leventhal, E. A. (1997). From compliance to social-self-regulation: Models of compliance process. In B. Blackwell (Ed.), *Treatment compliance and the therapeutic alliance: Chronic mental illness* (Vol. 5, pp. 17–33). Singapore: Harwood Academic Publishers.

Lieberman, A. F., Weston, D. R., & Pawl, J. H. (1991). Preventive intervention and outcome with anxiously attached dyads. *Child Development, 62,* 199–209.

Liebowitz, M. R., Salmán, E., Jusino, C. M., Garfinkel, R., Street, L., Cardenas, D. L., Silvestre, J., Fyer, A. J., Carrasco, J. L., Davies, S., et al. (1994). Ataque de nervios and panic disorder. *American Journal of Psychiatry, 151,* 871–875.

Loewenstein, D. A., Arguelles, T., Arguelles, S., & Linn-Fuentes, P. (1994). Potential cultural bias in neuropsychological assessment of the older adult. *Journal of Clinical and Experimental Neuropsychology, 16,* 623–629.

Lopez, S. R. (1988). The empirical basis of ethnocultural and linguistic bias in mental health evaluations of Hispanics. *American Psychologist, 43,* 1095–1097.

Lopez, S. R. (1997). Cultural competence in psychotherapy: A guide for clinicians and their supervisors. In C. E. Watkins, Jr. (Ed.), *Handbook of psychotherapy supervision.* New York: Wiley.

Lopez, S. R., & Guarnaccia, P. J. (2000). Cultural psychopathology: Uncovering the social world of mental illness. *Annual Review of Psychology, 51,* 571–598.

Lopez, S. R., Kopelowicz, A., & Canive, J. M. (in press). Strategies in developing culturally congruent family interventions for schizophrenia: The case of Hispanics in Madrid and Los Angeles. In H. P. Lefley & D. L. Johnson (Eds.), *Family interventions in mental illness: International perspectives.* Westport, CT: Greenwood.

Lopez, S. R., & Taussig, I. M. (1991). Cognitive-intellectual functioning of impaired and non-impaired Spanish-speaking elderly: Implications for culturally sensitive assessment. *Psychological Assessment: Journal of Consulting and Clinical Psychology, 3,* 448–454.

Lopez, S. R., Nelson, K. A., Snyder, K. S., & Mintz, J. (1999). Attributions and affective reactions of family members and course of schizophrenia. *Journal of Abnormal Psychology, 108,* 307–314.

Lopez, S. R., Nelson, K. A., Polo, J. A., Jenkins, J., Karno, M., & Snyder, K. (1998, August). *Family warmth and the course of schizophrenia of Mexican Americans and Anglo Americans.* Paper presented at the 24th International Congress of Applied Psychology, San Francisco.

Macias E. P., & Morales, L. S. (2000). Utilization of health care services among adults attending a health fair in south Los Angeles County. *Journal of Community Health, 25,* 35–46.

Malgady, R. G., Rogler, L. H., & Costantino, G. (1987). Ethnocultural and linguistic bias in mental health evaluation of Hispanics. *American Psychologist, 42,* 228–234.

Malgady, R. G., Rogler, L. H., & Costantino, G. (1990). Culturally sensitive psychotherapy for Puerto Rican children and adolescents: A program of treatment outcome research. *Journal of Consulting and Clinical Psychology, 58,* 704–712.

Malgady, R. G., & Costantino, G. (1998). Symptom severity in bilingual Hispanics as a function of clinician ethnicity and language of interview. *Psychological Assessment, 10,* 120–127.

Marcos, L. R., Urcuyo, L., Kesselman, M., & Alpert, M. (1973). The language barrier in evaluating Spanish-American patients. *Archives of General Psychiatry, 29,* 655–659.

Martin, P. P. (Ed.). (1979). *La Frontera perspective: Providing mental health services to Mexican Americans.* Tucson, AZ: La Frontera Center.

Martinez, R. E., Rodriquez, M. S., Bravo, M., Canino, G., & Rubio-Stipec, M. (1991). Utilizacion de servicios de salud en Puerto Rico por personas con trastornos mentales. *Acta de Psiquiatria y Psicologia, 36,* 143–147.

McGahey, R. (1986). Economic conditions, neighbourhood organisation and urban crime. In A. Reiss & M. Tonry (Eds.), *Communities and crime.* Chicago: University of Chicago Press.

Michultka, D., Blanchard, E. B., & Kalous, T. (1998). Responses to civilian war experiences: Predictors of psychological functioning and coping. *Journal of Traumatic Stress, 11,* 571–577.

Miranda, J., & Munoz, R. (1994). Intervention for minor depression in primary care patients. *Psychosomatic Medicine, 56,* 136–142.

Moscicki, E. K., Locke, B. Z., Rae, D. S., & Boyd, J. H. (1989). Depressive symptoms among Mexican Americans: The Hispanic Health and Nutrition Examination Survey. *American Journal of Epidemiology, 130,* 348–360.

Moscicki, E. K., Rae, D., Regier, D. A., & Locke, B. Z. (1987). The Hispanic Health and Nutrition Examination Survey: Depression among Mexican Americans, Cuban Americans, Puerto Ricans. In M. Gaviria & J. D. Arana (Eds.), *Health and behavior: Research agenda for Hispanics.* Chicago: University of Illinois.

Mukherjee, S., Shukla, S., Woodle, J., Rosen, A. M., & Olarte, S. (1983). Misdiagnosis of schizophrenia in bipolar patients: A multiethnic comparison. *American Journal of Psychiatry, 140,* 1571–1574.

Naglieri, J. A., & Bardos, A. N. (1999). *GAMA: General Ability Measure for Adults.* Minneapolis: National Computer Systems, Inc.

Narrow, W. E., Rae, D. S., Moscicki, E. K., Locke, B. Z., & Regier, D. A. (1990). Depression among Cuban Americans: The Hispanic Health and Nutrition Examination Survey. *Social Psychiatry and Psychiatric Epidemiology, 25,* 260–268.

National Center for Education Statistics (2000). *Dropout rates in the United States: 1999.* Retrieved July 25, 2001, from http://nces.ed.gov/pubs2001/dropout/StatusRates3.asp.

National Center for Health Statistics. (n. d.a). *National Health Interview Survey (NHIS).* Retrieved July 26, 2001, from http://www.cdc.gov/nchs/nhis.htm.

National Center for Health Statistics. (n. d.b). *National Hospital Ambulatory Medical Care Survey (NHAMCS).* Retrieved July 26, 2001, from http://www.cdc.gov/nchs/products/catalogs/subject/nhamcs/nhamcs.htm.

Ochoa, S. H., Powell, M. P., & Robles-Pina, R. (1996). School psychologists' assessment practices with bilingual and limited-English-proficient students. *Journal of Psychoeducational Assessment, 14,* 250–275.

Ortega, A. N., & Rosenheck, R. (2000). Posttraumatic stress disorder among Hispanic Vietnam veterans. *American Journal of Psychiatry, 157,* 615–619.

Ortega, A. N., Rosenheck, R., Alegria, M., & Desai, R. A. (2000). Acculturation and lifetime risk of psychiatric and substance use disorders among Hispanics. *Journal of Nervous and Mental Disease, 188,* 728–735.

Pachter, L. M., Cloutier, M. M., & Berstein, B. A. (1995). Ethnomedical (folk) remedies for childhood asthma in a mainland Puerto Rican community. *Archives of Pediatric Adolescent Medicine, 149,* 982–988.

Padgett, D. K., Patrick, C., Burns, B. J., & Schlesinger, H. J. (1994). Ethnic differences in use of inpatient mental health services by blacks, whites, and Hispanics in a national insured population. *Health Service Research, 29,* 135–153.

Population Reference Bureau. (1999). America's racial and ethnic minorities. Retrieved July 25, 2001, from http://www.prb.org/pubs/population_bulletin/bu54-3/where_minorities_live.htm.

Potter, L. B., Rogler, L. H., Moscicki, E. K. (1995). Depression among Puerto Ricans in New York City: The Hispanic Health and Nutrition Examination Survey. *Social Psychiatry and Psychiatric Epidemiology, 30,* 185–193.

Preciado Martin, P. (Ed.). (1979). La Frontera Perspective: *Providing mental health services to Mexican Americans* (Monograph No. 1). Tucson, AZ: La Frontera Center.

Price, C. S. A., & Cuellar, I. (1981). Effects of language and related variables on the expression of psychopathology in Mexican American psychiatric patients. *Hispanic Journal of Behavioral Sciences, 3,* 145–160.

Pumariega, A. J., Glover, S., Holzer, C. E., III, & Nguyen, H. (1998). II. Utilization of mental health services in a tri-ethnic sample of adolescents. *Community Mental Health Journal, 34,* 145–156.

Riche, M. F. (2000). *America's diversity and growth: Signposts for the 21st Century* (Population Bulletin Vol. 55, No. 3). Washington, DC: Population Reference Bureau.

Risser, A. L., & Mazur, L. J. (1995). Use of folk remedies in a Hispanic population. *Archives of Pediatric Adolescent Medicine, 149,* 978–981.

Roberts, R. E. (1981). Prevalence of depressive symptoms among Mexican Americans. *Journal of Nervous and Mental Disease, 169,* 213–219.

Roberts, R. E., & Chen, Y. (1995). Depressive symptoms and suicidal ideation among Mexican-origin and Anglo adolescents. *Journal of the American Academy of Child and Adolescent Psychiatry, 34,* 81–90.

Roberts, R. E., & Sobhan, M. (1992). Symptoms of depression in adolescence: A comparison of Anglo, African, and Hispanic Americans. *Journal of Youth and Adolescence, 21,* 639–651.

Roberts, R. E., Roberts, C., & Chen, Y. R. (1997). Ethnocultural differences in prevalence of adolescent depression. *American Journal of Community Psychology, 25,* 95–110.

Robins, L., & Regier, D. A. (1991). Psychiatric disorders in America: *The Epidemiologic Catchment Area Study.* New York: The Free Press.

Ross, H. E., Glaser, F. B., & Germanson, T. (1988). The prevalence of psychiatric disorders in patients with alcohol and other drug problems. *Archives of General Psychiatry, 45,* 1023–1031.

Rossello, J., & Bernal, G. (1999). The efficacy of cognitive-behavioral and interpersonal treatments for depression in Puerto Rican adolescents. *Journal of Consulting and Clinical Psychology, 67,* 734–745.

Rounsaville, B. J., Anton, S. F., Carroll, K., Budde, D., Prusoff, B. A., & Gawin, F. (1991). Psychiatric diagnoses of treatment-seeking cocaine abusers. *Archives of General Psychiatry, 48,* 43–51.

Ruef, A. M., Brett, T. L., & Schlenger, W. E. (2000). Hispanic ethnicity and risk for combat-related posttraumatic stress disorder. *Cultural Diversity and Ethnic Minority Psychology, 6,* 235–251.

Rutter, M. (1979). Protective factors in children's responses to stress and disadvantage. *Annals of the Academy of Medicine, Singapore, 8,* 324–338.

Sabogal, F., Marin, G., Otero-Sabogal, R., Marin, B. V., & Perez-Stable, P. (1987). Hispanic familism and acculturation: What changes and what doesn't. *Hispanic Journal of Behavioral Sciences, 9,* 397–412.

Salgado de Snyder, V. N., Diaz-Perez, M. J., & Ojeda, V. D. (2000). The prevalence of nervios and associated symptomatology among inhabitants of Mexican rural communities. *Culture Medicine and Psychiatry, 24,* 453-470.

Sandoval, J. (1979). The WISC–R and internal evidence of test bias with minority groups. *Journal of Consulting and Clinical Psychology, 47,* 919–927.

Scheffler, R. M., & Miller, A. B. (1989). Demand analysis of service use among ethnic subpopulations. *Inquiry, 26,* 202–215.

Schuerman, L., & Kobrin, S. (1986). *Community careers in crime*. In A. Reiss & M. Tonry (Eds.), *Communities and crime*. Chicago: University of Chicago Press.

Sclar, D. A., Robison, L. M., Skaer, T. L, & Galin, R. S. (1999). Ethnicity and the prescribing of antidepressant pharmacotherapy: 1992–1995. *Harvard Review of Psychiatry, 7*, 29–36.

Scribner R., & Dwyer, J. H. (1989). Acculturation and low birthweight among Latinos in the Hispanic HANES. *American Journal of Public Health, 79*, 1263–1267.

Shaffer, D., Fisher, P., Dulcan, M. K., Davies, M., Piacentini, J., Schwab-Stone, M. E., Lahey, B. B., Bourdon, K., Jensen, P. S., Bird, H. R., Canino, G., & Regier, D. A. (1996). The NIMH Diagnostic Interview Schedule for Children Version 2.3 (DISC 2.3): Description, acceptability, prevalence rates and performance in the MECA study. Methods for the Epidemiology of Child and Adolescent Mental Disorders Study. *Journal of the American Academy of Child and Adolescent Psychiatry, 35*, 865–877.

Skaer, T. L., Robison, L. M., Sclar, D. A., & Harding, G. H. (1996). Utilization of curanderos among foreign-born Mexican American women attending migrant health clinics. *Journal of Cultural Diversity, 3*, 29–34.

Snowden, L. R., & Cheung, F. K. (1990). Use of inpatient mental health services by members of ethnic minority groups. *American Psychologist, 45*, 347–355.

Spencer, G., & Hollmann, F. W. (1998). National population projections. In *U.S. Census Bureau, Population profile of the United States: 1997* (Series P23–194, pp. 8–9). Washington, DC: U.S. Government Printing Office.

Stroup-Benham, C. A., Markides, K. S., Black, S. A., & Goodwin, J. S. (2000). Relationship between low blood pressure and depressive symptomatology in older people. *Journal of the American Geriatric Society, 48*, 250–255.

Suarez-Orozco, C., & Suarez-Orozco, M. M. (1995). *Transformations: Immigration, family life, and achievement motivation among Latino adolescents*. Stanford, CA: Stanford University Press.

Suarez-Orozco, M. M. (1990). Speaking of the unspeakable: Toward a psychosocial understanding of responses to terror. *Ethos, 18*, 353–383.

Suarez-Orozco, M. M. (1989). *Central American refugees and U.S. high schools: A psychosocial study of motivation and achievement*. Stanford, CA: Stanford University Press.

Sue, S., Fujino, D. C., Hu, L., & Takeuchi, D. T. (1991). Community mental health services for ethnic minority groups: A test of the cultural responsiveness hypothesis. *Journal of Consulting and Clinical Psychology, 59*, 533–540.

Swanson, J. W., Linskey, A. O., Quintero-Salinas, R., Pumariega, A. J., & Holzer, C.E., III. (1992). A binational school survey of depressive symptoms, drug use, and suicidal ideation. *Journal of the American Academy of Child and Adolescent Psychiatry, 31*, 669–678.

Szapocznik, J., Santisteban, D., Rio, A., Perez-Vidal, A., Santisteban, D., & Kurtines, W. M. (1989). Family effectiveness training: An intervention to prevent drug abuse and problem behaviors in Hispanic adolescents. *Hispanic Journal of Behavioral Sciences, 11*, 4–27.

Tang, M. X., Stern, Y., Marder, K., Bell, K., Gurland, B., Lantigua, R., Andrews, H., Feng, L., Tycko, B., & Mayeux, R. (1998). The APOE-epsilon4 allele and the risk of Alzheimer disease among African Americans, whites, and Hispanics. *Journal of the American Medical Association, 279*, 751–755.

Telles, C., Karno, M., Mintz, J., Paz, G., Arias, M., Tucker, D., & Lopez, S. (1995). Immigrant families coping with schizophrenia: Behavioural family intervention v. case management with a low-income Spanish-speaking population. *British Journal of Psychiatry, 167*, 473–479.

Teplin, L. A. (1994). Psychiatric and substance abuse disorders among male urban jail detainees. *American Journal of Public Health, 84*, 290–293.

Teplin, L. A., Abram, K. M., & McClelland, G. M. (1996). Prevalence of psychiatric disorders among incarcerated women: I. Pretrial jail detainees. *Archives of General Psychiatry, 53*, 505–512.

Tracy, P. E., Wolfgang, M. E., & Figlio, R. M. (1990). *Delinquency careers in two birth cohorts*. New York: Plenum Press.

U.S. Census Bureau. (1996). National Survey of Homeless Assistance Providers and Clients. Washington, DC: Author.

U.S. Census Bureau. (1998). *Current population survey, March 1997*, Ethnic and Hispanic Statistics Branch, Population Division. Retrieved July 25, 2001, from http://www.census.gov./sociodemo/hispanic/cps97/.

U.S. Census Bureau. (2000a). *Coming from the Americas: A profile of the Nation's Latin American foreign-born* (Report No. CENBR/00–3). Washington, DC: Author.

U.S. Census Bureau. (2000b). *Educational attainment in the United States: Population characteristics, March 1999* (Current Population Reports No. P20–528). Washington, DC: Author.

U.S. Census Bureau. (2000c). *Projections of the resident population by race, Hispanic origin, and nativity: Middle series, 20001 to 20005*. Retrieved July 25, 2001, from http://www.census.gov./sociodemo/hispanic/cps97/.

U.S. Census Bureau. (2000d). *States ranked by Hispanic population, July 1, 1999*. Retrieved July 25, 2001, from http://www.census.gov/population/estimates/state/rank/hi sp.txt.

U.S. Census Bureau. (2001a). *Profiles of general demographic characteristics: 2000 Census of Population and Housing, United States*. Retrieved June 22, 2001, from http://www2.census.gov/census_2000/datasets/demographic_profile/0_National_Summary/.

U.S. Census Bureau. (2001b). *The Hispanic Population: Census 2000 Brief*. Retrieved May 28, 2001, from http://www.census.gov/population/www/cen2000/briefs.html.

U.S. Department of Health and Human Services. (1990). *Healthy People 2000*. Rockville, MD: Author.

U.S. Department of Health and Human Services. (1999). *The AFCARS (Adoption and Foster Care Analysis and Reporting System) Report: Current estimates as of January 1999*. Rockville, MD: Author.

U.S. Department of Health and Human Services. (2000). *Healthy People 2010*. Rockville, MD: Author.

Vazsonyi, A. T., & Flannery, D. (1997). Early adolescent delinquent behaviors: Associations with family and school domains. *Journal of Early Adolescence, 17,* 271–293.

Vega, W., Warheit, G., Buhl-Auth, J., & Meinhardt, K. (1984). The prevalence of depressive symptoms among Mexican Americans and Anglos. *American Journal of Epidemiology, 120,* 592–607.

Vega, W. A., Khoury, E. L., Zimmerman, R. S., Gil, A. G., & Warheit, G. J. (1995). Cultural conflicts and problem behaviors of Latino adolescents in home and school environments. *Journal of Community Psychology, 23,* 167–179.

Vega, W. A., Kolody, B., Aguilar-Gaxiola, S., Alderate, E., Catalano, R., & Carveo-Anduaga, J. (1998). Lifetime prevalence of DSM–III–R psychiatric disorders among urban and rural Mexican Americans in California. *Archives of General Psychiatry, 55,* 771–778.

Vega, W. A., Kolody, B., Aguilar-Gaxiola, S., & Catalano, R. (1999). Gaps in service utilization by Mexican Americans with mental health problems. *American Journal of Psychiatry, 156,* 928–934.

Velasquez, R. J., Ayala, G. X., & Mendoza, S. A. (1998). *Psychodiagnostic assessment of U.S. Latinos: MMPI, MMPI–2, MMPI–A results*. Lansing, MI: Michigan State University, Julian Samora Research Institute.

Vera, M., Alegria, M., Freeman, D., Robles, R. R., Rios, R., & Rios, C. F. (1991). Depressive symptoms among Puerto Ricans: Island poor compared with residents of the New York City area. *American Journal of Epidemiology, 134,* 502–510.

Vera, M., Alegria, M., Freeman, D. H., Jr., Robles, R., Pescosolido, B., & Pena, M. (1998). Help seeking for mental health care among poor Puerto Ricans: Problem recognition, service use, and type of provider. *Medical Care, 36,* 1047–1056.

Vernon, S. W., & Roberts, R. E. (1982). Prevalence of treated and untreated psychiatric disorders in three ethnic groups. *Social Science and Medicine, 16,* 1575–1582.

Villasenor, Y., & Waitzkin, H. (1999). Limitations of a structured psychiatric diagnostic instrument in assessing somatization among Latino patients in primary care. *Medical Care, 37,* 637–646.

Vigil, J. D. (1988). *Barrio gangs: Street life and identity in Southern California*. Austin, TX: University of Texas Press.

Wadsworth, M. E. (1979). *Roots of delinquency, infancy, adolescence and crime*. Oxford, England: Robertson.

Wechsler, D. (1968). *Escala de Inteligencia Wechsler para Adultos*. San Antonio, TX: Psychological Corporation.

Wechsler, D. (1981). *Wechsler Adult Intelligence Scale—Revised*. San Antonio, TX: Psychological Corporation.

Wechsler, D. (1989). *Escala de Inteligencia Wechsler para Niños—Revisada*. Orlando, FL: Psychological Corporation.

Wechsler, D. (1998). *Wechsler Adult Intelligence Scale–III*. San Antonio, TX: Psychological Corporation.

Wells, K. B., Sherbourne, C., Schoenbaum, C., Duan, N., Meredith, L., Unutzer, J., Miranda, J., Carney, M. F., & Rubenstein, L. V. (2000). Impact of disseminating quality improvement programs for depression in managed primary care. *Journal of the American Medical Association, 283,* 212–220.

Werner, E. E., & Smith, R. S. (1992). *Overcoming the odds: High risk children from birth to adulthood*. New York: Cornell University Press.

Western Interstate Commission for Higher Education. (1996). *Cultural competence standards in managed care mental health services for Latino populations*. Boulder, CO: Author.

Williams, S., & Kohout, J. L. (1999). *A survey of licensed practitioners of psychology: Activities, roles, and services*. Washington, DC: American Psychological Association.

Woodcock, R. W., & Munoz-Sandoval, A. F. (1993). *Language survey: Comprehensive manual*. Chicago: Riverside.

Young, A. S., Klap, R., Sherbourne, C. D., & Wells, K. B. (2001). The quality of care for depressive and anxiety disorders in the United States. *Archives of General Psychiatry, 58*, 55–61.

CHAPTER 7
A VISION FOR THE FUTURE

Contents

Contents, *continued*

CHAPTER 7

A VISION FOR THE FUTURE

Introduction

The extensive evidence reviewed in this supplemental report to *Mental Health: A Report of the Surgeon General* (1999) supports the conclusion that mental illnesses are serious and disabling disorders affecting all populations, regardless of race or ethnicity. This Supplement also concludes that culture and social context influence mental health, mental illness, and mental health services in America. Despite the existence of effective treatments, disparities lie in the availability, accessibility, and quality of mental health services for racial and ethnic minorities. As a result, these populations bear a disproportionately high disability burden from mental disorders. This Supplement underscores the recommendation of the original Surgeon General's Report on Mental Health: *People should seek help if they have a mental health problem or if they think they have symptoms of a mental disorder.* In addition, the literature reviewed herein suggests that mental health researchers, policymakers, and service providers must be more responsive to the social contexts, cultural values, and historical experiences of all Americans, including racial and ethnic minorities.

Lack of information regarding the mental health needs of many racial and ethnic minorities is also a critical disparity. Too often, the best available research on racial and ethnic minorities consists of small studies that cannot be generalized to today's increasingly diverse communities. While the research reported in this Supplement is the best science available, it represents a science base that is incomplete.

To better address the dynamic impact of culture, race, and ethnicity on mental health and mental illness, more research is needed on how to prevent and treat mental illness and to enhance the mental health of all racial and ethnic groups. Following an extensive consultation process with public health experts, service providers, and consumers, the Surgeon General released *Healthy People 2010* in early 2000 as a challenge to the Nation to address disparities in health care access and outcomes. For the first time, among the 10 "leading indicators" of the Nation's health on which progress will be regularly monitored is one mental health goal: increasing treatment of depression for underserved minority groups. This national agenda encourages the field to strive toward the highest possible quality of health care and health outcomes, with equally high standards of care across groups.

A public health approach to reducing mental health disparities will require a national commitment, bringing together the best of the public and private sectors, individuals and communities, Federal, State, and local governments, universities, foundations, mental health researchers, advocates, health service providers, consumers, and their families. Through active partnership, these stakeholders can generate the knowledge and resources necessary to improve mental health services for racial and ethnic minorities in this country. This chapter highlights promising courses of action that can be used to reach the ambitious goals of reducing barriers and promoting equal access to effective mental health services for all persons who need them.

Continue to Expand the Science Base

The mental health knowledge base regarding racial and ethnic minorities is limited but growing. Because good science is an essential underpinning of the public health approach to mental health and mental illness, systematic work in the areas of epidemiology, evidence-based treatment, psychopharmacology, ethnic- and culture-specific interventions, diagnosis and assessment, and prevention and promotion needs to be developed and expanded.

Epidemiology

In March 1994, the policies of the National Institutes of Health (NIH) regarding inclusion of racial and ethnic minorities in study populations were significantly strengthened (NIH Guidelines, 1994, p. 14509). This change requires inclusion of ethnic minorities in all NIH-funded research. The results of this policy will be apparent in the coming years as studies funded during this era begin to be published.

Several large epidemiological studies that include significant samples of racial and ethnic minorities have recently been initiated or completed. These surveys, when combined with smaller, ethnic-specific epidemiological surveys, may help resolve some of the uncertainties about the extent of mental illness among specific racial and ethnic groups.

The National Institute of Mental Health (NIMH) recently funded a collaborative series of projects that will make great strides in psychiatric epidemiology nationwide. The National Survey of Health and Stress (NSHS) will interview a nationally representative sample of adolescents and adults to estimate the prevalence of mental disorders in the United States. Although the NSHS will interview nearly 20,000 adolescents and adults, its samples of specific racial and ethnic minority groups will be proportionate to their size in the Nation's population, and, thus, not very large. To complement the NSHS, NIMH has funded the National Survey of American Lives (NSAL) and the National Latino and Asian American Study (NLAAS), which will include large samples of different racial and ethnic minorities. In the NSAL, approximately 9,000 African American adolescents and adults will be interviewed; about a quarter of them will be immigrants to the United States. In the NLAAS, a total of about 8,000 Latino and Asian American adults from a few specific ethnic groups will be interviewed about their mental health and service use patterns. Project investigators have made a substantial portion of the NSHS, NSAL, and NLAAS surveys similar to facilitate cross-study comparisons. Taken together, these studies will permit the most comprehensive assessments to date of symptom patterns, prevalence rates of disorders, access to services, and functioning for different racial and ethnic minority groups.

In addition, a major effort to examine the psychiatric epidemiology and the use of mental health services by American Indians has recently been completed. The American Indian Services Utilization, Psychiatric Epidemiology, Risk and Protective Factors Project (AI–SUPERPFP), sponsored by NIMH and conducted by the National Center for American Indian and Alaska Native Mental Health Research, is a large-scale, multistage study of prevalence and utilization rates among over 3,000 individuals in two large American Indian communities, a Southwestern tribe and a Northern Plains tribe. In this study, mental disorders are diagnosed in a manner that is culturally relevant, using methods similar to those employed by the National Comorbidity Survey. The results of this study will be available in 2002 and will add greatly to our understanding of the need for mental health care among American Indians.

The National Household Survey on Drug Abuse (NHSDA) is conducted annually by the Substance Abuse and Mental Health Services Administration (SAMHSA) and interviews approximately 70,000 respondents each year. The NHSDA conducts interviews in both Spanish and English and has generated samples of white Americans, African Americans, and Hispanic Americans large enough to allow separate data analyses by racial or ethnic group. Through this annual survey it will be possible to track changes in the prevalence of substance abuse and dependence, as well as certain mental health problems for several racial and ethnic groups.

It is important that findings from these studies serve as a basis for improving mental health services for all groups.

Evidence-Based Treatment

Research reviewed in the previous chapters provides evidence that ethnic minorities can benefit from mental health treatment. While the Surgeon General's Report on Mental Health contained strong and consistent documentation of a comprehensive range of effective interventions for treating many mental disorders (DHHS, 1999), most of the studies reporting findings for racial and ethnic minorities had small samples and were not randomized controlled trials. As discussed in Chapter 2, the research used to generate professional treatment guidelines for most health and mental health interventions does not include or report large enough samples of racial and ethnic minorities to allow group-specific determinations of efficacy (see Appendix A). In the future, evidence from randomized controlled trials that include and identify sizable racial and ethnic minority samples may lead to treatment improvements, which will help clinicians to maximize real-world effectiveness of already-proven psychiatric medications and psychotherapies.

At the same time, research is essential to examine the efficacy of ethnic- or culture-specific interventions for minority populations and their effectiveness in clinical practice settings. A good example of a well-designed study addressing these issues is the WE Care Study (Women Entering Care), a major effort to examine treatment for depression in low-income and minority women. Funded by NIMH, this study examines the impact of evidence-based care for depression on a large sample (*N* = 350) of white, African American, and Latina women who are poor. This randomized controlled trial is not only examining the impact of treatment for depression on this group of women, but it will also determine whether providing treatment to women who are mothers results in improvements in the mental health and functioning of their children.

Psychopharmacology

Some of the variability in people's responses to medications is accounted for by factors related to race, ethnicity, and lifestyle. Information about race and ethnicity, as well as factors such as age, gender, and family history, may provide a starting point for medical research aimed at developing and testing drug therapies tailored to individual patients. Identifying the various mechanisms responsible for differential pharmacological response will aid in predicting an individual's likely response to a medication before it is prescribed.

A few studies have examined racial and ethnic differences in the metabolism of clinically important drugs used to treat mental illnesses. As the evidence base grows, improved treatment guidelines will help clinicians be aware that differences in metabolic response, as well as differences in age, gender, family history, lifestyle, and co-occurring illnesses, can alter a drug's safety and efficacy. For example, clinicians are becoming sensitized to the possibility that a significant proportion of racial and ethnic minority patients will respond to some common medications at lower-than-usual dosages. Care must be taken to avoid overmedicating patients, because overmedication can lead to adverse effects or toxicity. However, because each racial and ethnic population contains the full range of drug metabolic activity across its membership, a clinician should not come to firm conclusions about higher or lower metabolic rates based on an individual's race or ethnicity alone.

Currently, there is little empirical evidence around improving systems of care for racial and ethnic minorities. To reduce disparities in quality of care, research is needed on strategies to improve the availability and delivery of evidence-based treatments, including state-of-the-art medications and psychotherapies. Consumers, communities, mental health services researchers, and Federal agencies have an opportunity to work together toward the development and dissemination of evidence-based treatment information to improve quality of care for racial and ethnic minorities. In particular, studies are needed that identify effective interventions for minority subpopulations, such as children, older adults, persons with co-occurring mental and physical health conditions, and persons who are living in rural areas.

Ethnic- or Culture-Specific Interventions

Clinicians' awareness of their own cultural orientation, their knowledge of the client's background, and their skills with different cultural groups may be essential to improving access, utilization, and quality of mental health services for minority populations. While no rigorous, systematic studies have been conducted to test these hypotheses, evidence suggests that culturally oriented interventions are more effective than usual care at reducing dropout rates for ethnic minority mental health clients. While the efficacy of most ethnic-specific or culturally responsive services is yet to be determined, models already shown to be useful through research could be targeted for further efficacy research and, ultimately, dissemination to mental health providers.

Because stigma and help-seeking behaviors are two culturally determined factors in service use, research is needed on how to change attitudes and improve utilization of mental health services. Some promising areas of study in racial and ethnic minority communities are reducing stigma associated with mental illness, encouraging early intervention, and increasing awareness of effective treatments and the possibility of recovery. These messages should be tailored to the languages and cultures of multiple racial and ethnic communities. Communities that can incorporate evidence-based knowledge about disease and treatments will have a health advantage.

Diagnosis and Assessment

Though the major mental illnesses are found worldwide, manifestations of these and other health conditions may vary with age, gender, race, ethnicity, and culture. Research reported in this Supplement documents that minorities tend to receive less appropriate diagnoses than whites. Further study is needed on how to address issues of clinician bias and diagnostic accuracy, particularly among those providers working with racial and ethnic minority consumers.

As noted in Chapter 1, the DSM–IV marked a new level of acknowledgment of the role of culture in shaping the symptoms and expression of mental disorders. The inclusion of a "Glossary of Culture-Bound Syndromes" and the "Outline for Cultural Formulation" for clinicians was a significant step forward in recognizing the impact of culture, race, and ethnicity on mental health. Further study is needed, however, to examine the relationship between culture-bound syndromes and existing disorders and the connection of culture-bound syndromes with underlying biological, social, and cultural processes.

Examining the extent to which culture-bound syndromes are unique idioms of distress for some groups or variants of existing syndromes or disorders is particularly important.

The fifth edition of the *Diagnostic and Statistical Manual of Mental Disorders*, now under development, will extend and elaborate concepts introduced in DSM–IV regarding the role and importance of culture and ethnicity in the diagnostic process. While striving to understand the processes that underlie disorders and syndromes, it is also critical to examine how clinicians apply cultural knowledge in their clinical evaluations. Further research is needed on the impact of culture in interview-based diagnosis and assessment techniques, as well as in the use and interpretation of formal psychological tests. Quality mental health assessment and treatment rely on understanding local representations of illness and distress for all populations.

Prevention and Promotion

Preventive interventions have the potential to decrease the incidence, severity, and duration of certain mental disorders or behavioral problems, e.g., depression, conduct disorder, or substance abuse. In addition, promotive interventions, such as increasing healthy thinking patterns or improving coping skills, may be integral to fostering the mental health of the nation. Unfortunately, only a handful of interventions to promote mental health, reduce risk, or enhance resiliency have been empirically validated for racial and ethnic minorities. As part of a public health approach to mental health and mental illness for all Americans, the growing knowledge base for preventive interventions must include racial and ethnic minorities.

Important opportunities exist for researchers to study cultural differences in stress, coping, and resilience as part of the complex of factors that influence mental health. Such work will lay the groundwork for developing new prevention and treatment strategies — building upon community strengths to foster mental health and to ameliorate negative health outcomes.

Study the Roles of Culture, Race, and Ethnicity in Mental Health

How do racial and ethnic groups differ in their manifestations and perceptions of mental illness and their attitudes toward and use of mental health services? What is it about race and ethnicity that helps explain these differences? The mental health community will benefit from a better understanding of how factors such as accul-

turation, help-seeking behaviors, stigma, ethnic identity, racism, and spirituality provide protection from or risk for mental illness in racial and ethnic minority populations. While no single study can shed light on all these issues simultaneously, scientific research will advance knowledge, increase our ability to prevent or treat mental illness, and promote mental health.

New studies will advance our knowledge about the social and cultural characteristics of racial and ethnic minority groups that correlate with risk and protective factors for mental health. As described earlier, researchers involved in the NSHS, NSAL, NLAAS, and AI–SUPERPFP large-scale epidemiological studies have collaborated on a set of core questions that will facilitate comparisons across populations. For example, across all four studies, it will be possible to assess how socioeconomic status, wealth, education, neighborhood context, social support, religiosity, and spirituality relate to mental illness among African Americans, Latinos, Asian Americans, American Indians, and whites. Similarly, it will be possible to assess how acculturation, ethnic identity, and perceived discrimination affect mental health outcomes for the four underserved racial and ethnic groups. These types of analyses go beyond straightforward epidemiological comparisons; with these groundbreaking studies, the mental health field will gain crucial insight into how social and cultural factors operate across race and ethnicity to affect mental illness in diverse communities.

Improve Access to Treatment

Race, ethnicity, culture, language, geographic region, and other social factors affect the perception, availability, utilization, and, potentially, the outcomes of mental health services. Therfore the provision of high-quality, culturally responsive, and language-appropriate mental health services in locations accessible to racial and ethnic minorities is essential to creating a more equitable system.

Improve Geographic Access

Racial and ethnic minorities have less access than white Americans to mental health services. Minorities are more likely to be poor and uninsured. Many live in areas where general health care and specialty mental health services are in short supply. An increasingly distressed safety net of community health centers, rural and migrant health centers, and community mental health agencies provides physical and mental health care services to racial and ethnic minorities in medically underserved areas (IOM, 2000). Innovative strategies for training providers, delivering services, creating incentives for providers to work in underserved areas, and strengthening the public health safety net promise to provide greater geographic access to mental health services for those in need.

Integrate Mental Health and Primary Care

Many racial and ethnic minority consumers and families prefer to receive mental health services through their primary care physicians. Explanations of this preference may be that members of minority groups fear, feel ill at ease with, or are unfamiliar with the specialty mental health system. Community health centers as well as other public and private primary health settings provide a vital frontline for the detection and treatment of mental illnesses and the co-occurrence of mental illnesses with physical illnesses.

The Federal Government, in collaboration with the private sector, is working to bring mental health care to the primary health care system. A variety of demonstration and research programs have been or will be created to strengthen the capacity of these providers to meet the demand for mental health services and to encourage the delivery of integrated primary health and mental health services that match the needs of the diverse communities they serve. Developing strong links between primary care providers and community mental health centers will also assure continuity of care when more complex or intensive mental health services are warranted.

For example, the Chinatown Health Center in New York City, a Health Resource Services Administration (HRSA)-funded community health center, participates in two important Federal projects. The first is a study of whether it is more effective to treat older Chinese American health center patients with mental illnesses in an integrated primary and behavioral health program or to have the primary care physician refer them to specialty mental health services. The second project is part of a "Break-through Collaborative" series co-sponsored by the Institute for Healthcare Improvement, the Robert Wood Johnson Foundation, and several Federal agencies. This intensive quality improvement program is aimed at transforming the way the health center treats patients with depression. These Breakthrough Collaboratives are changing the way safety net health providers engage and treat their patients who may have chronic physical health conditions as well as mental health problems.

Ensure Language Access

A major barrier to effective mental health treatment arises when provider and patient do not speak the same language. The DHHS Office of Civil Rights has published guidance on this subject for health and social services providers (DHHS, 2000). All organizations or individuals receiving Federal financial assistance from DHHS, including hospitals, nursing homes, home health agencies, managed health care organizations, health and mental health service providers, and human services organizations have an obligation under the 1964 Civil Rights Act to ensure that persons with limited English proficiency (LEP) have meaningful and equal access to benefits and services. As outlined in the guidance, satisfactory service to LEP clients includes identifying and documenting the language needs of the individual provider and the client population, providing a range of translation options, monitoring the quality of language services, and providing written materials in languages other than English wherever a significant percentage of the target population has LEP. Efforts such as these will help ensure that limited English skills do not restrict access to the fullest use of services for a significant proportion of racial and ethnic minority Americans.

Coordinate and Integrate Mental Health Services for High-Need Populations

The Nation is struggling to meet the needs of its most vulnerable individuals, such as those in foster care, jails, prisons, homeless shelters, and refugee resettlement programs. Accordingly, the attention being given to the development and provision of effective, culturally responsive mental health services for these populations is increasing. Because racial and ethnic minorities are over-represented among these vulnerable, high-need populations, the introduction, expansion, and improvement of mental health services in settings where these groups are is critical to reducing mental health disparities. Another promising line of research is the role of mental health treatment in preventing individuals from falling into these vulnerable populations.

One innovative Center for Mental Health Services (CMHS) demonstration program to reduce homelessness integrates housing supports with medical and mental health services. This program has successfully brought adults with serious mental illness off the streets and helped them stay in housing, reduced their illicit drug use, decreased minor crime, and increased their use of outpatient mental health services. It has also shown that it is possible for organizations with very different missions and funding streams to work together to deliver effective, integrated services when they are focused on a common goal: to meet the real and complex needs of vulnerable people. These grants have helped several thousand homeless adults with severe mental illness (over 50 percent of whom were racial or ethnic minorities) to move off the streets and into stable housing (CMHS, Rosenheck et al., 1998). Because of the over-representation of ethnic minorities among persons who are homeless, such programs may play an important role in reducing racial and ethnic disparities in access to the mental health system.

Reduce Barriers to Treatment

Organization and financing of services have impeded access and availability for racial and ethnic minorities. Therefore, reducing financial barriers and making services more accessible to minority communities should be aims within any effort to reduce mental health disparities. Shame, stigma, discrimination, and mistrust also keep racial and ethnic minorities from seeking treatment when it is needed. Therefore, effective efforts to increase utilization will target social factors as well as quality of services.

Racial and ethnic minorities do not use mental health services at rates comparable to those of whites or in proportion to the prevalence of mental illness in either minority populations or the general population. The reasons for lower rates of utilization are complex. Research suggests that cost and lack of health insurance, fragmentation of services, culturally mediated stigma or patterns of help-seeking, mistrust of specialty mental health services, and the insensitivity of many mental health care systems, all discourage racial and ethnic minorities' use of mental health care. Opportunities exist to remove barriers and to promote consumers' access to needed services.

Ensure Parity and Expand Public Health Insurance

Minorities are less likely than whites to have health insurance and to have the ability to pay for mental health services. Across racial and ethnic groups, lack of health insurance is a significant financial barrier to getting needed mental health care. Even for people with health insurance, whether public or private insurance, there are greater restrictions on coverage for mental disorders than for other illnesses. This inequity, known as lack of parity in mental health coverage, needs to be corrected. The

original *Surgeon General's Report on Mental Health* made clear that parity in mental health coverage is an affordable and effective objective for the Nation.

Another important step toward removing the financial barriers that contribute to unequal access to needed mental health care is the extension of publicly supported health care coverage to children who are poor and near poor. Federal legislation has created prospects for significantly expanding mental health coverage for the nation's 10 million uninsured children. The State Children's Health Insurance Program is a federally funded program enacted in 1997 that provides $24 billion over five years to ensure health care coverage for children in low-income families who are not eligible for Medicaid. If this program were modified to ensure adequate coverage for mental health and substance abuse disorders, it might substantially reduce the financial barriers to treatment and enhance access to health care for millions of children from all racial and ethnic backgrounds.

Extend Health Insurance for the Uninsured

Approximately 43 million Americans have no health insurance. Federal and State parity laws and steps to equalize health and mental health benefits in public insurance programs will do little to reduce barriers for the millions of working poor who do not qualify for public benefits, yet do not have private insurance. Today, the Nation's patchwork of health insurance programs leaves more than one person in seven with no means to pay for health care other than by out-of-pocket and charity payments. The consequences of the patchwork are many holes in the health care system through which a disproportionately greater number of poor, sick, rural, and distressed minority families frequently fall.

Efforts are currently underway to create more systematic approaches for States and local communities to extend health and mental health care to their uninsured residents. In 2000 and 2001, HRSA awarded planning grants to communities in 20 States to develop strategies to extend health coverage to their uninsured. Recipients of the grants will receive technical assistance to ensure that mental health needs of their uninsured residents are met in equal measure with other health needs. The program is modeled on a Robert Wood Johnson Foundation program, *Communities in Charge*, which is assisting 20 cities to stretch a safety net of health care insurance for people who have no health coverage. This and other efforts will have a significant impact on many racial and ethnic minority individuals who are uninsured.

Examine the Costs and Benefits of Culturally Appropriate Services

The burden of untreated mental illness is costly for all Americans. As the Nation looks into ways to remove financial barriers to mental health and addictions treatment, it is also important to look at the long-term cost-effectiveness of offering culturally appropriate services. Engaging and treating racial and ethnic minority children, adults, or older adults by reaching out to family members and other social supports may require a greater initial investment of resources, but it may also result in substantial decreases in disability burden. In addition, undertaking other case management services that do not involve direct client contact, such as discussing a coordinated treatment plan with a traditional healer, may not be payable through insurance. Nevertheless, such "ancillary" services may be essential to ensuring that those in need of services will enter and stay in treatment long enough to get help that is effective.

Similarly, bilingual or bicultural community health workers may be needed to bridge the gap between the formal health care system and racial and ethnic minority communities. Funds to support these community workers are scarce, and in the bottom-line environment of managed care, often nonexistent. Yet studies across many areas of health have shown that community health workers— neighborhood workers, indigenous health workers, lay health advisers, *consejera, promotora*—can improve minorities' access to and utilization of health care and preventive services (Krieger et al., 1999; Witmer et al., 1995). These community health workers can also bridge language differences that create communication barriers for a substantial proportion of racial and ethnic minority Americans receiving health care (Commonwealth Fund, 1995; President's Advisory Commission on Asian Americans and Pacific Islanders, 2001).

Many Americans, including members of racial and ethnic minorities, use alternative or complementary health care. The findings from a study of American Indian veterans' use of biomedical and alternative mental health care suggest that medical need drives service use, but the physical, financial, and cultural availability of services may influence the form that such service use assumes (Gurley et al., 2001). Research is needed to fully understand the effects of complementary care and their interactions with standard mental health interventions. In the meantime, it is important that mental health systems create avenues for working with complementary care providers to foster greater awareness, mutual understanding, and respect. Consumers and families may be more likely to take advantage of effective mental health treatments if both the formal mental health and complementary care systems work together to ensure that individuals with mental illness receive coordinated, and truly complementary, treatments.

Although providing services to meet the cultural and linguistic needs of more diverse populations may demand more of an initial investment than continuing services as usual, cost-effectiveness studies will help to examine the benefits of providing (or the costs of failing to provide) culturally appropriate services.

Reduce Barriers in Managed Care

Evidence cited in this Supplement suggests that managed mental health care is perceived by some racial and ethnic minorities as creating even greater barriers to treatment than fee-for-service plans. However, more systematic assessment of the treatment experiences, quality, and outcome of racial and ethnic minorities in managed care may help to identify opportunities for using this mechanism to improve access and quality of services. Because managed care organizations contract to provide all necessary services to beneficiaries at a fixed cost, managed care offers a potential means for increasing providers' flexibility to reach out and engage minority populations. For example, a health maintenance organization (HMO) might be able to support more outreach and engagement to people of color living in rural communities by removing inflexible billing methods based on individual office visits.

Overcome Shame, Stigma, and Discrimination

Shame, stigma, and discrimination are major reasons why people with mental health problems avoid seeking treatment, regardless of their race or ethnicity. The effects of negative public attitudes and behaviors toward people with mental illness may be even more powerful for racial and ethnic minorities than for whites (Chapter 2). For example, in some Asian American communities, the shame and stigma associated with the mental illness of one family member can affect the marriage and employment potential of other relatives. More research is needed to develop effective methods of overcoming this powerful barrier to getting people with mental health problems the help they need. Public education efforts targeting shame, stigma, and discrimination are likely to be more effective if they are tailored to the languages, needs, and cultures of racial and ethnic minorities.

165

Build Trust in Mental Health Services

Mistrust of mental health services deters many individuals from seeking treatment for mental illness. Although there are undoubtedly myriad complex reasons for this lack of trust, one of its major sources for racial and ethnic minorities may be their past negative experiences with the mental health treatment system. Mistrust is understandable in light of research findings that minorities receive a higher proportion of misdiagnoses, experience greater clinician bias, and have lower access to effective treatments that are evidence-based, as compared with whites. As detailed in the next section, one of the most essential steps to building trust in mental health services is reducing racial and ethnic disparities in the quality of available services. Minority communities also need more information about the effectiveness of treatment and the possibility of recovery from mental illness.

Improve Quality of Care

This Supplement identified racial and ethnic disparities in the quality of mental health services people receive. Therefore, the provision of high-quality services in settings where there is an appreciation for diversity and its impact on mental health is a priority for meeting current and future needs of diverse racial and ethnic populations.

Ensure Evidence-Based Treatment

As noted earlier, the recommended treatments available for all patients are those based on a strong and consistent evidence base and tailored to the age, race, gender, and culture of the individual. It is clear that the Nation's mental health service system needs to ensure that all Americans receive the highest standard of care. This Supplement finds that racial and ethnic minorities are less likely than whites to receive effective, state-of-the-art treatments. Therefore, frontline providers need incentives and opportunities to participate in quality improvement activities that will help them better manage medications and provide effective psychosocial treatments to racial and ethnic minority consumers, children, and families in ways that are both culturally and linguistically appropriate and consistent with practice standards.

Develop and Evaluate Culturally Responsive Services

Culture and language affect the perception, utilization, and, potentially, the outcomes of mental health services. Therefore, the provision of culturally and linguistically

appropriate mental health services is a key ingredient for any programming designed to meet the needs of diverse racial and ethnic populations. This programming should include:

(1) language access for persons with limited English proficiency;

(2) services provided in a manner that is congruent, rather than conflicting, with cultural norms; and

(3) the capacity of the provider to convey understanding and respect for the client's worldview and experiences.

The refinement and study of cultural competence may reveal a mechanism for helping mental health organizations and providers deliver culturally appropriate services. This approach underscores the recognition of cultural differences in consumers and families and then develops a set of skills, knowledge, and policies in an effort to deliver services more effectively. There have been, however, few direct empirical studies of cultural competence. Research is needed to determine its key ingredients and what influence, if any, they have on improving service delivery, utilization, treatment response, adherence, outcomes, or quality for racial and ethnic minorities.

Engage Consumers, Families, and Communities in Developing Services

One way to ensure that mental health services meet the needs of racial and ethnic minority populations is to involve representatives from the community being served in the design, planning, and implementation of services. Modeled on primary health care programs that successfully target recent immigrants and refugees, some minority-oriented mental health programs appear to succeed by maintaining active relationships with community institutions and leaders. These programs do aggressive outreach, furnish a familiar and welcoming atmosphere, and identify and encourage styles of practice tailored to racial and ethnic minority groups.

State, county, and local communities carry the primary responsibility for developing, organizing, and operating their own mental health services. Their leaders are frequently in the position to determine the investment of Federal, State, and local mental health resources. It is incumbent upon those who control the organizational structure of local programs to engage consumers, families, and other community members in the process of reducing mental health service disparities.

One organization that is successfully reaching out is the Feather River Tribe of California. With Federal seed-grant funds, this tribe has developed a plan for serving tribal children with serious emotional problems that is based on community members' assessment of needs and expectations from mental health treatment. Their effort has engaged tribal members so successfully that, through their own fundraising efforts, they have netted sufficient tribal, State, foundation, and Federal resources to implement a comprehensive, community-based children's services program. As a result, this community feels ownership and commitment to its mental health service delivery system, and Feather River children are receiving more and better quality services.

Support Capacity Development

Minorities are underrepresented among mental health providers, researchers, administrators, policymakers, and consumer and family organizations. Furthermore, many providers and researchers of all backgrounds are not fully aware of the impact of culture on mental health, mental illness, and mental health services. All mental health professionals are encouraged to develop their understanding of the roles of age, gender, race, ethnicity, and culture in research and treatment. Therefore, mental health training programs and funding sources that work toward equitable representation and a culturally informed training curriculum will contribute to reducing disparities.

Train Mental Health Professionals

Racial and ethnic minorities continue to be badly underrepresented, relative to their proportion of the U.S. population, within the core mental health professions — psychiatry, psychology, social work, counseling, and psychiatric nursing. Although it is certainly not the case that only minorities can understand or treat persons of like race or cultural background, minority providers treat a higher proportion of minority patients than do white providers. There is also evidence that ethnic match between provider and client encourages consumers to enter and stay in treatment.

The ability to reduce health disparities through the research proposed in the NIH 2001 Health Disparities Plan requires a strong commitment to training and supporting investigators in this area. Not only are there disparities in the number of studies that analyze their findings by race or ethnicity, but there are also disparities in the number of racial and ethnic minority investigators applying for and receiving grants to pursue mental health research.

Without concerted efforts by policymakers, educational institutions, and senior researchers, the shortage of providers and researchers equipped to address the needs of minority populations will contribute to the disproportionate burden of mental illness on racial and ethnic minorities. Programs that encourage students who are committed to serving racial and ethnic minority communities to enter the field of mental health will help to reduce the mismatch between needs and capacity. Furthermore, it is important that professional training programs include curricula that address the impact of culture, race, and ethnicity on mental health, mental illness, and mental health services. Hence, there is a need to encourage targeted Federal training or grant programs, educational programs for high school, college, and graduate students, outreach by graduate and professional schools, and continuing education by accrediting professional organizations.

Encourage Consumer and Family Leadership

Whereas the movement to give voice and leadership to the recipients of mental health services — consumers and family members — has been growing rapidly over the past 20 years, racial and ethnic minorities continue to be underrepresented in this arena. Although there have been recent Federal, State and local efforts to develop networks and leadership among minority consumers and families, concerted efforts are needed to give voices to these relatively unheard stakeholders of the mental health system.

Promote Mental Health

Mental health promotion and mental illness prevention can improve the mental health of a community. Therefore, dedicated efforts should investigate avenues for reducing the effects of historical social inequities and for promoting community and family strengths.

Address Social Adversities

Mental health is adversely affected by chronic social conditions that disproportionately affect America's poor and its racial and ethnic minority groups. These conditions include poverty, community violence, racism, and discrimination. The reduction of social adversities, while a formidable task, may be vital to improving the mental health of racial and ethnic minorities. Although there is substantial literature on the damaging effects of poverty on mental health, there is less empirical evidence for the effects of exposure to racism, discrimination, and community violence. As these relationships are examined, it is in the Nation's interest to reduce the impact of such social problems, as well as to promote respect and understanding among Americans of all backgrounds.

Build on Natural Supports

Efforts to prevent mental illness and promote mental health should build on intrinsic community strengths such as spirituality, positive ethnic identity, traditional values, educational attainment, and local leadership. Programs founded on individual, family, and community strengths have the potential for both ameliorating risk and fostering resilience. Furthermore, culturally appropriate efforts are needed to educate families and communities about mental health, mental illness, treatment effectiveness, the possibility of recovery, and the availability of services in their area.

Strengthen Families

Families are the primary source of care and support for the majority of adults and children with mental health disorders or problems. Given the important role of family in the mental health system, it is essential that efforts to reduce racial and ethnic disparities include strategies to strengthen families to function at their fullest potential and to mitigate the stressful effects of caring for a relative with mental illness or serious emotional disturbance. Furthermore, strong families are better equipped to cope with adversity and to provide mentally healthy environments for their children. As with mental health interventions, family support and family strengthening efforts need to be tailored to the linguistic and cultural needs of racial and ethnic minorities.

Conclusions

Mental Health: Culture, Race, and Ethnicity presents compelling evidence that racial and ethnic minorities collectively experience a disproportionately high disability burden from unmet mental health needs. Despite the progress in understanding the causes of mental illness and the tremendous advances in finding effective mental health treatments, far less is known about the mental health of African Americans, American Indians and Alaska Natives, Asian American and Pacific Islanders, and Hispanic Americans.

The Nation has far to go to eliminate racial and ethnic disparities in mental health. While working toward this goal, the public health system must support the strength and resilience of America's families. The demographic changes anticipated over the next decades magnify the importance of eliminating differences in mental health burden and access to services. Ethnic minority groups are expected to grow as a proportion of the total U.S. population. Therefore, the future mental health of America as a whole will be enhanced substantially by improving the health of racial and ethnic minorities.

It is necessary to expand and improve programs to deliver culturally, linguistically, and geographically accessible mental health services. Financial barriers, including discriminatory health insurance coverage of treatment for mental illness, need to be surmounted. Programs to increase public awareness of mental illness and effective treatments must be developed for racial and ethnic minority communities, as must efforts to overcome shame, stigma, discrimination, and distrust. The time is right for a commitment to expand or redirect resources to support evidence-based, affordable, and culturally appropriate mental health services for racial and ethnic minorities, particularly in settings where those with the highest need are not being adequately served, such as jails, prisons, homeless shelters, and foster care.

Clinical practice guidelines and program standards for culturally competent mental health services should be subject to rigorous empirical study. If they are found to be effective for racial and ethnic minorities, such standards should be disseminated and implemented with fidelity. For state-of-the-art, evidence-based interventions, it is critical that quality improvement processes be inaugurated, so that clinicians and programs actually use them and use them appropriately.

Building capacity for research, training, and community leadership is essential to meet the needs of racial and ethnic minorities in the 21st century. Where gaps exist in the evidence base about the prevalence, perception, course, detection, and treatment of mental illness in racial and ethnic minority populations, individuals must be trained and supported to carry out systematic programs of research. Where shortages of accessible services are evident, both mainstream and bilingual-bicultural providers and administrators must learn to create culturally appropriate and evidence-based systems of care. Where leadership is lacking in consumer and family groups, encouraging grassroots efforts will help to strengthen the voices of racial and ethnic minorities.

Accountability for making progress and providing state-of-the-art services will help to reduce disparities in the mental health and health care systems. This Supplement sets a foundation for national efforts to provide racial and ethnic minorities affected by mental disorders with effective and affordable treatments tailored to their specific needs. Public reports throughout the decade will provide excellent opportunities to gauge successes, evaluate directions, and chart necessary changes. Addressing disparities in mental health is the right thing to do for all Americans.

References

American Psychiatric Association. (1994). *Diagnostic and statistical manual of mental disorders* (4th ed.). Washington, DC: Author.

Center for Mental Health Servcies.

Commonwealth Fund. (1995). *National comparative survey of minority health care*. New York: Commonwealth Fund.

Gurley, D., Novins, D. K., Jones, M. C., Beals, J., Shore, J. H., & Manson, S. M. (2001). Comparative use of biomedical services and traditional health options by American Indian veterans. *Psychiatric Services, 52*, 68–74.

Institute of Medicine. (2000). *America's health care safety net, intact but endangered*. Washington, DC: National Academy Press.

Krieger, J., Collier, C., Song, L., & Martin, D. (1999). Linking community-based blood pressure measurement to clinical care: A randomized controlled trial of outreach and tracking by community health workers. *American Journal of Public Health, 89*, 856–861.

National Institutes of Health. (1994). NIH guidelines on the inclusion of women and minorities as subjects in clinical research. Retrieved July 27, 2001, from http://grants.nih.gov/grants/policy/emprograms/overview/women-and-mi.htm.

National Institutes of Health. (2000). *Strategic research plan to reduce and ultimately eliminate health disparities, fiscal years 2002–2006*. Draft, Oct. 6, 2000.

President's Advisory Commission on Asian Americans and Pacific Islanders. (2001). *Interim report to the President*. Rockville, MD: U.S. Department of Health and Human Services.

Rosenheck, R., Morrissey, J., Lam, J., Calloway, M., Johnsen, M., Goldman, H., Randolph, F., Blasinsky, M., Fontana, A., Calsyn, R., and Teague, G. (1998). Service system integration, access to services, and housing outcomes in a program for homeless persons with severe mental illness. *American Journal of Public Health, 88*, 1610–1615.

U.S. Department of Health and Human Services. (1999). *Mental health: A report of the Surgeon General*. Rockville, MD: U.S. Department of Health and Human Services, Substance Abuse and Mental Health Services Administration, Center for Mental Health Services, National Institutes of Health, National Institute of Mental Health.

U.S. Department of Health and Human Services. (2000a). *Healthy people 2010 (2nd ed.)*. With *Understanding and improving health and Objectives for improving health*. (2 vols.). Washington, DC: U.S. Government Printing Office.

U.S. Department of Health and Human Services. (2000b). Policy guidance on the Title VI prohibition against national origin discrimination as it affects persons with limited English proficiency. Retrieved July 27, 2001, from http://www.aoa.gov/network/lep /hhsguidance.html.

Witmer, A., Seifer, S.D., Finocchio, L., Leslie, J., & O'Neil, E. H. (1995). Community health workers: Integral members of the health care work force. *American Journal of Public Health, 85*, 1055–1058.

INCLUSION OF MINORITIES IN CONTROLLED CLINICAL TRIALS USED TO DEVELOP PROFESSIONAL TREATMENT GUIDELINES FOR MAJOR MENTAL DISORDERS

This appendix[1] examined the inclusion of racial and ethnic minorities in randomized clinical trials used to develop professional guidelines for treatment of four specific mental disorders: bipolar disorder, major depression, schizophrenia, and attention-deficit/hyperactivity disorder.

The American Psychiatric Association (1994) developed practice guidelines for treatment of patients with bipolar disorder. Their guidelines were based on a review of all relevant studies, including randomized controlled clinical trials. This appendix considered the representation of minorities in all randomized trials conducted in the United States during the most recent 10-year period (1983–1994). Results are presented in Table A–1. Seventeen of these studies represented 16 separate patient populations. Two articles reported on the same subjects, but these subjects are only included once in this review. Of 825 participants, 29 were identified as nonwhite, and 32 were identified as black. No analyses were conducted to determine if these participants differed from white participants in outcomes. As a result, the treatment guidelines for patients with bipolar disorder developed by the APA do not offer any information on expected outcomes for minority persons.

The American Psychiatric Association (1997) conducted a similar review to develop guidelines for schizophrenia. Results are presented in Table A–2. Twenty-five randomized clinical trials that occurred in the United States between 1986 and 1997 were included in this analysis. A total of 2,865 participants were included in these 25 studies. Of those participants, 316 were identified as nonwhite, 376 as African American, 40 as Hispanic, and 3 as Asian American. Although several studies had a modest African American sample (39–74), none analyzed results separately for African Americans or presented outcomes specifically for them. As a result, the guidelines developed by the APA to guide treatments for those with schizophrenia do not provide information regarding potentially different outcomes for African Americans or any other ethnic minorities.

The American Psychiatric Association (2000) conducted a similar review to develop treatment guidelines for major depression. Randomized clinical trials conducted between 1986–1997 were evaluated, with 27 studies included. Results are presented in Table A–3. A total of 3,980 patients were involved. Amoung them, 241 were nonwhite, 150 were African American, and 2 were Asian American. None of the studies analyzed minority participants separately. The one study with a sizeable African American population (N=123) did find similar clinical outcomes as a result of depression care, although there were differences in functional outcomes.

To examine the inclusion of ethnic minority children in research, this appendix reviewed the randomized trials of interventions for attention-deficit/hyperactivity disorder (AD/HD) used by a multidisciplinary team assembled by the Agency for Healthcare Research and Quality (AHRQ). These trials were used to develop an evidence-based report on treatment (AHRQ, 1999). Thirty-two studies from 1988 to 1999 were eligible for review. Results are presented in Table 4. These studies evaluated 1,657 children with AD/HD. Of those children, 126 were African American, 55 Hispanic, 4 nonwhite, and 1 each Asian American, Pacific Islander, East Indian, and Asian Indian. With the exception of the recent multisite study sponsored by the National Institute of Mental Health, the largest inclusion of minorities in any study was 5. However, in the recent NIMH trial, 115 African Americans and 48 Latinos were included. Although not analyzed separately in this Supplement, further reports analyzing outcomes for the ethnic minorities could still be forthcoming.

The American Psychological Association recently reviewed empirically validated therapies, namely, those therapies judged by a panel of scientists to be effective, according to explicit criteria for empirical studies (Chambless et al., 1996). Their report states;

Examining the citations for empirically validated therapies identified in the 1995 task force report, we find not a single study included tests of the efficacy of the treatment for ethnic minority populations. Most investigators did not spec-

---

[1] This Appendix was prepared by the Senior Scientific Editor for this Supplement.

ify ethnicity of subjects or used only white subjects. Out of about 41 studies cited, only 6–7 made any reference to race or ethnicity of subjects. No one used ethnicity as a variable of interest.

Overall, minorities are not represented in studies that evaluate the impact of interventions for major mental disorders. Furthermore, when minorities are included, rarely are analyses conducted to determine whether the treatments are as effective for them as they are for white populations. Although a great deal is known about efficacy of a wide range of interventions for treating common mental disorders, specific information about the efficacy of these interventions for racial and ethnic minority populations is unavailable.

References

Agency for Healthcare Research and Quality. (1999). *Treatment of Attention-Deficit/Hyperactivity Disorder: Summary, evidence report/technology assessment No. 11* (AHCPR Publication No. 99–E018). Rockville, MD: Author.

American Psychiatric Association. (1994). Practice guideline for treatment of patients with bipolar disorder. *American Journal of Psychiatry, 151* (12th suppl.), 1–36.

American Psychiatric Association. (1997). Practice guideline for treatment of patients with bipolar disorder. *American Journal of Psychiatry, 154* (4th suppl.), 1–63.

American Psychiatric Association. (2000). Practice guideline for treatment of patients with bipolar disorder. *American Journal of Psychiatry, 157* (4th suppl.), 1–45.

Chambless, D. L., Sanderson, W. C., Shoham, V., Bennett Johnson, S., Pope, K. S., Crits-Christoph, P., Baker, M., Johnson, B., Woody, S. R., Sue, S., Beutler, L., Williams, D. A., & McCurry, S. (1996). An update on empirically validated therapies. *The Clinical Psychologist, 49*, 5–18.

Table A–1: Representation of Minorities in Randomized Controlled Trials for Treatment of Bipolar Disorder.

Study	Sample	Information on ethnicity of sample	Analyses by ethnicity
Dubovsky, Franks, Allen, & Murphy, (1986)	N = 7	No	No
Giannini, Taraszewski, & Loiselle, (1987)	N = 20	All white, male patients	N/A
Cohn, Collins, Ashbrook, et al., (1989)	N = 89	No	No
Gelenberg, Kane, Keller, et al., (1989)	N = 94	No mention	No
Clarkin, Glick, Haas, et al., (1990)	N = 50	35 white 15 nonwhite	No
Gallagher-Thompson, Hanley-Peterson, & Thompson, (1990)	N = 91	No	No
O'Leary & Beach, (1990)	N = 36 couples	No	No
Himmelhoch, Thase, Mallinger, et al., (1991)	N = 56	52 white 4 nonwhite	No
Jacobson, Dobson, Fruzzetti, et al., (1991)	N = 60 couples	No	No
Pope, McElroy, Keck, et al., (1991)	N = 36	No	No
Small, Klapper, Milstein, et al., (1991)	N = 52	No	No
Garza-Treviño, Overall, & Hollister, (1992)	N = 20	No	No
Lenox, Newhouse, & Creelman, (1992)	N = 20	No	No
Bowden, Brugger, Swann, et al., (1994)	N = 179	127 white 32 black 20 other	No
Sachs, Lafer, Stoll, et al., (1994)	N = 15	No	No

Table excludes studies published before 1986.
Table excludes studies with samples outside United States.

continued on next page

References

Bowden, C. L., Brugger, A. M., Swann, A. C., Calabrese, J. R., Janicak, P. G., Petty, F., Dilsaver, S. C., Davis, J. M., Rush, A. J., Small, J. G., Garza-Treviño, E. S., Risch, S. C., Goodnick, P. J., & Morris, D. D. (1994). Efficacy of divalproex vs lithium and placebo in the treatment of mania. The Depakote Mania Study Group. *Journal of the American Medical Association, 271*, 918–924.

Clarkin, J. F., Glick, I. D., Hass, G. L., Spencer, J. H., Lewis, A. B., Peyser, J., DeMane, N., Good-Ellis, M., Harris, E., & Lestelle, V. (1990). A randomized clinical trial of inpatient family intervention. V. Results for affective disorders. *Journal of Affective Disorders, 18*, 17–28.

Cohn, J. B., Collins, G., Ashbrook, E., & Wernicke, J. F. (1989). A comparison of fluoxetine imipramine and placebo in patients with bipolar depressive disorder. *International Clinical Psychopharmacology, 4*, 313–322.

Dubovsky, S. L., Franks, R. D., Lifschitz, M., & Coen, P. (1982). Effectiveness of verapamil in the treatment of a manic patient. *American Journal of Psychiatry, 139*, 502–504.

Dubovsky, S. L., Franks, R. D., Allen, S., & Murphy, J. (1986). Calcium antagonists in mania: A double-blind study of verapolmil. *Psychiatry Research, 18*, 309–320.

Gallagher-Thompson, D., Hanley-Peterson, P., & Thompson, L. W. (1990). Maintenance of gains versus relapse following brief psychotherapy for depression. *Journal of Consulting Clinical Psychology, 58*, 371–374.

Garza-Treviño, E. S., Overall, J. E., & Hollister, L. E. (1992). Verapamil versus lithium in acute mania. *American Journal of Psychiatry, 149*, 121–122.

Gelenberg, A. J., Kane, J. M., Keller, M. B., Lavori, P., Rosenbaum, J. F., Cole, K., & Lavelle, J. (1989). Comparison of standard and low serum levels of lithium for maintenance treatment of bipolar disorder. *New England Journal of Medicine, 321*, 1489–1493.

Giannini, A. J., Taraszewski, R., & Loiselle, R. H. (1987). Verapamil and lithium in maintenance therapy of manic patients. *Journal of Clinical Pharmacology, 27*, 980–982.

Himmelhoch, J. M., Thase, M. E., Mallinger, A. G., & Houck, P. (1991). Tranylcypromine versus imipramine in anergic bipolar depression. *American Journal of Psychiatry, 148*, 910–916.

Jacobson, N. S., Dobson, K., Fruzzettii, A. E., Schmaling, K. B., & Salusky, S. (1991). Marital therapy as a treatment for depression. *Journal of Consulting Clinical Psychology, 59*, 547–557.

Lenox, R. H., Newhouse, P. A., Creelman, W. L., & Whitaker, T. M. (1992). Adjunctive treatment of manic agitation with lorazepam versus haloperidol: A double-blind study. *Journal of Clinical Psychiatry, 53*, 47–52.

O'Leary, K. D., Beach, S. R. (1990). Marital Therapy: Available treatment for depression and marital discord. *American Journal of Psychiatry, 147*, 183–186.

Pope, H. G., Jr., McElroy, S. L., Keck, P. E., Jr., & Hudson, J. I. (1991). Valproate in the treatment of acute mania: A placebo controlled study. *Archives of General Psychiatry, 48*, 62–68.

Sachs, G. S., Lafer, B., Stoll, A. L., Banov, M., Thibault, A. B., Tohen, M., & Rosenbaum, J. F. (1994). A double-blind trial of bupropion versus desipramine for bipolar depression. *Journal of Clinical Psychiatry, 55*, 391–393.

Small, J. G., Klapper, M. H., Milstein, V., Kellams, J. J., Marhenke, J. D., & Small, I. F. (1991). Carbamazepine compared with lithium in the treatment of mania. *Archives of General Psychiatry, 48*, 915–921.

Table A–2: Representation of Minorities in Randomized Controlled Trials for Treatment of Schizophrenia.

Study	Sample	Information on ethnicity of sample	Analyses by ethnicity
Hogarty, Anderson, Reiss, et al., (1986)	N = 103	81% white (n = 83.4) No other information	No
Carpenter, Heinrichs, & Hanlon, (1987)	N = 42	8 white 34 black	No
Claghorn, Honigfeld, & Abuzzahab, (1987)	N = 151	No	No
Marder, Van Putten, Mintz, et al., (1987)	N = 66	32% white (n = 21) 59% black (n = 39) 6% Hispanic (n = 4) 3% other (n = 2)	No
Csernansky, Riney, Lombrozo, et al., (1988)	N = 55	No	No
Hogarty, McEvoy, Munetz, et al., (1988)	N = 70	67% white (n = 47) No other information	No
Kane, Honigfeld, Singer, et al., (1988)	N = 319	65% white (n = 208) 23% black (n = 74) 10% Hispanic (n = 31) 1% Asian (n = 2) 1% other (n = 4)	No
Kramer, Vogel, DiJohnson, et al., (1989)	N = 58	No	No
Herz, Glazer, Mostert, et al., (1991)	N = 101	56 white 45 black	No
Salzman, Solomon, Miyawaki, et al., (1991)	N = 60	No	No
Borison, Pathiraja, Diamond, et al., (1992)	N = 36	20 white 15 black 1 Hispanic	No
Eckman, Wirshing, Marder, et al., (1992)	N = 41 (40 with ethnic data available)	14 white 23 black 3 Hispanic	No
Pickar, Owen, Litman, et al., (1992)	N = 21	No	No
Breier, Buchanan, Irish, et al., (1993)	N = 35	26 white 9 black	No

continued on next page

continued

McEvoy, Borrison, Small, et al., (1993)	N = 38	No	No
Marder & Meibach, (1994)	N = 388	244 white 144 nonwhite	No
Marder, Wirshing, Van Putten, et al., (1994)	N = 80	58 nonwhite No other information	No
Randolph, Eth Glynn, et al., (1994)	N = 41	14 white 19 black, 5 Hispanic 3 Asian	No
DeSisto, Harding, McCormick, et al., (1995)	N = 269	No	No
Hogarty, McEvoy, Ulrich, et al., (1995)	N = 128 (trial 1), same pool of subjects used for 2 subsequent trials	Trial 1: 74% white (n = 95) Trial 2: no information Trial 3: 83% white (n = 51)	No
Beasley, Tollefson, Tran, et al., (1996)	N = 335 (299 subjects with race reported)	*77% white (n = 230) 23% black (n = 69)	No
Drake, McHugo, Becker, et al., (1996)	N = 143	95% white (n = 136) No other information	No
Marder, Wirshing, Mintz, et al., (1996) (different study from Marder 1994 above)	N = 80	No	No
Schulz, Mack, Zborowski, et al., (1996)	No sample size reported (brief report of findings from "two large" studies)	No	No
van Kammen, McEvoy, Targum, et al., (1996)	N = 153 in evaluable data set with demographic information reported (205 randomized)	59% white (n = 90) 32% black (n = 49) 9% other (n = 14)	No

*information is approximate (numbers in published table do not add up to total sample size).

Table excludes studies published before 1986.

Table excludes studies with samples outside United States.

continued on next page

References

Beasley, C. M., Jr., Tollefson, G., Tran, P., Satterlee, W., Sanger, T., Hamilton, S., Fabre, L., Small, J., Ereshevsky, L., True, J., Nemeroff, C., Risch, S. C., Perry, P. J., Potkin, S. G., Borison, R. L., James, S., Meltzewr, H. Y., Igbal, N., Fann, W. E., Gewitt, G. R., Landbloom, R., Roybyrne, P. P., Tudson, V. B., Carman, J. S., Stokes, P. E., et al. (1996). Olanzapine versus placebo and haloperidol: Acute phase results of the North American double-blind olanzapine trial. *Neuropsychopharmacology, 14,* 111–123.

Borison, R. L., Pathiraja, A. P., Diamond, B. I., & Meibach, R. C. (1992). Risperidone: Clinical safety and efficacy in schizophrenia. *Psychopharmacological Bulletin, 28,* 213–218.

Breier, A., Buchanan, R. W., Irish, D., & Carpenter, W. T., Jr. (1993). Clozapine treatment of outpatients with schizophrenia: Outcome and long-term response patters. *Hospital and Community Psychiatry, 44,* 1145–1149.

Carpenter, W. T., Jr., Heinrichs, D. W., & Hanlon, T. E. (1987). A comparative trial of pharmacologic strategies in schizophrenia. *American Journal of Psychiatry, 144,* 1466–1470.

Claghorn, J., Honigfeld, G., Abuzzahab, F. S., Wang, R., Steinbook, R., Tuason, V., & Klerman, G. (1987). The risks and benefits of clozapine versus chlorpromazine. *Journal of Clinical Psychopharmacology, 7,* 377–384.

Csernansky, J. G., Riney, S. J., Lombarozo, L., Overall, J. E., & Hollister, L. E. (1988). Double-blind comparison of alprazolam, diazepam and placebo for the treatment of negative schizophrenic symptoms. *Archives of General Psychiatry, 45,* 655–659.

De Sisto, M. J., Harding, C. M., McCormick, R. V., Ashikaga, T., & Brooks, G. W. (1995). The Maine and Vermont three-decade studies of serious mental illness, I: Matched comparison of cross-sectional outcome. *British Journal of Psychiatry, 167,* 331–342.

Drake, R. E., McHugo, G. J., Becker, D. R., Anthony, W. A., & Clark, R. E. (1996). The New Hampshire study of supported employment for people with severe mental illness. *Journal of Consulting Clinical Psychology, 64,* 391–399.

Eckman, T. A., Wirshing, W. C., Marder, S. R., Liberman, R. P., Johnston-Cronk, K., Zimmermann, K., & Mintz, J. (1992). Technique for training schizophrenic patients in illness self-management: A controlled trial. *American Journal of Psychiatry, 149,* 1549–1555.

Herz, M. I., Glazer, W. M., Mostert, M. A., Sheard, M. A., Szymanski, H. V., Hafez, H., Mirza, M., & Vana, J. (1991). Intermittent vs. maintenance medication in schizophrenia: Two-year results. *Archives of General Psychiatry, 48,* 333–339.

Hogarty, G. E., Anderson, C. M., Reiss, D. J., Kornblith, S. J., Greenwald, D. P., Javna, C. D., & Madonia, M. J. (1986). Family psychoeducation, social skills training, and maintenance chemotherapy in the aftercare treatment of schizophrenia, I: One-year effects of a controlled study on relapse and expressed emotion. *Archives of General Psychiatry, 43,* 633–642.

Hogarty, G. E., McEvoy, J. P., Munetz, M., DiBarry, A. L., Bartone, P., Cather, R., Cooley, S. J., Ulrich, R. F., Carter, M., & Madonia, M. J. (Environmental/Personal Indicators in the Course of Schizophrenia Research Group). (1988). Dose of fluphenazine, familial expressed emotion, and outcome in schizophrenia: Results of a two-year controlled study. *Archives of General Psychiatry, 45,* 797–805.

Hogarty, G. E., McEvoy, J. P., Ulrich, R. F., DiBarry, A. L., Bartone, P., Cooley, S., Hammill, K., Carter, M., Munetz, M. R., & Perel, J. (1995). Pharmacotherapy of impaired affect in recovering schizophrenic patients. *Archives of General Psychiatry, 52,* 29–41.

Kane, J., Honigfeld, G., Singer, J., & Meltzer, H. (1988). Clozapine for the treatment-resistant schizophrenic: A double-blind comparison with chorpromazine. *Archives of General Psychiatry, 45,* 789–796.

Kramer, M. S., Vogel, W. H., DiJohnson, C., Dewey, D. A., Sheves, P., Cavicchia, S., Little, P., Schmidt, R., & Kimes, I. (1989). Antidepressants in "depressed" schizophrenic inpatients: A controlled trial. *Archives of General Psychiatry, 46,* 922–928.

Marder, S. R., & Meibach, R. C. (1994). Risperidone in the treatment of schizophrenia. *American Journal of Psychiatry, 151,* 825–835.

Marder, S. R., Van Putten, T., Mintz, J., Lebell, M., McKenzie, J., & May, P. R. (1987). Low-and conventional-dose maintenance therapy with fluphenazine decanoate: Two-year outcome. *Archives of General Psychiatry, 44,* 518–521.

Marder, S. R., Wirshing, W. C., Mintz, J., McKenzie, J., Johnston, K., Echman, T. A., Lebell, M., Zimmerman, K., & Liberman, R. P. (1996). Two-year outcome of social skills training and group psychotherapy for outpatients with schizophrenia. *American Journal of Psychiatry, 153,* 1585–1592.

continued on next page

continued

Marder, S. R., Wirshing, W. C., Van Putten, T., Mintz, J., McKenzie, J., Johnston-Cronk, K., Lebell, M., & Liberman, R. P. (1994). Fluphenazine vs placebo supplementation for prodromal signs of relapse in schizophrenia. *Archives of General Psychiatry. 51*, 280–287.

McEvoy, J., Borison, R., Small, J., van Kammen, D., Meltzer, H., Hamner, M., Morris, D., Shu, V., Sebree, T., & Grebb, J. (1993). The efficacy and tolerability of sertindole in schizophrenic patients: A pilot double-blind placebo controlled, dose ranging study. *Schizophrenia Research, 9*, 244.

Pickar, D., Owen, R. R., Litman, R. E., Konicki, E., Gutierrez, R., & Rapoport, M. H. (1992). Clinical and biologic response to clozapine in patients with schizophrenia: Crossover comparison with fluphenazine. *Archives of General Psychiatry, 49*, 345–353.

Randolph, E. T., Eth, S., Glynn, S. M., Paz, G. G., Leong, G. B., Shaner, A. L., Strachan, A., Van Vort, W., Escobar, J. I., & Liberman, R. P. (1994). Behavioural family management in schizophrenia: Outcome of a clinic-based intervention. *British Journal of Psychiatry, 164*, 501–506.

Salzman, C., Solomon, D., Miyawaki, E., Glassman, R., Rood, L., Flowers, E., & Thayer, S. (1991). Parenteral lorazepam versus parenteral haloperidol for the control of psychotic disruptive behavior. *Journal of Clinical Psychiatry, 52*, 177–180.

van Kammen, D. P., McEvoy, J. P., Targum, S. D., Kardatzke, D., & Sebree, T. B. (1996). A randomized controlled dose-ranging trial of sertindole in patients with schizophrenia. *Psychopharmacology, 124*, 168–175.

Table A–3: Representation of Minorities in Randomized Controlled Trials for Treatment of Depression.

Study	Sample	Information on ethnicity of sample	Analyses by ethnicity
Kocsis, Frances, Voss, et al., (1988)	N = 76	No	No
Liebowitz, Quitkin, Stewart, et al., (1988)	N = 119	No (subject description published in 1984 report)	No
Quitkin, Stewart, McGrath, et al., (1988)	N = 60	No	No
Elkin, Shea, Watkins, et al., (1989)	N = 239	212 white No other information	No
Feighner, Pambakian, Fowler, et al., (1989)	N = 45	No	No
Frank, Kupfer, Perel, et al., (1990)	N = 128	No	No
Quitkin, McGrath, Stewart, et al., (1990)	N = 90 (different sample from 1988 study)	No	No
Feighner, Gardner, Johnston, et al., (1991)	N = 123	No	No
Quitkin, Harrison, Stewart, et al., (1991)	N = 64	No	No
Kupfer, Frank, Perel, et al., (1992)	N = 20 (sample drawn from Frank, 1990)	No	No
Shea, Elkin, Imber, et al., (1992)	N = 239 (same sample as Elkin, et al., 1989)	No (1989 sample is 212/239 white, no other information)	No
Thase, Mallinger, McKnight, et al., (1992)	N = 16	No	No
Frank, Kupfer, Perel, et al., (1993)	N = 20 (sample drawn from Frank, et al., 1990)	No	No
Sackheim, Prudic, Devanand, et al., (1993)	N = 96	No	No
Cunningham, Borison, Carman, et al., (1994)	N = 225	No	No

continued on next page

179

continued

Fontaine, Ontiveros, Elie, et al., (1994)	N = 180	No	No
Schweizer, Feighner, Mandos, et al., (1994)	N = 224	No	No
Weisler, Johnston, Lineberry, et al., (1994)	N = 124	112 white No other information	No
Claghorn & Lesem, (1995)	N = 90	No	No
McElhiney, Moody, Steif, et al., (1995) (investigates post-ECT amnesia)	N = 91	No	No
Mendels, Reimherr, Marcus, et al., (1995)	N = 240	214 white 26 other	No
Kelsey, (1996)	Study 1: N = 60 Study 2: N = 312	Study 1: No Study 2: No	Study 1: No Study 2: No
Pande, Birkett, & Fechner-Bates, (1996)	N = 42	38 white 2 African 2 Asian	No
Schulberg, Block, Madonia, et al., (1996)	N = 276	153 white No other information	No (study notes significantly more attrition among non-whites in nortriptyline condition)
Chaudhry, Najam, & Naqvi, (1998)	N = 100	No	No
Keller, Gelenberg, Hirschfeld, et al., (1998)	N = 635	577 white 25 black 33 other	No
Bright, Baker, & Neimeyer, (1999)	N = 98	91 white (93%) No other information	No
Reynolds, Frank, Perel, et al., (1999)	N = 187	174 white (93.1%) No other information	No

Table excludes studies published before 1986.
Table excludes studies with samples outside United States.

continued on next page

References

Bright, J. I., Baker, K. D., & Neimeyer, R. A. (1999). Professional and paraprofessional group treatments for depression: A comparison of cognitive–behavioral and mutual support interventions. *Journal of Consulting Clinical Psychology, 67,* 491–501.

Chaudhry, J. R., Najam, N., & Naqvi, A. (1998). The value of amineptine in depressed patients treated with cognitive behavioural psychotherapy. *Human Psychopharmacology, 13,* 419–424.

Claghorn, J. L., & Lesem, M. D. (1995). A double-blind placebo-controlled study of Org 1770 in depressed outpatients. *Journal of Affective Disorders, 34,* 165–171.

Cunningham, L. A., Borison, R. L., Carman, J. S., Chouinard, G., Crowder, J. F., Diamond, B. I., Fishcer, D. E., & Hearst, E. (1994). A comparison of venlafaxine, trazodone, and placebo in major depression. *Journal of Clinical Psychopharmacology, 14,* 99–106.

Elkin, I., Shea, M. T., Watkins, J. T., Imber, S. D., Sotsky, S. M., Collins, J. F., Glass, D. R., Pilkonis, P. A., Leber, W. R., Docherty, J. P., Fiester, S. J., & Parloff, M. B. (1989). National Institute of Mental Health Treatment of Depression Collaborative Research Program: General effectiveness of treatments. *Archives of General Psychiatry, 46,* 971–982.

Feighner, J. P., Gardner, E. A., Johnson, J. A., Boltey, S. R., Khayrallah, M. A., Ascher, J. A., & Lineberry, C. G. (1991). Double-blind comparison of bupropion and fluoyetine in depressed outpatients. *Journal of Clinical Psychiatry, 52,* 329–335.

Feighner, J. P., Pambakian, R., Fowler, R. C., Boyer, W. F., & D'Amico, M. F. (1989). A comparison of nefazodone, imipramine, and placebo in patients with moderate to severe depression. *Psychopharmacology Bulletin, 25,* 219–221.

Fontaine, R., Ontiveros, A., Elie, R., Kensler, T. T., Roberts, D. L., Kaplita, S., Ecker, J. A., Faludi, G., & Louis, H. (1994). A double-blind comparison of nefazodone, imipramine, and placebo in major depression. *Journal of Clinical Psychiatry, 55,* 234–241.

Frank, E., Kupfer, D. J., Perel, J. M., Cornes, C., & Mallinger, A. G. (1990). Three-year outcomes for maintenance therapies in recurrent depression. *Archives of General Psychiatry, 47,* 1093–1099.

Frank, E., Kupfer, D. J., Perel, J. M., et al. (1993). Comparison of full dose versus half dose pharmacotherapy in the maintenance treatment of recurrent depression. *Journal of Affective Disorders, 27,* 139–145.

Keller, M. D., Gelenberg, A. J., Hirschfeld, R. M., Rush, A. J., Thase, M. E., Kocsis, J. H., Markowitz, J. C., Fawcett, J. A., Koran, L. M., Klein, D. N., Russell, J. M., Kornstein, S. G., McCullough, J. P., Davis, S. M., & Harrison, W. M. (1998). The treatment of chronic depression, part 2: A double-blind, randomized trial of sertraline and imipramine. *Journal of Clinical Psychiatry, 59,* 598–607.

Kelsey, J. E. (1996). Dose-response relationship with venlafaxine. *Journal of Clinical Psychopharmacology, 16* (Suppl. 2), 215–285.

Kocsis, J. H., Frances, A. J., Voss, C. B., Mann, J. J., Mason, B. J., & Sweeney, J. (1988). Imipramine treatment for chronic depression. *Archives of General Psychiatry, 45,* 253–257.

Liebowitz, M. R., Quitkin, F. M., Stewart, J. W., McGrath, P. J., Harrison, W. M., Markowitz, J. S., Rabkin, J. G., Tricamo, E., Goetz, D. M., & Klein, D. G. (1988). Antidepressant specificity in atypical depression. *Archives of General Psychiatry, 45,* 129–137.

McElhiney, M. C., Moody, B. J., Steif, B. L., Prudic, J., Devanand, D. P., Nobler, M. S., & Sackeim, H. A. (1995). Autobiographical memory and mood: Effects of electroconvulsive therapy. *Neuropsychology, 9,* 501–517.

Mendels, J., Reimherr, F., Marcus, R. N., Roberts, D. L., Francis, R. J., & Anton, S. F. (1995). A double-blind, placebo-controlled trial of two dose ranges of nefazodone in the treatment of depressed outpatients. *Journal of Clinical Psychiatry, 56* (Suppl. 6), 30–36.

Pande, A. C., Birkett, M., Fechner-Bates, S., Haskett, R. F., & Greden, J. F. (1996). Fluoxetine versus phenelzine in atypical depression. *Biological Psychiatry, 40,* 1017–1020.

Quitkin, F. M., Harrison, W., Stewart, J. W., McGrath, P. J., Tricamo, E., Ocepek-Welikson, K., Rabkin, J. G., Wager, S. G., Nunes, E., & Klein, D. F. (1991). Response to phenelzine and imipramine in placebo nonresponders with atypical depression: A new application of the crossover design. *Archives of General Psychiatry, 48,* 319–323.

continued on next page

continued

Quitkin, F. M., McGrath, P. J., Stewart, J. W., Harrison, W., Tricamo, E., Wager, S. G., Ocepek-Welikson, K., Nunes, E., Rabkin, J. G., & Klein, D. F. (1990). Atypical depression, panic attacks, and response to imipramine and phenelzine. A replication. *Archives of General Psychiatry, 47*, 935–941.

Quitkin, F. M., Stewart, J. W., McGrath, P. J., Liebowitz, M. R., Harrison, W. J., Tricamo, E., Klein, D. F., Rabkin, J. G., Markowitz, J. S., & Wager, S. G. (1988). Phenelzine versus imipramine in the treatment of probably atypical depression: Defining syndrome boundaries of selective MAOI responders. *American Journal of Psychiatry, 145*, 306–311.

Reynolds, C. F., Frank, E., Perel, J. M., Imber, S. D., Cornes, C., Miller, M. D., Mazaumdar, S., Houck, P. R., Dew, M. A., Stack, J. A., Pollock, B. G., & Kupfer, D. J. (1999). Nortriptyline and interpersonal psychotherapy as maintenance therapies for recurrent major depression: A randomized controlled trial in patients older than 59 years. *Journal of the American Medical Association, 281*, 39–45.

Sackheim, H. A., Prudic, J., Devanand, D. P., Kiersy, J. E., Fizsimons, L., Moody, B. J., McElhiney, M. C., Coleman, E. A., & Settembrino, J. M. (1993). Effects of stimulus intensity and electrode placement on the efficacy and cognitive effects of electroconvulsive therapy. *New England Journal of Medicine, 328*, 839–846.

Schulberg, H. C., Block, M. R., Madonia, M. J., Scott, C. P., Rodriguez, E., Imber, S. D., Perel, J., Lave, J., Houck, P. R., & Coulehan, J. L. (1996). Treating major depression in primary care pactice: Eight-month clinical outcomes. *Archives of General Psychiatry, 53*, 913–919.

Schweizer, E., Feighner, J., Mandos, L. A., & Rickels, K. (1994). Comparison of venlafaxine and imipramine in the acute treatment of major depression in outpatients. *Journal of Clinical Psychiatry, 55*, 104–108.

Shea, M. T., Elkin, I., Imber, S. D., Sotsky, S. M., Watkins, J. T., Collins, J. F., Pilkonis, P. A., Beckham, E., Glass, D. R., Dolan, R. T., et al. (1992). Course of depressive symptoms over follow-up: Findings from the NIMH Treatment of Depression Collaborative Research Program. *Archives of General Psychiatry, 49*, 782–787.

Weisler, R. H., Johnston, J. A., Lineberry, C. G., Samara, B., Branconnier, R. J., & Billow, A. A. (1994). Comparison of bupropion and trazodone for the treatment of major depression. *Journal of Clinical Psychopharmacology, 14*, 170–179.

Table A–4: Representation of Minorities in Randomized Controlled Trials for Treatment of AD/HD.

Study	Sample	Information on ethnicity of sample	Analyses by ethnicity
Fitzpatrick, Klorman, Brumaghim, et al., (1992)	N = 19 (analyzed)	No	No
Srinivas, Hubbard, Quinn, et al., (1992)	N = 9	No	No
Borcherding, Keysor, Cooper, et al., (1989)	N = 18	No	No
Castellanos, Giedd, Elia, et al., (1997)	N = 22	16 white 2 black 1 Asian 1 Hispanic	No
Efron, Jarman, & Barker, (1997)	N = 125	No	No
Elia, Borcherding, Rapoport, et al., (1991)	N = 48	No	No
Matochik, Liebenauer, King, et al., (1994)	N = 37 (analyzed)	No	No
Pelham, Greenslade, Vodde-Hamilton, et al., (1990)	N = 22	No	No
Rapport, Carlson, Kelly, et al., (1993)	N = 16	14 white 2 black	No
Arnold, Kleykamp, Votolato, et al., (1989)	N = 18 (analyzed)	No	No
Klein & Abikoff, (1997)	N = 89 (no break down given)	?? white ?? African American ?? Hispanic ?? Asian	No
MTA Coop Group, (1999)	N = 579	351 white 115 African American 48 Hispanic	No
Levy, Hobbes, (1996)	N = 10	No	No
Long, Rickert, & Ashcraft, (1993)	N = 32	No	No

continued on next page

continued

Borden & Brown (1989)	N = 30	No	No
Brown, Borden, Wynne, et al., (1988)	N= 71	No	No
Carlson, Pelham, Milich, et al., (1992)	N = 24	No	No
Hinshaw, Buhrmester, & Heller, (1989)	N = 24	17 white 4 black 1 Hispanic 1 Pacific Islander 1 East Indian	No
Pelham, Carlson, Sams, et al., (1993)	N = 31	29 white 2 black	No
Solanto, Wender, & Bartell, (1997)	N = 22	16 white 5 Hispanic 1 Asian Indian	No
Biederman, Baldessarini, Wright, et al., (1989) a+b	N = 73	69 white 4 other	No
Gualtieri, Keenan, & Chandler, (1991)	N = 12	No	No
Singer, Brown, Quaskey, et al., (1995)	N = 37 (34 completed)	33 white 1 black	No
Wilens, Biederman, Prince, et al., (1996)	N = 43	No	No
Gualtieri & Evans, (1988)	N = 9	No	No
Kupietz, Winsberg, Richardson, et al., (1988)	N = 58	No	No
Schachar, Tannock, Cunningham, et al., (1997)	N = 91	No	No
Gillberg, Melander, von Knorring, et al., (1997)	N = 62	No	No
Fehlings, Roberts, Humphries, et al., (1991)	N = 26	No	No
Linden, Habib, & Radojevic, (1996)	N = 18	No	No

continued on next page

References

Arnold, L. E., Kleykamp, D., Votolato, N. A., Taylor, W. A., Kontras, S. B., & Tobin, K. (1989). Gamma-linolenic acid for attention-deficit hyperactivity disorder: Placebo-controlled omparison to d-amphetamine. *Biological Psychiatry, 25,* 222–228.

Biederman, J., Baldessarini, R. J., Wright, V., Knee, D., & Harmatz, J. S. (1989a). A double-blind placebo controlled study of desipramine in the treatment of ADD: I. Efficacy. *Journal of the American Academy of Child and Adolescent Psychiatry, 28,* 777–784.

Biederman, J., Baldessarini, R. J., Wright, V., Knee, D., Harmatz, J. S., & Goldblatt, A. (1989b). A double-blind placebo controlled study of desipramine in the treatment ADD: II. Serum drug levels and cardiovascular findings. *Journal of the American Academy of Child and Adolescent Psychiatry, 28,* 903–911.

Borcherding, B. G., Keysor, C. S., Cooper, T. B., & Rapoport, J. L. (1989). Differential effects of methylphenidate and dextroamphetamine on the motor activity level of hyperactive children. *Neuropsychopharmacology, 2,* 255–263.

Borden, K. A., & Brown, R. T. (1989). Attributional outcomes: The subtle messages of treatments for attention deficit disorder. *Cognitive Therapy and Research, 13,* 147–160.

Brown, R. T., Borden, K. A., Wynne, M. E., & Spunt, A. L. (1988). Patterns of compliance in a treatment program for children with attention deficit disorder. *Journal of Compliance in Health Care, 3,* 23–39.

Carlson, C. L., Pelham, W. E. J., Milich, R., & Dixon, J. (1992). Single and combined effects of methylphenidate and behavior therapy on the classroom performance of children with attention-deficit hyperactivity disorder. *Journal of Abnormal Child Psychology, 20,* 213–232.

Castellanos, F. X., Giedd, J. N., Elia, J., Marsh, W. L., Ritchie, G. F., Hamburger, S. D., & Rapoport, J. L. (1997). Controlled stimulant treatment of AD/HD and comorbid Tourette's syndrome: Effects of stimulant and dose. *Journal of the American Academy of Child and Adolescent Psychiatry, 36,* 589–596.

Efron, D., Jarman, F., & Barker, M. (1997). Methylphenidate versus dexamphetamine in children with attention deficit hyperactivity disorder: A double-blind, crossover trial. *Paediatrics, 100* (6), E6.

Elia, J., Borcherding, B. G., Rapoport, J. L., & Keysor, C. S. (1991). Methylphenidate and dextroamphetamine treatments of hyperactivity: Are there true nonresponders? *Psychiatry Research, 36,* 141–155.

Fehlings, D. L., Roberts, W., Humphries, T., & Dawe, G. (1991). Attention deficit hyperactivity disorder: Does cognitive behavioral therapy improve home behavior? Journal of Developmental and Behavioral Pediatrics, 12, 223–228.

Fitzpatrick, P. A., Klorman, R., Brumaghim, J. T., & Borgstedt, A. D. (1992). Effects of sustained-release and standard preparations of methylphenidate on attention deficit disorder. *Journal of the American Academy of Child and Adolescent Psychiatry, 31,* 226–234.

Gillberg, C., Melander, H., von Knorring, A. L., Janols, L. O., Thernlund, G., Hagglof, B., Eidevall-Wallin, L., Gustafsson, P., & Kopp, S. (1997). Long-term stimulant treatment of children with attention-deficit hyperactivity disorder symptoms. A randomized, double-blind, placebo-controlled trial. *Archives of General Psychiatry, 54,* 857–864.

Gualtieri, C. T., & Evans, R. W. (1988). Motor performance in hyperactive children treated with imipramine. *Perceptual and Motor Skills, 66,* 763–769.

Gualtieri, C. T., Keenan, P. A., & Chandler, M. (1991). Clinical and neuropsychological effects of desipramine in children with attention deficit hyperactivity disorder. *Journal of Clinical Psychopharmacology, 11,* 155–159.

Hinshaw, S. P., Buhrmester, D., & Heller, T. (1989). Anger control in response to verbal provocation: Effects of stimulant medication for boys with AD/HD. *Journal of Abnormal Child Psychology, 1,* 393–407.

Klein, R. G., & Abikoff, H. (1997). Behavior therapy and methylphenidate in the treatment of children with AD/HD. *Journal of Attention Disorders, 2,* 89–114. (Same study as Gittelman-Klein, Klein, Abikoff, et al., 1976.)

Kupietz, S. S., Winsberg, B. G., Richardson, E., Maitinsky, S. (1988). Effects of methylphenidate dosage in hyperactive reading-disabled children: I. Behavior and cognitive performance effects. *Journal of the American Academy of Child and Adolescent Psychiatry, 27,* 70–77.

Levy, F., & Hobbes, G. (1996). Does haloperidol block methylphenidate? Motivation or attention? *Psychopharmacology, 126,* 70–74.

continued on next page

continued

Linden, M., Habib, T., & Radojevic, V. (1996). A controlled study of the effects of EEG biofeedback on cognition and behavior of children with attention deficit disorder and learning disabilities. Biofeedback and Self-Regulation, 21, 35–49.

Long, N., Rickert, V. I., & Ashcraft, E.W. (1993). Bibliotherapy as an adjunct to stimulant medication in the treatment of attention-deficit hyperactivity disorder. *Journal of Pediatric Health Care, 7*, 82–88.

Matochik, J. A., Liebenauer, L. L., King, C., Szymanski, H. V., Cohen, R. M., & Zametkin, A. J. (1994). Cerebral glucose metabolism in adults with attention deficit hyperactivity disorder after chronic stimulant treatment. *American Journal of Psychiatry, 151*, 658–664.

MTA Cooperative Group. (1999). 14-month randomized clinical trial of treatment strategies for attention deficit hyperactivity disorder. Multimodal treatment Study of Children with AD/HD. Archives of General Psychiatry, 56, 1073–1086. Pelham, W. E. J., Carlson, C., Sams, S. E., Vallano, G., Dixon, M. J., & Hoza, B. (1993). Separate and combined effects of methylphenidate and behavior modification on boys with attention deficit-hyperactivity disorder in the classroom. *Journal of Consulting and Clinical Psychology, 61*, 506–515.

Pelham, W. E. J., Carlson, C., Sams, S.E., Vallano, G., Dixon, M. J., & Hoza, B. (1993). Separate and combined effects of methylphenidate and behavior modification on the classroom behavior and academic performance of AD/HD boys: Group effects and individual differences. *Journal of Consulting and Clinical Psycology, 61*, 506–515.

Pelham, W. E. J., Greenslade, K. E., Vodde-Hamilton, M., Murphy, D. A., Greenstein, J. J., Gnagy, E. M., Guthrie, K. J., Hoover, M. D., & Dahl, R. E. (1990). Relative efficacy of long-acting stimulants on children with attention deficit-hyperactivity disorder: A comparison of standard methylphenidate, sustained-release methylphenidate, sustained-release dextroamphetamine, and pemoline. *Pediatrics 86*, 226–237.

Rapport, M. D., Carlson, G. A., Kelly, K. L., & Pataki, C. (1993). Methylphenidate and desipramine in hospitalized children: I. Separate and combined effects on cognitive function. *Journal of the American Academy of Child and Adolescent Psychiatry, 32*, 333–342.

Schachar, R. J., Tannock, R., Cunningham, C., & Corkum, P. V. (1997). Behavioral, situational, and temporal effects of treatment of AD/HD with methylphenidate. *Journal of the American Academy of Child and Adolescent Psychiatry, 36*, 754–763.

Singer, H. S., Brown, J., Quaskey, S., Rosenberg, L. A., Mellits, E. D., & Denckla, M. B. (1995). The treatment of attention-deficit hyperactivity disorder in Tourette's syndrome: A double-blind placebo-controlled study with clonidine and desipramine. *Pediatrics, 95*, 74–81.

Solanto, M. V., Wender, E. H., & Bartell, S. S. (1997). Effects of methylphenidate and behavioral contingencies on sustained attention in attention-deficit hyperactivity disorder: A test of the reward dysfunction hypothesis. *Journal of Child and Adolescent Psychopharmacology, 7*, 123–136.

Srinivas, N. R., Hubbard, J. W., Quinn, D., & Midha, K. K. (1992). Enantioselective pharmacokinetics and pharmacodynamics of dl-threo-methylphenidate in children with attention deficit hyperactivity disorder. *Clinical Pharmacological Therapy, 52*, 561–568.

Wilens, T. E., Biederman, J., Prince, J., Spencer, T. J., Faraone, S. V., Warburton, R., Schleifer, D., Harding, M., Linehan, C., & Geller, D. (1996). Six-week, double-blind, placebo-controlled study of desipramine for adult attention deficit hyperactivity disorder. *American Journal of Psychiatry, 153*, 1147–1153.

APPENDIX B

RESOURCE DIRECTORY

Federal Lead Agencies

Office of the Surgeon General (OSG)
5600 Fishers Lane
Rockville, MD 20857
Tel: 301-443-4000
Fax: 301-443-3574
www.surgeongeneral.gov

Center for Mental Health Services (CMHS)
Knowledge Exchange Network
P.O. Box 42490
Washington, DC 20015
Tel: 800-789-2647
Fax:301-984-8796
www.mentalhealth.org

National Institute of Mental Health (NIMH)
Office of Communications and Public Liaison
6001 Executive Boulevard
Room 8184, MSC 9663
Bethesda, MD 20892-9663
Tel: 301-443-4513
TTY: 301-443-8431
Fax: 301-443-4279
www.nimh.nih.gov

Substance Abuse and Mental Health Services Administration (SAMHSA)
Office of the Administrator
5600 Fishers Lane, Room 12-105
Rockville, MD 20857
Tel: 301-443-2271
www.samhsa.gov

Additional Federal Resources

Office of the Secretary
200 Independence Avenue, S.W.
Washington, DC 20201
Tel: 202-690-7000
www.hhs.gov/progorg/ospage.html

Administration for Children and Families
370 L'Enfant Promenade, S.W.
Washington, DC 20447
www.acf.dhhs.gov

Administration on Aging
National Aging Information Center
330 Independence Avenue, SW
Washington, DC 20201
Tel: 202-619-7501
Tel: 800-677-1116 (Eldercare Locator)
www.aoa.dhhs.gov

Agency for Health Care Research and Quality
Publications Clearinghouse
P.O. Box 8547
Silver Spring, MD 20907
Tel: 800-358-9295
www.ahcpr.gov

Centers for Disease Control and Prevention
1600 Clifton Road
Atlanta, GA 30333
Tel: 800-311-3435 or 404-639-3534
www.cdc.gov

Centers for Medicare and Medicaid Services
500 Securities Boulevard
Baltimore, MD 21244
Tel: 410-786-3000
www.hcfa.gov

Food and Drug Administration
Center for Drugs, Evaluation and Safety
5600 Fishers Lane, RM 12B-31
Rockville, MD 20857
Tel: 888-INFO-FDA (888-463-6332)
www.fda.gov

Health Resources and Services Administration
Clearinghouse on Maternal and Child Health
2070 Chain Bridge Road, # 450
Vienna, VA 22182
Tel: 888-434-4mch
www.nmchc.org

Indian Health Service
Headquarters East
Parklawn Building
5600 Fishers Lane
Rockville, MD 20857
www.ihs.gov

National Institutes of Health
Bethesda, MD 20892
www.nih.gov

National Center on Minority Health and Health Disparities
6707 Democracy Boulevard, Suite 800
Bethesda, MD 200892-5465
Tel: 301-402-1366
Fax: 301-402-7040
ncmhd.nih.gov

National Institute on Aging
Alzheimer's Disease Education and Referral Center
P.O. Box 8250
Silver Spring, MD 20898-8057
Tel: 800-438-4380
www.alzheimers.org

National Institute on Alcohol Abuse and Alcoholism
Office of Scientific Communication
6000 Executive Boulevard, Suite 409
Bethesda, MD 20892-7003
Tel: 301-443-3860
www.niaaa.nih.gov

National Institute on Child Health and Human Development
NICHD Clearinghouse
P.O. Box 3006
Rockville, MD 20847
Tel: 800-370-2943
www.nichd.nih.gov

National Institute on Drug Abuse
6001 Executive Boulevard, Room 5213
Bethesda, MD 20892-1124
www.drugabuse.gov

National Institute on Neurological Disorders and Stroke
Office of Communications and Public Liaison
P.O. Box 5801
Bethesda, MD 20824
Tel: 301-496-5751

www.ninds.nih.gov

National Clearinghouse for Alcohol and Drug Information
P.O. Box 2345
Rockville, MD 20847-2600
Tel: 800-729-6686 or 301-468-2600
Fax: 301-468-6433
TDD: 800-487-4889
www.health.org

National Clearinghouse on Child Abuse and Neglect Information
P.O. BOX 1182
Washington, DC 20013-1182
Tel: 800-FYI-3366 or 703-385-7565
Fax: 703-385-3206
www.calib.com/nccanch/

National Information Center for Children and Youth with Disabilities
P.O. Box 1492
Washington, DC 20013
Tel: 800-695-0285
Fax: 202-884-8441
www.nichy.org

Office of Minority Health Resource Center
U.S. Department of Health and Human Services
P.O. Box 37337
Washington, DC 20013-7337
Tel: 800-444-6472
www.omhrc.gov

Rehabilitation Services Administration
U.S. Department of Education
330 C Street, S.W. Room 3211
Washington, DC 20202
Tel: 202-205-5474
www.ed.gov/offices/OSERS/RSA

Rural Information Center Health Service
(A joint project of the U.S. Department of Health and Human Services and U.S. Department of Agriculture)
National Agricultural Library, Room 304
10301 Baltimore Avenue
Beltsville, MD 20705-2351
Tel: 301-504-5755 or 800-633-7701
www.nal.usda.gov/ric/richs

Substance Abuse and Mental Health Services Administration

Center for Substance Abuse Prevention
www.samhsa.gov/csap

Center for Substance Abuse Treatment
www.samhsa.gov/csat

Office of Minority Health
Rockville, MD 20857
5600 Fishers Lane, Room 10-75
Tel: 301-443-7265

Refugee Mental Health Program
www.samhsa.gov/centers/cmhs/cmhs.html
Special Populations, Refugee Mental Health

Veterans Health Administration
1120 Vermont Avenue, NW
Washington, DC 20421
Tel: 800-827-1000
www.va.gov/health/index.htm

General Federal Government Web Sites

Consumer Information Center
www.pueblo.gsa.gov

Health Finder
www.healthfinder.gov

The Center for Mental Health Services (KEN)
www.mental health.org

National Library of Medicine
www.nlm.nih.gov

National Women's Health Information Center
www.4woman.gov

Substance Abuse and Mental Health Services Administration
www.samhsa.gov

U.S. Consumer Gateway- Health
www.consumer.gov/health

Resources for Specific Racial and Ethnic Groups

African Americans

African American Mental Health Research Center
Institute for Social Research
University of Michigan
426 Thompson, Room 5118
Ann Arbor, MI 48106
Tel: 313-763-0045
www.isr.umich.edu/rcgd/prba/index.html

Association of Black Psychologists
P.O. Box 55999
Washington, DC 20040-5999
Tel: 202-722-0808
www.abpsi.org

Black Health Network
www.blackhealthnet.com

Black Psychiatrists of America
866 Carlson Avenue
Oakland, CA 94610
Tel: 510–834-7103
Fax: 510-695-9830

Minority Health Professions Foundation
3 Executive Park Drive, NE, Suite 100
Atlanta, GA 30329
Tel: 404-634-1993
www.minorityhealth.org

National Association for the Advancement of Colored People
National Health Coordinator
4805 Mt. Hope Drive
Baltimore, MD 21215
Tel: 410-486-9147
www.naacp.org

National Association of Black Social Workers
8436 West McNichols Street
Detroit, MI 48221
Tel: 313-862-6700
www.ssw.unc.edu/professional

National Black Child Development Institute
1023 15th Street, NW, Suite 600
Washington, DC 20005
Tel: 202-387-1281 or 800-556-2234
www.nbcdi.org

National Medical Association
1012 Tenth Street, NW
Washington, DC 20001
Tel: 202-347-1895
www.nmanet.org

American Indians and Alaska Natives

Association of American Indian Physicians
1225 Sovereign Row, Suite 103
Oklahoma City, OK 73108
Tel: 405-946-7072
Fax:405-946-7651
www.aaip.com

Indian Health Service
5600 Fishers Lane
Parklawn Building, Room 6-35
Rockville, MD 20857
Tel: 301-443-3593
www.ihs.gov

National Center for American Indian and Alaska Native Mental Health Research
University of Colorado Health Sciences Center
Department of Psychiatry, North Pavilion
4455 East 12th Avenue, Campus Box A011-13
Denver, CO 80220
Tel: 303-315-9232
www.uchsc.edu/sm/ncaianmhr

National Congress of American Indians
1301 Connecticut Avenue NW
Suite 200
Washington DC 20036
202-466-7767
fax: 202-466-7797
www.ncai.org

National Indian Child Welfare Association
5100 S Macadam Avenue, Suite 300
Portland, OR 97201
Tel: 503-222-4044
Fax:503-222-4007
www.nicwa.org

National Indian Health Board
Nez Perce Tribal Council
1385 South Colorado Boulevard, Suite A-707
Denver, CA 80222
Tel: 303-759-3075
www.nihb.org

National Native American AIDS Prevention Center
436 14th Street, Suite 1020
Oakland, CA 94612
Tel: 510-444-2051
www.nnaapc.org

Native Elder Health Care Resource Center
University of Colorado
Department of Psychiatry
4455 East 12th Avenue, Campus Box A011-13
Denver, CO 80220
Tel: 303-315-9351
www.uchsc.edu/sm/nehcrc

Society of Indian Psychologists
Oklahoma State University
215 N. Murray Hall
Stillwater, OK 74078
405-744-6027
jchaney@okstate.edu

Asian Americans and Pacific Islanders

Asian American Psychological Association
3003 North Central Avenue, Suite 103-198
Phoenix, AZ 85012
Tel: 602-230-4257
www.west.asu.edu/aapa

Asian and Pacific Islander American Health Forum
942 Market Street, Suite 200
San Francisco, CA 94102
Tel: 415-954-9988
Washington, DC area: 703-841-9128
www.apiahf.org

Association of Asian Pacific Community Health Organizations
439 23rd Street
Oakland, CA 94612
Tel: 510-272-9536
www.aapcho.org

National Asian American and Pacific Islander Mental Health Association
565 S. High Street
Denver, CO 80209
Tel: 303-765-5330
www.naapimha.org
naapimha@cs.com

National Asian Pacific American Families Against Substance Abuse
340 East Second Street, Suite 409
Los Angeles, CA 90012
Tel: 213-625-5795
www.napafasa.org

National Asian Women's Health Organization
250 Montgomery Street, Suite 900
San Francisco, CA 94104
Tel: 415-989-9747
Fax: 415-989-9758
www.nawho.org

National Research Center on Asian American Mental Health
Department of Psychology
University of California
One Shields Avenue
Davis, CA 95616-8686
Tel: 530-752-1400
nrcaamh.ucdavis.edu

Refugee Health Issues Center
American Refugee Committee
430 Oakgrove Street, Suite 204
Minneapolis, MN 55404
Tel: 612-872-7060
www.archq.org

South Asian Women's NETwork (Sawnet)
www.umiacs.umd.edu/users/sawweb/sawnet/health
.html Or www.api-healthline.net

Hispanics/Latinos

Association of Hispanic Mental Health Professionals
P.O. Box 7631, F.D.R. Station
New York, NY 10150-1913
Tel: 718-960-0208
www.hispanicfederation.org/agencies/ahmhp.htm

Centros Para el Control y la Prevencion de Enfermedades
(CDC Spanish Language Web Site)
1600 Clifton Road
Atlanta, GA 30333
Tel: 800-311-3435
www.cdc.gov/spanish

Latino Research Program Project (LRPP)
Center for Evaluation and Sociomedical Research
Medical Sciences Campus
Main Building 3rd Floor
GPO BOX 365067
San Juan, P.R. 00936-5067
Telephone (787) 758-2525 extensions 1422, 1423
latino.rcm.upr.edu/index.html

National Alliance for Hispanic Health
(formerly COSSMHO)
1501 16th Street, NW
Washington, DC 20036-1401
Tel: 202-387-5000
www.hispanichealth.org

National Hispanic Medical Association
1700 17th Street, NW, Suite 405
Washington, DC 20009
Tel: 202-265-4297
home.earthlink.net/~nhma

National Latina Health Network
1680 Wisconsin Avenue, NW, 2nd Floor
Washington, DC 20007
Tel: 202-965-9633
NLHN@erols.com

National Latina Health Organization
P.O. Box 7567
Oakland, CA 94601
Tel: 510-534-1362
Fax:510-534-1364
clnet.ucr.edu/women/nlho

National Latino Behavioral Health Association
www.nlbha.org

UCLA LatinoMentalHealth.net
www.latinomentalhealth.net

Multicultural

Association for Multicultural Counseling and Development
5999 Stevenson Avenue
Alexandria, VA 22304
Tel: 703-823-9800 or 800-347-6647
www.counseling.org

The Center for Multicultural and Multilingual Mental Health Services
4750 N. Sheridan Road
Suite 300
Chicago, IL 60640
Tel: 312-271-1073
www.mc-mlmhs.org

DiversityRx
www.diversityRx.org

National Center for Cultural Competence
Georgetown University
Child Development Center
3307 M Street, NW, Suite 401
Washington, DC 20007-3935
Toll free: 800-788-2066
Tel: 202-687-5387
Fax: 202-687-8899
www.gencd.georgetown.edu/nccc

National Minority AIDS Council
1931 13th Street, NW
Washington, DC 20009-4432
Tel: 202-483-6622
Fax:202-483-1135
www.nmac.org

Research Center on the Psychobiology of Ethnicity
UCLA Medical Center
Department of Psychiatry
1000 West Carson Street
Torrance, CA 90509
Tel: 213-533-3188
www.rei.edu/centers/Ethnicity_Center.htm

Search Institute
700 South Third Street, Suite 210
Minneapolis, MN 55415
Tel: 612-376-8955
Toll Free: 1-800-888-7828
Fax: 512-376-8956
www.search-institute.org

The Society for the Psychological Study of Ethnic Minority Issues
Division 45 of the American Psychological Association
www.apa.org/divisions/div45

Transcultural & Multicultural Health Links
www.lib.iun.indiana.edu/trannurs.htm

Y

Z